BY FAITH ALONE

Explorations in Philosophy and Theology

Series Editors: Kevin Hart (University of Virginia, USA) and Jeffrey Bloechl (Boston College, USA)

This series promotes philosophical and theological works committed to drawing on both disciplines, without either holding them strictly apart or overlooking important differences between them. The series favours philosophical approaches covered under the umbrella of 'continental European,' by which is meant a general commitment to developments sharpened since the work of Kant, German idealism, and Nietzsche. It provides a space for theological approaches historically informed and actively engaged via modern thought and culture. The series will focus on Christian theology in the first instance, but not to the exclusion of work in dialogue with multiple religions. Expanding the historical and cultural origins of both continental European philosophy and Christian theology, the series will embrace a global outlook. The series thus provides a platform for work from Africa, Asia, Australia, North and South America. Featuring edited collections, single-authored works, and translations managed by an active and global editorial board, the series is one of the main destinations for scholarship in the continental philosophy of religion today.

Editorial Board

Sarah Coakley, University of Cambridge, UK
Werner Jeanrond, University of Oslo, Norway
Jean-Yves Lacoste, Paris
Adriaan Peperzak, Loyola University of Chicago, USA
Pheme Perkins, Boston College, USA
David Tracy, University of Chicago, USA
Claudia Welz, Aarhus University, Denmark
Olivier Boulnois, École Pratique des Hautes Études, France
Nythamar de Oliveira, Pontifical Catholic University of Rio Grande do Sul, Brazil
James Heisig, Nanzan Institute for Religion and Culture, Japan
Robyn Horner, Australian Catholic University, Australia
Leonard Katchekpele, University of Strasbourg, France
Judith Wolfe, Durham University, UK

Forthcoming Titles

The Book of Experience, by Emmanuel Falque and translated by George Hughes
Anthropomorphism in Christian Theology, by William C. Hackett
The Poetics of the Sensible, by Stanislas Breton and translated by Sarah Horton

BY FAITH ALONE

The Medieval Church and Martin Luther

Lev Shestov

Translated by
Stephen P. Van Trees

BLOOMSBURY ACADEMIC
LONDON · NEW YORK · OXFORD · NEW DELHI · SYDNEY

BLOOMSBURY ACADEMIC
Bloomsbury Publishing Plc, 50 Bedford Square, London, WC1B 3DP, UK
Bloomsbury Publishing Inc, 1385 Broadway, New York, NY 10018, USA
Bloomsbury Publishing Ireland, 29 Earlsfort Terrace, Dublin 2, D02 AY28, Ireland

BLOOMSBURY, BLOOMSBURY ACADEMIC and the Diana
logo are trademarks of Bloomsbury Publishing Plc

First published in Great Britain 2023
This paperback edition published 2025

First published in 1966 in Paris, France as Sola Fide – Tol'ko Veroyu.
Grecheskaya I Srednevekovaya Filosofiya. Lyuter I Tserkov by YMCA-Press.

Copyright © Stephen P. Van Trees, 2023

Stephen P. Van Trees has asserted his right under the Copyright, Designs and
Patents Act, 1988, to be identified as Translator of this work.

For legal purposes the Acknowledgements on p. vii constitute
an extension of this copyright page.

Series design: Ben Anslow
Photography © Sashanna Hart

All rights reserved. No part of this publication may be: i) reproduced or
transmitted in any form, electronic or mechanical, including photocopying,
recording or by means of any information storage or retrieval system without
prior permission in writing from the publishers; or ii) used or reproduced in any
way for the training, development or operation of artificial intelligence (AI)
technologies, including generative AI technologies. The rights holders expressly
reserve this publication from the text and data mining exception as per
Article 4(3) of the Digital Single Market Directive (EU) 2019/790.

Bloomsbury Publishing Inc does not have any control over, or responsibility for,
any third-party websites referred to or in this book. All internet addresses given
in this book were correct at the time of going to press. The author and publisher
regret any inconvenience caused if addresses have changed or sites have
ceased to exist, but can accept no responsibility for any such changes.

A catalogue record for this book is available from the British Library.

A catalog record for this book is available from the Library of Congress.

ISBN: HB: 978-1-3503-6231-4
PB: 978-1-3503-6235-2
ePDF: 978-1-3503-6232-1
eBook: 978-1-3503-6233-8

Series: Explorations in Philosophy and Theology

Typeset by Integra Software Services Pvt. Ltd.

For product safety related questions contact productsafety@bloomsbury.com.

To find out more about our authors and books visit www.bloomsbury.com
and sign up for our newsletters.

TABLE OF CONTENTS

LEV SHESTOV, BY FAITH ALONE (SOLA FIDE)   1

YMCA EDITOR'S INTRODUCTION   9

Part I
GREEK AND MEDIEVAL PHILOSOPHY

GREEK AND MEDIEVAL PHILOSOPHY   13

Part II
LUTHER AND THE CHURCH

LUTHER AND THE CHURCH   83

Notes   201
Bibliography of Cited Works   222
Index   226

LEV SHESTOV, BY FAITH ALONE (SOLA FIDE)
TRANSLATOR'S INTRODUCTION

Introduction to Shestov

Lev Shestov (1866–1938) was a Russian philosopher. He is well known as one of the first modern existential religious philosophers, in the tradition of the writer of Job, Plotinus, Pascal, Luther and Dostoevsky. His work was devoted to exploring the limits of the rationalist world view and the access of faith. Something of the depth of his insight can be grasped from the description given him by Czesław Miłosz, the Nobel Prize-winning poet and essayist:

> [Shestov] was a man of the Scriptures. He would probably have gladly accepted the epithet Plato often hurled at his opponents in a dispute – *Misologos*, a hater of reason – but only to stress the absurd of the human condition, which is masked by Reason. There was a way out: 'The good is not God. We must seek that which is higher than the Good. We must seek God.' Which means that the despair that seizes us when we are faced with the Absurd leads us beyond good and evil to an act of faith. There is nothing impossible for God and for those who truly believe in him. An absurd affirmation, for who ever saw a mountain moved by prayer? But do we have a choice? The fruits of the tree of knowledge bring only death. It should be noted that Shestov was not a preacher; he tried only to present a dilemma in all its acuteness. Most definitely he was neither a moralist nor a theologian.[1]

Shestov's life

Who was Shestov? He was born in Kyiv. As a youth, he was held for ransom for six months. His father wouldn't pay. There is a mysterious lacuna, a breakdown and great spiritual crisis, of which he never spoke, even to his daughters. He was initially a law student: His submitted dissertation was never returned to him, citing revolutionary tendencies in his analysis of the worker situation. His parents were wealthy merchants, and he was obliged to help with the store. He had an illegitimate son, Pavel, who died in combat in the waning days of the First World

War. He married a Russian Orthodox woman, Anna Eleazarovna Berezovskaya, with whom he had two daughters. He felt the news would kill his father, so his wife and children lived in Western Europe until after his father died. Shestov returned regularly to Russia. He escaped Russia in 1921, after witnessing the October Revolution in Moscow and the Russian Civil War in Kyiv, in which his family's factory burned to the ground. He then escaped to Paris, where he lived the rest of his life.

Shestov's work

Early in his career, he wrote a series of books that were more literary criticism than philosophy: Shakespeare and His Critic Brandes, Tolstoy and Nietzsche, Dostoevsky and Nietzsche, Turgenev and The Apotheosis of Groundlessness.

Shestov wrote with deep insight on Tolstoy and spoke of seeking what is beyond the good – we must seek God. He was one of the early Russian writers on Nietzsche – relating his insights to those of the great Russians. His book on Dostoevsky was perhaps the first to establish the importance of Notes from Underground in his work.

Sola Fide – By Faith Alone marks a crucial transition point in Shestov's work. He had worked as a literary critic; this book is the transition from literary criticism to religious philosophy, albeit with a personal approach. It was written in Switzerland between 1911 and 1914 and was not published at the time.

In 1914, on returning to Russia, Shestov gave this manuscript to his brother-in-law, G.L. Lowtzsky, who lived in Geneva for all of the First World War. Shestov was not able to return to Switzerland during the First World War.

Sola Fide – the genesis

Shestov's daughter writes in her biography of her father:[2]

> Shestov didn't succeed in finishing even the 'draft' of the book Sola Fide on which he worked until his departure from Coppet to Moscow. He did not take the manuscript of the unfinished book (6 notebooks, 1100 pages) with him. It remained abroad until the end of the war. When in 1920 Shestov quit Russia and went to Geneva he found the manuscript.

She then discusses the content of the book.

> The manuscript of the book Sola Fide consists of two parts, with no indication of titles for the parts. The editors called these parts 'Greek and Medieval Philosophy' and 'Luther and the Church'.

The first section of the book traces the origin of Western religious thought in the Platonic and Aristotelian tradition and focuses especially on Thomas Aquinas and

Augustine. The section discussing Augustine's dispute with the Pelagians is key to the book. If man cannot be saved by his own efforts alone, where is his salvation? His salvation is only unmerited grace.

The second section presents Luther's access to faith. Luther was a believing Catholic, who became convinced he was lost without faith, that monasticism was not enough.

As his daughter says:

Shestov took the title of the book from Luther's translation of 'The Epistle of Apostle Paul to the Romans' III, 28. The words of the apostle in the original; Man is justified by faith' were translated by Luther as 'Man is justified by faith alone'. This arbitrary change of the text of the Holy Scripture evoked many arguments in theological circles.

Shestov took as the title of his book the pronouncement 'Sola Fide' probably, because it brilliantly characterizes young Luther's struggle for faith (cf. 2nd chapter of 2nd part). Among the people who Shestov visited in his 'pilgrimage through souls'³ hardly anyone was so close in spirit to him as was young Luther. This book bears more a philosophical than a literary character. Many ideas presented in it were at the basis of Shestov's later books. The book was written in a short time (8–9 months) with great effort and spiritual intensity. The absence of final rework makes it more immediate than Shestov's other books. It is in some sense a spiritual autobiography of the author.

Then she notes the publication history of the book: The book was published posthumously in Paris: the 2nd part came out in French in 1957, and the book was published in toto in Russian in 1966, per the draft manuscript, by the YMCA-Press publisher, under the title Sola Fide. By Faith Alone. It is the twelfth volume of Shestov's collected works. Chronologically its place is after volume six ('Great Vigils').⁴

The second part of the book appeared in a French translation. The complete book has never appeared in any language besides the original Russian. It is not mentioned in Bernard Martin's excellent introductions except as a precursor to Potestas Clavium.

Sola Fide – the thematic

Shestov's mature work talks of the dynamic between Athens and Jerusalem in Western thought. This he owes to Tertullian. Jerusalem for Shestov is the original biblical inspiration, whether this is the prophets, revelation, direct mystical experience, or the language of love. He then concerns himself with the Biblical access of faith.

Now, he says, in Genesis the serpent comes into the garden. The serpent offers knowledge. Consistent with the narrative, the serpent offers that men will be as gods, with knowledge of good and evil. But, Shestov says, precisely the opposite occurs – men wish to limit God and wish to reduce Him to the ambit of their minds.

Athens is the tradition of Plato, Aristotle and Aquinas. These are the great idealists, the positivists, the system builders. One of Shestov's favourite metaphors for the whole modern effort is the Tower of Babel.

The dynamic occurs when rationalism and scientism dictate to God. Shestov had not read Kierkegaard at the time, but he strikingly prefigures the Dane in his emphasis on the qualitative difference of God's ways.

Shestov himself expands on his key themes:

> One can say with conviction: the task of all religious genius is the destruction of extant religious authorities.
>
> (p.15)

One of the fascinating themes of the book is seeing Shestov take questions posed by Dostoevsky, Tolstoy or Chekhov and find their answer in Luther's search.

> Man does not wish to rise to God, he wishes to compel God to lower to himself, to become such as He is represented to our weak and limited minds.
>
> (p. 65)

This is one of the keys of Shestov. He repeats this from even his first book. Whatever one goes through, the final result cannot be predicted.

> The most difficult and horrible thing in that internal struggle, which Augustine recounts, is exactly that its upshot for him was impossible to guess in advance. Afterwards Augustine could say: You, Lord, knew to what my torments led me, but I knew nothing. But he could say this only afterwards, when, looking back at the past and the new present, he had the possibility of running the totals on his tormenting experiences.
>
> (p. 94)

And, of course, Dostoevsky was one of the key landmarks.

> If you too much value that already acquired, you will never discover anything new. In the case we're working – Luther, when he had to, staked everything he had, and if you wish to follow after him, you must be prepared for everything, you must not be afraid to jettison treasures into the sea, in order to lighten and save the sinking boat. Doubtless, the Catholic theologians are correct, when they affirm that Luther's struggle was a struggle against the church. It was not difficult for Dostoevsky, standing outside Catholicism and living in the nineteenth century to say that Catholicism committed the most terrible of crimes – put the Pope in the place of Christ, put itself in the place of God. From the outside, Dostoevsky judged of others' sins and crimes. Luther himself was a believing Catholic and before judging the Church to which he belonged, ought to have judged himself.
>
> (p. 131)

And this is Shestov's key theme – man's condition in seeking God.

God demands nothing from us. 'I am sought of *them that* asked not *for me*; I am found of *them that* sought me not', says the prophet (Is 65:1).

(p. 181)

Shestov once said[5] that it was not given to Schelling to be 'the Luther of philosophy' but that title could certainly be claimed by Shestov himself.

Shestov's later work

After Sola Fide, he turned to truly philosophical and religious themes in his books Potestas Clavium, In Job's Balances, Kierkegaard and the Existential Philosophy, and Athens and Jerusalem.

In In Job's Balances,[6] in 'The Conquest of the Self-Evident', Shestov's article on Dostoevsky for French readers, he says:

These are the questions that Hippolyte has learned to ask; Kant did not know how to question thus. It is only a few, rare natures in the history of humanity who are able to ask such questions. In our own day, there was Nietzsche, with his *Beyond Good and Evil*. Before him Luther, who taught that good works do not bring salvation. Luther had heard this from St Augustine, who in his turn was only developing the ideas of St Paul, which he again had gathered from Isaiah and from the supreme and terrible Bible story of the Fall.

Rereading Potestas Clavium,[7] we turn to the title article, which is indeed a short summary of the clairvoyance of Dostoevsky's analysis of the Catholic Church, and Luther's reaction to the church from inside the church.

Finally, the masterwork – Athens and Jerusalem.[8] Most of the first part, Parmenides in Chains (On the source of eternal truths), is devoted to the problematic that Shestov first identifies in Sola Fide.

But while Spinoza affirms that philosophy has no end other than truth and that the goal of theology is piety and obedience, Luther says, or rather cries out with all the force and ardor of which a man is capable when he struggles for his most precious good, that the source of truth is not knowledge, the knowledge that reason brings to man, but faith, faith alone. Strange as it may seem, Luther was convinced that the goal of philosophy is not truth but obedience and piety, while truth is obtained only through faith, *sola fide*. (p. 193)

Shestov's later career

Shestov's move to Paris allowed him to serve as the linkage between the great Russians and the new French existentialists. He was key to the reception of both Dostoevsky and Nietzsche in France. He wrote seminal articles on Dostoevsky, Nietzsche and Pascal for French readers. He was the mentor of Benjamin Fondane, the Romanian poet and writer. One would be hard-pressed to find anyone else who had dinner with both Tolstoy and Einstein.

Critical reception of Sola Fide

As the best example of Shestov's serving as a nexus in Paris, we listen to Ramona Fotiade:[9]

> Among the young French intellectuals of the 1930s on whom Shestov's thought had a decisive impact, Camus remains the most prominent representative of the absurd in twentieth-century French literature and philosophy. Yet critics and historians have rarely pointed out the fact that Camus's Mythe de Sisyphe is a barely disguised polemical reply to Shestov's arguments on the absurd, and indirectly pays homage to most of the recurrent themes in the Russian philosopher's writing (the 'wall of evidence', the revolt against reason, the existential fight against Husserlian scientific rationalism, the affirmation of freedom and personal, subjective experience, and so on).
>
> (p. 4)

> Man, therefore, has to content himself with the things that lie in his power and find consolation in ethics and self-knowledge, which is itself 'man's greatest good'. Thus, Shestov argues, begins the replacement of ontology by ethics in philosophy and the education of man's desire to accept the principle of the greatest good, which is also that of the truth.
>
> (p. 93)

> Faith opens up an alternative mode of understanding, the existential 'second dimension of thought', which is situated beyond good and evil, beyond virtue or 'merit', beyond logical arguments based on the dichotomy between truth and error. Man's salvation, his freedom and immortality, lie in faith alone (Sola Fide, as Shestov insisted, reiterating Luther's watchword).
>
> (p. 212)

Fotiade is an excellent source on the purer religious existential philosophy, at that moment before it was developed to the Absurd by later French and German existentialists, and her work led me to a deeper understanding of Shestov.

Alexis Philonenko is emeritus professor at the University of Rouen. He recently wrote an article on Sola Fide and captures the essential Shestov stance.[10]

> To understand Shestov and Luther, *the same disposition of spirit is necessary*. It is less in the *content* than in the structure of the formal intention which manifests itself in coincidence; the common postulate is that attitude expresses itself in aptitude, and reciprocally as well. What counts is not Being, but the manner of existence. Shestov's privileged place is that of the joys and sufferings of philosophers: their story and sometimes even their intertwined stories.
>
> (p. 31)

Michael Finkenthal is a physics professor at Johns Hopkins. His recent book contains a chapter on <u>Sola Fide</u>. In it he captures Shestov's leap:

> *Sola Fide* is on the surface a book about Luther and faith, but in fact it is much more than that: the text is summing up the results of an interference process between Shestov's efforts toward the deconstruction of the basic principles of a philosophy built upon the absolute rights of rational reasoning and his search for a *meta-sophia* based on faith in an absolute Transcendental.[11]
>
> (pp. 61–2)

A personal note

In closing, allow me to return to the words of Milosz one last time.

> What could Sorana Gurian, a young woman dying of cancer, get from her reading of Shestov? Not the promise of a miraculous cure. He did not maintain that you can knock down the wall of Necessity by beating your Head against it. To the sober-minded who criticized the Absurd of Kierkegaard and his faith in the impossible, he used to reply that Kierkegaard knew perfectly well the weight of reality: Regina Olsen would not be restored to him. Yet there is a great difference between our looking at ourselves as ciphers on a statistical sheet and our grasping our destiny as something that is personal and unique.
>
> (p. 118)

Milosz wrote this article in 1973, the year I took his Dostoevsky course at Berkeley. I wrote a paper on Kirillov for the course and then wrote an undergraduate thesis on the eschatological climate in Dostoevsky. I was his graduate assistant for several years in the late 1970s. I knew Shestov from his discussions and article. I have had the first edition of <u>Sola Fide</u> since Berkeley. It was not until recently (2018) that I saw a Russian-language edition in Ukraine.

In 2003, after the death of my late wife, I was at dinner with Martha, who is now my wife. We talked of our children and hopes and dreams, and that went quickly. She asked me what else I did. I said I was a Russian religious philosophy translator. She asked what I had done lately. Well, nothing, I said. Thirty years in aviation, other things intervened. So I told her about the Russians, about Fedorov, about Shestov, about Sergei Bulgakov – how important they were in Russia, in emigration, in the world, and how much of the work was still in Russian. She suggested I do something about it. So I started carrying a packet with a Russian philosophical text and a blank pad of paper. Whenever I had time, I translated. I spent a lot of time in the years 2006–2013 in waiting rooms and such. With that time, I translated all of Fedorov and all the remaining Shestov, going to the Library of Congress to get the Greek Philosophy course. Then, more events, and from 2011 to 2014 I had plenty of time to type it up, alone with the St Bernard.

Shestov's work has been translated in three waves. In the 1920s, D.H. Lawrence and S.S. Koteliansky translated his early works on Dostoevsky, Tolstoy and Chekhov. In the 1960s, Bernard Martin translated many of his later works from the French editions. Shestov's remaining works in this third wave include both earlier works never translated at the time and works released posthumously by his family.

So the initial version of this translation was done some ten years ago, extending my own and others' work at Berkeley, and as a Shestovian sublimation of the times in which it was translated. It took some fifty years to publish the Russian edition, and some fifty-seven years after that to publish this translation.

I had the pleasure of attending Ramona Fotiade's Fondane symposium at Yale in April 2018 and heard Kevin Hart's magisterial keynote on Shestov and Husserl. I talked to him and said I had all the remaining Russian-language Shestov done into English. He was very encouraging, and his comments have given me the pleasure of rereading Sola Fide in the original, and much improving the manuscript.

I offer my thanks to Kevin Hart at the University of Virginia, and Jeffrey Bloechl of Boston College, who first recommended the work for publication.

I thank Professor Ramona Fotiade and Professor Margaret Tejerizo at the University of Glasgow for their reading of the manuscript.

I thank the anonymous reviewers for their comments, which have much improved the manuscript. The comment on this lost work representing a link between Russian religious philosophy and Western philosophy was especially acute.

The team at Bloomsbury Academic, led by Suzie Nash, and Shamlipriya Vijayan, has been brilliant.

And thank you to Boris Jakim, the dean of Russian religious philosophy translators. I have read and profited from his many translations, as well as his reading of the manuscript.

I want to thank my parents, Harry and Diane; my wife Martha (you'll see her on page 48); our children, Robert (Alex), Rebecca, Gabrielle, Erikka (Dave), Jennifer (Greg) and Charlie (Lauren); our grandchildren, Savannah, Bekah (JT), Emily, Lillian, Logan, Quentin, Eleanor and Oden; and our great grandchildren, Adeline, Envy, Sophia, Charlotte and Lincoln.

YMCA EDITOR'S INTRODUCTION

From the Editor[1]

Among the papers left after Lev Shestov's death, there was an unfinished manuscript, entitled *Sola Fide*, written in Switzerland between 1911 and 1914. It was not published at the time.

In 1914, on returning to Russia, Shestov gave this manuscript to his brother-in-law G.L. Lowtzsky, who lived in Geneva all of the First World War. In 1920, when Shestov quit Russia, he found his manuscript and in 1920 published several of its chapters with several additions, in Paris, in the journal *Contemporary Notes*, no. 1 under the title *The Last Judgment* (Tolstoy's last words), which was then included in the book *In Job's Balances* (Paris, 1928).

The manuscript consists of two parts, without titles indicated. We have called these: *Greek and Medieval Philosophy*, and *Luther and the Church*. Shestov did not publish the manuscript *in toto* in 1920 probably because a part of the ideas expressed in it entered into the book *Potestas Clavium*, which was written in Russia between 1914 and 1918, and came out in Russian in Berlin in 1923.

More than fifteen years had passed since Shestov's death. Someone reading the unpublished part of the manuscript remarked: 'Yes, this is the key to Shestov's philosophy, a spiritual autobiography unique in Russian religious philosophy.' But this time too only a part, the second part, of the manuscript was able to be published, in French, under the title *Sola Fide, Luther and the Church* (translated from Russian by Sophie Sève), Presses Universitaires, Paris, 1957. Several chapters of this book also appeared in Russian journals.

Reading the work, twenty-five years on from Shestov's death, we are convinced that it is of great value and that to publish this book in the Russian language is a matter of great interest. The public appearance of this book is tied to the centenary of the birthday of the author (Lev Shestov was born in Kyiv on 31 January (12 February) 1866 and died in Paris on 20 November 1938).

The title of the book *Sola Fide (By Faith Alone)* is taken from Luther's translation of the *Epistle of the Apostle Paul to the Romans (Romans III, 28)*. The words of the apostle reading in Russian translation 'man is justified by faith', Luther translated: 'man is justified by faith *alone*'. This arbitrary change of the text of the Holy Writ evoked many disputes in theological circles.

Shestov probably selected the statement *Sola Fide* as the title of the book because it acutely characterizes the struggle of the young Luther for faith (cf. chapter II, second part). Among the people whom Lev Shestov encountered in his 'pilgrimage among souls', few were so close to him in spirit as Luther in his youth.

Part I

GREEK AND MEDIEVAL PHILOSOPHY

GREEK AND MEDIEVAL PHILOSOPHY

I

<u>Pati, domine aut mori</u> – sufferings, Lord or death – so prayed St Theresa, as she lived in the second half of the sixteenth century.

Two thousand years and a little more before her, one of the famous Cynics, Antisthenes, founder of the school and disciple of Socrates, exclaimed: 'better for me to go out of my mind, than to experience satisfaction in life'. Μανείην μᾶλλον ἤ ἡσθείην (Zeller II-1, 260).

Plato, per tradition, said that Antisthenes' disciple, Diogenes, was an insane Socrates. And Plato was right. Unconditionally, Diogenes, not only Diogenes, but also his teacher and his closest disciples were insane, and, as well, not only insane but really insane Socrates, i.e., insane sages. To fear satisfaction – at a time, when all of humanity, for the whole period of its existence, saw the meaning and essence of life in satisfaction – isn't this insanity, as well, 'systematic' insanity, just as systematic as Socrates' wisdom?

How the Cynics lived – more or less anyone knows that, and one hardly need expatiate on that, all the more since the horror of life, its difficulty and muck do not much attract modern man – the period of 'naturalism' is long past. We even run hurriedly over those lines of the prophet Ezekiel, in which he tells of his preparation for prophecy, of the flat cake which he ate at God's behest. One ought just not to forget that the Cynics considered themselves touched by the finger of God. They said: τοὺς ἀγαθοὺς ἄνδρας θεῶν εἰκόνας εἶναι – Good men are like gods (Zeller, II-1, 267). Just like Socrates, they obeyed the mysterious, incomprehensible impulse to give up the beauty and joy of existence in exchange for ugliness and horrors. They said that beauty and joy are not necessary, that they interfere with man's approach to God, that they yield <u>satisfaction</u>, and that satisfaction is worse than madness. One must run from satisfaction, they taught, as from the plague. As is well known, contemporaries hated and disdained the Cynics and called them dogs, and only a few, very sensitive people, like Plato and, if you believe the tradition, the disciples of Aristotle, were astonished or, at least, thought deep, on the strange life of these mad sages, these outcasts. I will not dwell on the arguments by which the Cynics justified their world view or, more accurately, their life. Despite the fact that their teaching, i.e., considerations, which they proposed in proof of their rightness, is lost in the depth of the ages, as everything that cannot be of use to men is lost, I do not think that their arguments would present very great interest for us, even in the case that they were very exact, witty and convincing. We have so many witty and convincing arguments – that, rightly, it's much more useful to forget some of them that we have already assimilated than assimilating new ones. All the more, since doubtless the life of the Cynics was in no way defined by their reasonings. There has not yet been a case where a man is headed to madness, directed by the proof of reason. And if such a paradox had turned out possible, if really reason could by its proof lead to insanity, then … then by this very point reason would forever have cancelled itself out. But, I repeat, doubtless reason is not culpable in the insane delirium and insane life of the cynics, as it is not culpable in the madness of Ezekiel. Madness has its independent source, its boldness and its force, and who knows, its rightness? Plato, the disciple of Socrates, said that the greatest misfortune is to become a hater of reason (misalogue). The Cynics, also disciples of Socrates, did not find misfortune in this at all; on the contrary, they saw the principle of any misfortune in what Plato considered reason. Plato attained completeness, explanation, pleasure, satisfaction. And all such spiritual conditions, the Cynics would say, if they knew medieval terminology, are from the deceiver. Why they thought so – more like felt so – hardly anyone can give an answer to that question.

There was something in the depths of the soul of the Cynics, which made them haters of any total organization on earth. Plato was right: there were two geniuses in Socrates: one, which found its expression through Plato's philosophy and especially Aristotle's – the genius of reason; the other, which attempted to attain its expression in the philosophy of the Cynics. Plate and Aristotle conquered the whole world. Here it's been 2,500 years that the great disciples of the great master have dominated human minds.

He who wishes to be listened to, he who wishes to leave a noticeable trace behind himself in history – he must pass the course at the school of the Greeks. Even the Middle Ages, even Catholicism, as we will see below, did not escape the common fate in this regard. Even though the opinion also exists, that in the Middle Ages philosophy was the handmaiden of theology, this is no more than a <u>fable convenue</u>. Theology had stakes for burning heretics at its disposal and thus it seemed that everyone obeyed it; it seemed that was it was an unlimited dominatrix. As a matter of fact, the relation of philosophy to theology always, both in the first centuries of Christianity and right up to the present day, was the same as the relation between the Romans and the barbarians who conquered the Roman Empire: the conquered dictated laws to the conquerors. Formally, power belonged, of course, to the Catholic clergy. But they dared not take a step without checking beforehand with the secular Greek teachers. Not for nothing did Thomas Aquinas call Aristotle simply <u>Philosophus</u>, i.e., eternal, unchangeable and indomitable lawgiver of thought. That which Thomas said, Catholic thinkers had already thought and done long before Thomas. And if they called Aristotle <u>praecursor Christi in naturalibus</u> – that's only because theology with its stakes for burning heretics demanded, as all conquerors do, the acknowledgement of its external superstitious rights. As a matter of fact, Aristotle was and remained for Catholicism the praecursor Christi in naturalibus, as well as in supernaturalibus. We would not exaggerate if we say that Aristotle dominated not only the thought but also the fantasy of European nations. Catholicism without Aristotelian philosophy is just as unthinkable, as it was unthinkable without Roman weapons. In order to conquer the proud and make nations bow before them, both Aristotelian reason and the Roman legions were necessary to Catholicism. Hic signes (by these signs) and only hic signes could it create for itself that firm position, which ere now has amazed historians and still can't amaze them enough.

If instead of Aristotle, the descendant of the rational Socrates, Catholicism had picked Diogenes, the descendant of the mad Socrates as its leader, history would have allocated Catholicism only a few unremarkable pages, as it today puts the doctrine and life of Cynics, Stoics or medieval heretics on the back pages – as losers. Stable victories are granted only to healthy common sense, which knows how to create great philosophical systems and organize expansive states with well-educated armies. The world is not ruled by the mad but rather by the good-sense Socrates. And nonetheless, no matter how strange it may be, two thousand years after Diogenes, St Theresa, canonized and acknowledged as great by the Catholic Church, repeats the words of the ancient cynic: pati aut mori – if she is not allowed to suffer, then she does not wish to live; she prefers to die.

II

The words of Antisthenes and St Theresa have been discounted as paradoxes among the innumerable collection of other paradoxes. Paradoxes, not necessary at all and worth little, are better fitted than anything else to reveal access to the domain to which I wish to recommend the attention of the reader. What kind of rational being Socrates was – everyone knows that or thinks they do. We have accepted measuring the value of all phenomena of life by rational Socrates. For Plato, when he called Diogenes the insane Socrates, had no doubt at all that by his sentence he forever deprived Diogenes of a place in the aeropagus of those weighing the fate of humanity. I would say further, Plato not only wished to deprive Diogenes of the right to be judge and weigh the fate of men, but he wished by this sentence to remove Diogenes even in the case that Diogenes pretended not to the role of law teacher or judge but just to the simple role of witness. Diogenes couldn't even be a witness, for Socrates, once out of his mind, is no longer Socrates, not even a man. One can take his life out of moral motives, but there's no reason at all to take him into consideration. So spoke and thought the ancient Greeks, in spite of the fact that in ancient time the idea still firmly held that madness had divine origin.[1] Modern thought then assimilated the conviction of Plato, as a self-evident truth, not submitted to proof or even judgement. If it's not always spelled out, that's only because it seems too self-evident. But without it our thought can't move from the spot; everyone knows that and never forgets it. In order not to look too far for an example, I'll point only to two historians – Harnack and Renan. They both say, 'One cannot disdain sound thought unpunished.'[2] They nowhere emphasize this and don't even find it necessary to establish the position as a 'prolegomenon' of their thinking. But try to deprive the cited writers of this prolegomenon, and all their huge historico-philosophical works lose the ground underneath it. Immediate experience, of course, is on their side; a disdainful relation to sound thought unconditionally passes unpunished in no man. But is it quite necessary at any cost to avoid punishment? What if Antisthenes and St Theresa are right? What if it's possible, if it's <u>necessary</u> to consciously disdain common sense and consciously bear the punishment? For man will not escape punishment, no matter how he wriggles! As man has appeared in the world, so he has to pay heavily: life is brought at the price of horror, of ineluctable death. You can forget it, but it's impossible not to know it. Even Anaximander considered any individual existence illegitimate, and all beings must redeem this illegitimacy by perdition, but yet new beings took on both illegitimacy and responsibility for the illegitimacy of their appearance in the world. And the big question is, would it be better in view of the impending punishment, were all the living to refuse the madness of existence, following the advice of Harnack and Renan – or the advice of the references of good sense.

It might be à propos here to recall that per the doctrine of Plato (Zeller II, 533), it's just as painful for a man to transition from contemplation of the sensual world to attainment of the truly existent, as it is for an eye used to darkness to transition to sudden light. And here immediately before the new life, there's the threat and danger of punishment. At some time a new life will ensue, and whether or not there'll be a new life – still the threat of punishment stands before us in all its concrete tangibility. And all the same Plato, condemning Diogenes, strove for pain, for the terrible. <u>Pati aut mori</u> – if the human 'ideal' consists in this, then, yes, the surest path to it is exactly in disdain of good sense, of any sense. Mad Socrates, i.e., Diogenes or Antisthenes, turn out to be more reliable guides than rational Socrates, i.e., Plato or Aristotle.

And further: good sense demarcates the path of the historians and philosophers (for every historian is a philosopher, he is compelled to wax wise, evasively wax wise – it seems now that is no longer a secret. Everyone who speaks of life must wax wise: one has to choose among what one sees, one must explain, one must evaluate – and – that's what philosophizing means). Once the danger of being submitted to punishment is acknowledged as a motive so serious, it stands to reason it's clear that danger should be avoided, and, it stands to reason; it's even clearer that one ought not to go where danger awaits. Despite Theresa, man saves himself from both death and from sufferings; despite Antisthenes, there is nothing worse than insanity, nor better than satisfaction and pleasure. And once the fundamental problem of life consists in this, then it stands to reason, philosophy, striving to give man wisdom, and must gain only such truths which help to avoid insanity and suffering and defer death to the longest possible term. Philosophy does just that – it acknowledges no dangerous truths. And in order to more surely attain its goal, it does not call dangerous truths truths but calls them errors. The same Protestant historian Harnack says that the possibility of harm from truth does not serve as a refutation of it. And not only the free-thinking Harnack, even an orthodox Catholic like Zahn affirms the same: in his own name, and in the name of the Catholic Church, who he represents in his work, he announces, that he gains the truth whatever it takes and is ready to accept any truth, not considering whether it will be useful or harmful, whether it will demand sacrifice or confer reward. I, of course, know that one cannot compare Zahn and Harnack. Harnack is a remarkable historian, whose name has thundered over the whole world; Zahn is a modest professor, known only in Catholics scholarly circles. To boot, Harnack is completely free from external constraints; Zahn beforehand submits to the censorship of his spiritual leadership. And nonetheless, in the given case they have completely converged. Both the one and the other are not indifferent at all to harmful truth. More than that, they both fuss in much larger degree over usefulness than over truth. Relative to Zahn, I think, no one will start an argument with me. For an orthodox Catholic it's not about usefulness – but the usefulness of truth has always been and is the highest criterion for the Catholic Church. But he'll never say this. On the contrary, he exclaims pathetically that truth is dearer to him than anything in the world. And you know, I am far from suspecting Zahn of a conscious lie. More likely, he is fully sincere, and he in point of fact thinks that serving the Catholic Church and serving the truth are one and the same. If he were to tell you that the Turks gained Constantinople because the schismatic Greeks refused to unite with the Florentine Uniates, if he were to tell you that at the hour when the dogma of the 'infallibility' of the Pope was proclaimed at the Vatican Council, God sent His thunder and lightning, like when he proclaimed His Testament on Sinai, he (Zahn) in point of fact thinks that he communicates only one truth and that nothing is necessary to him besides the truth. He validates his judgements with, it seems to him, a special, highest criterion. Harnack, of course, laughs at the gullible Catholic. He is sure nothing similar can happen with him – he's an historian tried and true, he knows how men have fallen into the holds of prejudice and superstitions, and he knows how to defend himself. It's only necessary to not disdain good sense – and science is guaranteed of itself. But concede that his presupposition is untrue, that good sense is a block for the truth, and that conversely, the dominion of truth is perdition for good sense, i.e., that the truth is as dangerous for good sense as it is for Catholicism. Would Harnack agree to accept it nonetheless? Would he have chosen such a dangerous truth or would he have preferred good sense? I suppose, there can't be two answers here. And, it stands to reason, Harnack's affirmation that truth is evaluated by him independently of its harm or use does not correspond to reality. It is pia fraus (pious lie), apparently necessary in the same degree to the positivist scholar as to the theologian. The truth becomes inapplicable for Harnack a lot earlier, i.e., in much less serious circumstances than we had judged. It will be rejected not only when it infringes on the rights of so-called good sense but even when it has to invalidate some other habitual and necessary conviction. If the truth required acknowledgement that Luther was in no way such an ideal German man as the Protestants depict him, if it were necessary to agree that the Reformation was the task not of a great prophet but, say, of an apostate, would Harnack have the courage to snatch their elevating deception away from his coreligionists? Even more: in view of all of the danger for Protestantism, for social morality, which the deposition of Luther from this pedestal threatens, could Harnack, with all his first-line conscientiousness, <u>see into</u> the true Luther? In order to see that which is, true desire is little, even courage is little, sometimes what is required is heroic readiness to make a knife cut on a living body. And, it seems, people are rarely, maybe never, capable of this. They see not because they wish to see but because they cannot not see. And until their hour, they remain Catholics, liberal Protestants or simply scholar positivists, materialists or idealists.

III

I have not named these three contemporaries at random: Harnack, Renan and Zahn. I wanted to point to those men, our contemporaries, who, per the problems of their activity, stand closest of all to religious creative work or at least to Judeo-Christian religious creative work. Per the common representation, dominant in our time, religious creative work in its essence is distinct and ought to be distinct from any other creative work. You'll be told this both by the man who has put his whole life to the study of ecclesiastical history and literature and by the man who knows nothing of religion, besides minimally binding findings taken from popular textbooks. But when you touch the questions – what exactly is the source of religious cognition, is there religious cognition, what are the criteria of the truth of religious cognition – here you won't soon get agreement. One person will start talking about revelation; another about internal experience; a third, à la Spencer, of animism, etc. And the more you try to probe, the clearer it becomes to you that each man, independent of whether he's studied religious movements a lot or a little, has his own sort of <u>credo</u>, drawn from who knows where, and already decisively inaccessible to any influences. Here we run into, apparently, some sort of predestination, <u>fatum</u>: before a man's birth, it is inscribed in the book of fate for him to be a Catholic, liberal Protestant or freethinker. Harnack, Renan and Zahn, all three, had before them the works of a huge quantity of inspired titans of the spirit – and they all flew past them, as though these books writ in fiery letters didn't exist at all. They knew what they knew and did not want to study men who lived before them. For Renan read both Isaiah and Jeremiah, he knew the apostle Paul, he read the fathers of the church, it's not enough that he read them, he valued them and loved them, as though they were for him near and dear beings – but he was not allowed to be inflamed by their fire. The saints, the great madmen, holy, great madness – that's his sentence. But the epithet mad, insane, ruins everything, no matter to which holy name you apply it. For Renan too the prophets and apostles were and remain beautiful madmen but predestined in their madness to eternally blunder in fantastic domains. Harnack will tell you the same. He, like Renan, is interested most of all in the history of past searches. Not that he didn't have religious convictions; compare his little booklet <u>Wesen der Christentums</u> with the huge <u>Dogmengeschicte</u> or with any other of historical works (always multivolume), and you'll see that actually speaking he has almost nothing to say about his faith, about his Christianity. Even the larger part of <u>Wesen der Christentums</u> is also dedicated to the <u>history</u> of Christianity and polemic with opponents. If Harnack were set the condition to write a book about his Christian faith, in which there were neither history nor critique of previous views, I don't know whether he could write more than two or three lukewarm pages. Attentively read his <u>Wesen der Christentums</u>, you'll probably be struck by the circumstance that almost every time, when he quits historical digressions, ceases to talk of history and sets to presentation of his personal thoughts, he is compelled to stop – and literally to catch some air, to exclaim: <u>meine Herrer</u>. The pathos of apostle and prophet is not in Harnack's essence. For it's characteristic of pathos to disdain good sense and bear the corresponding punishment, and we saw that Harnack, along with Renan, considers a rupture with good sense inadmissible. We'll see this with Catholic dogmatics as well. And thus he takes refuge in the now beloved historico-scientific method. You've got to say that Harnack is one of the most remarkable historians of our time. His <u>Dogmengeschicte</u> along with <u>Geschichte der Griechischen Philosophie</u> of Zeller is positive chef-d'oeuvre of their kind. He can excellently recount Athanasius the Great, and St Augustine, and Luther. And with a conviction which many envy, he shows that the whole sense of the history of Christianity reduces to what is now accepted to be called the liberal Protestant doctrine. Hegel would be so proud: one more time it's proven that the spirit has cognized itself over the extent of two millennia of historical development. All the Tertullians, Ambroses, Iraneuses, Augustines, Pelagiuses, medieval mystics, scholastics, even Luther himself existed, were tormented, searched, only such that now the truth of contemporary liberal Protestantism triumphed, which in a few words might be defined in the following manner: we believe in God, the father of all people living, who through Jesus proclaimed to us the forgiveness of sins. To boot, Jesus, through Harnack's doctrine, can thence in no way be acknowledged as the incarnation of God. As early as Schleiermacher and A. Ritschl, Jesus is considered a man, in his essence, like all other men. All the Gospel miracles, all the events of Old Testament history, prophecy and foretelling are arraigned at the court of reason and, in the absence of firm proofs, are rejected, as the product of fantasy, if not unhealthy, then uncultured. True, Harnack, per the example of his predecessors, never sharply emphasizes his rift with the Church past; he avoids overt dispute with the view dominant in orthodox Protestantism. Such is still the tradition of the Protestant theologians: they've always avoided sharp excursions and preferred to avoid seduction to pour new wine in old skins, i.e., to inject completely different content into old habitual words. Harnack never, for example, directly puts the question: was Jesus man or God; he asks: '<u>gehort Jesus in Evangelium?</u>', did Jesus belong in the Gospel? So then his opponents in dispute with him, in order to accuse him, select a sharper and more challenging formulation. Harnack's problem is first of all to show, by following the history and evolution of dogmatics in Catholicism, that history ineluctably led to the destruction and perdition of almost any dogmatic, and that the Reformation struck the ultimate and decisive blow to 'almost' any dogma. The present time strives to complete the task Luther began. Harnack considers that his understanding and exegesis of Christianity are the true attainment of the doctrine of Christ. The spirit in the domain of religion has already evolved to the ultimate limit and he now has to stop here and wait, so that in the remaining domains of human creative work it reaches a corresponding height, and then humanity can consider its history complete and then get by without Hegel. No need to say that I present Harnack 'in my own words'. Harnack is too smart, educated and talented to indict himself with this sort of revelation. He knows that 'truth', whatever it is, cannot stand completely naked even before its own creator. Harnack nowhere says that 'almost' all dogmatics perished – I put in the 'almost' myself. Harnack nowhere says that the spirit has already evolved to its ultimate limits in his, Harnack's, conception. He acts, as they acted before him, he only calls his concept of Christianity the true religion. But in essence there's no difference between his affirmation and my words. But an inessential difference can mean quite a bit in the eyes of competent judges – this I know, and thus I admit, that if the matter at this time concerned Harnack, I'd have to tell it completely differently. But no matter how significant and how interesting Harnack is in himself, at this time I cannot devote the requisite attention to his person. Harnack, in the history of religious movements, like Zeller in the history of philosophy, makes one concession, moot in the highest degree. He, following Hegel, thinks that spirit develops in time, and it stands to reason, each following epoch, compared with the previous, approaches the more to the ultimate goal of development. To boot, also following Hegel, he considers that our time already marks the end of development. I said that his position is moot – one ought to and can say stronger: the position is doubtless false. Human spirit in no way develops in time. Or even better: sometimes it develops; sometimes it doesn't. If we compare the nineteenth century AD with the eighth century BC, then we can say that in the religious sense men have gone backwards. Do we have psalmists like King David, do we have sages like King Solomon, and do we have prophets like Isaiah? Call up even a hundred Hegels – they'll do nothing with the circumstance. And meantime almost three millennia have passed. If the spirit had all developed, like Hegel wants it, what kind of Davids and Isaiahs we ought to have! It stands to reason, one cannot unconditionally apply Hegel's general formula here. The spirit breathes where it wishes and time is not its sign. That concept of true religion which Harnack gives can not only not be considered the highest point of development compared to the conception of King David but clearly and unequivocally it's a huge step backwards.

IV

Let's follow Harnack further. He is especially interesting for us in view of the fact that he, without exaggerating, can be called the modern 'normal' historian, just like the Catholics call Thomas Aquinas a normal theologian. Harnack is a Protestant and an admirer of Luther – it stands to reason, an implacable enemy of Catholicism. He mercilessly persecutes atavisms of Catholicism even in Luther himself. And he defines the difference between Catholicism and his own religion thus, completely free of any historical atavisms. Catholicism seeks narcotic stimulants in order to tear the human soul out of the power of the quotidian; liberal Protestantism then gives solid, nutritious, healthy food for the spirit. And for Harnack it is clear that a man faced with such a dilemma can't vacillate long. One must quit narcotics and use only healthy food. And just so, good sense well knows that one cannot use narcotics unpunished – it stands to reason, Catholicism ought to be rejected and yield its place to Protestantism; in place of the insane orgies of medieval religious intoxication, modern times ought to accept sober religious positivism, the last word in religious revelation. True, Harnack knows that even his modest religiosity, adapted to the spirit of our time, cannot be scientifically justified. No matter how willingly he concedes one after another the dogmata Protestantism inherited from Catholicism, all the same, if he wants to be like a religious man, he has to hold several statements, more or less paradoxical from the point of view of human people, holding a sober scientific point of view.[3] He denies the infallibility of the dogmata of the Church, denies the divinity of Christ, denies the sacraments, etc. But he acknowledges the Bible as the singular book of its type. He acknowledges Christ as the singular man of his type, whose equal in the world there never was and never will be, for neither Socrates, nor Mohammed, nor Buddha, nor even the Old Testament prophets – Isaiah or Jeremiah – can be compared with Christ. He acknowledges that the Bible ought to produce on all men an irresistible impression and if one reads it without prejudices and not under the direction of a Catholic priest, then it surely leads to that faith, to that concept of God, which Harnack considers singularly true and singularly Christian. What can one say – compared to the affirmations of Catholicism, the affirmation of Harnack cannot be called too paradoxical – although he himself, as I already remarked, does not deny that any affirmation of a believer cannot but be paradoxical (cf. note, p, 16). But, obviously, Harnack hopes that paradoxes in such quantity, despite his earlier adduced personal opinion, will not evoke too much anger among those of good sense and will not invoke the ineluctable punishment. More than that, Harnack, like all apologists, is inclined to think that his paradoxes will encounter a favourable reception with good sense and even, instead of punishment, will bring high reward. Such is a sense of his <u>Dogmengeschicte</u> and his <u>Wesen der Christentums</u>. I hasten to add that I have not exhausted all the 'the paradoxes' allowed by modern liberal theology. There's one more, especially interesting for us, in view of the fact that it is so close to the hated Catholicism in its character. Harnack almost allows the canonization of Luther. Citing one of the very boldest letters of the reformer, Harnack says: the Catholics are right, if they see in these words of Luther signs of a mania of greatness and insanity. Really, a man who allows himself to speak thus is a prophet, albeit insane.[4] That Luther was not insane in Harnack's opinion, of course, is well understood. It stands to reason, Luther was a prophet, in fact receiving revelation from God.

It seems to me that I have exhausted the main paradoxes allowed by Harnack. The natural question arises: once paradoxes, even though small, are conceded, how and in what can one distinguish between an allowable and unallowable paradox? Once it's allowed to consider Luther a prophet or almost a prophet, why not consider the doctor angelicus Thomas Aquinas or Swedenborg a prophet or almost a prophet? Or why not concede, more or less, such a paradox that narcotics are useful to humanity, and even more necessary than simple and healthy food? It looks as though one cannot in principle refer to good sense once it's acknowledged that in the religious domain it is no longer the supreme judge. And, so, to get out of this difficulty, Harnack proposes the court of history. It alone decides which paradoxes are allowed, and which aren't, to guide human life. In Harnack's opinion, as well as all other historians', everything that has no future, everything condemned to perdition, by the fact alone that it cannot stand up for itself, proves its internal unfitness; in this respect our historian of Christianity differs not a whit from other historians. This position likewise corresponds to both Hegelian doctrine and the judgement of actual unscientific experience, which, although it knows nothing of the development of the spirit, always naturally, almost instinctively, strives to justification of success. The question is only – for us this question has unusual importance – whether in the given case good sense dictates laws to everyday experience or, conversely, whether good sense itself this time receives directives from experience. On the basis of all those works of Harnack which I've had to read, I cannot decide how he would answer this question. I can only guess that he has not posed himself such a question. It seems to me that if he were asked directly, he would answer that it's not his task to bang his head against such difficulties. That's already the domain of the philosopher and he is only an historian and theologian. True, in antiquity theologians did not renounce philosophical questions: Origen, St Augustine, Thomas Aquinas, Duns Scotus, Occam and even Luther all tried their theological strength on these questions most of all. Something else is true, too: maybe Harnack didn't either want to pose this question but resolve it he did – and if not explicite, then implicite, you'll find the answer you need in his works.

I adduce a long quotation from his Dogmengeschicte.

> Noch hat es in der Welt keinen starken religiösen Glauben gegeben, der nicht an irgend einem entscheidenden Punkt sich auf eine äussere Autorität berufen hätte. Nur in den blassen Ausführungen der Religionsphilosophen oder in den polemischen Entwürfen protestantischer Theologen wird ein Glaube konstruiert, der seine Gewissheit den eigenen inneren Momenten entnimmt ... Jesus Christus hat sich auf die Autorität des Alten Testamentes, die alten Christen haben sich auf den Weissagungsbeweis, Augustin hat sich auf die Kirche, selbst Luther hat sich auf des geschriebene Wort Gottes berufen.[5]
>
> (Harnack D.G. III, 81)

You can see from this that Harnack, no matter how difficult this might be, has added a new mysterious paradox to the complex of paradoxes which are the very condition of the existence of religions. Not one faith of not one man affirms the historian, who his whole life has worked on the investigation of the two-thousand-year development of Christianity, who knows the religious literature, as who knows else besides him in our time might know it – not one faith of not one man can be maintained without external authority. Paul, too, needed an authority, and Christ, too, and as Harnack expresses himself, 'even Luther'. Why Harnack says even Luther, and not even Christ, if he'd had to have said it, would have said it I don't know and can't even guess. For all the same is Christ for Harnack a man, singular in religious consciousness? Or is Harnack first a Lutheran – then a Christian? But we won't trouble our head on this question, for whose resolution we have insufficient data, and we'll move to the essence of the matter. Per Harnack's opinion, based on the study of the religious literature of twenty centuries, the condition of faith is external authority. First of all, this is a deeply Catholic opinion.[6] As is well known, even Blessed Augustine affirmed that if he had not received the Holy Writ from the Catholic Church, he would never have believed in it. All Catholicism, all the faith of Catholicism, rests on the authority of the infallible Church. Catholic opponents of Luther have heretofore chiefly (if completely correctly) based all their objections to the reformer on the point that Luther came out against the authority of the Church. So that Harnack's last paradox is also purely Catholic. But Harnack cannot proceed without this, and understanding full well the risk to which he exposes the whole construct of his liberal Protestant ideas he, with his characteristic conscientiousness, has all the same exposed his weak spot, not waiting until his opponents did it. Faith without authority is impossible, the representative of the modern theology in Germany tells us. I again will not take up just dissecting and analysing this, and still less, evaluating Harnack's adduced judgement. We will speak of this anon. It's only necessary for me to establish that Harnack's experience, the experience, I repeat, of an excellent scholar, the most talented and smartest connoisseur of the religious literature, leads to such a conclusion of the significance of authority in religious questions. A little anticipating the presentation and running ahead, I here ought to say that I consider Harnack's conclusion completely incorrect. If he knew only the Apostle Paul and Luther, that would be completely sufficient for the opposite conclusion. I'm not even talking about medieval mystics and sectarians, who departed from the authorities on which they were educated. One can say with conviction: the task of all religious genius reduces to the destruction of extant religious authorities. The special characteristic of the life and the meaning of the tormented and intense existence of these people inhere exactly in that they themselves had to be authorities for others, at the same time as they had no such authority for themselves. Harnack didn't notice this, did not want to or could not notice? Probably, the reason here lies deeper. We recall that Harnack considers paradox licit in the domain of religion (Wes.d.Christ. 44). And along with that we know that even those paradoxes which the confessions of Christianity acknowledged by men allow, even the paradoxes of orthodox Protestantism, I'm not even talking about Catholicism, seem inapplicable to Harnack. How to find a criterion for paradoxes? Where to find the dam which would hold back the powerful and terrible stream of allowed paradoxical creative work? Can good sense and the threat of punishment hold back insane humanity? And, then, can good sense possibly be trusted? For it too does not have long to over-enthuse: it, soon as you look round, along with the other paradoxes repulsive to Harnack, imposes its <u>veto</u> and holds back even those which Harnack acknowledges as necessary and salvific. Good sense can also not be left to itself. The historian knows this. The historian remembers the desperate struggle of at least that same Luther with Thomas Munzer and [Andreas] Karlstadt. The historian remembers what a storm arose in Germany when Luther first rebelled against authority. The historian can also recall quite a few other analogous pictures from the recent and remote past. Good sense does not restrain men. Another force is necessary; a firm unshakable power is necessary. <u>Ferret vulgus nisi paveat.</u>[7] And it stands to reason, in that truth is one for all, then authority is obligatory for Luther, and for Augustine, and even for Jesus. On this we'll pause for now and put Harnack aside for a while.

V

Thus the moderate liberal theology, in the same measure as Catholicism, cannot get by without authority. In its capacity of true and devoted handmaiden of philosophy, theology does not trust itself, does not trust men, as adults don't trust children. Philosophy from olden times has established, as its unwavering principle, that any truth ought to be verified and that, prior to stepping out with some truth, man is obliged to devise a special philosopher's stone, which is called the criterion. The ultimate power, the decisive word – per general conviction – ought to belong to human reason. Man does not even accept his Creator, without having first checked whether such corresponds with the demands put forth by reason. I recall here Socrates' question in Eutiphrones: whether the good is good [потому ли добро хорошо] because the gods love it, or do gods love the good, because it is good.[8] In other words, standards exist, principles for distinction of good and evil. These norms are well known to human reason. And prior to accepting gods, we pose ourselves this question: are these gods subordinate to what our reason acknowledges good, or insubordinate. If insubordinate, they are not gods, not actual gods. <u>Potestas clavium</u>, the right to bind and loose, per Socrates' doctrine, belongs not to the denizens of heaven but to the dwellers on earth. Not only Socrates, not only Socrates' disciples but also the disciples of Socrates' disciples, both those who remained pagans and those who with their works laid the foundation of Catholic dogma, in equal degree always considered themselves rightly obliged to validate their judgements with some firmly established criteria. There's no need to say it, that both here, as everywhere, people artfully deceived themselves. Seizing the <u>potestas clavium</u>, they never resolved to admit to themselves that they had allowed themselves such a bold usurpation. I'll take the first example at hand. '<u>Jubes, quod ad probem</u>', writes Augustine, '<u>si quis dicat, tempus esse motum corporis? Non jubes</u>'. This means, he turns to God with a question, whether God will order him to agree with those who affirm that time is the movement of a body. And he himself answers for God: <u>non jubes</u> – you do not so order. I don't think it'd be necessary to long dwell on exegesis of this point. Better to adduce yet another reasoning of Blessed Augustine in the exegesis of a modern Catholic. Augustine says: <u>intellege ut credas, crede ut intelligas</u>[9] (understand to believe, and believe to understand).

Prior to coming to believe, one must sort out the legitimacy of the rights of the one who proposes that you believe him at his word; one must first of all decide the question, whom to believe – cui sit credendum; and from this point of view reason precedes faith – 'ipsa (ratio) antecedit fidem'.[10] Here it's equally curious and important to denote both the hidden human pride (I say pride, only adapting to the dominant word usage – in actual fact, as we'll see in the upshot, there's not that much pride here) and the humility on display.

If the adduced example is insufficient, I can offer a selection of many others. Anselm of Canterbury, rationalist par excellence, i.e., a man, who in the same measure as Socrates does not accept and hearken to a word, albeit it were the word of God, if it is not found in compliance with those norms of truth and falsity, good and evil, which must be obligatory for all; well, he wrote the book 'Cur deus homo', where it is proven modo geometrico, that God could not but incarnate Himself – the man writes 'non tento, Domine, penetrare altitudinem tuam, quia nullatenus comparo illi intellectum meum; sed desidero aliquatenus intelligere veritatem tuam, quam credit et amat cor meum' (Proslogion, chap I). (I do not try, Lord, to penetrate to Your heights, in that I can in no way compare my reason to them; but I wish somehow to attain Your truth, in which my heart believes and which it loves.)

If you turn to the king of the medieval scholastics, to the doctor angelicus, Thomas Aquinas, you'll see here too that it's the same matter. The same humility and the same internal pride of reason on display. Thomas Aquinas was an unusual man – he saw much live, that the majority of people never saw in their dreams. He conversed with saints long departed from the world; he entered into communication with the apostles. Once even, in time of prayer before the crucifix, Christ Himself came down from the cross to him and said to him: bene de mi scriptisti (you wrote well of me) and asked him, what reward he asked for himself. It would seem, such extraordinary events ought to shake Thomas' trust in existing authority, i.e., of the Philosophus and of reason elevated to the throne by the philosophers. But with Thomas it turned out completely the opposite. No one of the Catholic writers, neither before or since, could or wished to stand up for the eternal prerogatives of reason. For him, more than for anyone else, Aristotle was praecursor Christi not only in naturalibus but also in supernaturalibus.[11] When it was necessary to decide the question, whether some supernatural phenomena were applicable or inapplicable, they turned for corrections and pointers to Aristotle. One could not simply believe; before believing one must have answered the question cui est credendum – (whom to believe). And no one dared answer this question, besides Aristotle and those to whom Aristotle delegated his divine rights. I'll adduce now a curious example from Summa theologica.

The well-known question is posed. It still disturbs both the theologians and laity, able to distinguish the essence and meaning of internal struggle under the theological covering. Utrum ad justificationem impii requiratur motus liberi arbitrii (Summa Th. De Gratia, Q. 113, Art 3, Title – Is movement of free will required for justification of the sinner?). Everyone knows, what great significance the Middle Ages attributed to the question of freedom of will. Modern times has convinced itself that the statement of the question which seemed the most correct to the Middle Ages little corresponds to the condition of our scientific knowledge. For medieval man, the question of the freedom of will was unbreakably connected with the question of salvation of the soul and, it stands to reason, of the Last Judgement. Now it seems to all the learned men that to speak of the salvation of the soul and of the Last Judgement is frivolous, for there's no Last Judgement and the same fate awaits all souls. Thus, too, the question of freedom of the will acquires a purely theoretical significance, as the best means of resolving it is elimination of the question itself. And the question is well eliminated by one or another means. I suppose that modern times hardly gained much in saving itself from the question. More than that, I'll say now that this question ought to be and might be posed exactly as it was posed by the Middle Ages – i.e., in connection with the question of the salvation of the soul and the Last Judgement. For all such philosophical questions ought to be considered in such fantastic illumination. You can not believe that Thomas Aquinas conversed with prophets and apostles; that's up to you. But you cannot but acknowledge that a man who has not been in such a fantastic domain, where at least such illusions are possible, is not fit for philosophy. He who has not experienced at least once that alongside our ordinary life there's yet another life, in which events occur which are completely idiosyncratic and nothing similar to those to which the everyday attests, can be an outstanding ploughman, or botanist, or even historian, but he hasn't even approached to the doorway of the ultimate mystery. Such a man might be a Kantian, Hegelian; he might even, as the materialists do, acknowledge miracles, but philosophy will always be a closed domain for him. For the matter is not at all to resolve for oneself some paradoxical affirmation, as is accepted in the dominant philosophy. Kant struck people with the statement that time and space are only forms of our perception. Hegel impressed with the law of development. Materialists went even further: they say that their 'reason' is not all contradicted by the affirmation of the possibility of such an unusual miracle as the transformation of dead material into living consciousness. After one hundred or five hundred thousand years a stone, they say, is transformed into man. As is well known, now the affirmations of the materialist are mocked everywhere. Reason, they're told, cannot acknowledge such a miracle. And it seems to me that it's not completely easy for the materialists themselves to acknowledge the possibility of such a miracle, and the majority of them prefer to hide their ultimate metaphysical faith behind positivism. They continue to think that first there were only stones and that then out of these stones came men, but they do not wish to say this and they shield themselves with the scientific words <u>ignoramus</u> (we don't know) or the not so scientific <u>ignorabimus</u> (we won't know). Materialists, of course, know what they're doing and, if they hide then, it stands to reason, they must hide. But if one throws out social-political considerations, then one must say that the considerations presented against materialism completely failed to withstand criticism. True, their affirmations are completely fantastic, much more fantastic than the affirmation of the most unrestrained Catholic. For reason, it is much easier to accept that bread and wine are turned into body and blood than that a stone turned into man. But can unacceptability to reason possibly serve as objection against any sort of metaphysical affirmation? Can there still be people so naive that they think that in the domain of metaphysics one must take reason into consideration? For, if one can speak with conviction and firmness of anything directly or indirectly tangent with the domain of metaphysics, then it's just exactly that metaphysics is a domain completely insubordinate to reason and its laws. And with greater probability one can presuppose that the degree of truth of any kind of metaphysical affirmation stands in inverse proportion to its acceptability for reason. So that the extant objections against materialism, i.e., indications that it is not reconciled with the laws of our thinking, not only do not condemn it but rather justify it. From the fact that our reason does not understand how a stone might turn instantly or gradually into Socrates, it does not at all follow that a stone cannot turn into Socrates, but solely that our reason is not able to understand the miraculous. All the miraculous, freely arising, repulses our rational consciousness, which would wish at any cost to subordinate to itself life with its stormy, characteristic way. Curiously – I already noted this long ago – from the very first moment of the awakening of human thought, people have made attempts to put limits to the autonomy of life. Autonomy for some reason has always seemed threatening. True it is too, the man never knew how, even in his own head – to so represent life to himself, so as to completely flush out this element of free creative work, which so irritates him. Everything went to compromises; i.e., they agreed to concede arbitrariness, but in the smallest possible dose. Expressing it in the language of the scholastics, they accepted <u>potentia ordinata</u>,[12] i.e., once for all established, albeit by arbitrariness – order, but <u>potentia absoluta</u>[13] ran wild, like the heads of Medusa. Take, for example, that most ancient remarkable thinker Empedocles. He explains everything, or nearly everything, now here even dwelling too long on the question of why he accepts some explanations and others rejects. Where have living beings come from? Separate members of different bodies grew out of the earth and then began to unite one with another. At first one got malformed bodies – they perished. Then little by little harmony was garnered. And there are as many of such explanations as you like in Empedocles, and they all fully satisfied him. And he demanded that his explanations be acknowledged true – as exemplary. Obviously, in him – yes, even long before him there was the habit to gain not so much the truth as much as explanations. The idiosyncratic taste appeared; the ineradicable autonomous demand, which became the pathos of philosophical creative work, as is the pathos of religious creativity – the urge to no matter what reconcile man to the fate prepared him by the gods. The former wish to explain the world, the latter to justify it. But both the one and the other attain their explanations and reconciliations by one means: the generalization of observed discrete phenomena into general laws. In other words, having discovered something, people decide that they already know quite a lot, that they know almost everything, even simply know everything, that they have general positions, which give the possibility of orienting themselves in the mysterious and complex multiformity of real life. They create <u>a priori</u> positions for themselves, serving as the basis and appearing as the result of discursive thought. Kant was a lot more correct than might appear at first glance, when he affirmed that man dictates his laws to the world. Dictates, what else can I say! But young Schopenhauer was also correct, when he interpreted the doctrine of Kant in the sense that all our discursive judgement is only a net we throw over living reality, and that's why it says nothing and can say nothing about it; i.e., it gives us no knowledge. In modern times Richert has taken up the idea of Schopenhauer and developed it in detail in his huge work. Discursive thought only exists so that man had the illusion of most perfect knowledge. As a matter of fact, abstract concepts not only do not yield cognition of reality, but on the contrary, they lead away from reality. Reality is irrational, absolutely unknowable, and our science is only ideal unknowledge of life. Richert, true, despite Schopenhauer, at his own expense and risk, affirms that such an ideal unknowledge is the apotheosis of science. Science, leading away from reality to abstract positions, in the opinion of the modern philosopher, has all rights to be called the very best, most perfect knowledge. Why Richert so judges, why, having taken whole from Schopenhauer his theory of discursive thought, he did not resolve to go further after his teacher and seek, as Schopenhauer did, for other sources of knowledge – I cannot say with assurance. But all probabilities say that here triumphed the principle of <u>primum vivere deinde philosophare</u>.[14] The contemporary scholar feels that for him to renounce discursive thought would mean to lose the right to life. If generalizing science does not yield perfect knowledge then that poses the question of the very right to science's existence. For a botanist, physicist, mathematician such a posing of the question is not so terrible. They know that if their sciences don't, well, turn out perfect or the most perfect of possible knowledge, then – although this isn't very pleasant – no harm: one can still live, there are other justifications for them – of a purely practical character. But what justifications will philosophy dig up for itself in this case? It had no practical significance and, if it's just clarified, that it has no perfect knowledge, it must cease to exist, cease to live. Schopenhauer did not fear this. He boldly decided that if discursive thought, on which positive sciences are architected, no wise yields results in philosophy, then one can get by without it. One can find another source of philosophical knowledge as well – even more seductive and attractive. And exactly so, the source of Schopenhauer's philosophy was pure fantasy, which he, paying tribute to philosophical traditions, named intuition. It wouldn't enter anyone's head to call his magnificent delirium on love, music, the veil of Maya, etc., science, as it would enter no one's head to call Plato's inspired prophecies in <u>Symposium</u>, <u>Phaedo</u> or <u>The Republic</u> on Eros and immortality science. But there've been and are quite a few admirers, who wouldn't trade the thoughts of Schopenhauer and Plato for the most sober judgements. Richert, like the majority of contemporary philosophers, goes delirious but is not up to fantasy and prophecy and he has only one move left: to reason. After he has in such detail, following Schopenhauer, demonstrated that reasonings only lead from reality. <u>Primum vivere – deinde philosophare</u>,[15] the device turns out immovable.

VI

Such is the role of reason, which pretends to the highest superstitious rights. It's clear that beginning with Socrates and concluding with Kant and his modern disciples, reason set itself a definite problem. It struggled with arbitrariness and systematically persecuted all attempts of free creative work to transgress the previously ordained limits. A second point, I suppose, is no less clear: reason could attain its goals by only one path – decreeing defining laws to human principles. And it seems to me that people ere the present time have not given themselves account of the degree to which the lawgiving activity of reason limited their creative work. All proclaim Socrates for his great revelation: the dialectic. The critique of pure reason is nothing but a Protestant hymn to Socrates. We rejoice that after Socrates we no longer have the right <u>to affirm</u> everything that we consider just, true or necessary. On the converse, one can consider just or true only that which does not diverge from the positions prescribed by reason. By what means has reason so succeeded in terrorizing the human soul, which, as is known, is not inclined to subordination, being free, arbitrary, even by its nature? Catholicism or Mohammadism subdued by fire and sword. How did Socrates conquer? What charm did the ugly Silenus have, that he succeeded in enchanting even the tempestuous Alcibades with his dialectic? Alcibades, who had not submitted to the dread laws of the state, quieted before the unarmed, conversing Socrates. And now, two and a half millennia later, everyone, even Catholic scholars, humbly bows before him who the ancient oracle called the wisest of men! Savonarola wrote once of the <u>trionfo del croce</u>,[16] all Catholic apologetics trumpeted the same – as a matter of fact, yes, only Socrates' conquest can be called universal; only he alone in point of fact succeeded in subduing almost the entire world. And, if there are today little quarters in our world, in which the power of the ancient sage is not acknowledged, one can say with conviction that there won't be any tomorrow. And, conversely, with no less assurance one can say that on the day when people throw off the power of Socrates and acknowledge insane Diogenes as their leader, the end of the world will ensue. True it is, too, that the most irreconcilable descendants of Diogenes feared no such threats. More than that, they tied their best hopes to the end of the world and for 1,500 years struggled in the name of this mad idea. But the Middle Ages are over, and now even Catholicism, if it has not in principle renounced its idea, has tried to prettify and mollify it, to denature it by supplementary circumlocutions comprehensible to the modern mind, so that if Thomas Aquinas or the holy Satan, Pope Gregory VII rose from the grave, they would not believe that the modern Catholic Church is still the same Church to whose creation and defence they applied so much labour and genius. The Church, who thanks to considerations of humanism shares with anyone at all her <u>potestas clavium</u> – would seem to them no longer the body of Christ, but one of the numerous enterprises which have been created by humanity over the course of the centuries. For in the concession, in the admission, which Pohle makes (he's far from unique, of course), and which contemporary Catholics 'understand', only the blind could not see that the power of the heirs of the Apostle Peter has no longer secretly, but has been overtly, delegated to the heirs of Socrates. The Catholic Church has the right to bind and loose not all people but only those who belong to the Church. Otherwise it would be immoral and irrational; i.e., in other words, it is not for the Church, in force of the power belonging to it to define what is rational and what moral, but rather, the norms of rationality and morality exalted by the pagan Socrates are obligatory for the Catholic Church. In other words, lumen naturale – for Socrates had no other little light – is just as necessary to Catholicism as to any Hegel or Voltaire. The mystery of revelation also ought to be illuminated by the spark struck by the ancient pagans. I'll emphasize again what I said earlier: Catholicism could not get by without Socrates even in the Middle Ages. But then concessions to reason and morality were done only in fact – theoretically, though, de jure, the source of religious knowledge was considered to be only revelation. Now, though, even the magnificent edifice of Catholicism is shaken. Defending itself against its numerous enemies – chiefly against the Protestants – Catholicism has already resolved to accept that forum, which Socrates considered uniquely competent for resolution of all moot questions. The Church is prepared on the most important question to acknowledge the right of reason to a decision without appeal. In place of the fairy-glow illumination lent by the previous lumen supernaturale (supernatural light), modern man sees life in the pale white light of the Socratic lumen naturale (natural light). When the choice came down to the insane and the right-minded Socrates, even Catholicism no longer hesitated. The Vatican council just recently, almost before our eyes, established that if anyone comes to affirm that reason contradicts faith, he is subject to anathema – anathema sit.

> We can now return to the question of Thomas Aquinas: Utrum ad justificationem impii requiratur motus liberi arbitrii? (Summa Th. De Gratia, Ia-IIae, Art. 3, Questio) Here's his answer: Respondeo dicendum, quod justificatio impii fit Deo movente hominem ad justitiam: Ipse enim est 'qui justificat impium', ut dicitur Rom. 4, 5. Deus autem movet omnia secundum modum uniucujusque: sicut in naturalibus videmus quod aliter moventur ab ipso gravia et aliter levia, propter diversam naturam utriusque. Unde homines ad justitiam movet secundum conditionem naturae humanae. Homo autem secundnam propriam naturam habet, quodsit liberi arbitrii. Et ideo in eo, qui habet usum liberi arbitrii. Et ideo in eo, qui habet usum liberi arbitrii, non fit motio a Deo ad justitiam absque motu liberi arbitrii.[17]
>
> (Ib., Conclusio)[18]

Follow attentively the trajectory of Thomas' thought. He takes the position from the Epistle of Paul to the Romans that God saves the sinner. But what the Apostle Paul says means little to him. Or better yet: he dared not show his readers life in that fairy-glow illumination, which the lumen supernaturale of the great apostle yields. The human eye – and not just any one – can withstand such illumination only for the course of a few seconds. If Paul is right, if God saves sinners, and man is justified by faith, as said in Romans III, 28, independent of works – colligimus igitur, fide justificari hominem absque operibus legis,[19] – then the first real result of a position so improbable for human reason is the necessity of renunciation of lumen naturale. For, recall what Socrates taught, recall how he glorified works, how he convinced everyone, that it's just by works, by one's works alone, that one could then be saved. In the light of Paul's lumen supernaturale the Socratic lumen naturale flickers out. Or the opposite – all the fairy glow of Paul could not produce any impression, if it were presented in the daylight devised by Socrates. As is known – further on we'll have to dwell on this at length – the verse cited from the epistle of Paul served as the apple of discord between Catholicism and Luther. As opposed to Thomas Aquinas, Luther not only made no attempt to weaken the impression of the words of the apostle, but on the contrary, he resolved as early as his translation of the named text to arbitrarily add the intensifying and sharply signifying word – sola. He, despite the Greek text and its traditional interpretation, translated the words of the Apostle in the following manner: sola fide justificari hominem,[20] etc. That is, by his translation he completely cut off any possibility of reconciliation between Paul and Socrates, between Judaism and Hellenism. He solemnly renounced the sober lumen naturale for the sake of the fairy-glow lumen supernaturale. If he had in parallel with the Vatican council to give his formula of the relation of reason to faith, he ought to have said that he who professes that reason is not in radical contradiction with faith – anathema to him forever and ever. As we'll see in the upshot, he did say this. Thomas Aquinas, princeps scholasticorum,[21] in our presentation always connected with what is most fantastical, fairy glow and eternally enigmatic in Catholicism, himself feared the doctrine of Paul no less than any other man, be he Catholic or even, if you will, atheist or pagan. He firmly embedded himself into the visible world and dared not for a moment turn from it. God moves everything, explains the doctor angelicus, corresponding to its nature. We saw, says he, that in the natural order of things God puts into motion everything corresponding to its characteristics, the lighter by one means, the heavier by another. It stands to reason, and justifying men, He is consistent with the movements of the free will given to each man. The question naturally arises: in order to clarify the mystery of human salvation, the mystery of the grace of God, once we have to deal with our poor reason – as though the matter in question were not a most profound mystery, but the solving of one of those extreme evil puzzles [одна из тех хитроумних загадок-ребусов] which people invent for themselves, or which nature invented for people – what's the requirement to go look in the holy books? That's on one hand. On the other, who gave the right to the normal theologian Thomas Aquinas or better yet to the first passer-by modern Catholic professor, composing his multivolume dogmatus in the image and likeness of Thomas' Summa theologica, to limit the freedom of the creative work of God himself? The unnoticed sicut in naturalibus videmus[22] is for Thomas – and after Thomas, for all Catholicism, too, right up to our days, the key to the solution of the whole great mystery of divine creative work. For one can then ask, and, I hope, completely legitimately, what did the normal theologians see in naturalibus?[23] And here you've got, as I've already indicated, a striking phenomenon: in order to judge of the invisible divine mystery, we turn for analogies to the visible world. The lawgiver for that visible world turns out to be the same old Aristotle. Can there now be any doubt that the Philosophus was for Catholicism not only the praecursor Christi in naturalibus,[24] but also praecursor Christi in supernaturalibus;[25] i.e., in other words, the spiritual director of the devout Catholic was the pagan ignorant of revelation. The myth of the independence of philosophy and theology ought to be, among other myths, donated to the history museum of errors, very curious errors, those no longer good for anything, and even harmful. I do not wish to say by this that the spiritual creative work of the Middle Ages ought to be rejected. On the contrary, the more I become familiar with this epoch, named (not without basis) the epoch of deepest night, the more I'm convinced that one can indicate few historic periods, in which the spiritual activity of man attained greater intensity than in the Middle Ages. If one compares the age of Enlightenment – the eighteenth century, and the age of creative work of positive science – the nineteenth century – with the ages of the twelfth and thirteenth centuries, then the comparison will be far from the advantage of modern times. On the contrary, you'll rather become amazed at the superficiality and complete absence of curiosity of our closest ancestors and contemporaries. True, the Middle Ages are one long unbroken night. Everyone that was strong, restless, and talented headed to the monastery in order to devote oneself in solitude to dream and daydream. And perhaps, that's why they summoned the eternally encouraging Aristotle in order not to completely lose contact with what's called reality. How would Thomas Aquinas know what happened <u>in naturalibus</u>[26] and whether there was, as a matter of fact, any kind of <u>naturalia</u>.[27] In his monastery at the foot of the crucifix Thomas didn't even know for sure, whether there was something else in the world, besides that which he was told by saints and martyrs come from another world. And, when it was necessary to tell people of his faith, he learned a language from his <u>Philosophus</u>, which would be comprehensible to energetic and right-thinking people. Aristotle explained to him that men are incredulous and vain beings. If you tell them everything that happens in nocturnal visions before the eyes of the recluse, exhausted by fasts and vigils and which is so unlike the vain beings' diurnal visions, they'll never believe anything. It seems to them that they're deceived or they're being laughed at – the average man is always inclined to suspect that you want to get around him, deceive him, or you want to laugh at him and, in order to remove any suspicion from oneself, one must find a connection between day and night, between the prose of the everyday and the dissolute orgy of unrestrained fantasy. Man will come to believe in God only when God subordinates Himself to his, human reason – <u>sicut in naturalibus videtur</u>[28] and limit his eternal arbitrariness to the norms worked out in everyday practice. Moses, the prophets, Christ, the apostles, and the great teachers of the Middle Ages – beginning with Tertullian and concluding with Luther, Loyola, St Theresa, or John of the Cross – could only be valued by people inasmuch as they could be applied to human needs. Remember Dostoevsky's <u>Legend of the Grand Inquisitor</u>.

VII

The bitter and sharp polemic of Aristotle against Plato is known to all. It's also known that Aristotle chose Plato's doctrine of ideas as the central point of his attacks on his teacher. Plato affirmed that ideas have independent transcendental existence, i.e., that above the visible world accessible to usual cognition, there exists yet another invisible world, inaccessible to the senses, and that this world is attained in moments of inspired insight by certain people and that it, this world, fantastic from the point of view of ordinary consciousness, is indeed the singularly real world, in which the human soul always lived before its unification with the body, and whither it will return anew, when it will shed the fetters of its earthly existence. Only in a world beautiful and perfect does life have meaning and significance, that world alone is beautiful and attractive; the usual world then arouses in the enlightened one [в прозревшем человеке – 'the man who has seen' – Trans] only revulsion and disdain. The dialectic, chiefly, is directed to destroying our habitual attachments to that which does not deserve attachment. Revulsion at the visible world, dissatisfaction with its usual, even best goods is the beginning of purification, i.e., the beginning of wisdom, leading to the attainment of true and eternal good. While you value and love that which is considered valuable and good by the majority of men, while you hustle after honours, glory, fame, wealth, after the happinesses of life, you are a blind man, not suspecting you're on an express to the cliff, to eternal perdition. The problem of the philosopher consists in devaluing in his own eyes and the eyes of people around him all the goods [блага], so as to make usual life lukewarm and repulsive, and set, as a goal of life, a longing [тоска] for another world, where eternal good [добро] replaces the values transient, and thus little worth, which now draw in the crowd of people who know not what's necessary for them. In the seventh chapter of his <u>Republic</u> Plato tells his now well-known parable of the cave. We all sit in the cave, back to the true and beautiful life. Reality is not visible to us – we see only shadows from real things on the walls of our cave. And we are so used to the darkness of our gloomy habitat that the bright light of truth and reality is terrible to us. Like owls and other night birds we can live only in darkness. Light blinds us.

This Platonic doctrine of ideas seemed most unbearable to Aristotle; he, as I said, launched on his teacher with all the mercilessness of conviction believing in its righteousness. He forgot even the gratitude which obliges students to masters. Truth before everything. Friendship must bow before truth. Even the most fervent admirers of Aristotle find his attacks against Plato too sharp. But what's most curious, even the most fervent defenders of Aristotle ought to acknowledge two circumstances. First, despite his sharp polemical relations to Plato, Aristotle all the same in his metaphysics was obliged to accept much of his doctrine on ideas. And second, Aristotle's metaphysics is no freer from contradiction than Plato's metaphysics. And meantime, the critique of Platonic ideas in Aristotle is wholly (like any philosophical critique, by the way) based on the exposure of contradictions in the doctrine under analysis. The question arises: if, to replace doctrine rejected as contradictory, you have to propose another doctrine just as contradictory, what have you gained? And still more interesting – and for us an especially essential question – did Aristotle really reject Plato's doctrine of ideas out of the contradictions he denoted in this doctrine? If you will, pose the problem more generally – we'll have to do it later anyways – have we really gotten away from this or that doctrine because we have noted contradictions in it? Or is the decisive moment here something else?

I call attention to the indicated considerations: the Aristotelian doctrine of form and matters suffers no less contradiction than Plato's doctrine of ideas as true realities. Aristotle wishes to think that the singular reality is individual things. But he does not wish to depart from Socrates and Plato. He acknowledges that sensual perception cannot be the source of knowledge, that knowledge is directed not at the changing and transient, but at the eternal and unchanging. So, it stands to reason, the object of knowledge is not the personal, individual, i.e., what's singularly real, per his opinion, but the general, i.e., per his doctrine, as a matter of fact, what doesn't exist. This contradiction penetrates Aristotle's whole system of metaphysics. It turns out with him that knowledge, i.e., the highest, relates to something not real, and he can just as little derive his real, i.e., one-off, individual things, out of general concepts, as Plato can derive his physical world out of his invisible ideas. They both are hammering out true eternal knowledge, i.e., proven, well-founded knowledge. They both disdain the empiric and 'opinion' (δόξα) and strive to show, following Socrates, that people are not to be left to think whatever they think up, that there are true and false judgements, and that the former of these, <u>of necessity</u>, not allowing any objections, are derived from self-evident truths. And both sin the same: neither of them can even approximately state his problem. Instead of necessity, which they promised, arbitrariness ensues. They dreamed of creating a metaphysics, like mathematics, where any succeeding proposition will ineluctably derive from the previous – but they created doctrines, shot through with unbearable contradictions.

If we can speak of unity in Plato and Aristotle, it's maybe only of unity in intentions. Neither Plato nor Aristotle ever put on display their personal contradictions. On the contrary, each of them spoke in a quiet tone, which excluded any thought of possibility of contradictions in his personal system. But didn't they notice them as a matter of fact? As a matter of fact, didn't people of such great penetration, who know so well how to find out their opponents, see their own defects? Don't we have repeated here the story of the Gospel parable of the mote in another's and the beam in one's own eye? I think not, here the question is of a completely different order. After Plato and Aristotle there were many more great philosophers, and with each of them the same story ineluctably repeated. They noted contradictions in their opponents and called them out but remained silent on their own contradictions, as though they didn't exist at all. And even now, in our times, the same is repeated. Philosophers passionately accuse each other of contradictions, exactly as though contradictions were a mortal sin, and exactly as though at some time there existed philosophical doctrines free of contradictions. The strange bad faith of philosophical critique, elevated to a system, disturbs no one. Everyone is used to it; no one is uneasy about it; no one even talks about it, as no one talks of the commandment accepted among diplomats: don't tell the truth. I even recently read the affirmation by one recognized very learned philosopher that if in the system of a philosopher there's even one contradiction, it already loses any significance. But Aristotle, I am convinced, could not so think. He saw not only Plato's contradictions but his own personal ones as well. If he forayed out with a sharp criticism of the doctrine of his great predecessor, teacher and friend, it was not because he was uneasy with contradiction in affirmations but because Plato's very affirmations were unacceptable, interfered with the task, which he, correctly or incorrectly, considered the most important in life. This is all the more obvious, as Aristotle serenely and assuredly took from Plato with a big scoop, each time, as soon as it seemed to him that something created by Plato would avail him. I, per the problem I've set myself, cannot here dwell long on clarification of what Aristotle owes Plato. And there's no need for it: others have long ago done this without me. As I already said, it is considered generally accepted, that Aristotle in his doctrine of forms took almost all Plato's doctrine of ideas: he rejected only the position on their independent existence (the transcendentality of ideas). We need to clarify to ourselves what exactly in this affirmation of Plato so repulsed Aristotle. The indemonstrability and contradictoriness of the affirmation would not have so disturbed our philosopher – that seems to me indubitable. And here's yet one more indication, which will lead us by the path of negation to clearing up the enigma that interests us.

Several years ago Natorp, a very well-known scholar, of the so-called Marburg school, published a large investigation on Plato's ideas. And – no matter how strange it sounds – now 2,500 years after Plato, Natorp proves that all Aristotle's attacks on Plato are completely in vain, for it never entered Plato's head to consider ideas as transcendental realities. Although all indeed read Plato, no one heretofore understood Plato, as all looked at him with Aristotle's eyes. Aristotle, though, although he studied with Plato all twenty years, did not analyse his teacher, for in essence he was not able to grasp him, as generally dogmatics cannot grasp criticists. Natorp affirms that what Kant formulated was already clear for Plato: the object of our thinking cannot be things but only relations. But Aristotle, as a dogmatic, naively imagined that knowledge is knowledge of things. It thus seems to him that only individual things are real, and general concepts are not real. As a matter of fact, general concepts are the same categories of our reason as are individual things, and the predicate of being, it stands to reason, is applicable to them in the same measure. For Natorp, as a consistent Kantian, this means that the predicate of being is only a predicate given to our consciousness and, it stands to reason, says nothing of existence <u>an sich</u>. Plato knew this, and he affirmed this, only this. But Aristotle for whose limited understanding the predicate of being could be applied only to individual things, decided, on the basis of the fact that Plato considered ideas as existent, that Plato also took them as individual and, reasonably, as transcendental things. As a matter of fact, Plato affirmed nothing of the kind. For him ideas were only logical forms, only a method of scientific rework, only regularity – and the question of the transcendentality of their existence never even presented itself to him. Later readers of Plato, hypnotized by Aristotle, no longer read Plato with their own eyes. They repeated of the great philosopher what Aristotle showed them.

Such is Natorp's fundamental idea, which he develops all through his large book with the foundation and patience characteristic of German scholars. As far as I know, however, Natorp's book did not produce the desired effect. Plato's ideas, even now, as previously, are interpreted as Aristotle interpreted them. I personally have yet another, additional impression: in spite of all Natorp's malice in relation to Aristotle, Natorp is still a disciple not of Plato, but of Aristotle, his hated Aristotle. If one were to search for the psychological interpretation of this or that understanding of Plato, one wouldn't have to go far for Natorp's psychology. About one thing one can say exactly that his philosophical thought under the influence of Aristotle and all his heirs, right up to Kant himself, was so formed, that the very idea of transcendental essences seemed to him a monstrous inconsistency, a mortal sin. He values, he sees in Plato, only that which Aristotle did not reject, that through Aristotle became the estate of medieval, and then too modern philosophical thought. Only Aristotle had a dual quality before Natorp (and if you will, before the immediate teacher of Natorp – Kant): he first rebelled against the fantastic element in philosophy – that's one, and the other, that he had the boldness to openly demarcate and subject to criticism the illegal elements in the doctrine of his divine teacher. No small qualities, especially the former. Aristotle was most of all obliged to it for his millennium-long influence. Thanks to Aristotle – no one will come to deny this – modern science became possible. Kant himself with his transcendental deduction became possible.

I repeat, Aristotle's metaphysics is just as contradictory as Plato's metaphysics. But yet Kant's theory of cognition, which displays pretensions to the rights once belonging to metaphysics, is filled with no less contradictions. If it too were fated to play such a decisive role in the history of human thought, it's in no way due to its shape and logical completeness. I said, I say and I will not tire of repeating: the myth of the existence of logically complete philosophical systems, containing no internal contradictions, that myth must be considered gone to history. For logical completeness is the same kind of idol as Perun. It's got beard and moustache of silver and gold, but it's not God. Kant's service (if it's a service) is that he long flushed out of philosophy the element of mystery and supernatural. He, like Aristotle, allocated consciousness to the 'primordial' truths, i.e., to those truths, without which, in his opinion, science is impossible, and these truth become guards, holding off all attempts at further curiosity. No matter what Natorp said, the difference between the critical philosophy of Kant and the metaphysics of Aristotle is much less significant than the difference between the synthetic ideas of Kant and Plato's ideas. Yes, and Natorp himself knows this in fact. Analysing <u>Phaedo</u>, he in passing, as though not even considering that this could raise confusion in anyone, allows himself to affirm that the contents of this dialogue has no relation to immortality of the soul, and that, if there were such a problem in Plato, then it needs to be considered completely unsuccessful, for Socrates was able to prove the thesis of the immortality of the soul only thanks to an illicit logical leap. Thus speaks Natorp of <u>Phaedo</u> and Plato's other dialogues in which the question of the immortality of the soul is raised and analysed. For Natorp this is metaphysics, unallowable, just like Plato's doctrine of awareness – and, it stands to reason, this is not the chief thing. The chief thing is Plato's doctrine of synthetic doctrine <u>a priori</u>, that is of the idea, as method, i.e., of science, which has its source not in reality – and not, God forbid, in sensual impression (sensualism is the most accursed word in our time), but in 'consciousness in general', and the logical completeness, to which one might attribute the predicate of being because this predicate is applicable to individual things as well, only per order of that same 'consciousness in general'. If Natorp allows Plato to speak of eternity, then it's only in a very conditional sense. One can speak of eternity in the moment, i.e., that eternity, which Schleiermacher found in Spinoza and which is passed down in the inheritance of modern Protestant theology. Such eternity was in Plato – this Natorp does not deny.

One must also remember that albeit Natorp really for the first time (together with Cohen) resolves to submit Plato to the above-described castration, his task was already fully prepared. It had already even been completed, if you like, by history – and just in the fact of the triumph of Aristotle over Plato. For to deprive Plato of his ideas means to put him under Aristotle's hand. Before Natorp, as we know, historians of philosophy had not done this. But it wasn't necessary for them to do this. Although they, presenting Plato's philosophy, presented his doctrine of memory, of immortality of the soul, eros, mania, of the judgement beyond the grave, and devoted enough space to his ideas, it turned out that these ideas are something which Plato, in essence, could have renounced, as he could have renounced his myths. Science would not have suffered at all from this – even would have gained, for science got no use out of Plato's 'ideas'. Aristotle criticized them, but history respectfully escorted them into a neighbouring domain, at well-defined separation from philosophy, that'd be poetry.

Who doesn't know that Plato was a great poet – and that the better half of his philosophical baggage, it stands to reason, cannot sustain the inspectors of philosophy. And the main contraband, of course, is ideas. There is something else, also dangerous and not allowed – of which we'll speak anon – but 'ideas' are at the forefront. As a product of poetic creative work, they can be allowed – the poet is allowed to carry whatever rubbish he wants. But the philosopher has the right to present only demonstrated truths. And one is not allowed to doubt that such truths existed and exist in humanity. And here, in the name of these proven truths, previous historians escorted Platonic ideas to the domain of poetry. Natorp interprets them in the sense in which they could have still satisfied Kant and, no doubt, would not have drawn Aristotle's resistance. And what kind of proven truths there are, in the name of which history pronounced its judgement on Plato, that's what we'll speak to now.

VIII

In Plato's <u>Phaedo</u> we read the following:

Κινδυνεύουσι γὰρ ὅσοι τυγχάνουσιν ὀρθῶς ἁπτόμενοι φιλοσοφίας λ ε λ η θ έ ν α ι τοὺς ἄλλους, ὅτι οὐδὲν ἄλλο αὐτοὶ ἐπιτηδεύουσιν τε καὶ τεθνάναι (<u>Phaedo</u>, 64 a).

It means that those who wholly devote themselves to philosophy <u>conceal</u> from the unenlightened, that they do nothing else than practise for dying and death. If you glance in any of the modern textbooks of philosophy and seek a definition of the science therein presented, you'll find there whatever you like, but you'll not find even a hint, that philosophy is practice for death and dying. If you go into the textbooks of the history of philosophy to acquaint yourself with Plato's doctrine, you'll again discover much, but it will still remain hidden from you that Plato gave philosophy the aforementioned definition. As before in Phaedo, so now for the great majority of people this mystery – even after Plato revealed it to man – remains a mystery. Why did this happen? Many have read Plato's works, of those many read Phaedo specifically. But so then, so now, not only the general public but also learned specialists do not know what Plato's main problem was. And meantime in Phaedo this admission is repeated twice. Over a couple of dozen pages (Phaedo 80 e) Socrates again affirms that in philosophizing, the soul practises for dying. And so, if you will, all of Phaedo is only a development of this basic theme: to philosophize is to move towards death; it means to tear oneself away from visible life and enter in the domain of the eternal mystery-denominated death. Everyone has read this, both the learned and the unlearned – and no one believed this. Not for nothing, in the same Phaedo (Phaedo 69 e). Plato affirms: Τοῖς δὲ πολλοῖς ἀπιστίαν παρέχει – unbelieving crowd. No one would agree to acknowledge that one could trade real, tangible life for problematic practice for death. Who needs it, for what? But if it's so, if on one hand the whole task of philosophy is reduced to preparation for death and dying, on the other hand, the crowd, i.e., all people, only believe when they are forced to faith by self-evidence, or a force equal to self-evidence, then how to be a philosopher turning to people with speeches? If he says simply what he knows or what he's seen, he will not be believed: we didn't see it, it follows it doesn't exist, this is what they'll answer him. Worse: they'll oppose usual life experience to his penetration and his wisdom, as having equal rights, as the singularly decisive. Plato was a witness, how two men in the crowd dared to throw down a challenge to the wisdom of Socrates. They didn't glance at the fact that the oracle acknowledged Socrates as the wisest of men. He's no sage, he's a criminal, they announced. And Anitus and Melitus triumphed. The court of Athenian citizens declared Socrates guilty and submitted him to the most disgraceful and terrible punishment. Force turned out on the side of the τῶν πολλῶν, that same crowd, who does not believe, who acknowledges nothing freely, who concedes only under compulsion.

Socrates felt this and understood it long before his task arose. He knew that he was one man, and it was all versus one. And in his solitary soul there was the embryonic idea of the possibility of struggling with the crowd with a special weapon – dialectic. Crowds rule people by the fist, rule even by the word – they can speak beautifully, but they cannot prove – and here for his self-defence Socrates did invent a special art of struggle, of argument – the basic condition of which is the proposition that there is a series of unarguable truths obligatory for all. In the course of decades, Socrates went in the squares, the bazaars and other common places and convinced people of only one thing: there is nothing arbitrary in the world; over all the living, not only over people but also over the gods, there stands an eternal, unchangeable law, able to stand up for itself. As early as Eutiphrones, as I noted in passing in one of the early dialogues, Socrates puts this question with unusual acuity: why is the good good because the gods love it, or do the gods love the good because it is good (Eutiphrones 10 a)?[29] And he decides it in the second sense. Even the gods are not allowed arbitrariness, and they are bound in their love and their hatred. In Apology and in Ion Socrates expressed his disdain of poets; they may see and know divine things, deeply significant things; they know them accidentally: οὐ τέχνῃ ... ἀλλὰ θεία μοῖρα.[30] They themselves do not understand, i.e., do not know how to explain and prove that of which they speak. Through all Plato's works there runs like a red thread the opposition of ἐπιστήμη – knowledge and θεία μοῖρα – i.e., inspiration, divine security (Phaedrus 244 c; Zeller II-1, 498 commentary). He is against those who do what they do not through wisdom, but somehow by nature, in a fit of inspiration (οὐ σοφίᾳ ποιοῖεν ἃ ποιοῖεν, ἀλλὰ φύσει τινὶ καὶ ἐνθουσιάζοντες. Apology 22 c; Zeller II-1, 498).

And although θεία μοίρα ... ἄμευ νοῦ actually means divine inspiration, there is no definite concept here. Plato considers that such virtue, such knowledge is negligible and compares it to chance (Meno 100 a). He values only those virtues which man, as teacher, can transmit to people. For him therefore virtue and knowledge are synonyms. In Protagoras Socrates forces his opponent to admit that the crowd is mistaken, supposing that knowledge is impotent and cannot dominate.[31] Knowledge is first of all force and the most powerful force on earth. In his defence speech he, in answer to the accusations of Anitus and Melitus, proudly and assuredly answers: what can Anitus and Melitus do to me? Haul me into court; slander me. They can even gain my condemnation in court, my death sentence. All that is so, but they cannot bring me harm. For a bad man can never harm a good man.

There is another position in connection with this, which is especially striking by its boldness and unusualness for that time (and indeed for our time): Socrates affirms that if one had to choose, it is better to endure injustice oneself than to be unjust. This is also spoken of in Phaedo, and in other works of Plato, but Plato never succeeded in developing this idea with such force as in the dialogue Gorgias; Socrates is opposed by an opponent of such huge force that for some people after reading through this dialogue there's even doubt whether Socrates could be considered the victor in this contest. Several people on this basis even refuse to acknowledge Plato as the author of the dialogue. And exactly, Calliclus speaks with true inspiration, but, it seems to me that this does serve exactly as proof of the original nature of the dialogue. Plato feels what he takes on himself, stepping up with such a statement. One must remember that it's one matter in our time, 2,500 years after Plato, to repeat rote phrases of the superiority of moral force over physical force; it's another matter to first see and express such a thought. It's not the point that our contemporaries penetrated more into it and attained it. I am convinced that both now, as in antiquity, you will find in all the world the most insignificant number of people, who could, putting their hand on their heart, say that they more feared to be unjust than to experience injustice. For it is difficult, infinitely difficult to endure denigration, be conscious of oneself as weak and helpless, be unable to defend one's rightness and along with that preserve proud consciousness of one's superiority. Calliclus spoke of this inimitably. But just because Plato could put such an inspired speech in the mouth of Socrates' opponent, thus one can judge the depth of the source from which Plato's creative work flowed. It's true that when Calliclus spoke, the picture of the death of Socrates stood before Plato unstinting. Yes, Socrates, the great teacher, the best and wisest of men, fell helpless before the blow of the negligible homunculi, Anitus and Mellitus, as Pushkin fell in our time, struck by the bullet of D'Anthes, a man not worth a thing to anyone. Socrates said that Anitus and Mellitus could not harm him, that the bad is not dangerous for the good. Anitus and Mellitus live, and Socrates is poisoned as tormentors poison wild dogs. Perhaps Socrates was incorrect, maybe all the same Anitus and Mellitus were stronger than him? For Plato this was not an abstract question; for him this was a question of life and death. This wasn't even for him a question in the sense in which the word is now understood.

With Socrates' death, the soul of Plato was no longer what it was previously. Some kind of internal shift occurred, after which everything was seen and heard differently. The same sky, the same stars, the same men, but there is something else that was not seen and heard before. Something remote, unclear, intangible, and invisible, but strongly compelling, acquired enigmatic power over the soul. Plato continued to live even after Socrates' death and lived a long time thereafter, almost fifty years. Perhaps, towards old age the impression was weakened and effaced. But there forever remained the engulfing and tormenting feeling of anguish and dissatisfaction. And to the end of his life Plato continued to prove insistently that it is better to endure injustice than to be unjust.

IX

Continued to prove … one asks, what were the proofs for? Why did Plato have to so insistently strive for <u>acknowledgement</u> of his truth? Is it insufficient that the truth is the truth? Is it insufficient that Socrates himself knew that Anitus and Mellitus could not harm him? Is it necessary that Mellitus and Anitus acknowledged this? And, to boot, is this attainable? The crowd's characteristic is unbelief and you will not overcome it; you might not believe it; you might triumph in consciousness of your strength. But neither Socrates, as we said above, nor Plato, nor even one of the philosophers living after them could endure. We have already had to speak more than once on this theme, but now it's especially incumbent to dwell on this. It's known to all, what a colossal role Socrates and Plato played in the history of European thought. One can say without exaggeration that our science began with Socrates. He first expressed and made man accept the position that truth unexplained and unproven is not truth. The basis of the world is a certain harmonious link of relations, eternal, invisible to the naked eye but accessible to intense thought. Perhaps this conviction of his was especially successfully expressed in <u>Gorgias</u>:

Φασὶ δ' οἱ σοφοί, ὦ Καλλίκλεις, καὶ οὐρανὸν καὶ γῆν καὶ θεοὺς καὶ ἀνθρώπους τὴν κοινωνίαν συνέχειν καὶ φιλίαν καὶ κοσμιότητα καὶ σωφροσύνην καὶ δικαιώτητα, καὶ τὸ ὅλον τοῦτο δυὶ ταῦτα κόσμος καλοῦσιν, ὦ ἑταῖπε, οὐκ ἀκοσμίαν οὐδὲ ἀκολασίαν.

(Gorgias, 507 e)

That is, wise men affirm that earth and heaven, gods and men are held together by friendship, communality [общность], and order, reasoning and justice and thus everything is called cosmos – order, and not acosmos and not acolasia, i.e., disorder and dissipation. And after a few more lines there's added:

ἰσότης ἡ γεωμετρικὴ καὶ ἐν θεῖς καὶ ἐν ἀνθρώποις μέγα δύναται.

(Gorgias, 508 a)

Geometric equations, i.e., ideal order, have great significance both among gods and among men.

In these few words the most sacred thought of Socrates and Plato is expressed. If there exists an eternal order, established from the beginning of the world, so stable and unchangeable such that neither on earth, nor in heaven, nor among the gods does it allow digression, it means all our forces must in no way be directed to realize our random and transient desires. For this order is not something invented, embryonic in the head of a wise or stupid man. Order is an all-conquering force. You can ignore it; you cannot know it, but you cannot escape it, no more than you can escape the laws of geometry. This order is everywhere and in everyone, in the very soul of man. Try to wrestle out of its power: your struggle will be in vain. And, conversely, one can gradually lead everyone, even the most ignorant man, by the path of simple questions, to that place, and to him, heretofore blind will momentarily be revealed all the greatness and symmetry of the cosmos founded on unchangeable principles. He will be struck and blinded by the heretofore unseen marvellous spectacle and along with that will be compelled to acknowledge that that knowledge is not completely new for him, that it already once in another life was communed to him [приобщен] and only having stepped on earth forgot that better part which was once given to his lot. Plato and Socrates discovered the great art of revealing this invisible world of harmony and called it dialectic. The condition of the possibility of dialectic is obviously the proposition of the universality of human reason. That which people before Socrates considered the source of cognition – experience – cannot grant cognition. Experience, consisting of sensual perceptions, is deceptive and inconstant, just like all sensual perceptions. That which now seems cold previously seemed hot; objects in the forward field which were square from afar seemed round; what seemed bitter to the sick, to the healthy seems sweet. Even the predecessors of Socrates right up to the Sophists extraordinarily artfully demonstrated the undependability and instability of knowledge based on sensual experience. Heraclitus with his affirmation that everything flows, all constantly changes, nothing stays in the same state, it is impossible to swim twice in the same river (later they affirmed that one can't even swim once in the same river), and the Eleatics furnished Socrates and Plato excellent material for critique of knowledge based on sensual experience.

Such knowledge leads exactly to acosmism, to the acknowledgement of the impossibility of a well-formed system of the universe. The doctrine of the Sophists is a completely legitimate deduction from the proposition that the unique source of knowledge is sensual experience. But the doctrine of the Sophists was the most unacceptable and hateful for Socrates. For, if the Sophists are right, in that case Anitus and Mellitus are right, and Socrates fully deserved being submitted to a shameful punishment. And Calliclus' hymn to force is the last word in human wisdom. The one who is right in this world is the one who by truth or untruth attained success. Geometry knows order, but the basis of the universe undermines even the very idea of order.

What could Socrates oppose to visible reality and to those numerous opponents, who, referring to this reality, condemned the doctrine of the great sage? How could Socrates win? How could he seduce the souls of numerous Athenian youth who sought his spiritual direction? The answer to this question presents exceptional interest for us. From all the preceding presentation, I hope one thing is now clear. Socrates was obviously far from so wrong when he affirmed that morality and true knowledge are one and the same. You see that the whole time his searches for the ideal man and the ideal knowledge led him to the same place. The source of science, as well as morality, is in the cosmos. The fundamental presupposition, expressed in modern language, of the possibility of the existence of science, as well as the possibility of morality, is pre-eternal order, in dominion in heaven, as on earth, obligatory for men, as well as for gods. And the second presupposition: man is allowed to attain this order. Try to renounce one of these concessions, and the whole task of Socrates and Plato falls down. It's clear, it follows, that all the strength of the patriarchs of philosophy ought to be directed to the aspect of the proofs of the named presuppositions. Exactly of <u>proofs</u> – for no one accepted their immediate self-evidence. On the contrary, immediate self-evidence spoke for the opposite affirmations. Visible reality both before and now affirms the rightness of Anitus and Mellitus, Calliclus, the Sophists. There is no unshakable order either in the external world or in the moral world. For in the former randomness is a usual thing, in the latter, success, force, cleverness and indiscrimination in means guarantee the victory.

Socrates found, as we know, an exit from this difficult position. He first among philosophers established the general concept that our knowledge relates not to the individual but to the general. He accepted whole the critique of empirical knowledge presented by his predecessors. But empirical knowledge is not knowledge. Here the talk can only be of opinions, and opinions, as a matter of fact, can be and are multiform, as they are based on sensual perceptions. But beyond the limits of sense perception there is something general, not-sense, attainable only by reason. For the rational is the object of true knowledge. The sage seeks and finds only <u>this</u>. The method of finding the general was the well-known method of questions. Socrates, true, concentrated all his attention on the questions of morality and not pure science. Even Plato, continuing Socrates' task, applied his method in all domains which aroused human inquisitiveness. And this is no accident that <u>science</u> took its beginning from ethics, that first the cosmos was revealed in the human soul, and only after that in the external world.

If one follows Socrates and Plato's reasonings, then it may seem as though their consistency was of another sort. Socrates usually began his investigations with an analysis of simple and uncomplicated external phenomena and only then transitioned to more complicated ones. His fundamental question, serving as the ultimate goal of all his dialogues, is the question of the essence of good; in large part it was not the departure but the arrival moment of his reasoning. At the beginning of the colloquy there's talk of smiths, pilots, doctors and their occupations. What is the difference, he asks, between a cook and a doctor? Both the one and the other worry over the needs of the body. But the cook pleases the body and gives it what is pleasant to the body, the doctor – that which is useful to the body. From a series of such examples from everyday life the difference between usefulness and pleasure is clarified, and corresponding to this – that between science and empirical knowledge. And that is exactly what Socrates and Plato did demand. It turns out that in unmediated terms, man does not know what is necessary to him as a matter of fact. Only he can judge of his true needs, who has drawn his evidence not out of the roiled source of the empiric but from the pure source of abstract knowledge. This is the first step. Once it is clarified that there can be two sources of cognition, of which the former yields false knowledge and only the latter yields truth, then Socrates has ground under his feet. Is the actual source accessible to Anitus and Mellitus, Protagoras and Gorgias? Do they know what knowledge is? They think that it yields only evidence. But they think so only in their ignorance and their limitation. Socrates is not interested in 'evidence'. A little more, little less evidence – man's life will not change thereof. Plato, too, although his interests, in this respect, are much broader than Socrates' interests, never identified philosophy with science. Such an identification was first introduced by Aristotle. For Plato philosophy is still the mystery of communing with another world – a world full of ideas, and to philosophize means to practise for death and to die.

Still this means to strive for good. Socrates first spoke up for good. He spoke of science, of the 'general concept', only because for him that was a stage to the good. The cook pleases the body; the doctor heals the body. And in the domain of the spirit? What do the Sophists do? They also please the soul. They know not the true needs of the soul. They think that the pleasant and the good are one and the same. Not only are they not one and the same, they are completely the opposite. Let Calliclus speak as eloquently and as inspired as he likes of the terrible position and helplessness of man, not able to defend oneself and one's friends from the injustice of enemies – this doesn't scare Socrates or Plato. They do not envy the triumphant Archelaus, who attained power and wealth by the path of murders and other crimes.[32] He's got it good, but he's not all good [Ему хорошо – но он не хорош]. He received what the cook can give, but if you take him to the doctor, the doctor would diagnose him hopelessly, incurably sick with the most horrible illnesses as can only exist in the world.

This is the most important and most remarkable revelation of Socrates. Man needs not fortune, nor success, but the good. Fortune and success are given and taken by chance; only man himself can gain himself the good: no one can give it or take it from man. The bond that this was so for Socrates and Plato was their reason. This reason which affirmed nothing arbitrarily, which can establish and prove any of its positions, which deduces the error-free nature of its affirmations and demonstrates it exactly such, that all of people or gods – gods as well for sure – cannot avoid the acknowledgement of the justice of their claims. Here's what it's necessary to prove to all – to Anitus and Mellitus, and Gorgias and Protagoras. Here's why dialectic is so important; here's why science is more important.

Anitus and Mellitus are strong, of course; they killed Socrates. But they did not win the ultimate victory – the bad man can never harm the good man. The bad man harms only himself.

X

I've had up to now to speak of Socrates and Plato as one person. It's impossible otherwise. It's hard to separate where Socrates' task ends and Plato's task begins. But I consider that in view of the problem of the present work there's no special harm in this. If they are not identical, they complement one another. Now I can transition to Plato alone. Socrates left him afar from easy problem as inheritance, not only by his doctrine but by his life, and especially death. The difficulty was of a dual character. The bad man cannot harm the good man, Socrates taught. Once that's so, it means the chief problem of man in life is to be good [добрым] and a good person [хорошим]. And in that it is insane to pose oneself an unattainable problem; it stands to reason, one must acknowledge that man, first, knows very definitely what the good is in this life, and second, if he wishes, he can fulfil the demands set him by the good, i.e., be a good person.

One must here remark that all the schools derived from Socrates (chiefly I have in mind the Cynics and Stoics) proceeded from this proposition. More than that, even the medieval scholastics could never free themselves from this principle. The well-known argument of Bl. Augustine and Pelagius, which aroused, and even now arouses, such disturbance and discord among Catholic teachers, in essence, passed without a trace. Plato affirmed that the judge beyond the grave would never have refused his reward in the other world φιλοσόφον τὰ αὑτοῦ πράξαντος³³ (Gorgias, 526c) And more: the soul can be saved only in this world. If it is not saved here, there will be too late. Thus in consequence both Thomas and others proved that facienti quod in se est deus infallibiter dat gratiam.³⁴ No matter where you look, no matter what system of morality and philosophy you get acquainted with, you unavoidably encounter the position that the meaning and chief problem of our life consist in realizing a definite moral problem within the limits of our strength. Even Spinoza, who, as we know, in opposition to Plato rejected the idea of reward for good and evil, who affirmed that ratio bonitas is completely alien to God, looked on the life problem of man exactly from the point of view of realization of a clear idea of good. In Spinoza even, if you will, this side shows up internally in special deep relief – only per the strange arbitrariness of fate it received the scantiest expression externally. I personally can indicate only one place in Spinoza in which he completely throws off the heavy armour of the philosopher, who considers himself called to accept the dictatorship of pure reason and obey only logic. Perhaps, exactly in force of the special internal intensity of all his being, he so feared to take off his armour. Even alone with himself he never took off his weapons. It seems, he even slept – if only this man ever slept – in armour. In the depth of his soul, the ineradicable conviction lived that if he did not defend himself, then no one would intercede for him. And Anitus and Mellitus do not doze. Listen to his story:

> 'Tractatus de intellectus emendatione' (Introduction): Videbam enim me in summo versari periculo, et me cogi, remedium, quamvis incertum, summis viribus quaerere; veluti aeger lethali morbo laborans, qui ubi mortem certam praevidet, no adhibeatur remidium, illud ipsum, quamvis incertum, summis viribus cogitur quaerere, nempe in eo tota ejus spes sita (1).

Spinoza was in such a position, per his personal words. Where to seek help, remedium? The usual means beloved by the crowd promised him nothing:

> Illa autem omnia, quae vulgus sequitur, non tantum nullum conferunt remedium ad nostrum esse conservandum, sed etiam id impediunt, et frequenter sunt causa ineritus eorum, qui ea possident, et semper causa ineritus eorum, qui ab iis possidentur.
>
> (Spinosa, Tract. de intellectus emendation, Introductio, p. 9)[35]

In such circumstances Spinoza then set himself this question: what ought a man to strive for – the changeable and transient goods of life or something stable and unchanging? The endgame of his reasonings was this: the goods of life are changeable, that's without a doubt. To boot, it's also indubitable, to some it is given, to some it is not. That which he set himself as the goal of life can also be unattainable, but if it is attainable, then it has one great advantage over the wishes and strivings of the crowd: it is unchanging.

> Sed amor erga rem aeternam et infinitam sola laetitia pascit animum ipsaque omnis tristitiae est expers; quod valde est desiderandum, totisque viribus quaerendum.
>
> (Spinosa, Tract. de intellectus emendation, Introductio, p. 11)[36]

Here, in short, but very expressive words is the history of what Spinoza sought and founds. He came to philosophy not in order to amuse himself or pass the time, not in order to educate his mind, to learn to converse easily and interestingly and strike his interlocutors with the abundance of multiform and multilateral evidences. To the majority of modern learned philosophers, this seems almost improbable, to such a degree has philosophy become a specialty and discipline along with all other specialties – chemistry, etc. No, Spinoza came to philosophy not as to science, but as to the spring of a new life, as to the source of dead and living water. 'Summus viribus' (with all his strength) he sought means of salvation from inescapable destruction. And – now for us this is the main thing – he was convinced that only by his own efforts could he be saved.

For all the opposition of the systems of Spinoza and Plato, they have one common trait. They were both convinced that man could be saved by his own personal efforts and that, it follows, he himself had to then find this path to salvation.

You see how many presuppositions were already accumulated, from which was constructed the granite foundation for future great philosophical systems. I don't know whether the reader has noticed that every presupposition is at the same time a limitation. One can be saved only by one's own efforts – for Socrates, Plato and Spinoza this is the source of the greatest hopes. This is the condition of the possibility of philosophy as a doctrine which encompasses all existence. For only he, who along with that supposes that human reason can penetrate into all the mysteries of life, can thus affirm. Otherwise, one can also with equal right oppose the opposite affirmation to all these affirmations. Perhaps we know the path to salvation, perhaps not. Perhaps we can so distinguish good from evil, perhaps we can't. Maybe cosmos – order – is obligatory for both people and for gods, but perhaps higher life is realized in acosmosia. And, finally, φιλοσόφον τὰ αὑτοῦ πράξαντος (Gorgias, 526 c);[37] there might be nothing at all to expect, and there's nothing to expect for the ordinary mortal, hustling his life away on trivial mercenary tasks.

I'm not even mentioning that the argument between Calliclus and Socrates allows a third resolution, which the arguers didn't even mention. Is it better to experience injustice or be unjust? In serious cases, of course, the one and the other are very bad. It would be horrible if Socrates killed innocent people, but it's also horrible that they killed an innocent Socrates. Socrates himself, answering the stated question, remarks that he, personally, so thinks. He says: if it were within my power, I would prefer to not be faced at all with such a dilemma, but once one has to choose – I would prefer to endure the insult, than to be the insulter. And I think that Plato recalled, tormented, the life of Socrates even after many years. But the position was such that once the first presupposition was accepted, once it was decided, that man could be saved by his efforts alone, one then had to accept all remaining presuppositions. One had to build the fortress, in which one can wait out the attacks of Mellitus and Anitus, i.e., of all the randomness of empirical life.

But a fortress, albeit it defends, deprives one of freedom as well. In a fortress a man is as in prison, as in captivity. But when one has to save oneself, one doesn't think of this. One values first of all and most of all the inaccessible stronghold. The sole sure defence which Plato could devise was the consciousness of his moral superiority over the crowd, the consciousness of his moral irreproachability. It's even little to be simply a moral man, honourable, righteous, courageous, just, disinterested. One must be conscious of oneself as such. One must definitely know what it means to be a good man, and one must also be definitely conscious that one is an active participant, for only by this means does one defend against the attacks of the evil, which have physical force at their disposal – the sword, fire, poisons, etc. Plato did directly say that one can acknowledge oneself unskilled as a doctor or pilot, but no one will acknowledge himself as not a good man.

After Plato the posing of the question of the essence of morality was preserved unchanged in the main philosophical systems. Everyone who spoke of morality was compelled and attracted by the possibility established by Plato of communing even here on earth with the highest good. Not in vain did Plato say that morality was a Siren, attracting all philosophers with sweet singing. For what could be sweeter than conviction of one's superiority over other men. Socrates is partial to good and knows this. And I, and any man, who wishes it, can like Socrates commune with the good, and this is the great mystery, and its force extends beyond the limits of earthly existence; it is generally limitless. We weak, limited people have attained a great mystery – are we not equal to gods? And is our capability, thanks to which we have penetrated into this mystery, not divine? This capability – it is already long time to pronounce the word – is our reason. For reason there are no limits – one can doubt anything you like, one just can't question the rights of reason. The greatest misfortune, says Plato, is to become a misologue in the same manner as misanthrope. And Plato is apparently correct, elevating reason to the throne – for it's reason that both gained cosmos and withstood impending acosmia, for reason gave us assurance in our strength, in our superiority over others. For reason saved Socrates from Anitus and Mellitus. Is it not due highest honours?

XI

We recall, however, what we previously said as well. Plato affirmed that to philosophize means to practise death and to die. Plato taught that ideas are transcendental essences, that our visible life is a shadow from the real, actual [реальной, действительной] life. Finally he affirmed that the source of our higher cognition is eros and mania; i.e., to see 'ideas' with the spiritual eye is to also see real life, given only to those found in conditions of insanity or ecstasy.

All of these affirmations of his, as we have already said, were not preserved in philosophical science as acknowledged truths. They remain only in philosophical museums as curious images of a bold, but dissipated fantasy. I'm not even talking about Plato's doctrine of existence beyond the grave and about the vengeance awaiting man at the just court of the gods. That all these affirmations were for Plato an essential element of his philosophy – this, it seems to me, no one except Natorp has denied or is set to deny. It's enough to read through Gorgias and Phaedo in order to be convinced how seriously Plato held to his doctrine of life beyond the grave. He tells in the most detailed fashion what awaits the soul after death. Natorp is only right about one thing: Plato never succeeded in 'proving' all this fantasticality, and if one considers that the only things essential in a philosophical system are those positions which are afforded truths, then one would have to strongly cut off Plato.

One would have to no less cut him off if its historical role is considered the criterion of value of a philosophical system. The fantasticality of Plato was rejected by history and, as we say, had no future. But I suppose that both these critical devices can give us nothing – can only detract, and that quite a lot. One must take Plato as a whole, with his sobriety and his intoxication. And an even larger question, from which we gain more: when will we utilize criteria and when proceed by guess. Let Aristotle criticize the doctrine of ideas; let Natorp recut it to a modern pattern – we must pose ourselves the question: didn't Plato 2,500 years ago, in an access of philosophical inspiration, see that which rare people succeeded are seeing only in flashes, in the fortunate minutes of spiritual uplift?

The critique of Aristotle and his heirs proceeds from the presumption which, true, Plato, too, shared, which he himself, following Socrates, introduced and developed – there are rules of reason of which one is conscious. Higher control over all human judgements belongs to them by right. One can't deny, and there's no need to deny, that Aristotle could crush Plato, citing Plato himself. But the conclusion thence will not at all be that which is usually drawn. One must pose the very question otherwise. Doubtless, there is a strange paradox in the admixture of opposed elements in Plato's philosophy for all those who find that philosophy ought to be science, i.e., a system of positions, logically interconnected. But for such people not only philosophy but all life as well is paradox, disorder, which is allowed only because limits are set to their reason. Such people resolve the question simply: the insight, made in a minute of inspiration, ought not to have any superiority over usual speculations. Even the converse, it demands an especially careful validation of all its claims. Eros and mania, per their opinion, are the most dangerous companions of philosophy. One can believe a man in love? They themselves cannot believe their own insanity when the impulse passes. Doesn't it seem to the one in love that his loved one is the most beautiful and best of all in the world? And can it be, when time cools his ardour, he is not convinced along with everyone else that she is the most usual woman? But what's still worse, can even his personal experience teach man to regard more carefully the inspiration of Eros? We know that the second, third and even for some the tenth love deceives just as much as the first. Recall how well Schopenhauer spoke of this in <u>Metaphysics of Love</u>. His result is that the special problem of Eros is to deceive people; it affords Schopenhauer special pleasure to depict this idiosyncratic real unusual art of the small god or demon. Nature requires that Steve and Martha give it a new man, and it so blinds them that Martha seems to Steve the incarnation of all which can be the very best in life, and the other way around; and the modest weak people, hitherto in no way outstanding for others, are made heroes. Try to put a barrier between the lovers; they sweep it all away. But time passes, nature got what it wanted, a new man exists, albeit in the mother's womb, and Eros damps her magic fires, and Martha and Steve themselves do not understand their previous inspiration. In the usual light of day, she sees in him a stolid, average man; he sees in her a commonplace, ordinary woman. The deceit is revealed; reason enters into its rights.

Thus, just so, Schopenhauer limns love, as all men understand it in general. No one doubts that Steve judges falsely of Martha, and Martha of Steve, when they saw each other in the unnatural light of the rays of Eros, and that they evaluated each other correctly, when they represented in the usual flat illumination. And 'proof' of that – in the former case, their judgements diverged from general judgements, in the latter – converged. And yet the correctness of judgements presupposes their generally obligatory nature. That which is true might and ought to be represented and accepted <u>always</u> and <u>by all</u> as true. The special characteristic and the chief distinction of reason is exactly that it, and only it, is the source of unarguable, constant truth. And everything, that is opposite to it, that contradicts it, that is not of it, is the source of lie and error. As the icon lamp pales before the rising sun, so the lights of eros flicker out before the light of the true, reason, always in the same state.

So speaks Schopenhauer, so speaks Trubetskoi;[38] so say they all, so Socrates and Plato taught people to speak and think. And this manner of looking at life has so engrafted with the soul of man that, apparently, it never for a moment entered anyone's head, that there could be an error here, that any another resolution of the question is allowable, that **Steve and Martha were right just when they saw in one another what no one else saw in them, what they did not see in themselves, neither before nor after that solemn moment, that Eros did not deceive them, but only showed them a new reality inaccessible to reason**, which then was forever closed to them, as soon as Eros snuffed her fires.

If this is true, what Plato tells of his ideas may also be true. The 'real' Steve, visible to all everywhere, and the 'real' Martha are really ordinary and uninteresting people. They eat, drink, curse and organize their petty deals. But this Steve is only the shadow of the actual Steve, and Martha is only the shadow of Martha. In order to see true people, of which our quotidian reality is only a weak and crude hint, what's necessary is not 'method' and logic, not levelling reason. All method, and logic, and reason – all are means which conceal reality from us. And uplift of the soul is necessary; what's necessary is a capability to be rescued from method, from any control imposed on us by 'logic'. What's necessary is a burst, rapture. When Diogenes said to Plato: I see the lion, but I do not see the leonine, Plato answered him: you have eyes to see the lion, but there is no organ to see the leonine.

In this answer there's also an untruth, very characteristic for Plato and all of us. In order to see a lion, one exactly needs eyes, a special organ, but in order to see the idea of the lion, the leonine, an organ is no longer necessary. One can't even generally speak of the conditions of such vision. For the conditions of vision, i.e., the coincidence of definite circumstances necessary so that this or that phenomenon were possible, are allowable only while we speak of the empirical world, of that world where the lords and masters of the position are those Anituses and Melituses, in struggle with which Plato had to exert all his inventiveness. They are strong because they conquer because they acknowledged these conditions, adapted to them and used them. There's no ideas of Steve and Mary for them. For them only the tangible Steve and Martha exist, filthy, ragged, crude. They are so convinced of themselves because they do not sense spectres. They don't even know that Socratic demons can exist, restraining men from acts doubtless useful to them. The instinct of averageness prompts them, that any connection with the invisible and mysterious brings some terrible destruction after them. They also invented that one cannot unpunished disdain good sense. The instinct of averageness is first of all the instinct of self-preservation so hymned in modern times. And Plato didn't have to talk of the organ of perception of ideas – for not only has Diogenes no such organ, neither does Plato himself. But expressed here is the special characteristic of the spiritual makeup of a man or, if you wish, the special characteristic of the position of man in the world.

Borrowing an answer from elementary physics, we can say that two forces rule us: centripetal and centrifugal. On one hand, we are all posed the goal of organizing ourselves in the visible world. Only that is good, only that is also valuable, that enables our organization. We strain all our spiritual capacities to attainment of this goal. We do more: without giving ourselves account, instinctively almost, there occurs in us a 'natural', as the learned men would say, summoning of spiritual capabilities and special characteristics. We cultivate in ourselves those capabilities which enable the centripetal direction, and mercilessly, as much as our strength allows, eradicate opposite characteristics, which interfere one way or another with the realization of this problem.

That which relates to characteristics also relates to our ideas and beliefs. That perhaps explains the striking phenomenon that in spite of its self-evidence, the huge majority of men do not even suspect that death awaits them and they live as though they are fated to exist eternally on earth so that the arrival of the mortal hour for everyone, even for the old, always appears in some measure unexpected, as well as terrible. All their life has been directed to creating, and suddenly such an absurd senseless destruction is impending, so arbitrary, capricious, beyond connection with all the past. Remember Tolstoy there in <u>Death of Ivan Il'ich</u>? Even in high school he went through the syllogism: all men are mortal, Socrates is a man, therefore Socrates is mortal. But that was Socrates who, obviously, was supposed to fall into the syllogism, Ivan Il'ich supposed and supposes another one. He was supposed to rise in the civil service ladder and not to die. And what Ivan Il'ich said, many would say, almost all people would say – only not all have the skill to tell themselves, like that skill with which Tolstoy endowed Ivan Il'ich.

But there is yet another force – centrifugal. In opposition to the former, hardly anyone feels it and knows it, and all quake and fear it. But it does its terrible task with tranquillity and indifference, which men call implacability. Just as our organism at the beginning of life grows, firms up, and develops, and then gradually starts to head to fading, desiccation, decomposition, so in the soul unconsciously and against its will there begins the strange work, so absurd to view, of decline, destruction and corruption. Man himself gradually buckles under that, on which deployment [сооружение] he so long and tirelessly laboured. It gets eerie for him, if only he remarks on what an ugly task he's engaged on, as it becomes weird at the approach of madness. He knows that he does not do what is necessary but that which is necessary no longer has its previous power over him. And just like birds or squirrels, hypnotized by the snake, with a despairing cry, but apparently unmotivated by anything external, throw themselves into the maw of the monster, just so man heads to encounter death, torn from kin and habitual place by an enigmatic and mysterious will.

Doubtless, both forces rule man. Doubtless also all people know how to see, be conscious of, and – chiefly – approve only the centripetal force. In our life, such seisms occur often, after which the earlier stable, firmly knit sleeve of time is ravelled. Over us there is no singular azure cupola, covering over infinity: over us cracks occurred, and through them something new is revealed, so dissimilar to the previously seen, that we cannot even resolve to say, under which category to classify it – to the category of the existent or non-existent. Whether exactly we see it, or it only seems to us that we see it. And in order to be convinced that we are not raving and we are not hallucinating, we try to inject the new into the same frames in which we are used to distinguish the old. It seems to us that we add <u>rights</u> to existence to it, if we prove it, if we connect it to our previous reality, if we validate it by those methods, which they've taught us previously in order to distinguish truth from error, dream from waking. And more: the sneaky human heart hopes that by this means one will be able to change the direction of active forces – not by itself to exit from the habitual milieu but to attract the newly discovered to the centre, to make it serve the traditional old goals.

We already talked about what impression the death of Socrates left on Plato. We already talked about the shift of his soul. But the role and significance of Plato's philosophy are comprehensible only if we do not forget about the two forces indicated above. Unrestrained it drew the philosopher to the liminal aspects of life. He saw, doubtless, that there is some other kind of life, new, great, unlike ours – but that was little to him. He wished to draw the new into service, to the service of the old. To philosophize means to practise for death and to die. True, great truth! While death has not yet appeared on man's horizon, he is still a youth in philosophy. Only great upheavals reveal the ultimate mystery to man. But why look in the visible world for a <u>guarantee,</u> <u>securing</u> our future existence? Why think that in our world over our short fast-flowing life we're able to discover so much that we can dictate laws to the gods as well? Plato wishes to think that we not only prepare for dying, for death, i.e., not only head to meet the new unknown. He needs assurance that the new is known. And he speaks of it with the same definiteness, with which Socrates taught his disciples and interlocutors to speak of usual life matters. He himself prepares everything for the future life, literally fearing that if even the smallest amount of freedom is left to the gods, they will ruin his whole task. Recall with what insistence he proposed in the second book of <u>The Republic</u> to flush out of the <u>Iliad</u> all those verses in which Homer says that upon investigation, the gods are the disposers of good and sorrow among men. 'Our first law and our first rule on the gods, that we oblige our citizens to acknowledge, orally or in their works, that God is not the creator of all, that He is only the creator of the good' (<u>The Republic</u>, book 2, 380c). The meaning of this principle will become even clearer if we juxtapose it to the corresponding places from <u>Phaedo</u> on the final judgement on human souls. He who will judge us will be directed by the principles and laws worked out by us here. Archelaius and other tyrants will fall into the nether world; those who succeeded in purifying their souls with philosophy in this life will find themselves haven on the isles of the blessed.

And no matter what Natorp said, this conviction is the cornerstone of Plato's philosophy; they were near and dear to him both in early youth, and in his full maturity, and in old age. Justice is the same on heaven and earth. And, chiefly, we on earth know this: both what justice is, what good is, and that good, as the highest law, directs all, equally powerful over people and over gods.

XII

It seems to me that we have now already sufficiently clarified the sources of Plato's philosophy. That circumstance, strange at first glance, now astonishes us the least of all, that it is all represented as interwoven of such irreconcilable contradictions. Even if Plato had heard nothing on dialectics; if he had not so solemnly announced that the greatest crime is to affirm that you know something, when you do not; if he had not demanded that any knowledge took mathematics as its model – in a word, if he had renounced one of his sources of cognition, even then there would have been ample arena for contradiction. For, if one concedes, that Eros can lead man, then where is the surety that this enigmatic demon will always lead man per the same paths? And we know that Socrates too, who, by tradition, was much more restrained and inclined to look things over than was Plato, often without murmuring submitted to the inspiration of his daemon, i.e., that means that, despite his own theory, just like those poets he despised, he took decisions, not being able to give himself account of what had defined his choice. In other words, if we do not establish once and for all that gods, demigods and people are directed by one and the same motivations; if, on the contrary, we concede that we, people, not only are not in condition to penetrate into the mysterious intents of the gods, but we can't even judge of the laws of their thinking, of the logic of the gods – and yet this latter judgement has all the probabilities for it – then how can we rely that all the judgements we receive from above will not be contradictory? That what happened with the lovers is not repeated with the philosophers, that they, on the inspiration of the gods, will come not to humble themselves to the truth but rule over it, not being prior restrained by earlier established laws – even the law of contradiction?

I ought to say here that the Platonic doctrine of ideas, even if you don't count it with the positive parts of his philosophy, is distinguished least of all by unity. Per their existing habit, each of Plato's readers made a judgement himself of what Plato actually meant as ideas, but no one could prove his judgement was uniquely correct. And the surest way, for my part, would be to openly acknowledge that Plato himself as well never could definitively say what he meant by ideas. He at moments saw something – that's almost indubitable. He strove to something and fled something – that's now simply indubitable. But did this possess some kind of continuity, which would have given him the possibility of finding clear and distinct predicates for it? That's the big question. I am well aware that in uttering such a judgement I go athwart both the traditional representation of Plato and the numerous explanations of Plato himself. Plato wished to convince us, and the majority of those readers are convinced that for him ideas and concepts are synonyms. What attracted him in the 'idea' was exactly the same thing that attracted Socrates in the original concept – i.e., exactly that continuity, unchangeability. All flows, appears and disappears, is born and dies; everything is not constant, is corrupt, passing, but in the stream of the transient, in the eternal multiformity of the sensual, there stands immovable the General, accessible to reason alone.

That Plato spoke like that, and that those who so accept his doctrine of ideas have all formal bases on their side – I won't argue against that. But that for Plato, ideas were not general concepts – that is also indubitable for me. And perhaps, if Plato were not fated to live so long, if the centripetal force were not so powerful over him, we would have heard much from him on ideas, but that he took with him to the grave. For me the beginning of the VII book of the Republic – the story of the cave – represents the most successful place of all those in which Plato expresses his ideas. But if that's so, then the identification of his ideas with general concepts is devoid of any basis. For them it's the opposite – then that true life, of which our earthly existence is the pale and grey reflection, must be represented not as more abstract but rather more concrete. Other dialogues of Plato then, as a matter of fact, are completely not tied up with this 'realness'. On the contrary, in Plato one observes fear before concreteness, just as though under every bush, under every blade of grass, bloodthirsty Anituses and Melituses lurk. And he tramples all the concrete and will not be at peace until there remain pure abstract concepts, hiding nothing, transparent clear through, 'purified' geometric figures, even simply numbers.

Only when he has done this terrible destructive work to the end does the heavy worry depart from his face. He can trust only lines and numbers, only they no longer conceal anything, no longer no way burst out of the law he set down, only they do not deceive, do not betray. Everything that is in the world, therefore, ought to be likened to numbers and figures: all science ought to be constructed in the image and likeness of mathematics. And Plato said this. Plato, in whose soul eros and mania lived. Plato, who always hoped and dreamed of the higher, most beautiful life! Try in actual fact to fulfil all his commands – what'll remain of life! Instead of music – harmony and melody – the correlation of sound waves, numerically expressed in the corresponding proportionality. Instead of nature – the laws of acceleration and gravity, which can also be reduced to numbers. But to so represent Plato to oneself means to take his soul out of him, all the same as he who expresses nature and music – although schematically and accurately – in mathematical formulas, takes out their soul. And no matter how many quotations from Plato you adduce, you'll all the same not convince – if you wish, even yourselves – that for him ideas and general concepts are identical.

And all the same Plato's dialectic was fated to play a colossal role in the history of human thought, especially in the history of philosophy. No matter how strange it is, and perhaps, it's not strange, who'll figure out what's strange, what's not strange in this world! – people accepted only his dialectic from Plato's whole philosophy. Τοῖς δὲ πολλοῖς ἀπιστίαν παρέχει.[39] No one believed Plato when he, inspired, told his prophetic dreams. But all seized on those of his reasonings, in which he convinced people to believe nothing without basis, to demand proofs for all affirmations. This seemed comprehensible, possible and, chiefly, desirable to all.

Anitus, Melitus and all those Athenians who condemned Socrates were not disturbed by the sobriety of the great sage. Perhaps, it was just this feature of Socrates that met with the greatest sympathy. His enigmatic nature, his mysterious nature repelled one from Socrates. The sensitive Greeks guessed that sooner or later from the egg of Socrates' wisdom, the little snakes, future Cynics and Stoics, must peck their way out. Along with who knows what, what kind of Holy Fools, as a matter of fact dangerous both for the popular religion that has withstood the ages, and for a stable state. It was not the method of seeking the truth which frightened the Greeks – Socrates' method (the near future showed this) was just exactly what was most of all necessary to humanity – what scared them was how Socrates applied his method. Even the point that Socrates went with his method equally to kings distinguished statespeople, to exalted philosophers, along with that to craftsmen and slaves. And spoke with all in one and the same tone of disrespect. Neither statesman, nor philosophers, nor poets, nor slaves, nor carpenters – no one knows anything, all alike are negligible and equally disdained. And the higher a man stands on the social ladder, the less respect he deserves. The first must not only be compared with the last but be put after the last.

Does Socrates' method presuppose in and of itself such a relation to the prevailing mores? The method prejudged nothing, but in Socrates' breast there lived profound disdain – we will not enquire where it came from – to historical forms of life and to the majority of those people, with whom fate drove him together, and he never missed a chance to show that one way or another. The essence of the method predefined nothing – and the schools which derived from Socrates might serve as the best proof of this. The Cynics, and the Stoics, and Plato, and Aristotle – all are fledglings of the Socratic nest. If this still seems unconvincing, I'll adduce two examples of the application of the Socratic method, which will show completely clearly how much arbitrariness the method he accepted still leaves to the thinker.

Epictetus reasons: you're told some unknown man died. Hearing this, you say: nothing special here. Per the existing laws of nature, once a man falls ill with an incurable disease, he has to die. But here someone told you your son died. You're in despair. Nothing's good, it seems to you that all must share your sorrow. But wouldn't it be more correct if you à propos of the death of your son recalled which you said when you learned of the death of the peripheral man: per the inescapable laws of nature, etc. That's true philosophy.

So Epictetus reasons. And his reasoning seems striking in its consistency. But it's possible with no less consistency to reverse it. One can say, your son died and you're in despair. Now a peripheral man has died and you're serene. Why? Recall how you were shocked at your son and then take as close to your heart the sorrow of a father unknown to you. That's true philosophy.

Both reasons are constructed per the same method and are equally logically correct. The results are directly opposite.

One more example. Speaking of human passions, Marcus Aurelius in almost every one of his aphorisms with true Socratic insistence repeats that it is mad to value and useless to devote oneself to the joys of life, for all finish the same: death awaits both the winner and the loser. The indicator of the corruptibility of all that exists always introduces the irrefutable element of conviction into our reasoning. But one must not forget that this element belongs to a number of those which can, as you wish, be evoked, even by not very thoughtful incantations. And to eliminate it, expel it once it's evoked, is no longer in the will of man. True, he who recalls death disdains the joys of life. But does he retain respect for those ideals, of which Marcus Aurelius speaks so much? How to stop the destructive action of this omnipotent spirit? For not only joys and sorrow are transient. Everything, that is of man, sooner or later, is submerged in the abyss of oblivion. The feast, orgies and evil-doing of men are forgotten, but the memory of Marcus Aurelius won't live eternally either. And now, and after all that long time that passed after the death of the philosopher on the throne, does humanity know much of his thoughts and deeds? Scholars read his work and argue the meaning of this or that of his statements, but the world, all men, recalls just as little of him as of his disgraced predecessors on the Roman throne. Time destroys equally the good and the evil. And Marcus Aurelius' argumentation is likewise dangerous for both the Epicureans and the Stoics. Where death reigns, the rights of reason cease. Worse: the problem of reason consists, apparently, in leading man into that domain subordinate to death and its laws, more exactly – its lawlessness. It seems to me that Marcus Aurelius and all other philosophers knew this well – and if all the same they didn't say this, that's exclusively based on the calculation, completely accurate, that not to anyone is it given to evaluate and understand its all-destroying action. People accept only that which is demonstrated to them <u>ad oculos</u>.[40]

Philosophy silently set the conditions to use the reminder of death only for defined goals. And the habit becomes law. But not in vain. Renan indicated that all the meditations of Marcus Aurelius are penetrated with a deep sorrow. He felt that the argumentation destroyed a great deal more than was necessary. If annihilating death lies before us, then one common lot awaits those who live consistently with nature and those who live inconsistently with nature. Death equally justifies both insanity and reason, and the philosopher has no means to protect the latter from it and give it the former as sacrifice. And if all the same they elevate reason to the throne, that from their side is an indubitably arbitrary act: <u>sic volo, sic jubes – sit pro ratione voluntas</u>.[41]

And maybe this is the same kind of unsearchable mystery of philosophy as the one of which Plato spoke in <u>Phaedo</u>. No one knows that philosophy is practice for dying; no one knows that the source of philosophy is arbitrariness. Even Plato himself didn't know this, if by knowledge is understood what is usually accepted by that word since the time of Socrates – i.e., conviction, clear and definite, expressed in concept. The German mystic of the seventeen century, the poorly educated Jacob Boehme allowed himself – the only one, it seems, among all those having written on this theme – to say that he himself only understood what he wrote just in those minutes when God extended His right hand over it. When then He withdrew it, the words he himself had written earlier seemed senseless to the philosopher himself, as all that he had said about Martha seemed senseless to Steve when he's fallen out of love. As expressed in Pushkin's language, the amusements of the vain world seemed to the poet the full and exhaustive expression of everything that life can give until Apollo calls him to this holy sacrifice. All of Socrates, and Plato, and Boehme, and Pushkin might be the most negligible among the negligible people of the world – until Apollo calls them to his holy sacrifice, and they knew this in torment.

Thus they so insistently sought firm principles and beginnings. Thus Pushkin affirmed that the deception which elevates us is worth more than low truths. And – this is the main thing – all of them wished that this deception was similar to the low truth, i.e., that it seemed to all just as stable, constant and indubitable. And they were prepared for whatever sneak attacks and sacrifices, so only to present their deception in the form of truth. They cut it up and distorted it by the hour: they had to have it ever ready with them, as other people have prepared low truths. Death and arbitrariness are terrible to all – even Plato.

And no 'science' has the strength to compare with them. The problem of science is to get rid of mysteries and enigmas. Aristotle understood and actualized this. He took from his genius predecessors all in their philosophy that was indubitable and stable and eliminated all the problemata. He damped the anguish of dissatisfaction, and sang the great hymn of triumphant knowledge, sure of itself.

XIII

One of the greatest services of Aristotle, as we know, consists in his being the creator of the theory of proofs. We already saw earlier that both Plato and Socrates struggled with all their strength against arbitrary, unproven affirmations. And we already know why they feared arbitrariness and to what sacrifices they resorted in order for their cosmos to withstand the chaos shrugging beneath it all and always threatening to burst out of the vice of reason. But in face of all that, Socrates did not renounce his demon, nor did Plato renounce his myths and eternally living ideas. The mystery did not seem terrible to them in its essence – it seemed terrible and inaccessible to them to give up the mystery to the disposition of the people. Perhaps thence emanated Plato's idea of the creation of the Republic, at the head of which the philosophers would stand. It's hard to think up another explanation, in that, obviously, Plato was ruled least of all by practical considerations when he thought up his ideal state arrangement. At the present time you'll find, probably, not many people whom the modern state construct would satisfy. But compared to that which Plato proposed, the most primordial sociality seems to have huge advantages. And if we begin to judge his <u>Republic</u> from the point of view of the practical consistency of the directive composition we would have to come to the most negative assessment. Marriages are arranged per the calculation of special commissions, people belong to define castes, everything that anyone does is subject to the most pedantic control of a special censor – except the philosophers, who have the highest power and can do as they wish, all the others become almost marionettes or mannequins, whose every hour and even minute is exactly defined beforehand by the omniscient oversight of the higher authority. In history only Sparta, for a time, while Lycurgis' laws existed, in a greater or lesser degree, realized the political ideal of the Platonic republic. Only the philosophers were not selected as rulers. I well understand that from Plato's point of view this 'only' meant a great deal, meant, if you will, everything. The meaning of the whole dialogue is revealed here. The crowd is supposed to obey, philosophers to give orders. Laws for all – philosophers are the source of laws. But in order to stabilize obedience, a higher levelling instantiation is necessary before which all are equal, both simple denizens and their rulers. It is necessary that the source of rights and laws is something consistent and unshakeable. A fiction acknowledged by all is necessary, to the effect that philosophers, too, obey reason like all others. In Plato's <u>Republic</u> there is no talk of arbitrariness, as there is not in his other dialogues. That which he demands, he demands in the name of the eternal and unchanging reason, which is revealing to the elect, i.e., philosophers, its ultimate mysteries. Philosophers then lead yet other people to the ultimate, higher goal, by paths revealed to them. They tear them away from everyday busyness, free them from the power of imaginary reality, and bring them together with true reality. And only philosophers alone, only philosophy alone can awaken humanity from the heavy nightmare sleep to the light divine vigil.

I repeat and insist: if one flushes the doctrine of ideas out of the Platonic <u>Republic</u>, if one looks at the work as a political tract, then one can't take it seriously. This is a direct challenge to good sense, in places simply the delirium of a maniac. And although many suppose that Plato took his political ideas completely seriously and even travelled to Sicily in the hope that he'd be able to realize them, this all the same does not shake my affirmation. If you will, it confirms it. Plato thought so little of what everyone calls reality and so eloped to his 'true' reality, that he was the least capable of men to direct people and organize society. He ran from the centre; he was drawn to the liminal regions, where, per the data of our experience, there can be nothing. For him our reality was a dream – could he rule it or direct it?

And here Aristotle had to enter into battle with the centrifugal tendency of Plato. The most mistaken approach to the argument of Aristotle and Plato would be if we started to verify the argument adduced by the one and the other in defence of the correctness of their doctrines. The matter here is in no way in argumentation. Afore one can say: neither the one nor the other had exhaustive arguments at his disposal. Aristotle himself says: 'those who demand that the foundation of everything be presented, demand a foundation where it is not, for the principle of proof is not proof' (Metaphysics IV, 6 1011, a 8; Zeller II-2, 202).[42] And again, 'there can't be proofs of everything' (Metaphysics III, 2; 997a, 7; Zeller II-2, 235).[43] Further he expresses it more strongly; 'the sign of lack of education – is not to distinguish for which things one must ask proofs and for which one must not' (Metaphysics IV, 4 1006, a, 6; Zeller II-2, 235).[44] And doubtless, the further we move from the centre of life, the more we distance ourselves from any possibility of proofs. At the liminal regions the question arises – do proofs have meaning, and are they necessary? But, if they are not, if Aristotle himself, so much and so successfully labouring on the theory of proofs, comes to the conclusion that the 'principle of proof is not proof', then how to resolve the dissonance here arising? True, Aristotle proceeds from the presupposition that in essence such sorts of dissonances are impossible. I took the above-cited places from the fourth book of his metaphysics, where he treats the well-known law of contradiction. Can anyone doubt the truth value of this law in the formulation Aristotle gave it? 'It is not allowable, that any man supposed, that one and the same thing existed and also did not exist. Heraclitus, true, per some opinion, affirmed this. But it is not at all obligatory, that a man always has the opinion which he expresses in words.'[45] This is Aristotle's fundamental rebuttal to those who doubt the law of contradiction. One must, by the way, not forget that although the honour of the first classical formulation of the law of contradiction belongs to Aristotle, Socrates and Plato already put it at the bases of all their reasonings, for without it dialectics, which takes its principle from it, is absolutely impossible. Aristotle, perhaps, might be named the creator of the theory of proofs, only in the sense, that he was fated to be the first to present it systematically and exhaustively. For us this is important to remember especially in view of the fact that consequently all of the critiques of Platonic ideas in Aristotle is maintained on positions wholly taken by him from his teachers. Now he simply completely devalues Heraclitus's words, by the simple statement that it cannot be that Heraclitus thinks what he says. He says that one and the same object can be and not be, but he cannot think that. And further, if you asked Aristotle, wither his assurance of Heraclitus' insincerity, he would consider it superfluous to respond. He would put your question to the account of ἀπαιδευσία – not raised right. And not only in the cases when argument flared up on the law of contradiction did Aristotle display such assurance that he had gone to such limits where proofs become superfluous and doubts indecent. He displays no less assurance on the resolution of questions of physics and mechanics. Heaviness and lightness, he affirms, are a quality of objects. When it is characteristic of an object to strive for the centre of the world, it is heavy; when it is characteristic of it to strive for the limits of the earth, it is light. To those who expressed doubts on the correctness of such an affirmation, he answered: if this were not the case, in a vacuum all bodies would fall at the same speed. The unthinkability of the last concession seemed to him just as obvious, as the unthinkability of the objection of Heraclitus against the law of contradiction. One can talk thus, but no one thinks thus, and the words of a man who would come to affirm that in a vacuum all objects fall at the same speed would not at all express his thought. Or another example: a body can be moved only unless and until it is immediately forced by something into motion. And this truth seems so self-evident to Aristotle, not allowing either proofs or doubts, on the contrary, serving as basis for proofs and elimination of doubts. I purposely cited these two curious examples of indubitable error of the genius mind, one of a kind in genius, in the domain of those affirmations which are considered free from obligation to present proofs, i.e., in that domain where any objection is taken as an intentional bad-faith interference to the normal flow of thought. Perhaps it would be useful here to recall Kant's reasoning on

Beharrlichkeit der Substanz from Critique of Pure Reason. For Kant the principle of conservation of substance was required as a necessary link in his transcendental deduction of categories. It was necessary to show a series of synthetic judgements a priori, by which the natural sciences are maintained, just like arithmetic and geometry maintain their own. That is, it was necessary to expose those principles and show that they are taken not from experience, that they are dictated by reason, not allowing converse affirmations. For us it is now unimportant that Kant, as opposed to Aristotle, acknowledged the obligatory nature of the affirmations of reason only for the world of phenomena. We are now interested only in the question of the source of self-evident judgements – per Kant's terminology – a priori, per Aristotle's terminology – ἀρχὴ ἀποδείξεως (that which precedes proof). So as to eliminate the final doubt of the right of judgement of Beharrlichkeit der Substanz to be called a priori, Kant recalls the reasoning of the 'ancient philosopher'. When he was asked how to find the weight of smoke, he said: one must subtract all the ash remaining from the weight of the tree. From this Kant concludes with assurance that even the ancient philosopher, who was deprived of the possibility of coming to his conclusion by experience, no whit doubted that matter is indestructible. That means the source of this knowledge is in reason. Reason does not allow the possibility of another judgement; the position – matter appears, matter disappears – is unthinkable. Per Kant, as per Aristotle, it is unthinkable that bodies in a vacuum fall at the same speed, or that a body is moved per inertia. The 'unthinkabilities' of Aristotle have long ago become elementary truths of physics. The 'unthinkability' of Kant is now far from impressing anyone. After the discovery of radio, many were already inclined to acknowledge that energy transitions to matter, and conversely, as some once acknowledged that motion transitions to heat (this admission would have led the ancient philosophers with their codex of unthinkabilities into such horrors!). Obviously 'unthinkability', as a criterion of judgement, is an idiosyncratic pseudonym for a special kind of want list of the human soul. Why did Heraclitus reject and Aristotle so affirm the law of contradiction? Why did Plato 'see' ideas, and Aristotle mock them? Before answering these questions one must once and for all renounce Aristotle's manner of seeing malevolent lying opponents in those who don't agree with you. Perhaps, even more is necessary; one must renounce several devices introduced into philosophy by Plato. Plato affirmed that philosophy is reasoning (διάνοια); it is the colloquy (λογος) of the soul with itself (Teatet 189 e; Zeller II-1, 481). This is unconditionally inaccurate.[46] Worse, this mistake is directly fatal. And, chiefly, such a definition of philosophy is least of all applicable to the process which occurred in the soul of Plato himself. If formal proof is necessary, I recall the definition introduced in one of the preceding chapters: philosophy is practice for death and dying. And I think that if Aristotle allowed himself to say of Heraclitus that a man does not always think what he says, it would be more accurate to recall this à propos Plato's words on διάνοια. Not, of course, that Plato wished to deceive or argue with anyone. Here there's another reason: the eternal incapacity of man to find words that exhaustively and adequately express what he already 'knows'. Plato attained what he was allowed to attain, but not at all in colloquy with his soul.

Ideas are revealed only in great internal silence and only to those who know the art of long and stubborn silence. Words interfere with man approaching the ultimate mystery of life and death. Words scare away the mystery. They apply; they are useful, when the man, after having witnessed for a moment, wishes to give his insight generally useful utilization – to make it necessary and useful for all. They are good for, expressed in Socrates' words, a midwife, helping the soul relieve a burden. Then he turns to logic and dialectic with the help of self-evident truths (in Kant synthetic judgements <u>a priori</u> transforming the momentary and unexpected into the constant and necessary). Both Socrates and Plato, as we already know, ascribed huge significance to the logical reworking of life events. They wished that everything that exists existed always and for everyone – otherwise there could not be positive knowledge. But such a demand is fulfilable only on the condition that it were conceded beforehand that that which does not exist always and for everyone must be relegated to the domain of non-being. This of course is <u>petito principii</u>, an unallowable presupposition. But, if you do not accept it, you must forever renounce scientific knowledge. And if Plato wished to and knew how to be consistent, he would have to humble himself before Diogenes, who denied ideas, and not rebut, as he did, that Diogenes has eyes to see the lion and no organ to see the leonine, for to demand a special organ for attainment of the truth means to deny that truth is for all. Plato himself proved that even a completely uneducated man could be convinced of the truth of geometric propositions. Here the question can't be of a special organ: the learned philosopher and the ignorant slave are alike compelled to come to the conclusion that the sum of the angles in a triangle is equal to two right angles. In order to attain the ideas of the leonine and justice, a special organ is required. Or, more accurately, not an organ – a special gift of eros and mania is necessary! But can science possibly maintain itself on a gift of insight? No matter how you put it, one can allow that scientific truths are first attained by such marvellous and unexpected insight. Perhaps, man is allowed to first see the truth only in the condition of intoxication or madness. But then, why couldn't Plato convince Diogenes? Why did Aristotle not bow before his divine teacher? It's clear that philosophy for Plato was in no way the colloquy of the soul with itself, and philosophical truths were not revealed to him in dialectical reasonings. The power and significance of dialectic are limited. In the onward movement of human creative work a moment occurs, when dialectic becomes an interference and even the law of contradiction does not liberate but rather binds. At this limit the spirit of the seeker is indeed tried. Will he resolve to renounce previous experience? Will he dare to cross over the marker separating him from the unknown? Will he be bold enough, being used to the known, defined, and stable, to trust the <u>absolutely</u> unknown? I emphasize the word <u>absolutely</u>, for any limited assurance in the future, any attempt to look back, where there are norms and laws worked out by experience, chains man to the past with unbreakable chains. We know that both Plato and Socrates, who had so much sincere, passionate striving to wrest out of the reality, that was stultifying to them and accessible to all, did not dare to head forward without looking back. Plato was drawn to his ideas, but he wished that there was nothing unexpected in the domain of new real life. It still seemed to him that the unexpected, created without him, not at peace with his representation of the good and rational, was unacceptable for him. Good in the other world must be the same as in this one. He carefully sought out the signs of the good in the activity of the carpenter, pilot and doctor and then exclaimed assuredly: and over that border the good will have the same signs. Aristotle did focus all the blows of his polemic on the indecision and half-measures, on this contradiction. If it's so, if we find there what we have already found here, then ideas are not transcendental. They in no way either have independent self-sufficient existence. They are only characteristics of objects. The doctrine of Plato on all of ideas, and of eros and of mania, is contradictory and unproven. And the truth cannot endure contradiction. And truth can be proven such that any man can acknowledge it – in no way is a special organ necessary, a special gift, in order to attain it – it can always be 'proven'.

XIV

There can't be a moment's doubt that Aristotle was correct in his merciless critique of Plato's ideas. Once the hallowed dream of Socrates – of perfect knowledge, of science – was fated to be realized, humanity had first of all to renounce inspiration and ecstasy. In order that truth was always in the hands of the mortal, one had to clip its wings. Put another way, one must decide to only acknowledge as truth that which one can always and everywhere hold in one's hands and have at one's disposal. Aristotle indeed decided on this step and in this inheres his permanent role and significance in the history of human thought and human struggle. It's understandable that the winged Platonic ideas, child of insane eros and mania, appearing by arbitrariness and disappearing by arbitrariness, seemed incarnations of the lie to Aristotle. They also caused Plato himself no little unease. Thus, probably, in different periods of his life he interpreted them differently. Thus, probably, we nowhere find in Plato a precise definition of what he actually meant by ideas. For Aristotle they were completely unendurable. He saw in them a completely unnecessary bifurcation of reality. Thus his argument of the third man: the concrete man, the idea of man, and then, the idea of the idea of man and the concrete man. And, then, how to derive the multiformity of our reality from the unchanging always steady-state ideas. These arguments seemed irrefutable to Aristotle. And, exactly, if one could rebut Plato by argument, then one must acknowledge Aristotle's rebuttals correct. To split reality for no good reason, and from a single idea, you'll never derive the multiplicity of concrete beings. True, as I already indicated above, Aristotle did not succeed in freeing himself from contradiction, he who replaced the Platonic doctrine of ideas with his own doctrine on forms, which in essence are no different from ideas, except that they have been deprived of the predicate of transcendentiality and that they acknowledge existing objects as immanent. But it wasn't contradictions that disturbed him, not from those that he fled. Forms, in Aristotle's eyes, had that huge advantage that they were always in one's sight and did not head off to infinity, hiding even from mental gaze and accessible only to intoxicated imagination.

Aristotle, following Plato, sets the strictest demands for knowledge and maintains them most consistently. The first condition of the possibility of the very existence of science is the strict delimitation of its boundaries. One cannot encompass the infinite; therefore, the object of our cognition ought to be finite. And if the object of cognition ought to be definite, then the same demand is made of the subject as well. Those who concede that our reality is not the infinite reality, who doubt whether we are awake or asleep, those who do not resolve to give the healthy normal mind unconditional preference over the sick and abnormal mind – Aristotle without any hesitation puts them aside, as people incompetent or intentionally operating in bad faith and uninteresting for philosophy. He doesn't even believe that anyone could make such propositions seriously. This is how people talk, people who are useless, vacuous ranters. Aristotle was strong in his conviction. In this were his gift and his providential mission. One of his biographers says that he was μέτριος εἰς ὑπερβολήν – moderate to an extreme. And this is very accurately noted. Aristotle was a genius of moderation, the like of which is unknown in the history of humanity. That which was out of bounds, not that it didn't interest him, for him it did not exist. Everything in the world is in continuous motion – the source of which is the unmoved mover, God, who has no other significance for us than that He defines the boundary of possible and necessary knowledge and, therefore, of human searchings. The unmoved mover holds the whole universe firmly in his hands. His unchanging nature binds both man and nature; it then secures the consistency of relations accessible to study. Knowledge in Aristotle, as in Plato, is knowledge of that which exists necessarily, i.e., of that which cannot but exist. And, in this sense, Aristotle is true to the traditions of Plato, for whom, just as for his teacher, it's a self-evident truth, that only that knowledge is actual knowledge which can be derived by necessity from some general position. That within this Platonic self-evident truth there lurks an unsolvable contradiction – this, I think, any reader at all experienced in these questions will easily grasp. Aristotle's position is complicated further by the point that, in view of his polemic against the Platonic transcendental ideas, he had to emphasize with special insistence another new self-evident truth: only individual things really exist. But individual things can in no way be derived from anything! That's not all; Aristotle himself, following Plato, acknowledges that the object of cognition can only be general concepts. That means, is all of reality inaccessible to knowledge? Aristotle sails past this contradiction with equanimity, as though it's not his task to eliminate contradictions in his work, as though it's already enough that he discovers contradictions in his predecessors. Transcendental ideas are a myth, an invention, absolutely inapplicable for reason. In the world there are matter and forms. So that forms of themselves, separate from things, do not exist; forms are immanent to things – in this lies their distinction from Platonic ideas – but as opposed to matter, which presents as chaos, having no internal law, forms are defined by eternal and constant principles. Thus Aristotle sees in matter the source and principle of all which is random and inconsistent in the world: Τῆς μὲν γὰρ ὕλης τὸ πάυχειν ἐστὶ καὶ τὸκινείσθαι, τὸ δὲ κινείν καὶ ποιείν ἑτέρας δυνάμεως (gen. et corr. II, 9. 335, b. 29; Zeller II-2, 331).[47]

He has to eliminate matter; he has to be liberated from all that can interfere with his returning back to Platonic ideas, so as to preserve for them those sovereign rights which the master allocated them. He thus calls it a passive element, he says, that it no longer exists other than only in 'possibility'. But nonetheless it does influence existence. Let it influence destructively; let it violate the harmonious consistency of the creative work of form; let it be the blind, meaningless necessity of the dead principle. But still a force it remains. And knowledge, which must study equally all influences, cannot ignore arbitrarily that which does not fit in pre-established frames and does not correspond with demands. And, of course, in fact Aristotle, who was much interested in empirical reality, was far from neglecting the influences of purely material forces in his observation. He considered them insofar as a man was allowed in his time to penetrate the construct of the visible world. And blind necessity in no way frightened him, as it does not frighten modern natural scientists and the majority of modern philosophers, who are long habituated to bowing unmurmuring before the deductions of positive sciences. Where there is defined order, no matter what kind it is, Aristotle knew how to find his own. For him, in the upshot, consistency and order were synonyms. His anxiety began where the thread of phenomena ended, or arbitrariness began, that is, possible chaos on one pole and the self-determined [самозаконный] beginning on the other. In nature there ought not to be disorder – and thus knowledge is knowledge of eternal forms. Man cannot freely create, and thus Platonic ideas, as transcendental essences, exactly consequent on their independent existence, ought to be rejected. Μέτριος εἰς ὑπερβολήν[48] – the special gift of avoiding extremes, a gift that no one before or after Aristotle possessed with such unusual mastery, which helped Aristotle demarcate those borders, within the limits of which even now our knowledge and our curiosity move. Where there is no order, there cannot be being, there cannot be thinking; where freedom rules, there cannot be creative work. Here's what Aristotle worked for and achieved. That's why his reason so sought necessity; here's why only that knowledge seemed knowledge to him, which could be compellingly extracted from reality by the path of exact and definite mythological devices. I repeat – Aristotle was not the first philosopher directing his wishes to the organization of our knowledge on the principles of compulsion and obligation. Plato and Socrates, already, as we saw, strove for this. And even to them indefiniteness seemed a monster. They wished, at any cost, to acquire firm knowledge of how it works in this world as well as in the other world. And they knew how to sacrifice many, that their goal be achieved. But they had not the courage and decisiveness to go through to the end. Socrates wish to still lord it over the world beyond the grave, where he hoped to be a witness of how the evil Melitus and Anitus, and he, the good Socrates, got what they deserved. Plato left himself a world of ideas, in which he felt himself full lord and master. Aristotle renounced this as well. He dragged everything into this immanent world because that which he knew was already such, it seemed to him, that one could really compel anyone to this knowledge; all of them – the tyrant, and the slave and the learned, and ignorant man. No need to wait until the god of love gave man wings – one could teach each man by a simpler and more natural means. Knowledge is acquired by the path of slow circumspect accumulation of validated and systematized evidence. We need know nothing of the mystery of the unmoved mover; it's enough for us that he clearly demarcates the limits of the universe and, by his unchangeability, his continuity, he guarantees us order and shape in the world. Any mystery, it's not that it's inaccessible; it's unnatural – it contradicts cognition, for it allows unforeseen, unforeseeable possibilities. And what is the sense of knowledge if the unforeseeable is allowed?

Even from our short presentation of the fundamental ideas of Aristotelian metaphysics, it's already clear, I suppose, in sufficient degree that Aristotle had no more theoretical 'proofs' of his correctness than had his predecessors and teachers. His constructs are confused and contradictory and, if they were to be evaluated from the point of view of logical consistency, we'd have to reject them whole. I want to say that if someone, more or less, brought us as proof of the proposition that people existed on Mars, the kind of considerations such as those which Aristotle brought forward in proof of his doctrine of matter and forms, we would know no more of life on Mars than we do now. It must be added that in the given case I am not even expressing my own opinion. Take any history of ancient philosophy, and you'll see that all of Aristotle's positions which I analysed no longer seem convincing to anyone. In the interest of fairness – this is for the unenlightened – one must only add that Aristotle is in no way an exception in this case. All the great philosophers suffer from the same thing. All of them have great contradictions, even those who are praised precisely for their consistency and logicality. And that did not prevent them from playing a great historical role, and it doesn't prevent us from valuing them and being interested in them. Only one thing ought to be established: that all philosophical systems are shot through with contradictions – therefore, their values and their interests are in no way defined by their logical qualities. And still less is the historical significance of philosophical systems defined by their consistency. Aristotle conquered Plato not by the force of his proofs but by the stability of his assurance in the singular truth value of that which is accessible to all men. For attainment of the ultimate truth neither talent nor inspiration is necessary. It is everywhere, it is in everyone, it is accessible to all – and conversely, that which is not everywhere, which is not accessible to all, ought to be relegated to the domain of the spectral, non-existent. This and only this marvellous talisman of Aristotle is the source of his world significance: he did not reveal mysteries to people; he only defined, with the instinct for moderation so characteristic of him, the distance people must maintain from the mystery. People felt this, and they knew how to value this. Modern science and modern philosophy cannot egress from the path shown them by Aristotle. It's a big mistake to think that Kant broke free of Aristotle's power. His statement of the question – is metaphysics possible as a science – includes Aristotelian presuppositions. It's clear that here lurks Aristotle's fundamental presupposition: the single worthwhile knowledge is scientific knowledge. The natural sciences ought to be constructed like mathematics, metaphysics like the natural sciences. That is, each science ought to be a system of positions, organically connected with one another and mutually conditioning one another. Mathematics possesses general positions – axioms, which hold all its particular truths in subordination; natural sciences (Kant had no doubt of this) also possess their axioms – metaphysics can't have the same kind. (Kant was sure that he had proven this.) Therefore, metaphysics as science cannot exist. And more, therefore (this is the essence of the critique of practical reason), once metaphysics can't be science, then one must either completely eliminate it or replace it with surrogates, which will be all the easier to invent, in that they do not dare claim to independence and are constructed on the old ready models.

XV

From the preceding it is clear that even if in ancient times the fathers of philosophy wished to see in philosophy science κατ' ἐξοχήν (par excellence),[49] if among the modern philosophers Spinoza considered it possible to derive from the concept of substance everything that is in the world, and Kant with such pathos preached of the royal path of mathematics, then from this it follows least of all that their ideal of 'knowledge' is as a matter of fact a limit of that attainable by man or even, as it seemed to them, by any rational being. Kantians, perhaps, will rise up to protest against the identification of Kant's method with the method of practical philosophy. But it is enough to point to the critique of practical reason, to be convinced that 'freedom' in Kant in no wise differs from Spinoza's necessity and even from that necessity, which Kant acknowledged regnant in the world of phenomena. The kingdom of freedom for Kant, as well as for all Catholic theologians, was a fictive kingdom. Just as the medieval theologian began his definition of God from the point that God is outside any definitions, so Kant too for the moral world established the principle of freedom only at the beginning of his investigations. Then, by the path of the device μετάβασις εἰς ἄλλο γένος[50] so habitual, unavoidable and thus almost legitimate in philosophy, freedom, which ought not to apparently be limited by any prepared norms, unnoticeably fell under the power of the a priori principle – and nothing remains of it, save its proud name. Act such that you can acknowledge that all men ought to act as you do, so that one can see in your act a principle of universal conduct. Where did Kant get this synthetic judgement a priori? I do not share, more accurately, cannot share, the suspicion of those people who see in this principle the inspiration of ordinary life experience. Of course, only very credulous Kantians could deny the flight of utilitarianism in it, but all the same this is not the usual utilitarianism of the practical man. It's more accurate to see here the trace of ineradicable rationalism. Kant, like Spinoza, like Socrates, dreamed of internal necessity, likewise binding both God and man in the philosopher's metaphysical freedom. Even God cannot do all – chiefly God is not able to desire anything he pleases. We know how Socrates insisted on this. With no less conviction, Kant too insisted on this. Freedom for metaphysical beings is defined by internal necessity exactly as phenomena are defined for us, people, by external necessity. The only difference is that regularity in the world of phenomena is conditional – in the world of freedom, in the metaphysical world it is already unconditional and unchanging. No matter how you interpret Kant, you'll never get unstuck from this conclusion. After a long journey to the domains of relative rationalism, Kant was compelled to return to absolute rationalism. The grasshopper jumps high, using Goethe's expression, but he has ineluctably to be back in the grass. Prologomena[51] to any future metaphysics did not protect Kant either from an unscientific theory of cognition nor from unscientific morality and metaphysics. More than that, one can say, that Kant is the patriarch of all that confusion and mess, which now lives in the heads of modern philosophers. All are busy, as we all know, with the theory of cognition; i.e., all are writing, here for about a century and a half, their prolegomena, per Kant's example. They ask what conditions must be fulfilled, so that metaphysics is possible as a science. And each one who asks gives his own specific answer. Such that Husserl, the new star on the European philosophical horizon, has not said in vain that now in the domain of logic what you have is bellum omnium contra omnes.[52] It would be even more accurate to say, from the philosophical point of view, that after Kant the position of an arbitrarily constructed metaphysics that convinced no one has been taken by a theory of cognition just as arbitrarily constructed, just as little convincing anyone. It's not that our era is poor in philosophical talents. I would say the opposite: not for a long time has the philosophical field been worked by such a large number of such gifted workers. But some sort of fatal force prevents them from working the common task. It's clear to each one of them that his neighbours make mistakes and go round in circles, and each one of them can excellently show the mistakes of his comrades. The best and most convincing places in modern investigations of the theory of cognition are those which are devoted to the critique of existing theories. The weakest, although in their weakness all the same the most interesting and edifying, are those where they make an attempt to eliminate reigning errors and contradictions. In them, in these feverish desperate attempts at salvation, one feels that in our contemporaries, in the literal sense of the word, they've lost their mind to reason [ум заходит за разум]. The critical capability is refined to an extreme degree. The fear of contradiction has elevated directly to painfulness. And, in order somehow some way to conceal from themselves the hopelessness of the position created, people invent the most complex and cleverest theories, in which new terms and concepts are piled on in such a terrible quantity that it sometimes seems that their mission is not always clear to the one who created them. The closer you look and the more you think on the meaning of these tense attempts, the more you're convinced that on the plane in which they occur, they're always fated to remain attempts. They wish at any cost to justify scientific knowledge – just as Socrates, Plato, Aristotle or Kant wished to. But does scientific knowledge require justification? I do not wish to say by this that any doubts (of the necessity of such justification) have ceased. After Kant all are convinced that such justification may be attained – just have to put your thinking cap on. But, hey, they've thought and think enough – and all the same they have not come to a positive result in the sense in which it's accepted to understand these words. Not only have they not created a theory of the sources of the sovereign rights of scientific knowledge, but they haven't succeeded in attaining even temporarily the most modest consensus sapientum.⁵³ The biggest thing – each of the gnoseologies has succeeded in attaining for himself personally that ἀταραξια (serenity), which factually puts an end to the curiosity of the investigator. They simply no longer wish to know, don't wish to seek – as it was with the ancient Sceptics, who had the clear conscience and boldness, to reject indubitable truth, but who even passed on before probable truth. Why does probable truth have preference over indubitable? Put another way: even probable truth won't fall in your lap. From the multitude of judgements one must be chosen as the most probable, as the doubtless most probable – otherwise you'll deprive yourself of any direction in practical life. One cannot say that ice is cold and ice is hot, that the earth moves and the earth is immobile – judgements are equally probable. Even a Sceptic won't say that. He says with assurance that ice is cold, that birds fly, that lions can't – and only this assurance can guarantee the serenity (ἀταραξία), that which the Sceptics saw as the goal of all their philosophical seeking. And so long as ἀταραξία (serenity) implicite or explicite⁵⁴ will represent the problem of philosophical creative work, the device and method of validation will remain unchanged. No matter how much the gnoseologues chipped away, they will not escape their enchanted circle. No need to justify existing knowledge as the uniquely possible, uniquely perfect knowledge. This self-satisfaction, this assurance, that we already have everything and it remains only to consider how we inherited that which we inherited, had rendered modern philosophers impotent, as their satisfaction rendered the Sceptics impotent. The royal paths of mathematics seduced Kant and he forgot that there are divine paths, on which, just for a moment, Plato's fantasy went. Between Plato and Kant stood Aristotle, once and for all instilling in humanity distrust in everything flying too far afield. Aristotle's principle is 'not too much, not too little'. In all one must seek the faithful, never deceptive mean. So one might live, so one must die – so one must also philosophize – for, you know, to philosophize means to live and to die. It seems, they've forgotten and forget about this, but one must recall this without tiring. While you live, Aristotle teaches, no need to think of death, no need to tormentor yourself with unattainable goals. Human thinking, seeking ought to have a defined end, as it has a defined beginning. One of Aristotle's favourite expressions – any regressus in infinitum – denotes a defect in thinking, for the problem of thinking is to get rid of enigmas and depict the world in the aspect of a closed, complete whole, constructed per an accurately defined plan. Only on such a presupposition is it possible to deify reason. Socrates and Plato already knew this well, as we recall. But they did not have the restraint to limit their philosophical searches with the necessary consistency. Like all Greeks they highly honoured moderation and the mean. But their love was not exclusive, and thus they allowed other elements into their reasonings which shook the foundations of positive thought. The Cynics derive from Socrates; Plotinus derived from Plato. Only Aristotle with all decisiveness accepted the faith of the omnipotence of human reason. Only he elevated that which is near to an ideal, and solemnly, for himself and all his heirs, as befits a great monarch, renounced claims to that which is far. As reward for this exploit, history considers him the founding father of science – and European; humanity beckoned him not only for resolution of peripheral questions but also when it had to assimilate new mystical truth come from the Far East. Here too, as we'll see, the theory of the mean rendered great service. Just like the eye sets its defence against the undefined, creating above itself a sky-blue, visible, and soothing cupola, so Aristotelian reason too knew how to turn the uneasy human heart from the far and the undefined, and problems that are difficult to approach, nailing them to the near, habitual, familial and comprehensible. The philosophy of the mean yields satisfaction, for it obviates the unexpected. Everything that may be is already included in that which is. Attempts to find something beyond the limits of the given, attempts at journeys at great distances are annulled forever. Bliss – the highest and ultimate goal of human life – we ought to find on earth:

> Therefore all acknowledge that the blissful life is the condition of joy, and thus – with full bliss – the condition of joy stands in the closest connection with bliss. For action cannot be complete if it encounters interference; bliss is complete and, therefore, the blissful need both corporeal and external goods and success, so that nothing would interfere with it. Those who affirm that the good man can be blissful under torture voluntarily or involuntarily speak rubbish.[55]

The adduced passage from Aristotle, directed chiefly against the Cynics, and perhaps also against Plato, can without exaggeration be considered the source of the philosophical creative work of Aristotle. Bliss on earth – he's convinced of this – is the ultimate goal of man. He is further convinced that bliss is possible only on the condition that successes accompany man through life, and when fate sends him many or enough external goods. And he is further convinced that under torture or under heavy blows of faith, man cannot be blessed. His ultimate conviction is that those people who do not agree with him, voluntarily or involuntarily, sin against the truth. You see how many 'convictions' are concealed in a few lines. You probably also see that if one were to demand proofs of his convictions from Aristotle, then he could not present anything in his justification except the consideration that he knows what he knows and that someone who judges other than he does is either a fool or a liar. And meantime, what we need to establish is the fact – that both during Aristotle's life and after him there were quite a few people who sought 'bliss' exactly where it – if you base yourself on Aristotle's assurances – cannot be. I ask, what gave Aristotle the right to relegate these people and deprive them of the right to vote in questions that concern them no less than him? Why do they voluntarily or involuntarily lie? Why do they head off from the mean illuminated by reason and come to search at the dark liminal regions? That is all that Aristotle could answer, if one could draw him into an answer à propos the assurances uttered by him in such a tone, brooking no dissent. He was not at the dark borders, he did not experience the heavy blows of fate, but he didn't need them. He had reason, which created the theory of the mean, and he well and firmly knew where one could and could not search. Not too much and not too little – the synthetic judgement <u>a priori</u> was a magic wand in Aristotle's hands, with which he marked an enchanted circle, which people ought not to step over. All the virtues of humanity were defined by Aristotle as a middle path between two extremes; even truth seemed to him a mean between two errors; man must seek μέσον between ὑπερβολήν and ἔλλειψις (i.e., a mean between too much and too little). Τὸ δὲ μέσον ἐστὶν ὡς ὁ λόγος ὁ ὀρθὸς λέγει[56] (Eth. VI, 1; Zeller II-2, 633) – right thinking. This testament of Aristotle was taken by humanity as the Good News. After Aristotle any attempt to suspect the mean and search at the liminal regions was met not with suspicion but with hatred. There were people, and quite a few people, to whom Aristotle's news did not seem good, who tried to wrest from themselves the heavy yoke of great sin. But such people were condemned to solitude and tormented fruitless struggle. Their deeds, their creative work at times found temporary response, but always, sooner or later, they were swept mercilessly from the historical highways over which marched triumphant and victorious humanity. If you will, Aristotle was adjudged in history even greater triumphs, one can indicate more than a few cases, when the most remarkable, bold people, filled with inflamed hatred towards him, after many years of long and stubborn struggle, humbly and voluntarily returned anew under his principle and acknowledged that they ἢ ἑκόντες ἢ ἄκοντες οὐδὲν λέγουσιν.[57] We will speak of them further on. Right now we'll only formulate in a few words what we've said in the preceding chapters. First Socrates and Plato, in their striving to parry the blows of Melitus and Anitus, created a theory of knowledge, obligatory for God and man. Aristotle took this theory from them. Gods and the divine were expelled by him to the borders ὑπερβολήν,[58] as forbidden and dangerous. Obligatory, rational and, yes, integral knowledge, yielding full satisfaction to man and teaching him a perfect life, was constructed by him on slightly changed but essentially the same foundations, which had been worked out by his teachers. The mean became the ultimate truth and the ultimate goal. The borders were equated to ends and to the non-existent. The mean – as the ideal of cognition and as satisfaction, as the ultimate goal of our existence on earth and as the ideal of morality – here's what humanity inherited from Aristotle and here's what it put at the basis of its science and its ethics and here's what it stands for with all its strength even now, as the eternal, validated and uniquely necessary.

XVI

We already know, how great Aristotle's power was over humanity. We also know that the force of Aristotle's ideas was in no way rooted in their logical convincingness. Aristotle could just as little prove the correctness of his own, and avoid contradiction, as other philosophers. The Stagrite completely owed his charm to that decisiveness, which gave him the possibility to wall off the human mind from the importuning inquest of the soul. He wished and knew how to limit himself and be satisfied with the achievable – and that's all the same, in human understanding, as seeking out the ultimate goal of existence. There are ends; there are beginnings – as limits – and there is the clear, illuminated mean, accessible to cognition, as the singular indubitable reality. This great discovery was greeted as good news by European humanists (I speak of European humanity because the life of Asian people still remains for us an unsolved mystery). Everything that was strong and healthy in Europe seized on the doctrine of Aristotle, as on an anchor of salvation. Even Catholicism – which always loved to consider itself independent from general culture – willingly assumed the yoke of the philosopher, truly feeling that the yoke is good. The time of the flowering of Catholic theology is the time of Aristotle's greatest triumph. And, conversely, the time of the decline, of the fall of Catholicism – the period preceding the Reformation and the Tridentine council – was the most unreceptive for the great philosopher. Even Duns Scotus began to express ideas threatening the wholeness of the world view expressed by Thomas Aquinas; the last great representative of scholasticism, William of Occam, decisively broke with Aristotle's traditions. The decline and decadence of scholasticism coincides with the scholars' loss of faith in Aristotle. It may even be identified with it. This is the loss of faith in what he called reason, in which he found direction for life.[59]

The cupola created by Thomas Aquinas on the basis of Aristotelian philosophy, so firm, sky blue, adorned by myriads of gleaming lights, no longer seemed even a beautiful work of art. They began to feel that there's a sky beyond the cupola and that art ought to be more penetrating and more profound. Why is that so? Why did Aristotle live for centuries and seemed to all a normal natural philosopher? Why did Thomas Aquinas still trust him, and post-Tridentine Catholicism again believed him, and Duns Scotus and Occam seek other sources? I do not have the opportunity to dwell in detail on the representatives of the decadence of Scholasticism. I'll confine myself to only an indication of one moment which will show us what exactly in Aristotelian philosophy was especially unacceptable for the last great Scholastics. This is important in view of the point that this will at once discover both the force and, if you will, the weakness of Aristotle. Duns Scotus and Occam departed tradition not because one or another specific resolution of theological questions did not satisfy them, and still less because they were insufficiently fervent Catholics. Their orthodoxy is just as indubitable, as the orthodoxy indeed of Thomas Aquinas himself. But what repelled them from Thomas was exactly what so attracted all other believers, convinced Catholics: his know-it-all attitude; his assurance that with Aristotle's help, theology could be turned into a science, just as exact almost as mathematics. We recall, by what means Aristotle wrought his omniscience. He, following Socrates and Plato, acknowledged that human reason is allowed to set laws for the universe. That which he acknowledges as true and good will also be acknowledged good and true in the other world, and what he rejects as lie and evil remains such in saecula saeculorum (for all the ages). Before adducing the corresponding judgements of the scholastics, I once more recall the formulation of Socrates or Plato in Eutiphrones: whether the good is good because the gods love it or, conversely, whether the gods love the good because it is good.[60] The answer of Socrates spake: the gods love the good because it is good – i.e., reason is given potestas clavium, power of the keys. We also know already that Thomas Aquinas did not allow another resolution veritati fidei christianae non contrariatur veritas rationis;[61] therefore he, like Anselm of Canterbury as well, considered himself justified to penetrate to the ultimate mysteries of revelation. Anselm of Canterbury was proving that per reason God ought to have been incarnated in man, that there was no other way to save the world. The time of Tertullian had long passed already. And by the by, his words, his explanation of the mystery of incarnation and Christ's death on the cross found no response in the history of Catholic thought. And even, if you like, Tertullian himself did not know what further to do with such explanations. He said: <u>crucifixus est Dei filius; not pudet quia pudendum est; et mortuus est Dei filius – prorsus credibile quia ineptum est; et sepultus resurrexit; certum est quia impossibile est.</u>[62]

If this 'explanation' were presented at Aristotle's court, he probably would say that Tertullian talks that way but does not think as he talks. Aristotle was not allowed to judge Tertullian, but history, i.e., historians and life, has approximately so regarded this explanation. You'll encounter these remarkable words in almost all books on the history of Christianity, but they do not speak of them seriously. Usually they're relegated to commentary, as a model of a curious but feral and completely unnecessary paradox. As early as Bl. Augustine, he found it possible to prove that reason more or less understands the incarnation and death of Christ, that such a means of redemption of the Adamite sin was <u>conventor</u> (consistent); consequently, as I already said, theologians proved that this was already even necessary, and that mortal reason could even define the value of the sacrifice offered by Christ. All definitions are based, obviously, on the conviction earlier uttered by Socrates on the power of our reason. If one allows that it was not Socrates and Aristotle that knew the truth, and that logic with its laws and reason with its scales are not the ultimate instance for resolution of all doubts, in a word that the <u>quia</u> (because) of Tertullian, i.e., his theory of cognition, ought not to be eliminated, as it was earlier voided by the <u>quia</u> of Aristotle. If this is so, then, of course, all the theological constructs of the scholastics turn out built on sand. For some this is most terrible, and thus they do not allow Tertullian and thinkers akin to him within firing range of their questions; for others, conversely, Aristotle with his reason, which defines everything in advance, and thus they head out on any path you like, only one not predefined by him. For them <u>sicut in naturalibus videtur</u> (as occurs naturally) is not a conclusion but a rebuttal. And here Duns Scotus, literally re-establishing the rights of the forgotten Tertullian theory of cognition with its overturned '<u>quia</u>' and literally throwing the gauntlet down to Socrates and Aristotle, writes:

> <u>sicut omne aliud a Deo ideo est bonum, quia a Deo volitum, et non e converso, sic meritum illud tantum bonum erat, pro quanto acceptabatur; et ideo meritum, quia acceptatum, not autem e converso quia meritum est bonum, ideo acceptatum; Christi meritum secundum sufficientiam valuit procul dubio quantum fuit a deo acceptatum si quidem divina acceptation est potissima causa et ratio omnis meriti.</u>[63]

Here's how Duns Scotus poses the question and here's how he answers it:

> <u>Divina acceptatio est potissima causa et ratio omnis meriti.</u>[64]

That is, that the good is good because and insofar, inasmuch as God accepts it, and the unique source of valuation of human conduct is the will of God, unlimited by any norms known to man and unshakable. It's clear that, as opposed to Socrates and Aristotle, Duns Scotus strives not to establish an unbreakable link between human and divine reasoning, but rather to dig an abysmal gap between them. Perhaps it's not so obvious, but the following presentation will clarify this – in opposition to Anselm of Canterbury and Thomas Aquinas, Duns Scotus not only did not humbly agree to transfer the potestas clavium to Aristotle but rather exerted all his strength to wrest from Aristotle's hands the power already given him by the Catholic Church and transfer it to where it belonged. We cannot attain the basis per which God acts, for bases are obligatory for men and not for God. On man's scale, norms exist by which he must be guided in his acts, wishes, valuations. But the divine will is free of all this: we cannot name the conditions by which it is defined.

> Et ideo hujus quare voluntas voluit hoc, nulla est causa, nisi quia voluntas est voluntas[65]
>
> (Duns Scott. Sent. I, dist. 8, quaest. 5, 24. – Seeberg, Die Theologie des Duns Scotus, Leipzig, 1900, 162).

God created the world as it is, not because he could not create it otherwise, but because He wished to create it thus. He established the known order of things potentia ordinata (by established power) – he could by his potentia absoluta establish another order as well.

> Sicut potest (Deus) aliter agere, ita potest aliam legem statuere rectam, quia, si statueretur a deo, recta esset, quia nulla lex est recta, nisi quatenus, a voluntate divina acceptatur
>
> (Seeberg, Ibd.)[66]

Therefore Duns Scotus feared not to even affirm that if God so wished, the redemption of the human race could be imposed on an angel or on a purus homo (sinless man), free from original sin or overshadowed by grace. For the valuation of the redemptive sacrifice is defined uniquely by the sovereign will of God; the service of an angel, taking on itself torment for another's sins, might be valued by God as highly as only He wished.

All these paradoxical affirmations – so strange, as well as unnecessary, at first glance, so insultingly unacceptable for usual thinking, naturally hewing to the logic of Anselm of Canterbury and Thomas Aquinas, who convinced people that divine reason exceeds but does not contradict human reason – how was it conceived in the soul of the medieval scholastic? The Protestant theologian Seeberg, wishing to weaken the significance of the admissions, incomprehensible from his point of view, says: 'Duns Scotus, as philosopher, could consider such possibilities (potentia absoluta), but in the limits of his theology they could have only one mission – to the more brightly illuminate the idiosyncrasy of positive Christianity.' Theological themes do not occupy us here, and the theological theories of a scholastic of the thirteenth century can occupy us least of all. But I suppose, that it's a great mistake on the historian's part to so arbitrarily cut off the living person of the man that interests him. And for our contemporaries such purposeful specialization is unallowable. In the Middle Ages, any scholar was pretty much an Encyclopaedist. Only a man having taken a position beforehand could artificially separate his philosophical views from their religious roots in Duns Scotus. Even Loofs and Harnack – also Protestants – found it necessary to protest, albeit weakly, against Seeberg's decisiveness.

This theory, putting God above the norms of usual morality, is the actual <u>crux interpretuum</u> for followers of Luther, the same as Plato's ideas were for Aristotle. As we'll see below, the philosophy of Duns Scotus was completely accepted by Luther – to boot again in that idiosyncratic and still sharper formulation which Occam had lent it. The value of the acts of a man is defined not by any immanently inherent qualities but by the free, arbitrary, no wise bound, decision of God. No matter how much the Protestant theologians write exegeses to the effect that religion ought not to be identified with morality, it ineluctably loses any point of support, as soon as they make an attempt to transition to incarnation of these conversations of theirs. God, standing above morality, seems to them an intentional challenge to common sense, and no one is allowed to disdain common sense unpunished. The difficulty then of the position of modern Protestant theologians is increased and becomes straight unendurable in view of the fact that Duns Scotus' doctrine of <u>acceptatio</u> came through Occam, who formulated it, as we'll now see, still more sharply, to their common teacher – to Luther. <u>Divina acceptatio est ratio omnis meriti</u> (Divine agreement is the reason of all merit). Luther constructed all his philosophy on this affirmation – all his objections to Catholicism.[67] It stands to reason that Protestant theologians in good time before they had to move to judgements on the revolution which Luther brought to the evaluation of the relation of men to God would try to undermine the trust in the idea of <u>acceptatio</u>. Harnack's argumentation is instructive for us in the highest degree. Citing in the commentary the words of the historian Werner,[68] who as opposed to Seeberg does not fear to characterize Duns Scotus in terms especially sharply emphasizing the idiosyncratic position he occupied, Harnack utters the following judgement: Doubtless Duns Scotus, compared to Thomas, took a significant step forward, strictly defining God as will and person, separate from the world, but all the advantages of such a concept are turned into defects from the moment it's clear that <u>one can no longer count on such a God</u> (Harnack said just this literally – I'm only translating – <u>wo man sich auf diesen Gott nicht mehr verlassen kann</u>) because it does not allow Him to think as acting by higher morally unshakable principles (<u>nach den höchsten Kategorien sittlicher Notwendigkeit</u>) and when consequently, the goods of the created (i.e., of man) consist, as Scotus' disciples taught – in subordination to the will of God. God's motives are unattainable for us, and are manifest only in revelation. This representation of God, as of will, i.e., of arbitrary will, leads to the same difficulties to which the representation of God as all-defining substance led to. For in both cases His being is bedecked with a cover of darkness. The Scholastics did not wish to go by that narrow path which leads to a stable and comforting concept of God, by the path of faith in God, as the father of Jesus Christ (Harnack III; 525, 526). It's important for us to uncover the basis of his religious views in these objections of Harnack. The thought of Duns Scotus and Occam that, as Werner expresses it, one cannot apply to God our usual little measures leads, in Harnack's opinion, to the most terrible result: once we don't know whether God is subordinate to our norms or not, then, therefore, we can't depend on Him. We can depend on a God, who along with us is subordinate to a general law – to a God validated and approved by us. We cannot trust a mysterious God, unattainable, covered in darkness, and what if he demands from us something that goes athwart our concept of good and evil? Of the rational, the highest? Harnack first wishes to decide – and is convinced that he has full possibility to do this – how God ought to be, per his concept – and then if God turns out as He ought, Harnack will agree to acknowledge Him and be subordinate to Him. Allow for a minute the opposite – allow that God is allowed to prescribe to Harnack, to teach Harnack – what ought to and ought not to be; what is good, what bad – Harnack would not go for that. This would mean to stand 'beyond good and evil'; this would mean to follow Nietzsche's example – to acknowledge that Nietzsche was no atheist but rather a believer. You won't tempt Harnack to such a step. He serenely and decisively renounces the authority of the Church; he passionately disputes with the Catholic Pope his <u>potestas clavium</u> – power of the keys, but to believe God, who does not take moral imperatives from men, Harnack's not about to do that. First one must ask <u>cui est credendum</u> (whom we ought to believe). Harnack, following Socrates, presents the power of the keys, taken from the Church, to reason and only to reason. And he's not even shook up by Luther's example, whom, as we recall, he is ready to consider a prophet.

XVII

Harnack, along with Thomas Aquinas and the Vatican council, was profoundly convinced that there can be no contradiction between religious truth and the truth of reason and that his moral principles are the highest criterion by which one might unmistakably test even the rights of the Creator. We will not validate the legitimacy of Harnack's claim – neither now or later. It seems to me that for anyone who gave himself the assignment of attentively looking into and thinking over the material I've gathered in the preceding chapters it will become obvious of itself, what the source of the assurance of the modern liberal German theologian is. Harnack is not alone. Harnack, in his convictions and presuppositions, is a person in the collective sense. Harnack is everyone, and everyone not even of today but, if it's allowable so to express oneself, he is everyone, <u>Herr omnes</u> ('Mr. Everyman'), as Luther said, of all times and all nations. To refute his theoretical objections is useless, for, as we can already be convinced, outside of certain limits theoretical considerations lose their power and all charm. We can do only one thing: show that there are people for whom to believe in that 'which they all believed always and everywhere' represents not a mistaken but rather a terrible and fatal error.[69] We saw that Aristotle, Thomas Aquinas, i.e., all of official Catholicism, and along with them the Protestant liberal theologian Harnack, as representative of modern scientific methodology, most of all fear to break the thread connecting the visible, known or, as it's accepted to say, the natural order of things with the ultimate mystery. For Thomas Aquinas the consideration – <u>sicut in naturalibus videtur</u>[70] – is decisive and final. In other words, the usual, ever repeating, experience, accessible to all, serves as the pledge that the unchanging order, rational by our lights, has dominion in all the universe, that the ultimate principle, the ultimate mystery, albeit unknown to us but yet is to be found in perfect correspondence and perfect harmony with that truth which we've already gained. That is, expressing in the terminology of the Scholastics, God in His <u>potentia absoluta</u> (unlimited power) cannot represent anything unexpected for man, cognizing Him in the world created by His <u>potentia ordinata</u> (established power). We have so profoundly penetrated into the ultimate goals of the Creator that we can with assurance even foretell that which awaits us in future life. Truth and justice are everywhere the same, and man, from his short life can, if he wishes, know exactly what he must do in order to be saved. We see manifest in all these reasonings that centripetal force of which we've already had to speak. Man does not wish to rise to God; he wishes to compel God to lower to himself, to become such as He is represented to our weak and limited minds. Fearing to destroy the even serenity of our bourgeois existence, we wall ourselves off from all that is new and unknown. Whatever else they'll demand of us there, it'd be better for us to demand it ourselves: we already know what's good, what's bad; we already know what the ultimate truth ought to be. It's not astonishing that the attempts of Duns Scotus and Occam to undermine the trust in rationalist theology evoked and continue to evoke such a sharp reaction. God, as freedom, unlimited by nothing, even – <u>horrible dictu</u> – by our reason – can man possibly sincerely and convincingly so think? Normal theologians and normal philosophers decide without vacillation that there's a dirty deal here. It cannot be, they say, that anywhere in the world, anyone, even more the Higher Being, entered into contradiction with our reason and our conscience. And, therefore, we are right to affirm: everything that does not reconcile with the ideals of good and evil living in us is relegated to the domain of the irreal, non-existent, and we, people, and our Creator are equally obligated to acknowledge well-known norms. Of course, once such a conviction lives in people, once they so profoundly believe in the uniquely salvific nature of the ideals worked out by them, such systems as the systems of Duns Scotus and Occam arouse the liveliest dissatisfaction in them. It seems to them they're being robbed, that an attempt is being made on their proudest possession. <u>Facienti quod in se est Deus infallibiter dat gratiam</u>[71] – it's not God's right to refuse His grace to him who has done everything in his power, says medieval theology, almost literally repeating Socrates' words. But Occam writes: '<u>Ex puris naturalibus, nemo possit mereri vitam aeternam nec etiam ex quibuscumque donis collatis a deo, nisi quia deus contingenter ex libere et misericorditer ordinavit, quod habens talia dona posit mereri vitam aeternam, ut deus per nullam rem possit necessitari</u>

ad conferendum cuicunque vitam aeternam'[72] (Occam, in Sent. I, dist. 17, qu. 1 L – PRE XIV, 276 – Ockam von R. Seeberg).

So Occam, the disciple of Scotus, affirms: by no means, i.e., by no moral exploits can a man compel God to give him eternal life. God saves whom he wishes, and Occam trusts more the free, nowise-fettered will of God and then the noblest reasonings of the most moral man, be he Socrates or Thomas Aquinas. It's understandable that Occam is an enfant terrible for theology and philosophy, which wish to be 'sciences'. And thus it's understandable that Catholics tie his ideas on to Protestants, and Protestants on to Catholics. For both the one and the other seek, expressing in Harnack's words, a God on Whom 'one can depend' – and how to depend on a God, if, per Occam's words, He does not consider our elementary concepts of justice – God can reject him, he who his whole life tried to please Him, and conversely accept him, who never thought of Him? But this general affirmation is insufficient for Occam. This doctor subtilissimus set himself as his life's goal to capsize and devalue the treasures accumulated by centuries of efforts of the most remarkable people. He disputes all the pretensions of human reason and conscience. Against the tradition established in Catholic theology, Occam does not even fear to utter such judgements: non potest demonstrative probari, quod tantum est unus Deus.[73] And again: non potest naturaliter demonstrari, quod voluntas non potest satiari nec quietari in alique citra Deum.[74] And finally: non potest probari sufficienter quod Deus sit causa finalis.[75] His disciple says of him that Occam: 'concedit nec reputat inconveniens, quin voluntas creata possit meritorie Deum odire, quia Deus possit illud praecipere'[76] (Denifle II, 304, 305, 306). And if a still more challenging formulation is necessary, proceeding from the very same epoch of the decline of Scholasticism, we can adduce the following statement: Deus potest praecipere rationali creature, quod habeat ipsum odio, et ipsa obediens plus meritur, quam si ipsum diligeret, quoniam hoc faceret cum majori conatu et magis contra propriam inclinationem[77] (Denifle, II, 306).

All these statements, as though selected, were literally foreordained to deprive people of assurance and hope that 'one could depend on God', i.e., that we can guess, to what the higher will directs us, penetrate into the mysterious intents of the Creator. He (Occam) with a sharp, almost crude mockery rejects all attempts of theologians to explain the mystery of incarnation:

> 'Est articulus fidei, quod Deus assumsit naturam humanum. Non includit contradictionem, Deum assumere naturam asininam; pari ratione potest assumere lapidem vel lignum'.[78]
>
> (Occam, Sentilog. Concl. 6 – Werner, Scholastick, II, 356)

You see how far Occam moved from Anselm of Canterbury and even from Gregory the Great.[79] Gregory the Great also considered that he knew what directed God, sending His Son to earth. When Adam sinned, said the great Pope, God accursed man and gave him into the eternal power of Satan. From that time man ceased to belong to God and became the property of the devil. Then God had pity on men, but He could not take them from Satan – God had no right to break His word even to the devil. And thus God thought up such a means: He sent His Son to earth in the image of man. Satan did not notice God under the external image of man, as the fish does not notice the hook under the worm; he attacked Christ and dealt Him a shameful death. In this Satan overstepped his rights: he could kill men but had no right to kill God. In this manner, God, having hooked the sly devil on this line, was also freed from the promise He made and could return to Himself the descendants of Adam once torn away from Him. Here's how Gregory the Great explains the mystery of incarnation. And such an explanation satisfied him: probably he considered his 'explanation' much more 'rational' than that which is contained in the earlier adduced words of Tertullian. Not even just him but also Harnack ought to have acknowledged that no matter how unacceptable the explanation of Gregory the Great is for him, in it there are at least some flashes of reason. Even more than that – from the purely formal logical side, it is irreproachable. From Tertullian's words there wafts a real insanity, that insanity which is ready to accept complete unknown, impenetrable darkness – as the ultimate goal. God sent Abram, and he went, not knowing where he was going. And here, just like Tertullian, we have Occam. He disdains his reason; he feels that if somewhere there is something that is necessary to him, then it's not in those places to which reason might lead him. He seeks revelation, and he is gladdened that revelation gave him not what reason seeks, not what it hopes for. Looking into the church dogmata he is convinced that they are not reconciled with his rational expectations, but this does not disturb him and does not scare him. Or, perhaps, it both scares and disturbs him, but he least of all interprets his fear and disturbance as an objection against revealed truth. No matter how fearsome it is to our limited reason, it must be accepted. Our problem is not to validate the Divine by the earthly, but on the contrary, to get used to, still living on earth, the thought of another life, so little similar to our present life and, it may be, on our measure, more similar not to life but to death. And the chief obstacle in this task is reason's assurance in its infallibility, in its all-encompassing nature. Corresponding to this, all our strength ought to be directed not to justification of our knowledge but to upheaval of those bases on which knowledge is supported. Here's the origin of the unrestrained nature of the Occam critique, exceeding all limits allowed by common sense. Here's why Occam so assiduously and stubbornly demonstrates that the truth of revelation is in implacable contradiction with rational truth. Dogmatic assertions cannot be proven – their source is not reason but faith: 'Nulla ratione naturali potest probari, esse plures personas in divinis; sed quod sunt plures personae, quarum una est Pater et alia Filius, et quod Filius vere generatur a Patre, est sola fide tenendum'[80] (Occam, Sentilog. I, dist 9, qu. 1 – Werner, Scholastik, II, 356).

I think what's been said of Duns Scotus and Occam will be enough for our goals. We ought only not to think that Occam's ideas are something completely new, first conceived in his learned head and alien to all historical development. Not in vain, as early as the first centuries of Christianity, Tertullian attempted in his explanation of the birth, death and resurrection of Christ to create a new theory of cognition, not considering either Socrates or Aristotle. This tendency never died in Catholicism; it's observed, as we'll see, in the great mystics of the seventeenth century; it lives in it, probably even now – but official Catholicism has managed to oppose to it the discipline of the powerful theology supported on Aristotle and Thomas Aquinas. We encounter expressions in the early mystics, which, if we take them seriously and think on them, have an inherent acknowledgement of the irreconcilability of our reason and faith, which called Occam's philosophy to life. Take just Dionysus the Areopagite: <u>Nihil eorum, quae sunt ... explicat arcanum illum omnem rationem et intellectum superans superdeitatis super essentialiter supra omnia superexistentis.</u>[81]

One can write that, one can say that, but hardly anyone would resolve to affirm that which lurks beneath the quoted words (I don't even know how to translate them into Russian!) can be in any connection with our rational knowledge. If that is light, then it's that <u>lux inaccessibilis, quem nullus hominum vidit nequere videre potest,</u>[82] i.e., if one drops the metaphors, it's exactly that <u>nox mystica</u>, which ordinary philosophy, like its correlate, normal Catholic theology, fears more than anything on earth and which it uses as the ultimate and unconquerable objection. This is that hidden God, of whom Harnack wrote, that one cannot depend on Him, and thus He ought to be rejected. And just the same, Dionysus the Areopagite affirms τῷ μηδὲν γιγνώσκειν ὑπὲρ νοῦν γιγνώσκων.[83] In other words, reason, each time it gets the wish to direct man in his ultimate searches, is an obstacle and only an obstacle. One must forget all that one knew; one must forget that generally there might be knowledge, if you want to enter on the path which leads to God. It's that <u>docta ignorantia</u> (learned unknowing), which Nicholas of Cusa praised in his time. <u>In rebus divinis scire est scire, non ignorare.</u>[84] One only must not, of course, confuse this unknowing with the <u>ignoramus</u> (we don't know) or <u>ignorabimus</u> (we won't know) of modern philosophy. For all the external likeness, leading man into comprehensible error, the formulas of the positivists and Dionysus the Areopagite are more different from one another than day and night. The <u>ignoramus</u> (we don't know) of Emil du Bois-Reymond[85] indicates the end – μηδὲν γιγνώσκειν (unknowing) in the Areopagite – the beginning. One must say the same of Occam as well. He, as Werner says,

> by his decisive denial of any internal ideal connection between moral guilt and its corresponding punishment or repentance, extended to its most extreme limits the doctrine of Scotus on the random nature of the moral order, based on absolute divine will (i.e., on arbitrariness), whose laws – beyond the exception of the commandment, that one must love God more than anything[86] – know completely no internal necessity.
>
> (Werner II, 319)

And then, as we recall, even with the Greeks the very possibility of knowledge conditioned the existence of that internal necessity, which itself defined the linkage and connection of disparate elements of the world architecture. As opposed to Occam and the mystics, Anselm of Canterbury assimilated exactly the Greek point of view. The Protestants are correct when they speak of the Hellenization of Catholicism. The Greek spirit, attaining its most perfect expression in the philosophy of Aristotle, the spirit μέτριος εἰς ὑπερβολήν (moderate to extremes) laid its powerful hand on the whole movement of European thought. But the Protestants err greatly, supposing that they have avoided Hellenization themselves, that their attempts to return to the pure Judaism, as it is expressed in the Old and New Testaments, in actual fact lead them to any kind of serious results in the domain of religious searching. The borderlands scare both the Protestants and the Catholics equally. The epistles of the apostle Paul are equally unacceptable both for Erasmus of Rotterdam and for the modern commentaries of the Lutheran servo arbitrio. Albrecht Ritschl, patriarch of modern liberal Protestant theology, responds to this work of Luther as ungluckliches Machwerk (unsuccessful makework). Corresponding to this, Occam too with his philosophy, attempting to overturn the limits marked by Aristotle to the limits of human seeking, likewise arouses the same dissatisfaction in both Harnack and Werner or in such Catholics as Denifle and Weiss. Here's how Harnack judges:

> the historical consequences of Occamism teach us that thinking humanity never has agreed to accept for long a religion founded uniquely on revelation, and sever all the threads by which revelation is connected to the general world view. From Occam one either returns back to Thomas Aquinas or heads forward to Socianism.[87] But can it be impossible that the history of religion shows the service to those seeking ideas, which heretofore the idealistic world views of Plato, Augustine and Thomas showed them? One cannot, of course, get by without the absolute, but it can be attained as experience, and not gained by the speculative path.
>
> (Harnack III, 646)

If the absolute, as experience, did not have really inherent the union of two completely contradictory concepts, perhaps Harnack would have succeeded in resolving the dilemma he set himself – to leave Occam and not proceed to Thomas Aquinas. But experience is experience exactly because it does not present in the logical form obligatory for the absolute which ought to be acknowledged quod semper, ubique, et ad omnibus creditum et credendum est. One can build a positive religion without dogma only on revelation. Otherwise 'the experiences' of Muslims, Buddhists and even idolators are equally privileged in their claims with Harnack's experience. If we're now talking about history – if we even take the Dogmengeschichte of Harnack himself – then one of the very brightest facts of the thousand-year development for humanity, a development, one of the links of which is the modern liberal Protestant theology, is the fear to supplant the absolute with experience. And this is understandable. Once the idea of Duns Scotus and Occam that deum necessitari non posse[88] leads the theoreticians of religion of all confessions and trends, then how can they allow the thought that no longer God, but rather man, in his weakness and limitation, is allowed to be supported on 'the arbitrary' of experience, perhaps completely random and transitory? And how can experience be called the absolute? We already recall what Harnack said earlier, there cannot be faith without authority. This is a sincere overt idea, common between him and Catholicism. It is indeed expressed in the contradictory union of two so dissimilar words. It seems to Harnack that the absolute totally absorbs experience in the final end, and thus, one could return to Thomas Aquinas, on an abbreviated and shortcut path attuned to modern requirements.

And I think that I won't exaggerate, if I say that Harnack's objections to Occam have the same source as Werner's objections. Werner (<u>Die Scholastik der späteren Mittelalters</u>, II, 320) says in the old way that Occam's 'mistake' is 'in the complete absence of the ideal world view … the thought of moral order which bears the law within itself, is alien to him, he explains everything by Godly edicts and laws'. And how could Occam, to whom the internal content of life seemed inaccessible to rational thinking, think other than this? For him the church doctrine of salvation, understood by him in his way, completely replaces the metaphysics of the moral order; it was the singular and exclusive support of his moral thinking.

I suppose, as I said, that Werner much better expressed Harnack's thoughts (and his own, of course) than Harnack himself. They both consider the fundamental defect of Occam's thinking to be the absence of what drew them both, voluntarily or involuntarily, to Thomas. Thomas knew, but Occam did not know, the metaphysics of the moral order. And this means, I think, that after the foregoing no new explanations are required of me – Thomas feared to allow God the arbitrary and subordinated him to the control of Aristotelian principles; Occam feared the arbitrary of Aristotle and went, perhaps with both a weird feeling, but also not without the triumph known to but few, to meet the completely unknown. Who of them was right – Thomas Aquinas and Catholicism and Harnack, who decided to give over the whole fullness of the potestas clavium to Aristotle, or Occam, unreservedly giving up all his soul to the Creator? In other words, is it that one might just find God only when you agree to break with reason, the usual companion and lead of our life, or is reason necessary even for remote, transliminal journeys?

Editor – The seven following chapters of the first part of the manuscript went with some changes and additions into Shestov's book <u>In Job's Balances</u> (pp. 83–138) under the title <u>At the Last Judgment (Last Works of L. N. Tolstoy)</u>.

Part II

LUTHER AND THE CHURCH

LUTHER AND THE CHURCH

I

Dostoevsky's Legend of the Grand Inquisitor in intent ought to represent a merciless critique of Catholicism. I very much doubt that Dostoevsky had the opportunity and leisure to become fundamentally acquainted with the past and present of Catholicism. He knew, of course, all of the powerful popes, cruel and venal, and of indulgences, of Jesuits, not stinting at any available means, and of the Inquisition – everyone knows that. He knew what everyone knows about the Reformation, too, and of Luther, rebelling against Catholicism. But he regarded both Luther and Catholicism with equal hatred, chiefly because everything that came out of Europe was of low account with him, instilling only suspicion in him.

The idea developed in the Legend about the internal meaning and mission of Catholicism, if one thinks deeply on it, can be related as a matter of fact to the whole spiritual life of Europe as it was drawn by Dostoevsky. The chief sin of Europe is its unbelief. And no matter what our Western neighbours did, no matter how their creative work manifested itself, in science, literature, philosophy, theology, in all ought to have been the mark of Cain, of unbelief.

European Christianity is no better than European science. Just as science in Europe trusts only itself, i.e., human reason, so European religion depends only on what man himself can understand, can himself do. In this sense, the Legend of the Grand Inquisitor says even more than it seems at first glance. It totals the accounts of the two-thousand-year history of Europe. You have done much, very much – announces Dostoevsky to his Western neighbours, but you have paid a terrible price for what you have gained. And you yourself know, you cannot but know, what sacrifice you have brought to the altar of your civilization, and the best, the most perceptive among you are tormented, exhausted under the burden of the colossal responsibility you have taken on yourselves. The Grand Inquisitor – the incarnation of all that was most human and most significant in Europe – ought to acknowledge before Him from Whom nothing is hidden – that for Europeans, the good news brought from the East that the world is ruled by He who stands above man and his reason has turned out to be unacceptable. The light come from the East appeared as impenetrable darkness to Western people. For historical reasons one could not openly renounce the proclaimed truth – and Catholicism was left one way out – gradually, in the course of centuries, to change out the mysterious divine word for one humanly comprehensible. It did just that – on that place where there ought to have been truth, it erected the visible Catholic Church, accessible to humanity. The Grand Inquisitor directly and openly says to his mysterious guest:

> We are not with You, but with him, i.e., with your eternal irreconcilable enemy. Our actual leader and lord is the devil, Antichrist. Him we can understand, him we can serve, for he speaks an accessible and comprehensible, rational language with his weak impotent creatures. That which You demand from us – subordinate reason to faith – we cannot fulfil. For us, people, the source of light always was and will be reason and where the power of reason ends, there begins an eternal, impenetrable darkness – the most terrible that could ever be invented. And we've never been and are never going there – into that darkness, which You wish that we consider light. Our holy Catholic Church corrects Your work. It gives people what is necessary to them. It gives them stability and assurance instead of Your freedom – it gives them an order founded on firm unchanging authority. It shows the mystery but does not demand that people are in communion [к ней приобщились] with it. It promises miracle – and people see it before their very eyes, although it will not be. For the crowd – the spectators, along with the actors – the elect are equally interested that the miracle, as well as the mystery, always be held at a distance. No one will come to look into, and validate; no one will come to penetrate the mystery. Our authority and our infallibility will justify themselves otherwise. Per its fruits will they judge the tree. And we gave humanity that which is most necessary of all – we gave it stable unchanging order – identified in its understanding with the ultimate and greatest truth. You wished freedom, unlimited. You wished that man became God – and we left You. Your enemy offered us limited reason – for reason cannot be unlimited – and we accepted his gift as gospel, and rejected You. We are not with You, but with him.

So speaks Dostoevsky in the Legend of the Grand Inquisitor on the Catholic Church. I don't know whether the Catholic world responded to the dread accusation of the Russian writer. In those quite numerous Catholics tracts, theological writings with which I've had to become familiar, his name has not once been mentioned. And I think this is not a simple accident. For the same accusations which Dostoevsky levelled against Catholicism have already once and long ago been levelled against it, and with still greater, many times greater force and passion of conviction. Three and a half centuries before Dostoevsky, Luther called the Pope Antichrist and the Catholic Church antichristian.

As I remarked earlier, there's every basis to suppose that Dostoevsky had the scantiest information about Luther and his work. This is all the more probable, since in the final count very few – if one excludes specialist theologians and scholars – know of the work and problems of Luther not only in Russia but in Germany, homeland and classical land of Lutheranism. More than that, I am convinced that if one shows the pious Lutheran the most remarkable of Luther's works, for example, <u>De servo arbitrio</u>, he would stagger back from it in horror. I fear that Dostoevsky himself as well, in <u>Legend of the Grand Inquisitor,</u> literally repeated everything that lived in Luther's soul, when he stepped out, a still completely unknown monk, with his lectures on the Epistles of the Apostle Paul to the Romans – Dostoevsky himself, if you showed him <u>De servo arbitrio</u> – or even <u>On the Babylonian Captivity of the Church</u> – would prefer better to remain with Catholicism and then head after Luther. Put another way, it seems to me that it would hardly be in Dostoevsky's power to deal with the truth revealed to Luther. We, of course, cannot judge what connection existed between the spiritual development of Dostoevsky and what was done prior to him by Luther. Luther's thought, despite the fact that the Reformation, as we'll see below, tried to adapt them to the needs of the everyday, and for this end performed an operation on the ideas, the same which, per Dostoevsky's words, Catholicism performed on the exploit of Christ – Luther's thoughts all the same did not pass trackless for humanity, even through the thicket of centuries might seep to individual people with high spiritual receptivity. Perhaps, without Luther Dostoevsky would indeed not have penetrated to the ultimate mystery of Catholicism, i.e., maybe it wouldn't have entered his head to seek unbelief in the secret reaches, the most deeply hidden, of the human soul. But, one way or another, whether by following Luther, or completely independently (I do not even exclude such a possibility and, if such a supposition turned out true, for us it would be especially interesting and edifying), Dostoevsky came to his evaluation of Catholicism – we ought to dwell on a striking, almost improbable fact: there where all people in the course of tens of centuries saw the most powerful and dependable support of faith, there was a haven of the most terrible and dangerous unbelief. Humanity did not affirm overt unbelief, and the enemy of the human race – let the prediction be fulfilled – deceived people, slyly bedecking himself with the icon frame of true piety. '<u>Una, sancta, vera ecclesia</u>', that church which for millennia preached – and even now preaches that outside itself there is no salvation – '<u>extra ecclesiam nemo salvatur</u>' – led hundreds of thousands, millions of believers on the straight path to destruction. So too Luther affirmed, so too Dostoevsky told us the same thing, 350 years after Luther. What kind of horrible world do we live in if such seismic improbable deceptions are possible?

II

I said that in the <u>Legend of the Grand Inquisitor</u>, Dostoevsky only repeated what Luther had said long before him. Despite the widespread opinion, Luther's struggle with Catholicism in no way had its beginning in his conflict with Tetzel à propos indulgences. This conflict occurred in 1517 (Luther's thesis on indulgences was hung on 31 October 1517), the internal break, already factually tearing Luther away from Rome, occurred much earlier. The well-known Catholic scholar, the Dominican monk Heinrich Denifle only recently, in 1904, extracted from the Vatican archive Luther's hitherto unpublished work <u>Vorlesung über den Römerbrief</u>, which he put as the basis of his large, much-discussed investigation of Luther. These lectures were composed in 1515/16, i.e., a long time before the story with Tetzel – and in it there's already poured out, if not all, then almost all, that had accumulated in the soul of the monk then still young (Luther was all of thirty-three then). Now these <u>Vorlesungen</u> are already published and accessible to all, but back in 1906, such a strong German critic as Loofs could use these words only per extracts made by Denifle. Thus so, in these <u>Vorlesungen</u>, I say, we already find all that explosive material which, obviously, had already long accumulated in Luther's soul and awaited only any external stimulus to liberate the destructive (or creative) force concealed within it. In the commentary to the Epistles to the Romans Luther in no wise touched on either the Pope or Catholicism. On the contrary, he starts out as a true son of the Church; it seems to him that he preaches only what he has himself accepted from Catholicism. It's not that he did not notice the disgraceful life of his contemporary clergy. It was no secret either for him, yes, or for any perceptive person, that Church life of the end of the fifteenth century and beginning of the sixteenth century was far from the level of not only the Christian but of the most modest pagan ideal. This, of course, much disturbed and pained all the true sons of Catholicism; this challenged them to struggle and protest. But the struggle was not against the Church but for the truth – against its unworthy servants who disgraced its high dignity. Catholic theologians to the present day express their profound regret that the brilliantly gifted Luther directed his talents otherwise than at the indictment of the sores of his contemporary clergy. If he had struggled in that direction, the Church would have taken his side and would have glorified his memory, as it glorified the memory of other of Her devoted sons. Priests and monks forgot their divine mission and devoted themselves to mundane cares and petty passions; the Church herself knew that it was necessary to make a terrific effort in order to raise anew a clergy fallen so low up to the requisite level. There were also other questions and worries, which demanded huge intensity of mind and will on the other side of the best representatives of faithful Catholics.

All were conscious that church life required radical transformation that many urgent and difficult problems of a purely theological character had matured.

But Luther went past all this. He did not wish to direct corrupt monks on the path to truth; he did not worry about specific theological questions. That is, when he, per his positions of professor or senior proctor for the monastery of his order, had to give a lecture or pull an unrestrained brother in line, he, as it does behove an actual monk, conscientiously fulfilled the obligations imposed on him. But his thought was far from his everyday occupations. His worry, that worry which he wished, or not wished, to which he devoted the best forces of his soul, which deprived him of sleep and spiritual peace, out of which afterwards grew his service, had nothing in common with his usual obligations. Even, rather on the contrary, the more conscientiously and insistently he fulfilled the vows he imposed on himself, the more his tormenting worry grew. So that one could say that there was an indubitable internal connection between his monastic service and the rebirth occurring in his soul. And this will become comprehensible, if we, somewhat anticipating the following presentation, will meanwhile formulate in several words the new problem presented before Luther.

Luther was a monk and believing Catholic. Therefore, he was convinced that each man at his time will stand before the dread and unhypocritical judge, Who pronounces on him His ultimate sentence. Either eternal bliss or eternal perdition awaits each of us. As we'll see, Luther doubted in all things. He did not fear to head along with Occam to the most extreme limits in critique of generally accepted moral, philosophical and theological presuppositions. He did not fear to suspect servants of the Antichrist in the Roman Pope and the whole Catholic Church. But the question never even entered his head, that perhaps his representations of the terrible judgements were false. Perhaps, no one, nowhere, never did, and never would judge anyone. Just exactly, that proposition, which at the present time is so easily conceded by people, which seems so natural and even irrefutable – it was absolutely unacceptable for Luther. With the conviction, with which at the present time any positivist or materialist presupposes the principle of evolution or the natural connection of phenomena as basis of all his ratiocinations, with the same, even yet with greater conviction, which only the fantastic or frenzied know, Luther spoke of the terrible judgement. For him there was no question whether really perdition awaited certain people, and eternal life awaited others. He asked himself only one thing – how is a man to save himself, how is he to avoid eternal death. And, if Luther, if Luther's life and task attain in our eyes such an unusual, exclusive interest, that's only because he had to stand face to face with this dread question. I wouldn't undertake to say – whether the huge person of Luther made his question so grandiose or, the opposite – Luther grew to such gigantic dimensions in view of the fact that he had to stand face to face with such a colossal and fearsome problem. Perhaps, the ensuing presentation will clarify a little something for us. For the nonce I'll only note the following: in all Tolstoy's works which I analysed earlier, in his unfinished <u>Notes of a Madman</u>, in <u>Father Sergei</u>, in <u>The Light that Shines in Darkness</u>, in <u>Death of Ivan Il'ich</u>, and in <u>Master and Man</u>, we see the same thing as in Luther. I, chiefly, took up Tolstoy anew, in order through his works, written for all in accessible modern language, to throw a pontoon bridge to the end of the Middle Ages and to Luther and thence, through Luther and partially through Bl. Augustine, to the most remarkable and problematic proclaimer of Gospel grace, the Apostle Paul. Tolstoy not only was no theologian; Tolstoy, as we know, was the most implacable enemy of theology. He never read Luther, but if Luther's works turned up in front of him, he would have rejected them with revulsion and dissatisfaction. For Luther took from the Apostle Paul exactly that doctrine of salvation by faith, which Tolstoy branded with that mercilessness characteristic of him alone as an immoral and blasphemous doctrine. And it wasn't enough for Luther that he took this doctrine from the great Apostle – he considered it necessary and possible with all the sharpness and force of which he was capable – and he wasn't short in either department – to emphasize exactly those places in the doctrine of the Apostle, which most of all insult both common sense and our moral holies. Roman III, 28 he considered the key to the whole Gospel. In these words – how and under what circumstances, we'll see below – he found the answer to the question tormenting him. He was so convinced that here lurked the greatest secret of Gospel revelation and thus believed that for the first time in the fifteen centuries of the historical existence of Christianity, he had succeeded, finally, in attaining this mystery in all its fullness, that consequently he allowed himself even in his transition to change – and in essence very significantly change – this verse which already was acceptable with such difficulty to human consciousness.

In the Greek text is denoted λογιξόμεθα γὰρ δικαιοῦσθαι πίστει ἄνθρωπον χωρὶς ἔργων νόμου. That is, we conclude that man is justified by faith without the works of the law. Luther made an addition in his translation: δικαιοῦσθαι πίστει ἄνθρωπον (man is justified by faith) he translated: 'justificare hominem <u>sola</u> fide', i.e., by faith alone. And when he was shown that he had arbitrarily changed the form of the text of the Holy Writ, even more arbitrarily and daringly answered: 'sic volo, sic jubeo – sit pro ratione voluntas'.[1] Simultaneously with this he allowed himself no less daring. The epistle of the Apostle James, from of old belonging to the Holy Writ, he pronounced apocryphal – chiefly because there were words in it, most often adduced by his opponents in objection against his understanding of justification – 'faith without works is dead' (James II, 17, 24 and 26). By faith, by faith alone, and only by faith is a man saved – that is that good news, which Luther wrested from the Antichrist Catholic Church.

He, like Dostoevsky, was convinced that the Catholic Church knew full well that the good news brought by the Gospel was completely in these words. But the Catholic Church did not wish to accept the truth of God. She was not with Him but with His eternal foe. And in order not to allow humanity to salvation, they traded His divine doctrine for their own human one. In place of faith they put works and convinced man to seek eternal life with his own strength. In this is its terrible crime – and in order to free people from the chains of the Antichrist, Luther resolved to lift the great weight – to step forth against the Church, to declare holy war on the Pope.

It goes without saying that if one were to present Luther's doctrine to Tolstoy in such a form, he would have left it with the same dissatisfaction, to which Nietzsche's <u>Beyond Good and Evil</u> led him. More than that, he, probably, would not have understood either – why Catholics rose up against Luther and what so insulted Luther in Catholicism. Could the Catholic Church at any time have rejected the Apostle Paul? And could it be, further, that the Catholic Church herself did not consider its fundamental dogma to be the dogma of redemption? Didn't she teach that man cannot be saved by his own efforts and that the Son of God descended to earth and was incarnated exactly so as to save men from perdition? For the question of 'justification' was raised over a thousand years before Luther, and in the famous dispute of Bl. Augustine with Pelagius, the Church without hesitation took the side of the former and condemned the doctrine of Pelagius as heretical. Just because Pelagius, albeit he did not reject grace, rather acknowledged it in a limited degree and attributed too much significance to the exploits of personal perfection. All this is correct and we'll have yet to speak of this. But just so that the modern reader, who's forgotten or never knew theological terminology, would not think that all these eccentric and archaic ideas, in the sphere which the great tragedy of Luther's apostasy was played out, have lost all meaning for us, I'll say here that for all their external dissimilarity, Tolstoy and Luther said and did one and the same thing. Luther wore the cassock and took the tonsure – Tolstoy went around in a sheepskin coat and boots and grew out his beard and hair. And the external difference was so great that neither the one nor the other would ever have suspected to what extent they were spiritually close to one another. But in fact it was so. Tolstoy, like Luther, rejected works. Not only Ivan Il'ich and Brekhunov are saved only when, suddenly by some kind of impulse, some force taking them up from who knows where, appearing exactly when, exhausted by hopeless attempts to wrest by their own strength out of the terrible position, they submit to fate and no longer head where they wish to go and no longer seize on to what's there to be grasped – even Father Sergei, the glorious and great religious hero [подвижник], giving his whole life to service of neighbours, had heaped up nothing to which he might latch onto and to which he might refer in the terrible ultimate minute. And Tolstoyan heroes are convinced that works yield nothing – that before the divine justice, Ivan Il'ich, Brekhunov and Father Sergei are equal. Worse than that, not only evil works but also good ones emburden him whom ultimate trial awaits. And even good works emburden more than bad ones. It's easy to renounce bad ones; it's hard to quit good ones, impossible for some. They fetter to the earth; man wishes to see in them the eternal meaning of his existence. He cannot tear away from them, and because of them he struggles with that force, unknown to him and still alien, which against his will draws him into that domain, where everything is new to him and thus terrible and so tormentingly unnecessary.

Tolstoy told us this in his secular language. Luther also related this to us, but in terms and images so remote and unhabitual for us, that on the first time it seems as though he speaks of something completely different.

Perhaps it's also relevant to add in order to dissipate (or conversely to intensify) the suspicions of the reader and inure him to the idea that the external appearance of man, i.e., the theory in which he clothes his ideas, often of itself has no significance, and to say right now, that not only Tolstoy but also Nietzsche lived in those same domains where fate tossed Luther. This is still more striking. Tolstoy, if he did reject the Church, at least, did consider himself a Christian and revered the Bible. Nietzsche the opposite. He belongs in the number of the most implacable, clearly frenzied opponents not of the Church but of Christianity itself. He expressed himself on the Gospel more sharply and blasphemously than Tolstoy did of the Church. And nonetheless – now this sounds like a paradox, but the further presentation will support my words –Nietzsche's formula 'beyond good and evil' and Luther's formula taken from the apostle Paul '<u>hominem justificare sola fide</u>' mean <u>literally</u> one and the same. Only Luther was bolder and more consistent than Nietzsche.

True, Luther the monk, unknown to all, all by himself in his cell was bold. When fate dragged him out of his cell and bade him create history, he didn't have the boldness. He made history like, or almost like, all people make history. Thus

Catholics do say that Lutheranism is better than Luther. This is true. Lutheranism did not dare – would that it had tried! – to follow the apostle Paul!

But we're speaking here of Luther. He dared – and dared as much – as Tolstoy's Brekhunov or Father Sergei. Actual, ultimate daring is indeed only born in that fantastic circumstance, which is afforded by the solitude of the cell, that solitude of which Tolstoy told us that there is nothing more complete than it, neither under the earth nor at the bottom of the sea.

One more remark. One of the Catholic biographers of Luther, the Jesuit Grisar, noted that Luther's doctrine recalls the Nietzschean <u>Beyond Good and Evil</u>. It's understandable what a find this was for the Jesuit heart. And all the same, Grisar did not dare to illumine his investigation with this idea. For all his hatred for the 'Reformer', he pitied him? Or the clever and devious Jesuit feared lest he justify Nietzsche?

III

Even a thousand years before Luther inside the bounds of the Catholic Church, then acknowledged as catholic, there first played out the great argument on the meaning of faith. The opponents on one side were Blessed Augustine, on the other, Pelagius with his allies, Celsetius and Julian of Eclanum. Both Catholic and Protestant historians converge on one conviction – the arguing sides were above all suspicion as to their sincerity. Bl. Augustine said something of which he was profoundly convinced; Pelagius as a matter of fact was prepared to defend his ideas even with his life. Both of them, to boot, were faithful sons of the Church – it seemed to the one and the other that they were in no way innovators, not inventors, that they defended not their patrimony, but that received from the ancestors.[2] The external sources, too, for both were one and the same, as for all Catholics at the beginning of the fifth century. They read the Holy Writ and in the Holy Writ found their justification. And nonetheless, for all their wish to find the truth and for all their fear to induce schism among the believers, they could no way come to agreement. Unending disputes and explanations occurred, a multitude of large and small books were written, but this did not resolve matters. Pelagius and his comrades insisted on their own; Bl. Augustine, on his. The Church, as we know, condemned Pelagius, took the side of Bl. Augustine and obligated all Catholics to maintain the doctrine of salvation by faith. But the condemned did not understand the meaning of the stern sentence pronounced on them. It seemed to them they had stepped up their defence of the truth, God's truth – why did they not have the strength to conquer such a clear error? Why did Bl. Augustine, whom all honoured and respected, not see what presented to them as so obvious? We will begin with this question and then enter into the essence of the great argument.

Both the Protestant Harnack and the Catholic Duchesne univocally affirm that the mutual lack of understanding of Bl. Augustine and Pelagius is rooted in the variety of their individual experience.

> Dort ist es ein heissblütiger Mann, der nach Kraft und Seligkeit gerungen hat, indem er nach Wahrheit rang, dem die sublimsten Gedanken der Neuplatoniker, die Psalmen und Paulus das Rätsel seines Inneren gelöst, und den die Erfahrung des lebendigen Gottes überwältigt hat. Hier sind es ein Mönch und die ein Eunich, beide ohne Spuren innerer Kämpfe, beide begeistert für die Tugend, beide erfüllt von dem Gedanken, die sittlich träge Christenheit zur Anspannung des Willens aufzurufen und sie zur mönischen Vollkommenheit zu bringen, beide mit den griechischen Vätern wohl vertraut, Beziehungen zum Orient aufsuchend, in der antiochenischen Exegese bewandert, vor Allem aber jener stoisch-aristotelischen Popularphilosophie (Erkenntnistheorie, Psychologie, Ethik und Dialektik) huldigend, die unter den gebildeten Christen des Abendlandes so viele Anhänger zählte.
> (A. von Harnack, Lehrbuch der Dogmengeschichte, Bd. III, S. 168)

Duchesne says the same thing. And he, like Harnack, sees the reason of the heteroglossia between Augustine and Pelagius in the dissimilarity of their past spiritual experience.

> Augustin, qui était venu á la vertu en passant par le vice et qui n'etait sorti de ses désordres qu'en se sentant appréhendé très fortement par la main de Dieu. Augustin devait á sa propre expérience un profond sentiment de l'infirmité humaine et du secours divin.[3]
> (Duchesne, Histoire Ancienne de l'Eglise. Vol. III, p 203. Ed. Fontemoine, Paris, 1911)

Pelagius did not have the internal experience which Bl. Augustine had. Pelagius did not know the tormented internal struggle, those fits of self-doubt and despair, of which Augustine tells so much in his Confessions. In his past everything was smooth, as opposed to Augustine, who only accepted baptism when he was fully mature. He knew not, as Augustine did, sudden marvellous enlightenings but also knew not the falls. Heading to faith and to virtue, he successfully obviated those domains, in which vice and unbelief rest. It would seem a priori that all advantages are on the side of the pure and strong Pelagius. He firmly went the direct path to his high goal – can that not be a great merit? His path was not easy, but it also lacked real difficulties. Didn't this guarantee at least moral success? Didn't it give him a right to satisfaction, to consciousness of his rightness, his superiority over those who only under the influence of late repentance fulfilled the behest of God? And could it be that not him, the righteous man, but rather the man who erred, was given to attain and proclaim faith to the world? No matter how you resolved the question, no matter how all your sympathies drew you to the righteous Pelagius – history, as I said, decided the argument in favour of Augustine. And not only the Catholic Church – whose authority many, of course, do not agree to accept – but also the representatives of modern thought, I've already named two remarkable scholars who without hesitation and even with special triumph join their authoritative voices to the verdict of history.

Here's how Harnack formulates the essence of the Pelagian dispute:

Die beiden grossen Denkweisen – gilt die Tugend oder die Gnade, die Moral oder die Religion, die ursprüngliche unverlierbare Anlage des Menschen oder die Kraft Jesu Christi?
(A. von Harnack, Lehrbuch der Dogmengeschichte, Bd. III. S. 1660)

Bl. Augustine saw the singular possibility of man to save himself in grace, in supernatural, in the marvellous force of Christ, in religion; Pelagius then based all his hopes on morality, on virtue, on human principles embedded in nature. The uninitiated might ask with astonishment – is there or can there be here any kind of contradiction? Can religion and morality possibly be at odds with one another? And wasn't Pelagius a religious man? How could it enter Harnack's head to so formulate the essence of the Pelagian dispute? Meantime, Harnack is doubtless right. But, it seems, I will not be mistaken if I say that Harnack hardly gave himself a clear account to what such a statement of the question obligates one to and hardly did he, like Duchesne, see the consequences which naturally issue from the psychological explanation he proposed of the Augustinian concept of grace. If one can come to true religion only through sin, and if he who has not sinned cannot come to believe, then, therefore, sin is the necessary condition of faith. And inasmuch as per the conviction of Harnack and his constant opponents, the Catholics – faith is the highest value, then, that means, its necessary condition, sin – ought also to be highly valued. And, conversely, that virtue, which led the unfortunate Pelagius to his errors, ought to be rejected by us. No matter how strange and absurd it seems, indubitably the whole Pelagian dispute revolved, as about its axis, around the concept of sin. It would be incorrect, or inaccurate to say, that Pelagius rejected the doctrine of grace. He says:

Deus, per doctrinam et revelationem suam, dum cordis nostri oculos aperit, dum nobis, ne praesentibus occupemur, futura demonstratat, dum diaboli pandit insidias, dum nos mulitformi et ineffabli dono gratiae caelestis illuminat ... Qui haec dicit gratiam tibi videtur negare?[4]
(Tixeront, Historie des Dogmes, Vol, II, p. 445)[5]

Then, faith, proceeding from the idea that God ought to be just – and that people, knowing, what is just and what is unjust – can attain the essence of Divine judgement, he affirms:

ibi vero remunerandi sint qui bene libero arbitrio utentes merentur Domini gratiam et ejus mandata custodiunt.[6]

And in point of fact, if our concepts of justice are worth anything, i.e., if expressing in Socrates' words the norms of the rational are likewise obligatory for both the mortal and the immortal, what can be more just than Pelagius' reasoning? Or isn't he right when he says:

> Praesciebat ergo (Deus) qui futuri essent sancti et immaculati per liberae voluntatis arbitrium, et ideo eos ante mundi constitutionem, in ipsa sua praescientia, qua tales futuros esse praescivit elegit. Elegit ergo antequam essent, praedestinans filios quos futuros sanctos immaculatosque praescivit; utique ipse non fecit, nec se facturum, sed illos futuros esse praevidit.[7]
>
> (Tixeront, II, 446)

If Socrates were presented all these reasonings, they would seem to him, maybe, to a certain degree fantastical in their bases, but indubitably profoundly consistent and highly moral. Tolstoy, doubtless, also would accept them with the most insignificant and non-essential demurrals. For if God is all-knowing and just, and if we, using the words of omniscience and justice, know what we're saying, then there's not a thing about which to reproach Pelagius. He preaches the same high ideals of eternal justice and the last true unhypocritical judgement, which ere now strikes all readers in the Platonic Phaedo. Or do our contemporaries too err, bowing to pagan virtues – 'virtutes gentium splendida vitia sunt'?[8] But let us look how the indictment against the Pelagians was formulated. Here are nine positions, extracted from the works of Celestius and others like-minded to Pelagius.

> Adam mortalem factum, qui sive peccaret, sive non peccaret, moriturus esset.
> Quoniam peccatum Adae ipsum solum laeserit, et non genus humanum.
> Quoniam Lex sic mittit ad regnum quemadmodum Evangelium.
> Quoniam ante adventum Christi fuerunt homines sine peccato.
> Quoniam infantes nuper nati in illo statu sunt in quo Adam fuit ante praevaricationem.
> Quoniam necque per mortem vel praevaricationem Adae omne genus hominum mortiatur. Neque per resurrectionem Christi omne genus hominum resurgat.
> Posse hominem sine peccato, si velit, esse.
> Infantes, etsi non bapizentur, habere vitam aeternam.
> Divites baptisatos nisi omnibus abrenuntient, si quid boni visi fuerint facere, non reputari illis, neque regnum Dei posse eos habere.[9]
>
> (August. De gestis Pelagii; Tixeront, II, 447)

Now, per the cited analysed affirmations of Pelagius, we can already to a certain degree see what repulsed Bl. Augustine from this doctrine. And, along with that, it will become comprehensible to us why Duchesne and Harnack so assuredly ascribed to Bl. Augustine the psychological motivations of the sinner.

One must, by the way, make a clarification – both the ideas of Augustine and the ideas of Pelagius were in no way first uttered by them. The Catholic Church had already long known both the one and the other. In the Pelagian dispute they were only for the first time expressed in that high relief, which made clear to self-evidence to all their eternal irreconcilability.

Pelagius, and this is the source of all his doctrine, believed that posse hominem sine peccato esse et Dei mandata facile custodire, si velit[10] (Harnack, III, 178) – man, if he wishes, can be without sin. Why Pelagius so believed, I don't think that anyone could give a satisfactory answer to this question. But one thing, apparently, is indubitable, and in this one can agree with Harnack – Pelagius and Celsetius did not feel themselves sinners. And from their side this was not a hypocrisy or pharisaism. Even the opposite – in the word 'facile' (it's not encountered everywhere) – there's heard some modesty and humility. In the mouth of Pelagius (not Celsetius, of course) it was an exaggeration, even significant: from the evidence preserved on him, it's apparent that even his enemies, of which there are quite a few, were obliged to give good reports of his life.[11] His word never diverged from his deed. And, of course, once so, once in point of fact he did not diverge from God's commandments, it wasn't easy for him to live. And the fact, with what insistence he repeated that man can be sinless, shows us that perhaps this consciousness of his purity and righteousness before God was his chief and even only comfort in life.

Omne bonum ac malum, quo vel laudabiles vel vituperabiles sumus, non nobiscum oritur, sed agitur a nobis; capaces enim utriusque rei, non pleni nascimur.[12] (Loofs, Leitfaden zum Studien der Dogmengeschicte, 427). For evil and for good we deserve condemnation and praise – can there possibly be any doubt of this? And if it's so, if we deserve praise and condemnation for our deeds, then it's absurd to allow that it's not in our will, not in our possibility to act one way or the other. And still less can we allow that we have no right to experience pleasure from deserved praise or remain equanimous to condemnation. Or can the works of man, his life be completely insusceptible to moral valuation? All men are equally laudabiles (worthy of praise) and equally vituperabiles (worthy of condemnation). But know you, what that means? Have you given yourself account that you have come up to that terrible formula, which, of course both Harnack and Duchesne, who so boldly step up in the name of religion against Pelagius, have never accepted and will not accept? This indeed is 'beyond good and evil'. It seemed to Pelagius, as to Socrates, that to efface the distinction between the good and the evil between laudabiles and vituperabiles means to annihilate religion and God himself. All are equally good; all are equally right; Anitus and Mellitus will stand before the Last Judgement just as pure and just as immaculate, as Socrates and Plato. And Nero and Caligula have no advantages over those fearless Christians, whom they sent ad leones (to the lions)?

For the sole advantage in this life for the good man is the consciousness of his goodness – and they wish to take that too. They wish to force him to think that all his labours are in vain, that Adam's sin, from a forefather so distant, is bequeathed to him as inheritance, that already by his very own nature he is infected and with such a terrible illness, with which he has not the strength to struggle. And that if he is fated to be saved, then that salvation is not in his will and does not depend on his efforts. All the labour which he has applied to observe the command of God is in vain.

Besides this, that such consciousness takes from the righteous man his moral support, the point that the salvation of man does not depend on himself leads to such horrible consequences. Pelagius says: <u>Wenn ich uber die Sittenlehre und die Grundsätze eines heligen Lebens handle, so weise ich immer zuerst die kraftvolle Fähigkeit der menschlichen Natur nach und zeige, was sie leisten kann, ne tanto remssior sit ad virtutem animus ac tardior, quanto minus se posse credat et dum quod inesse sibi ignorat id se existemet non habere</u>[13] (Pelag. <u>Ep. Ad Demetr.</u>, Harnack, III, 171). And so, this is true: if the problem of man is moral perfection, then, yes, he first of all has to know that he has the strength to fulfil it; otherwise, naturally, he'll drop his hands and instead of struggling with seductions inimical to him, he'll submit to them. Thus Pelagius and his allies so much and so insistently talk of freedom of the will – freedom is nothing other than the nowise encumbered movement of the soul. All his doctrine actually is a development of two principles – the principle, uttered by Socrates and accepted by all his heirs – by Plato, Aristotle and the Stoics and even preserved, in the upshot, in Neo-Platonism as well – that the norms of good stand above God, and not the other way about, and the corresponding principle of freedom of the will. <u>Libertas arbitrii, qua a Deo emancipatus homo est, in admittendi peccati et abstinendi a peccato possibilitate constitit</u>[14] (Tixeront II, 438). The herald of Pelagianism is in these short words – Julian truly and accurately formulated the fundamental idea of that current, whose representative he was. Harnack too says this. The adduced position of Julian is actually the key to the whole construct of thought: freely created man completely independently opposes God in his own personal sphere. God is only in the consequent (at judgement). But Harnack is right only inasmuch as he saw the key to the Pelagian system in the position of Julian. But there is no way to agree that the Pelagians wished to liberate themselves, i.e., distance themselves from God. As far as I'm concerned, this is a completely unnecessary distortion of their whole doctrine. It's much more accurate, when Harnack, along with all other historians, both Protestant and Catholic, speaks of the rationalism of the Pelagians. But this is completely not it; rationalism in no way excludes religiosity. One can believe in God, one can love God, and along with that think that God has revealed higher truths to us in reason. Even more than that, it's most natural of all for man to love and honour that God, Who is revealed to him in reason – for the arcane [сокровенное] does not attract but rather scares people.

And I here can ask Harnack and those who think likewise – let them answer, hand on their heart – whether they feel the readiness to believe in the mysterious and unknown. We already recall what Harnack said assuredly: one cannot unpunished disdain good sense. We know that Renan too affirmed this along with Harnack. And even Catholicism, openly preaching the possibility of the miraculous, fears the irrational no less than do the most usual positivists. They condemn to anathema those who resolve that faith is not reconciled with reason. Faith knows more than reason; it is supra-rational, but not antirational. This is a dogma, not just Catholic; this is a doctrine almost of general humanity. Perhaps, even the limiting 'almost' might be deleted. That is, I wish to say that even the rare person who vaunts in actual fact to reject <u>ratio</u> is capable of such daring only in rare moments of exclusively spiritual uplift. And from his transliminal excursions in the domain of the unattainable he usually brings back with him nothing for usual existence. They recall that they were somewhere, where everything is completely on another construct than in our everyday life. But they cannot clearly and definitely tell what they saw and felt there in another existence, neither to others, nor even to themselves. True, rarely does anyone admit this. Rarely does anyone have the courage because this 'other', attained by them for a moment and in the moment of attainment available, as the highest, unique of its kind, does not possess those characteristics, which would yield the possibility to fixate it, to hold it in hand and impress it on other people; few people are capable of believing something which appears and disappears. All are used to thinking that the value of all that is valuable is first of all in its constant necessity and utility. And even in general – necessity, in general – utility. That which is not necessary to all and always, what does not meet with general acknowledgement and sympathy, that per se is acknowledged as 'subjective', i.e., second rate. And if this subjective does not have constant power even indeed over those to whom it is revealed can one possibly grant it, not the highest value, but generally even any kind of value? Isn't it more accurate to relegate it, per exactly this sign of randomness and inconstancy, to the category of the spectral? And, therefore, to disdain them? When people are faced with this sort of dilemma, they almost don't hesitate. They prefer better to distort, disfigure their revelations to unrecognizability, than to renounce the right to fit them into that frame, which by general conditions of human perception is the conditio sine qua non of the quality not just of value, but even of the reality of spiritual visions. Harnack and the Catholics, with their critique of Pelagianism as an unsuccessful attempt to inject a rationalist element into religion, could evoke the reproach of bad faith – if we could impose on them responsibility for their critique. But in point of fact, they have no personal guilt here. The infinite millennial tradition speaks by their lips. So it was, so, surely, it will always be. Reason retains dominion over man – for, no matter how much men are disturbed by it, they cannot exist without it, any more than air. Catholicism rejected Pelgianism, but Catholicism lives on the ideas of Pelagius. Harnack is enraptured with Bl. Augustine and Luther but fears more than anything on earth to insult common sense. Preserved in the works of Bl. Augustine is an excerpt from the lettre de condoleance of Pelagius to the widow Livania. Whether the letter really belongs to Pelagius or not, we don't know, but it is extremely characteristic, and Harnack's relation to it is still more instructive. Pelagius writes, 'Ille ad deum digne elevat manus, ille orationem bona conscientia effundit qui potest dicere, tu nosti, domine, quam sanctae et innocents et mundae sunt ab omni molestia et inquitate et rapina quas ad te extendo manus, quemadmodem, justa et munda labia et ab omnia mendacio libera, quibus offero tibi deprecationem, ut mihi miserearsis'[15] (Harnack III, 175). That is, only he can actually pray, who has prepared himself for the opportunity, turning to God, to say that he has done nothing unjust, nothing bad; has not stolen; and has not consciously lied. Citing this passage, Harnack remarks: Pharisee and tax collector in one person.

I again recall Socrates and Plato with their doctrine of catharsis or purification. For what Pelagius said – if the adduced excerpt belongs to him – could have been said, even was said, by Socrates and Plato in Phaedo. Only the prayer of a pure, just man, prepared to better accept any kind of injustice than himself do something bad, reaches to God. More than that, for the very catharsis, the very readiness to renounce evil for the sake of good is the one path to God. Prayer is only the verbal continuation of a virtuous life. In this indeed is the essence of the Socratic and Platonic philosophy. And Harnack boldly brands it with the most insulting words: in the person of Socrates he sees both the Pharisee and the tax collector. How can one unpunished insult common sense! Harnack said, one cannot. And for himself he was right. We'll see further that one little-known Protestant pastor, in his book directed against Harnack's Das Wesen des Christentums, reproaches the latter of the same thing of which he reproaches Pelagius.

Warum Harnack diese grossen Erfahrungen nicht gemacht hat, die ihm das Auge gegeben hätten für alle objectiven 'Wunder'? Velleicht war es noch nie recht 'krank'. Velleicht war es noch nie am 'Abgrund der Hölle gestanden'; vielleicht noch nie ganz 'nichts'. Only they can attain the mystery of Divine Redemption inaccessible for Harnack, die nämlich nicht bloss Harnacksünden, moralische Fleckender 'Unwissenheit und Uebereilung' haben, sondern 'blutrote' Sünden, Laster, Greuel, vor denen einem gebildeten und ehrbaren Rabbi (m.e. Harnack) schauert (Ed. Rupprecht, Das Christentum von D. Ad. Harnack, 33, 59).[16] He blames him – no matter how strange this sounds – that Harnack does not know, i.e., did not experience, what sin is. Harnack's sin, in the words of the same Rupprecht, is only a play-toy, theoretical sin. In other words, in Rupprecht's opinion, Harnack understands Christianity so 'flatly' and 'positively' because, like Pelagius, he was too virtuous, more exactly too little vicious in his life. And such people cannot be religious and will never attain the profound mystery of redemption preached by Christianity. It was easier for the thief on the cross to turn to the true faith than for the virtuous monk Pelagius and the honourable professor Harnack.

IV

The reader sees what impassable debris the Pelagian dispute has led us into. And yet we have only just touched it. We have ere now talked only of the doctrine of Pelagius himself – and what has crossed us up is only that such a clear and noble doctrine, rooted in the best traditions of Hellenic philosophy, can encounter condemnation just exactly where it might hope to find a fervent and even triumphant reception. Why can one not allow that man may fulfil divine commandments? And – having fulfilled them – be sinless? Or was the affirmation of the Pelagians incorrect that the sin of Adam harmed only him alone – and not the whole human race? Or, finally, doesn't his doctrine correspond to the words of Christ cited in the Gospel that the rich man, even indeed a Christian, will not enter the heavenly kingdom if he does not renounce all? For in these words what Christ told the rich youth is almost literally repeated? What is the matter here, what so disturbed Bl. Augustine that forced him with such indefatigability to persecute the Pelagians until he finally attained their condemnation by the Church?

Much has been said of the opposition of Hellenism and Judaism, paganism and Christianity. But, perhaps, not in any one of these dogmata has this opposition presented itself with such sharpness as in the dogma of salvation by faith. This dogma, if Catholicism (or Protestantism ensuing) could and wished to implement it in life in a somewhat restrained and consistent manner, would have dredged a forever impassable abyss between the two periods of human existence. Harnack offers the opinion that the doctrine of Athanasius the Great and the decrees of the Nicene ecumenical council especially sharply rent Christian thought from the pagan (in Harnack's understanding, on this point, from the singularly true).

> The Nicene council sanctioned the doctrine of St. Athanasius the Great. One of the most serious consequences of this was that henceforth dogmatics were for times eternal torn away from clear thinking and from attainable concepts and habituated to the contradictory – that not agreeing with reason. Disagreement with reason came to be considered – albeit not now, but soon enough after the Nicene council – the characteristic sign of the holy. In that they everywhere sought mysteries, then each doctrine already served to conceal a mystery in itself, in that it was in contradiction with usual clarity. The irreconcilable contradiction in ὁμοούσιος[17] drew after itself a whole series of new contradictions, as human thought moved forward.
>
> (Harnack, II, 226)

No doubt, St Athanasius the Great and the Nicene council played a huge role in the history of Christian dogmatics with their doctrine of the one being of the three persons of the Divinity. But I cannot agree with Harnack, who in this sees almost the first instance of overt acknowledgement of the right of the human mind to contradiction. First of all, it seems to me an exaggeration to speak of official sanction. Contradiction with the usual laws of human thought was allowed, but no one elevated it to a principle. And, thence, it is completely incorrect to affirm that contradiction only first entered on the historical arena in the doctrine of Athanasius the Great. We recall that Greek philosophy was also not much free of contradictions. Not even speaking of Heraclitus, who as a matter of fact tried to make contradiction almost the law of human thinking, all of classical philosophy, as we recall, was least of all capable of purifying its systems from clear contradictions. Aristotle accused Plato of allowing obvious absurdities. And Aristotle himself was no less guilty of the same sin. The sole reproach which Harnack might from his point of view make to Athanasius the Great and his heirs is possibly that they allowed themselves to issue new personal contradictions not yet sanctioned by the traditions of Hellenism. But, of course, it's still a long way from here to the right of seeing signs of purposeful paradoxicalism in the creative work of the Eastern fathers. Never was there nor can there be on the borders of human thought that pacific clarity which we are completely legitimately accustomed to consider the criterion of truth and without which our usual, everyday existence is unthinkable. I'll say even more. In his argumentation, in the conclusions with which Athanasius the Great defended his position from the Arians, one still too much feels the trust in the Hellenic method of seeking the truth. Athanasius the Great did not resolve to put forward his dogma of the one being of Christ with the Father without having introduced considerations accessible to reason in his justification. From the purely logical side – and now that's exactly what interests us here – in Athanasius the Great we already find all those elements which Anselm of Canterbury consequently used for his reasoning on the theme Cur Deus homo (why God is man); i.e., Athanasius the Great stood on a point of view complete opposite to that which Tertullian put forth. He not only did not overturn all the traditional quia (because) he, on the contrary, re-established all their traditional rights. In words of one syllable all his reasoning reduces to the following. If Christ, as the Arians affirmed, was only like[18] God, and not equal to him in essence then, therefore, His very manifestation for people cannot be decisive in its significance. Only in the case, that he was one in being, i.e., put in other words, only in the case, that God Himself could take on human image on earth, do men have the right to hope that they are allowed 'to become gods'.[19]

Here, at its basis, is the reasoning of St Athanasius. It's completely clear that it didn't enter his head to elevate das Widervernünftige[20] into a principle. Yes, on the contrary, rather here it is à propos to speak of rationalism, of elevating to a principle that 'clarity' of which Harnack dreams. There's contradiction in the metaphysical concept of the Triune and Single God – fully legitimate even from the point of view of Hellenic logic – for not one philosopher was in condition to present this ultimate principle, principle of all principles, in a form free from contradiction. And yes, this was not required. It would be another matter, if Athanasius the Great reasoned like Tertullian. But Tertullian himself as well, despite the fact that he had once too to utter his paradoxes which thundered round the world, never had the courage, nor even the desire to take it with him into life in the capacity of a constant guide. A Montanist, believing in the possibility of prophecy even after the appearance of Christ, he was and remained an admirer of autoritas et ratio (authority and reason).

So that Harnack and his like thinkers were more correct when they spoke of the Hellenization of Catholicism, i.e., of its subordination to Hellenism than when they tried to indicate attempts to wrest past the limits of logic and methodology prescribed by the ancients. All attempts of this sort – and there were quite a few – always encountered decisive opposition from the most influential representatives of the Church. Catholicism strove, and completely consciously, for unity of doctrine and ere now regards with implacable enmity those who did not acknowledge their eternal right of lawgiving. For it is not accidental that the pagan Aristotle became and to this day remains the official philosopher of the Catholic Church, as it's not accidental that the dogma of the infallibility of the Pope was proclaimed – albeit late, only at the Vatican council of 1871. Unity is necessary to Catholicism exactly because unity is the condition of rationality, the condition of logic. In this sense Catholicism eventuated more restrained and consistent than those from whom it took over restraint and consistency.

No matter how much Aristotle believed in his truths, no matter how much Plato valued his philosophy, all the same it would never have entered their heads to elevate the principle of their infallibility. Only Catholicism dared to make this ultimate conclusion from the principle of single truth. But not for nothing do they see complexio oppositorum (union of opposites) in Catholicism. The historical conditions of this development and the very problems which they set themselves often demanded the simultaneous acknowledgement of the most opposite demands. And the opposites, when there was no other way, in the event, lived together, and even peacefully. But, I repeat, that which was de facto was de jure condemned and not acknowledged. The peripheral critical eye espied contradictions, but Catholicism in principle recognized only oneness. And look even at modern Catholic theologians. They continue to glorify Aristotle, even Socrates as their teacher. And hardly anywhere else will you find such masters of reconciliation of contradictions as among Catholics. They have developed the art to an unusual perfection, that art which they took over from the Hellenic philosophers – to utter mutually exclusive affirmations is such a tone as though they mutually conditioned one another. One can easily convince oneself of this, getting acquainted with any of the official Catholic dogmatics. And, internally, they are right. For they have one goal: to establish that authority which Dostoevsky speaks of in The Grand Inquisitor. In other words, to arrogate to him who has been proclaimed the heir of Peter on earth the whole fullness of potestas clavium. The Catholic Church never forgets this and thanks to this all the specific contradictions preserved by her in their nuclei, no matter how great they are, are in no way dangerous for her. Even affirmations clearly offending common sense are not dangerous for her – those which Harnack and Renan so fear. For the interpretation of the doctrine lies wholly in the power of the Pope – and he is allowed to interpret in what measure this or that of the elements of the depositum fidei (treasury of the faith) are allocated to influence life or remain inactive. The Catholic Church, arisen on the ruins of the Roman Empire, preserved and protected those devices of direction of human thought, which themselves conditioned a stable and unshakable power.

This perhaps explains that circumstance, strange at first glance, that Catholicism did not fear to take under its aegis doctrines of just such a type, which, apparently, least of all corresponded to the problems it set itself. Montanism, allowing prophecy, was unacceptable for it. But the doctrine of the one being of the three persons of the Godhood in no way threatened the stability of the erected building. And even in the dispute with Bl. Augustine, Catholicism stood without hesitation on the side of the latter – although, as we'll now see, Pelagianism was and always remained the soul of Catholicism. In one point, perhaps, Catholicism turned out insufficiently perceptive. It did not foresee that one thousand years after the condemnation of Pelagius, that same Bl. Augustine, whom it supported, would raise in the person of Luther the most terrible and merciless opponent of Papism.

Now we observe the most paradoxical phenomenon. Both Catholics and Protestants consider Bl. Augustine their own. And yes, with equal right. With equal right Luther in his doctrine refers with respect to the invisible church and with respect to grace to that same source, which fed and ere now feeds the most orthodox Catholic theologians. Luther had no need at all to falsify Augustine, as the Catholics had no need to renounce him. For Augustine himself was a believing Catholic, i.e., accepted that first and basic condition, without which Catholicism is impossible – he identified Christianity with the Catholic Church.

He affirmed that he would not believe in the Holy Writ if he had not received it from the Church.[21] Once this affirmation is made, i.e., once it's accepted, expressed in Dostoevsky's words from the Legend of the Grand Inquisitor, that Christ give over all his power to the Church and can no longer add or subtract anything which now already is in its possession – the Church can be serene. Its authority is acknowledged, and it can already direct humanity by means of those devices of which the old inquisitor tells in Dostoevsky.

Authority stood over the Holy Writ; therefore, no miracle, no mystery could any longer violate the order established by this authority. Even the converse, the self-assured authority loves to effuse in fantastic colours that don't belong to it, for in its own characteristic colourless greyness it, perhaps, would not turn out attractive enough for people and many would be scared away. And in this sense Bl. Augustine had an invaluable significance for the Church. He knew how, like no one before him, to lead man to the living mystery of the universe. And he was allowed this. Perhaps, for us now the tone of Augustine's writings no longer seems so attractive. Often, reading it, one would wish greater sternness, greater restraint, even greater compression. There is too much art in it – one hears the former rhetorician. And this is especially notable in view of Augustine's inclination to quote the Psalms. One cannot, of course, demand from him more than he has – and the gift of King David remains even now unsurpassed and unique. But one would wish – involuntarily – that David, and not Cicero or Seneca, served as model for he who has to speak of the greatest mysteries of life. Augustine seizes us most of all because he still belongs to that epoch of which Tertullian could say fiant non nascuntur Christiani (Christians are made, not born). He was born a pagan and his conversion to Christianity already in full maturity, of course, is an event out of the normal course – if you wish, a true miracle, like the conversion of Saul is also a miracle. I want to say that in the thread of usual, everyday events of human life such phenomena as the impossibility of remaining in the sphere in which you're born and raised is incomprehensible and enigmatic to such a degree that it doubtless violates the natural thread of cause and effect. It's natural that a man hold tightly to the foundations which he was given at birth. It's natural that the atmosphere in which we end up at birth seems to us the most favourable condition of development and existence. How strange it would be for us to hear of a fish, who rushed to the dry land, or a man, living on the bottom of the ocean. The conversion of Augustine (and still more, of course, of Saul) bears exactly such character. As he tells in his Confessions, it became impossible to live in his natural element. 'Jam rebus talibus satiatae erant auras meae'[22] (Bl. Augustine, Confessions, V, 6).

Everything that seemed good, right, elevated, pacifying suddenly becomes evil, cruel, challenging, insulting. Without any visible cause a tormenting, clearly insane unease suddenly was born in his soul. It was not that Bl. Augustine knew something better, where he must go, and clearly saw the bad, from which he must run. On the contrary, as known from his Confessions, he tried to seek out the path everywhere it was possible to seek it. He went through the ancient holy places, i.e., studied the works of the well-known philosophers. He was with the Manicheans. He, as one lost, wandered without any plan, without any calculation from side to side, in no way foreseeing, where all his desperate staggering would lead. Even in the last moment before his conversion, he just as little knew that his wanderings were near an end, as he knew several years before that. Here's the words in which he later expressed his last tension:

> <u>Illuc me abstulerat tumultus pectoris, ubi nemo impediret ardentem litem, quam mecum agressus eram, donec exiret, qua tu (i.e., God) sciebas, ego autem non: sed tantum insaniebam salubriter (i.e., salvific frenzy) et moriebar vitaliter, gnarus, quid mali essem, et ignarus, quid boni post paululum futurus essem.</u>[23]
>
> (<u>Confessions</u>, VIII, 8)

This moment was, apparently, singular and the most decisive and significant in Augustine's life. At least, in the <u>Confessions</u>, and in his other works, nothing is said of his secondary conversions. And, perhaps, generally speaking, it's a rare man who has the strength to twice experience that spiritual bottom [перелом], of which we speak here. The most difficult and horrible thing in that internal struggle, which Augustine recounts, is exactly that its upshot for him was impossible to guess in advance. Afterwards Augustine could say: You, Lord, knew to what my torments led me, but I knew nothing. But he could say this only afterwards, when, looking back at the past and the new present, he had the possibility of running the totals on his tormenting experiences. Until everything had finished, Augustine couldn't even guess that the torments to which he himself or fate submitted him had even any kind of meaning. He knew that in the present was horror, but he did not suspect that in the nearest future such a great reward awaited him – '<u>Gnarus, quid mali essem, et ignarus, quid boni post paululum futurus essem</u>'.

Perhaps, this is the most characteristic trait for Augustine's experiences. Man begins to voluntarily submit himself to torments – not knowing why he does this. He loses the usual sense prompting him that one must flee 'evil' and with all one's strength protect oneself from it. Reason, heretofore directing him on clear and definite paths, loses its power over him. As previously, he continues to believe only in the conclusion of reason, as previously he fears evil and wishes what he is used to consider and cannot but consider good – but he wishes one and involuntarily does the other.

I above recalled that Augustine only once in his life experienced such a spiritual bottom, and I uttered the proposition that it's a rare man who is allowed twice in his life to experience what Augustine experienced. But if this were indeed allowed I think that the second, third, and even tenth bottom would be no less burdensome in its torment than the first. And that the second time man would be compelled to experience the same unknowing and repeat the same thing that Augustine expresses in the concluding works of the adduced excerpt from <u>Confessions</u> – '<u>Gnarus, quid mali essem, et ignarus, quid boni post paululum futurus essem</u>'.

Such experience, even if it was indeed repeated, does not teach man to see through into the unknown future. Or, better said, such experience is not susceptible to generalization – and that may be its most striking trait, distinguishing it from all other forms of experience.

Here's something else that's indubitable: if someone could free Augustine from those horrors, which he had to experience in the garden, by whatever means, albeit purely external, Augustine would consider him his benefactor – in the moment, where he knew only quid mali essem. But, if then post paululum someone had proposed to him to strike from his life the pages connected with his garden, he would not have agreed to this for anything in life. These torments, once they were past, became dearer to him than all joys ever experienced. But, I emphasize, this same Augustine likewise would not agree for anything in the world that these torments, which seem so valuable to him in retrospect, would be repeated.

I'll make only one emendation – very important. 'Gnarus, quid mali essem, et ignarus, quid boni post pailulum futurus essem', said Augustine himself. This means, he was fully conscious of the meaning and significance of the experience. Relative to the possibility and necessity of new future trials, he judged otherwise. He wished to think, he thought, that the new bonum revealed to him is already the ultimate, best summum bonum (highest good). In any case, he did not allow the thought that life would sometimes demand from him new tests of his righteousness, new renunciations, and that the new renunciations would be accompanied with the same difficulties which he experienced when it was necessary to renounce pagan ideals.

V

Perhaps, just in view of the point that Augustine's internal struggle demanded from him an extreme, exhaustive intensity of all spiritual forces and that he felt himself decidedly incapable after the exploit he accomplished of undertaking something else new, the conviction grew on him that he had already gone to the extreme limits of attainment accessible to man. The Confessions begin and end with a word of praise to God, as an eternally pacifying principle. 'Tu excitas, ut laudare te delectet, quia fecisti nos ad te et inquietum est cor nostrum, donec requescat in te'[24] (Confessions, I, 1). So it says in the first chapter. The last chapter, explaining why the seventh day of creation had no evening, when the Creator rested after labours, is a short triumphant hymn to eternal rest. 'Pax quietas, pax sabbati, pax sine vespera'[25] (Confessions, XIII, 35) is the object of rests of those, who were not born but made a Christian:

> Dies autem septimus sine vespera est nec habet occasum, quia sanctificasti eum ad permansionem semptiternam, ut id. quod tu post opera tua bona valde, quamvis ea quietus feceris, requievisti septimo die, hoc praeloquatur nobis vox libri tui; quod et nos post opera nostra ideo bona valde, quia tu nobis ea donasti, sabbato vitae aeternae requiescamus in te.[26]
>
> (Confessions, XIII, 36)

No need to say that the ideal of the eternal, ultimate and unchangeable rest was revealed to Augustine long before his conversion to Christianity. Pagan philosophers, with which he was directly acquainted in his youth, always set themselves the same ideal. In the purely philosophical sense Christianity gave nothing new to the professor of rhetoric, educated on Hellenic wisdom. On the contrary, Bl. Augustine Romero remained a true disciple of Plotinus until old age. Through him the fundamental motifs of Neo-Platonism penetrated into Western European theology, as they penetrated the theology of the Eastern Church through Dionysus the Areopagite. But pure Neo-Platonism in the expression which Plotinus gave it could least of all satisfy not only Augustine himself, with his internal disarray and exhaustion – all Greco-Roman-educated society bore this doctrine as a heavy and tormenting cross. And, on the contrary, as well, for Plotinus incarnated in his life and his philosophy that decadence to which the collapsing Roman Empire ineluctably headed. We already recall that the elements of decomposition were essential to the philosophy of Plato. He, who himself defined philosophy as practice in death and dying, can least of all give men a firm and serene world view. But along with that we recall that history overcame Plato, that even Plato himself overcame himself in a significant degree. Aristotle at once extirpated from Plato's doctrine all the disturbing and inconstant elements. In the doctrine of Plotinus they resurrect anew and with a double, perhaps a ten-fold force. Although Plotinus did fear to in any small measure digress from his divine teachers and officially presented only as follower and epigone of Plato, but in actual fact his internal closeness with his teacher was exhausted by an unquenchable, eternally gnawing angst for the unattainable, invisible. If for Plato ideas were the singular reality in theory, then for Plotinus in actual fact, what only existed was that which was not in ordinary representation at all.

Plotinus did not ruminate on the ideal state, did not strive to the creation of all – encompassing science. His problem – to commune [приобщиться] with a new existence. In his last deathbed words, as Porfiry relates them, he let out a breath, saying that now he transferred that divine, which was in him, to that divine which was in all[27] – the accounts are summed of all his life task, all his 'philosophy'.

True, the historians of philosophy, who consider it their obligation to take from philosophers only that which consequently achieved its scientific justification, i.e., that which could be accepted as 'positive', corresponding to the existing criteria of the true – according to this view, the doctrines of Plotinus were considered as the very least of doctrines, though one could not but acknowledge their exceptional idiosyncrasy. Zeller says:

> Es steht mit der ganzen Richtung des klassischen Denkens in Widerspruch und es ist eine entschiedene Annäherung an die orientalische Geistsweise, wenn Plotin nach dem Vorgange eines Philo das letzte Ziel der Philosophie nur in einer solchen Anschauung des Göttlichen zu finden weiss, bei welcher alle Bestimmtheit des Denkens und alle Klarheit des Selbstbewustseins in mystischer Ekstase verschwindet.
>
> (Zeller, V, 611)[28]

Zeller, of course, is also correct in his characterization of Plotinus, as he is correct too that European thought even when it attains its higher uplift stands in fear before the necessity of renouncing definition and clarity. This criterion, inherited from Aristotle or, more accurately, always characteristic of the nature of European man and only receiving from Aristotle its exhaustive formulation, always was and probably always will be considered scientific par excellence. Where there is no definiteness and definition, there cannot, obviously, be truth either – for the indefinite, i.e., the truth not in a steady state is not truth and cannot be the object of study and knowledge.

Plotinus himself knew this full well and told of the fear and vacillation the soul experiences when it has to draw near to the singular, unformed: All the more, that the soul, when it nears to 'things' without form, cannot grasp this 'thing', for it is indefinite: in it nothing is delimited and one can say there is no imprint. Then the soul vacillates and fears lest it possess nothing more[29] (Enneads VI, 9–3).

But he knew also that man is not allowed to ceaselessly endure such a condition over the course of any kind of extended time. For that condition of momentary ecstasy, for seconds of participation in the divine, man has to pay heavily in impotence, exhaustion, illnesses. And the chief thing, which, apparently Plotinus didn't acknowledge either, just like Philo, through whom Eastern wisdom found its way to Plotinus, is that truth, which is attained through participation in the divine, can by its very essence in no way be submitted to logical rework, i.e., to take the form of generally obligatory logically exclusive judgements. He who communes with God loses his basic 'sacred' right, which belongs to man as a political being, as expressed in Aristotle's language and, if you prefer modern language, as a social being. That is, his judgements are deprived of any kind of sanction and therefore lose that prerogative to be called truths, a prerogative so seductive and valued by all. Each man can then with equal right oppose opposites to it – and there is no authority in the world in whose name one could reconcile the disputants.

When Plotinus teaches of the one and the ultimate, and so speaking, supposes that beyond that with which he is enabled to participate, there was not or could be anything – he then completely illegitimately applied the characteristics of empiricism to that, which, per his doctrine, had nothing in common with empiricism. He allows an antipathy to experience, completely legitimate and self-justifying in the visible world, but clearly pretentiously limiting the indefinite. In this is the same fear before the infinite and formless, under which influence Aristotle and his heir worked out and brought to life the theory of the mean.

At one time Plato traded his creative eros for the unshakable system of idea numbers, so Plotinus too in the final account, under threat of being exiled from the ideal state of the rational ones, possessing the rights, acknowledged by all, to speak in the name of truth, renounced his ecstasies. For no one could attest that these half-human half-divine conditions of spirit would always engender the constant and the steady state if they were not subordinated to the control of reason. And, doubtless, if Plato and Plotinus did not believe in rights not belonging to them, the history of philosophy could not canonize them, count their names among the names of the righteous of science. From his point of view, Zeller, of course, is right. The historical significance of Plato and Plotinus is not that they were enabled to experience and see, but in how they projected their specific, exclusive, perhaps unrepeatable experience on the plane of societal existence. And Bl. Augustine, doubtless, to the end of his days under the influence of Plotinus, received from him the Eastern revelation already Hellenized, all the more, such that Philo himself, being the intermediary between Asia and Europe, exerted all his strength to agree Judaism and Hellenism. Philo, in order to lay the historical path for the prophecies of Judaism, had to justify the Eastern attainment of truth before the educated Greeks. He, thus, more than anything else had to show that Biblical 'wisdom' was not in contradiction with scientific truth as it was represented in the works of the Greek sages. He wished that a Greek, who knew Plato and Aristotle, 'understood' the psalmists and the prophets. Of course, this was already an unallowable compromise on Philo's side. And along with that, his problem was factually unimplementable. Hellenism could not justify neither Moses, nor King David, nor Isaiah, nor Ezekiel. And first of all because the prophets and singers of the Holy Book never sought and never worked on justification. They preached the truth, as one having power. They accounted to no one – they called everyone to account. They did not justify themselves; they themselves judged. And if one were to reject these claims of theirs, then all that remained for them was silence. They never had any kind of proofs on them, and in essence there could not be, for, despite the Aristotelian theory of the mean, that which uniquely created the possibility of the very idea of proofs and criteria, the prophets never knew what the mean was. And if we're already talking of the kinship of Hellenism and Judaism, then right here one must concentrate on those old-fashioned elements in Neo-Platonism [нужно сосредоточиться на тех елементах старо и неоплатонизма], which were completely unacceptable for scientific consciousness and are atavisms even at the present time, unnecessary ballast, burdening the already huge histories of philosophy. An ecstasy in no way limited, insane eros, knowing no bounds, was the source of the creative work of the Judaic prophets. Hellenism in its pure form never could accept this. The question ineluctably arose, how to verify the prophet, where's the guarantee, that he passing himself off as a prophet is really the voice of truth and the emissary of God, and not the devil.

Plotinus sought out a modus vivendi – for himself. But his answer, obviously, could not satisfy Augustine. He accurately felt that exactly that which was most necessary to him, i.e., assurance, which would put an end to the vacillations tormenting him, could not be given by philosophy, and especially Plotinus.[30] Plotinus' philosophy, swooping up all the destructive elements accumulated over the ages, undermined in the end any possibility of assurance. It stripped naked the powerlessness and impotence of the human mind and presented the pitiful and weak man to himself and to his negligible little powers. While the healthy instinct of life still preserved the spirit of Aristotle in Hellenism and held men at a definite separation from tormenting mysteries and enigmas, philosophy could be the directress of life. But Plotinus, who had developed disdain for the visible empirical world to extreme limits, that were heretofore unknown even to the Stoics and Cynics, broke down all the barriers holding back the heretofore unrestrained strivings of the human spirit. Woe to him who wishes to know what was and what will be, what is found under the earth and what is higher than the sky, better for him had he never been born in this world, says popular wisdom. Plotinus, himself poisoned by the decadence decomposing Hellenism, infected Bl. Augustine as well with his spiritual powerlessness. The new attainments revealed to him did not convey on the plane of existing scientific systems. One must either renounce these ecstatic visions or renounce the philosophical criteria of truth.

As we know, Plotinus himself and his nearest followers sought out and found asylum in pagan doctrine. But paganism no longer satisfied Augustine – he had long outgrown it. He had outgrown not only its weak but also its strong sides. His polemic with paganism, to which a large part of the huge tract De civitate Dei is devoted, written, true, many years after his conversion, but still bearing the traces of immediate struggle with that in which he once believed, strikes one with its unnecessary crudeness and injustice. Bl. Augustine in no way wishes to be just to paganism, for his problem is not to evaluate paganism but to annihilate it, stomp it out. Whether it's guilty or not guilty of those transgressions which Augustine ascribes to it is already indifferent. For, even if it weren't guilty, it is all the same already condemned and cannot count on defence. Its guilt is that, it, like salt having lost its flavour, can only instil revulsion. If Augustine needed to be just, he would have said other things of paganism in another tone. Now his polemic astonishingly recalls, in both sharpness of device and in the passion and unrestrained volley of attacks, Tolstoy's Critique of Dogmatic Theology. Augustine cannot forgive the pagan gods that they have not the power to give what they promised, and mercilessly mocks them – beats the stuffing out of the inhabitants of Olympus already pretty near dead. Why don't they give stability? Why don't they show the one true path? He is specially struck by the comparison of the feeble, expiring faith of the pagans with the young inspiration of the Christians.

> 'Surgunt indocti et caelum rapiunt; et nos cum doctrinis nostris sine corde ecce ubi volutamur in carne et sanguine. An quia praecesserunt, pudet sequi, et non pudet nec saltem sequi, et non pudet nec saltem sequi.' Dixi nescio qua talia, et abripuit me ab illo aestus meus, cum taceret attonitus me intuens. Neque enim solita sonabam; plusque loquebantur animum meum frons, genae, oculi, color, modus vocis, quam verba quae, promebam.[31]

(Confessions, VIII, 8)

These people, these ignorant people, who knew neither Plato nor Plotinus, had what was more necessary to Augustine than anything else in the world. And only they had it. 'Ignorance', which Augustine was so used to disdain, had one colossal advantage. It did not bind man. One who did not know Aristotle might search anywhere: the free spirit breathes where it wishes. The learned man though, like the majority of Augustine's contemporaries, had no right to go in those places where, per the traditions of science, truth never is to be found. And Augustine, having thrown off false self-love, headed after those who, per his previous representations, ought to have attended his own rhetoric classes. But it would be mistaken to think that Augustine, after his conversion, completely renounced his old spiritual treasures. The Neo-Platonist went to the Christians for what he didn't have. From the Church he sought authority, support for those unusual spiritual experiences, which were already revealed to him in Plotinus' school. When he writes:

> Tu autem, Domine, bonus et misericors et dextera tua respiciens prounditatem mortis meae et a fundo cordis mei exhauriens abyssum corruptionis. Et hoc erat totum nolle, quod volebam, et velle quod volebas.³²
>
> (Confessions, IX, 1)

When he writes that his salvation consists only in renouncing all his personal desires, and wishing what God wishes, the new element, compared to that which Augustine experienced when he was only a Neo-Platonist, is only the willingness to subordinate himself to the orderer rather than the teacher. That is, the readiness, following those ignorant people, bruit of whose life so disturbed him, to give himself wholly into the power of the Church. This was hardest of all, and most necessary of all for Bl. Augustine. He felt that he no longer had the strength to endure the burden of his freedom [бремя свободы], the burden of internal aporia [безначалия]; all his previous authorities, as I said earlier, had lost their previous charm for him. He did not fear the sternness and demanding nature of the new power. Stories of monasticism and of the life of St Anthony led him to rapture.

The difficulties of the life of religious heroism, only such huge difficulties, could humble the ceaseless anarchy living in his soul. But to head to difficulties – only for the sake of difficulties, or so as to put an end to internal struggle, neither Aristotle nor anyone else had the initiative for that. Above that, Augustine was and remained too much the philosopher, too much the seeker of truth and ultimate truth – like that time too when he studied the Ciceronian Hortensia – to dwell on such a quotidian and prosaic decision. The new idea ought to be higher and ultimate; the new truth ought to exceed all the preceding in brilliance, beauty and depth. And – the very main thing – the power of the prophets and apostles proclaiming the one God will resolve all doubts – i.e., fulfil the demands which Hellenic philosophy imposed but could not itself fulfil. Under the direction and defence of the Church, who possessed the revelation of the Holy Spirit, it's no longer fearsome to enter those domains whither Plotinus beckoned. The unusual upheavals, ecstasies are not fearsome – the interpenetration with the ultimate great formless is not fearsome. Thus, for Bl. Augustine Christianity resolved the tormenting questions, advanced but not resolved by all the previous development of Hellenism. Paganism, in searching for the criterion of truth, undermined in principle any possibility of any kind of stable philosophical knowledge. There eventuated a union of fresh self-assured unknowing with the exactitude of a too demanding and intellectually developed soul. In this and only in this one ought to and can see the Hellenization of Christianity. The Greek spirit, demanding clarity and definition and outside this condition not allowing the possibility of existence, subordinated itself to this form of truth imported from outside, in order only to be rescued from the unbearable burden of truth.

This is also the reason that Catholicism always remained a complexio oppositorum.³³ Doubtless, the ultimate dogma of the infallibility of the Pope symbolizes the whole evolution of Catholicism. Catholicism needed whatever kind of authority – only not to return to past freedom. And even modern Catholics, explaining the positions of the Vatican council, are in no way restraining themselves from seeing the infallibility of the Pope as a specific miracle of the Divine, showing people on earth the worries and cares of Providence [попечение Промысла] as to their earthly organization. But something else is indubitable. The assurance in the divine force of the Church and in the authority of revelation gave, if not to all, at least to some believing Catholics the boldness to penetrate into such remote domains, as men would never have gone at their own risk.

And Bl. Augustine himself, probably, would not have dared to step up against Pelagius, i.e., against all Hellenic wisdom, with his declaration of grace – so much did it seem and now seems to be repulsive to reason and disturbing to common sense – if he did not feel the possibility in his exclusive experiences to rely on the divine authority of the apostle and the prophets.

VI

So that – although this seems paradoxical – one must say that the elements of 'vulgar Catholicism' accepted by Bl. Augustine, as the Protestant theologians and historians love to call them, were not something external for him, which he could under other circumstances renounce. The authority of the one Holy Catholic Church, preserving eternal truth in its nucleus, was a new criterion of truth for Augustine, raised on Greek philosophy. Christianity preserved what the pagan had lost and so regretted. And only under the shadow of the new unshakable authority could the spiritual authority of the newly converted develop. Now he resolved to boldly speak not only to others but to himself, things which in the light of usual reason, i.e., before the criteria of mind and truth worked out by Hellenic philosophy, seemed madness and even worse than madness.

Tertullian, rebutting those who were disturbed at the very possibility of the admission that God might lower himself to an undignified death on the cross, wrote:

> Parce unicae spei totius mundi. Quid destruis necessarium dedecus fidei. Quodcumque deo indignum est, mihi expedit. And further: salvus sum, si non confundor de domino meo.[34]
>
> (De carne Christi, V, 760)

In another reading instead of dedecus (without honour) there's the opposite decus (honour) and how about that? In Tertullian's reasonings such a change has no influence on the meaning of what was said!

This new possibility of creativity, having all the stability and assurance of which Hellenic science ever dreamed, and along with that unbound by the reins of usual restraints imposed by the traditional criteria of truth, also gave Bl. Augustine the opportunity to manifest those sides of his spirit and internal experience which would have remained hidden, if he had had to the end of his life moved only within the limits of the freedom set by ancient philosophy. The 27th verse of the 72nd Psalm became the first fundamental motif of Augustinian creativity, me adhere Deo bonum est,³⁵ and to commune with God is my good, that verse which in the course of the whole thousand-year existence of Christianity inspired the mystics. The second motif is the inscrutability of the paths of God and the mystery of his eternal justice. We recall that Socrates based all his hopes on his moral force and righteousness. Take away from Socrates the conviction that a philosopher, doing everything on earth that's in his power, will attain the right to demand acknowledgement of his righteousness in the land of eternal repose – and all his philosophy tumbles into dust.

More than that, as we recall, Socrates was firmly convinced that he by his life personally realized the ideal of the philosopher. He serenely headed to meet death – knowing beforehand that if we are given life beyond the grave, he would ascend to the Preternal with a light spirit. The experience of his long life gave him firm faith. Here on earth the evil may triumph – but in the other life the good and only the good – and Socrates in that number – are guaranteed the ultimate great victory. Socrates always felt that in him reason, the better part of his being, dominated over sensual impulses. The seductions of the flesh were not terrible to him in life, and he serenely prepared for death. He always preferred to bear injustice and never was himself unjust. He rejected the spells of Alcibades. Everything that we know of his life attests that it was a continuous triumph of virtue. Posse hominem sine peccato esse et mandata Dei custodire.³⁶ Pelagius only repeated what Socrates expressed and proved by his life. Augustine could not say this of himself. He himself, in the Confessions, says the following:

> At ego adolescens miser, valde miser, in exordio ipsius adolescentiae etiam petieram a te castitatem et dixeram; da mihi castitatem et continentiam, sed noli *modo*. Timebam enim, ne me cito exaudires et cito sanares a morbo concupiscentiae, quem *malebam* expleri quam exstingui.³⁷
>
> (Confessions, VIII, 7)

Thus, even in early youth Augustine felt in his soul that duality, which, apparently, did not quit him through the end of his life. By himself, he never could come to any kind of definite decision. He simultaneously prayed to God so that He would heal him from fleshly lusts and so that He didn't hurry with his help. What was the truth? What was necessary to man in point of fact? Augustine, despite his great reading and his complete philosophical education, never himself could answer this question.

He was torn by constant contradiction; he waged a constant war with himself – at the same time as he valued more than anything internal peace and spiritual serenity. This spiritual struggle, with no end in sight, also threw Augustine from the plane of common thinking. One can say it otherwise and more strongly: Augustine felt that all thinking, no matter how intense and recherché it might be, would yield him nothing. What's necessary is not thinking but something else. What? He could not answer that question. And yes he could never answer it; i.e., he never could make the inference necessary for him from the presuppositions which he received prepared from the Hellenic philosophers. No matter how much 'reason' convinced him that Socrates was the ideal of philosopher and saint, all Augustine's being felt that he could not follow Socrates. One of two things was necessary: either acknowledge that there is no exit or reject Socrates. And here the Holy Writ came to his aid. For Socrates and for all pagan wisdom the <u>Genesis</u> story of the sin of Adam, transmitted to all humanity, would seem an undignified mockery both on reason and on morality. A God who would punish the remote descendants for the sins of their ancestor would seem to him the incarnation of injustice. Therefore both Pelagius and his friends, allowing no possibility of thinking badly of God, affirmed with such assurance that Adam's sin harmed only himself alone and that the people born later were no way culpable for his weakness. <u>Nihil potest per sanctas scripturas probari, quod justitia non potest tueri</u>.[38] And well, from the point of view of human justice, what could you invent more disturbing to moral feeling than the decision of God to punish Adam in the person of his innumerable posterity? Doubtless, Augustine himself, as his opponents, likewise little knew how to justify God in His wrath.

Had to do something else. Had to allow that the human concept of justice is incomplete. That <u>justitia cujus munus est sua cuique tribuere</u>[39] (<u>De civitate Dei</u>, XIX, 4, v. III, 203) consists not at all in awarding each his own but in something completely different. For Socrates and Plato, for the whole ancient world, such a position was absolutely unacceptable. For them this was equivalent to spiritual death. And this is no image, no exaggeration. These are adequate words. They shook; they rocked the foundations on which the moral life of men held. And not only for Socrates but for the huge majority of 'thinking' contemporaries. To put on mankind collective responsibility [*круговая порука*], to make Socrates responsible for the sins and crimes of Anitus and Melitus, what could be more unjust and unreasonable? This means to issue the great parchment of liberty to all criminals. They will violate the laws, commit filth and evil deeds, and the just shall have to answer for violation! And God himself so established it! Yes, says Augustine, God in His inscrutable justice put it just so. The sin of Adam is passed hereditarily and continues to pass to his posterity, as a consequence of the Fall of our forefathers. All of present-day humanity is just <u>massa peccati, massa perditionis</u>.

Augustine throws down a challenge to his contemporary Hellenic philosophy to the whole conscience of ancient nations. It has blundered on the chief thing. It affirms that a man who follows the guideline of wisdom in this life can attain bliss in this world. As a matter of fact it is indubitable that pagan philosophers, while correctly understanding the goal to which one must strive, were completely helpless and could not seek out means by which one can head to this goal.

<u>Quando quid nulla est homini causa philosophandi, nisi ut beatus sit: quod autem beatum facit; ipse est finis boni: nulla est igitur causa philosphandi, nisi finis boni; quamobrem quae nullum boni finem sectatur, nulla philosophiae secta dicenda est.</u>[40]

(<u>De civitate Dei</u>, XIX, 1, v. III, 191)

Having established this position in agreement with antiquity Augustine asks: could they, these pagan philosophers, come to the goal which they have set for themselves? And without hesitation he answers that they can't. They affirm that for bliss it's enough for a man to be conscious of himself as virtuous. But that is a lie, voluntary or involuntary, conscious or unconscious. He does not believe the eloquence dispensed by Cicero in honour of the blissful life of the Stoic sage:

> Illi autem qui in ista vita fines bonorum et malorum esse putaverunt, sive in corpore, sive in animo, sive in utroque ponetes summum bonum; atque, ut id explicatius eloquar, sive in voluptate, sive in virtute, sive in utraque; sive in voluptate simul et quiete, sive in virtute, sive in utrisque; sive in primis naturae, sive in virtute, sive in utrisque: hic beati esse, et a se ipsis beati fieri mira vanitate voluerunt.[41]
>
> (De civitate Dei, XIX, 4, v. III, 200)

In order to demonstrate the justice of his words, Bl. Augustine describes in the very strongest expressions the pathetic helplessness of the mortal. He is prey to all possible randomness – today he's rich, tomorrow he's poor, today esteemed, tomorrow fortune disgraces him, he can fall ill, go blind, go deaf, he can lose friends, family, etc. All that, by the way, was well known to pagan philosophers as well; there's nothing new in this. Exactly due to the point that philosophers were conscious of the instability of earthly goods, they always sought refuge and comfort in virtue. What's new in Augustine is only that he attributes to virtue no advantage over other earthly goods – for him it's all the same, whether the sage seeks his highest goal in natural data or in virtue.

> Quamdiu ergo nobis inest haec infirmitas, haec pestis, hic languor, quomodo nos jam salvos; et si nondum salvos, quomodo jam beatos illa finali beatitudine dicere audebimus? Jam vero illa virtus, cujus nomen est fortitudo, in quantacumque sapienta evidentissima testis est humanorum malorum, quae compellitur patientia tolerare.[42]
>
> (De civitate Dei, XIX, 4, v. III, 204)

And Augustine considered the Stoic's doctrine on suicide to be the indubitable proof of his rightness (he, like all Catholicism as well, in this respect remained to the end of his life a devoted disciple of Socrates: he believed in truths, no less than any educated Hellene). If virtue had an intrinsic value, if there is bliss in virtue, why, he asks with the triumph of the dialectician assured of the irrefutability of his conclusion, do Stoics allow suicide?

> Hanc in his malis vitam constitutam, eos non pudeat beatam vocare. O vitam beatam, quae ut finiatur mortis quaerit auxilium! Si beata est, maneatur in ea: si vero propter ista mala fugitur ab ea, quomodo est beata? An quomodo ista non sunt mala, quae vincunt fortitudinis bonum, eamdemque fortitudinem non solum sibi cedere, verum etiam delirare compellunt, ut eadem vitam et dicat

beatam, et persuadeat esse fugiendam? Quis usque adeo caecus est, ut non videat quod, si beata esset, fugienda non esset? Sed si propter infirmitatis pondus, qua premitur, hanc fugiendam fatentur: quid igitur causae est, cur non etiam miseram fracta superbiae cervice fateantur? Utrum, obsecro. Cato ille patientia, an potius impatientia se peremit? Non enim hoc fecisset, nisi victoriam Caesaris impatienter tulisset. Ubi est fortitudo? Nempe cessit, nempe succubuit, nempe usque adeo superata est, ut vitam beatam derelinqueret, desereret, fugeret. An non erat jam beata? Misera ergo erat. Quomodo igitur mala non erant quae vitam miseram fugiendamque faciebant?[43]

(Ib., 205)

I purposely wrote out this long excerpt from Augustine's works; to my mind there's expressed with especial expressiveness the revulsion of Bl. Augustine to everything by which the best representatives of Hellenism lived and what they deified – beginning with Socrates and ending with Marcus Aurelius – and what was reborn also in the most modern philosophy and which even in our time is considered the life nerve of all spiritual creative work. The same challenge which here Bl. Augustine flung down on the ancient world was in our time flung down on modern philosophy by Friedrich Nietzsche. When I had to speak of the great dispute of world views of the two opposite geniuses of our time, Tolstoy and Nietzsche, I thus formulated the essence of the positions they defended: 'the Good is not God, one must seek what is higher than good – one must seek God'.[44] Tolstoy knew this no worse than Nietzsche, but Tolstoy never resolved to say this openly. It seemed to him to deprive the good of independent force and significance – meant to kill life, to kill the best that is in life. That was his rational a priori, imbibed by him with his mother's milk or, more accurately, with the first word which he heard from his educators, and with the first phrases he read in books. If the good is not an eternal and high law, a law for mortals and immortals, then all of life ought, it seemed to him, collapse like a building from which the foundation has been pulled away or like a human body from which the skeleton has been extracted. All of philosophy, ancient and new, held to this conviction. And only experiences especially profound, exclusive in their force, unusual spiritual uplifts and upheavals force man out of those ruts into which he's fallen since youthful years, thanks to the condition of his existence. That's why this 'truth' is accessible only to those people who are compelled to judge of life sub specie its unexperienced mysteries. That's why Kant so serenely could create his critique of pure reason, in the consciousness that he had never insulted anyone in his life, the critique based on the conviction that he, Kant, knew what his duty was and that he had fulfilled his duty. And here's why Spinoza, flailing like one incurably ill, in spite of all his glorified rationalism, wrote:

Fateor, hanc opinionem, quae omnia indifferenti cuidam Dei voluntati subjicit, et ab ipsius beneplacito omnia pendere statuit, minus a vero aberrare, quam illorum, qui statuunt, Deum omnia sub ratione boni agere.[45]

(Ethics, Pars I, Prop. 33, Schol II)

I don't know how true Loof's statement is that Spinoza was under the influence of Bl. Augustine. Perhaps the thought was instilled in the Protestant theologian by the desire to explain the influence of Spinoza on Schleiermacher. But, even if Spinoza did know Augustine, it's indubitable, that such ideas can only be received from another when one's personal experience is sufficiently broad to open access to them. All of Spinoza's philosophy proceeds from the conviction that 'ad Dei naturam neque intellectum, neque voluntas pertinere'[46] (Eth. Pars I, Prop. XVII, Schol II). What this means he explains himself a little further on:

Nam intellectus et voluntas, qui Dei essentiam constituerent, a nostro intellectu et voluntate toto caelo differre deberent, nec in ulla re praeterquam in nomine, convenire possent; non aliter scilicet, quam inter se conveniunt canis, signum caeleste et canis, animae latrans.[47]

(Ethics. Pars I, Prop. XVII, Schol II)

The meaning of the polemic of Augustine with pagan philosophy and with Pelagianism consists in the point that his opponents found it possible to draw conclusions from what they knew, to what they knew not. It seemed to them that the Divine will and reason is human will and reason, but taken in some very excellent degree. And therefore, that God could be cognized, although yet imperfectly via superlationis eminentiae, as modern Catholic dogmatics express it. The Pelagians also expressed this in their affirmation nihil potest per sanctas scripturas probari, quod justitia non potest tueri.[48] They were convinced that God acts sub ratione boni and that therefore they, also striving for the good, always can discover error-free what is good, what is bad, what is true, what is false. Augustine knew that it's not so. That a man no matter how wise and honourable he might be cannot not know what is good, what is bad, nor even less, how to realize good and evil. His experience explained to him what he read in the holy books. He unmediated felt his nature as sinful. Not just now, in mature age, was he sinful, i.e., always naturally strove for the bad. He recalls the years of his early childhood and is compelled to acknowledge that then he was no better than now. Ita imbecillitas membrorum infantilium innocens est, non animus infantium[49] (Confessions, I, VII). Everything in himself inspires him with revulsion – not only his body, as with Plotinus, but also his soul. With all his being he feels himself belonging to the massa perditionis, massa peccata.

For him it is clear that he appeared on earth not pure and not immaculate but already with a difficult burden of ineffaceable sins. The same evil which he sees outside himself, he also sees inside himself. Whither is it? Why does struggle naught avail? Why too even now, when the Holy Writ and the Catholic Church have revealed the truth to him, he likewise, as expressed in St Paul's words, wishes the good but does evil? One can't blame God. God is the creator of all; God is omnipotent and all good – this means the guilt is in man, the guilt is in our remote forefather, who committed the most horrible of crimes. Adam, before the Fall, lived in paradise – he was given the opportunity of living with God – the opportunity of not sinning; he did not take advantage of them; he rejected the Divine and wanted his own. This crime is so horrible that an appropriate punishment could not even be devised for him. By his own power, man, as sinful, as having renounced God, can no longer be saved. He generally can no longer even desire the good. He has so distorted his natural nature given him from God, that he has become capable only of doing evil.

And if God judged him per justice, then there could be only one sentence: eternal torments and eternal death. But God is not only just – God is merciful. In His infinite love for fallen humanity, he resolved on the greatest sacrifice: to send on earth His only Son and give Him over to torments and death, so as at such price to redeem the terrible sin of Adam. Why exactly it was necessary to send the Son on earth, Augustine does not explain. He doesn't even affirm, as Gregory the Great later did, or especially Anselm of Canterbury, that God had no other means of saving humanity. He says only that this means was <u>coventius</u> (convenient).

Nor does he answer the question of why the sin of Adam was bequeathed to all of humanity. The question is all the more difficult for him as at that point the Church had already condemned as heretical the doctrine of traducianism, to the effect that human souls, like their bodies as well, are naturally reproduced by birth. Only bodies are born; souls then of all new-born are created by God.

Doubtless, Augustine's position was very difficult – and Julian of Eclanum persecuted him with constant indications that the doctrine of original sin leads unavoidably to Traducianism.[50] And all the same Augustine remained unshaken. He well understood that the force of logic is on the side of his opponents[51] and that he could not defend the position he'd taken with compelling arguments. But, when he had to choose between the necessity of renouncing an explanation and renouncing a reality indubitable for him, Augustine, whom they already mockingly called the <u>Philophraster Poenorum</u> and <u>Aristoteles Poenorum</u> (Carthaganian philosopher and Carthaganian Aristotle), preferred the latter. And this is highly remarkable for Augustine, who was living, as Harnack says, in an epoch when the inability to answer all questions was considered a sign of criminal ignorance and unbelief (Harnack, III, 202). Augustine felt that inexplicable reality did not cease to be reality. That one must deal with it – although it was not reconciled with reason. It is one step thence to the general and ultimate 'conclusion' that reality has no need of the sanction of reason, that reason ought not to rule, but rather be subordinated, that its power extends only to defined limits, that what reason considers impossible is possible. Augustine made no such conclusion. As far as I know, no one ever overtly made such a general conclusion. But in the question which occupies us here Augustine made such a decision as though he had made that conclusion. But because the arbitrariness of the indefinite all the same was no less fearsome for Augustine than for those philosophers with whom he polemicized, thus he thence made the directly opposite conclusion: in the place of the philosophical, rational criterion of truth he put the principle of the unshakable authority of the Catholic Church. This made him akin as well with 'vulgar Catholicism', like trust in common sense made Harnack akin to 'vulgar' philosophy. This then led to the phenomenon, incomprehensible at first glance, that the historical significance of Augustine in the West, for all the respect which he enjoyed even during his life, was comparatively very limited. He had influence only inasmuch as he developed 'vulgar-Catholic' ideas. His original ideas found acknowledgement in wide circles only much later.

VII

<u>O domine, Deus noster, in velamento alarum tuarum speremus, et protege nos et porta nos. Tu portabis, tu portabis et parvulos, et usque ad canos tu portabis, quoniam firmitas nostra quando tu es, tunc es firmitas, cum autem nostra est, infrmitas est.</u>[52]

(Confessions, IV, 16)

Our strength is only strength when God is with us; without God we are powerlessness incarnate. The little ones are just as weak beings, as are the old men with grey in their hair. The reason of the adults can no more raise them to the truth than can the unreason of babies.

The laws of natural reason, in opposition to what the ancient sages thought, are not universal. They have their limits, their limitations. Say for the usual course of life these limits seem huge, even unlimited: practically, the space occupied by the Roman Empire seems unlimited for the human mind, and the power of the tyrant, disposing of the life and property of his subject, seems limitless. And can a man, completely engulfed and burdened by the evils of the day, think that visible reality does not exhaust all the possibilities? That expanses exist in comparison with which the extensive possessions of the Roman Caesar are negligible that there might be a force, annihilating the power of the omnipotent tyrant?

This is so hard for a man to conceive! How to allow that the laws of nature, before whom the unconquerable Caesar bows, are second to some other force in their unchangeability? The more enlightened the mind, the more it has measured the power of natural forces, all the more does it incline to allowance of their eternal significance. This is exactly what, under the name of the unity of the forces of nature, gave wings to thinking people by hopes for the possibility of resolution of the ultimate mystery of the universe. Only by such allowance can the intensive and extensive multiformity of life phenomena be accessible to subjugation, as expressed in the language of modern philosophy. Allow that the laws of nature are limited in their significance by space and time, i.e., that order, which we now observe, was not so one hundred thousand years ago and would not be so in one thousand years, or that outside at least our solar system, bodies are not subject to the 'laws' of gravity, and all the grandiose dream of philosophy as science disintegrates in dust. For no matter how much Kant and his followers rumbled around, scientific philosophy must proceed from the Spinozan presupposition: <u>Res nullo alio modo, neque alio ordine a Deo produci potuerunt, quam productae sunt.</u>[53] Or, expressed in the language of the same Spinoza:

Naturae leges et regulae sunt ubique et semper eadem, atque adeo una eademque etiam debet esse ratio rerum qualiumcumque naturam intelligendi.[54]

In other words, per that which is, what we have already experienced and discovered, we can judge of what will be, what generally might be.[55] And, if no one fully repeats following Spinoza – ordo et connexio idearum idem est, ac ordo et connexio rerum[56] (Eth II, 7) – then only in the sense that not any philosopher is ready to concede the psychological parallelism. But, I suppose, that for Spinoza himself too the centre of gravity in this formula too is not the mutual correspondence between the phenomenon of matter and spirit, but the eternal and unchanging order and correspondence between phenomena – i.e., ordo et connexio. For, in the upshot, even psychological materialism can go no further. That is, one can say, for example, that definite psychic changes always correspond to known changes in the nervous system. But there is no possibility of penetrating into the mystery of the connection between two orders of different phenomena. And, apparently, even Spinoza himself was not too interested in penetrating the mystery of this connection. He is satisfied with only the establishment of principles: cogitatio attributum Dei est, sive Deus est res cogitans and Extensio attributum Dei est, sive Deus est res extensa[57] (Eth., Pars II, Prop. I et II). Why from the infinite attributes of God only two were selected and indicated remains unclarified, and still less is it clear, why such a modest result fully satisfied such a demanding philosopher. Just so it remains unclarified in what manner the infinite quantity of moduses, i.e., all reality, derive from God.

True, this last question was and remained to our time the true crux philosophorum. Even Heraclitus was disturbed by all the individual, bursting to the surface of being and then again falling without a trace. Anaximander considered the existence of the individual directly illegitimate, and criminal, and saw just punishment in the perdition of the individual in redemption of criminal existence. We recall that it wasn't easy for Plato to be reconciled with the multiformity of the real world, and he was compelled to consider it spectral and hide away from it in the sphere of ideas. The same for Aristotle and even for Plotinus.

Spinoza crisply formulates what all philosophers since ancient times have thought when he says:

Nam ut ex propositionibus 21, 22, 23 constat, ille effectus perfectissimus est, qui a Deo immediate producitur, et quo aliquid pluribus causis intermedis indiget, ut producatur, eo imperfectius est.[58]

(Eth., Pars I, Prop. XXXVI, Appendix)

I will not here analyse the theories which Spinoza here invokes, but an attentive analysis of the cited excerpt sufficiently reveals that in relation to the problem he set himself Spinoza was in no better position than his predecessors.

And exactly the fundamental position of Spinoza is that God is the most perfect being. He constantly bases himself on this position in all his reasoning. Several pages before this, proving that things could not be otherwise than they entered into reality, he defends his affirmation with the indication that if things could be otherwise then that would prove that God is not completely perfect. But, as such, once it's affirmed that God is the most perfect being and that we ourselves have so far attained the idea of the most perfect being, then we can exhaust all its content and, in this manner, draw irrefutable conclusions from it – then in what manner can we be reconciled with the idea that the creative work of the perfect being can yield imperfect things? For it's the contrary: the idea of the perfect being presupposes that all, too, proceeding from it is perfect. Spinoza allows that the more intermediate links are required between God and the thing created by him, the more imperfect will the thing be? Again the same question? First, why are these intermediate links required? Why could not God create all that exists unmediated? Second, why should the existence of intermediate links reflect on the quality of the created works?

Not only does our reason not see necessity in this but also empirical reality accessible to us refutes Spinoza. Were people and animals of the time of Nebuchadnezzar any worse than in Spinoza's time? Weaker, uglier, stupider? Swallows and nightingales, horses and elephants are just the same now as they were several thousand years ago. There is even much foundation to think that the chain of causae intermediae, as evolutionary theory teaches, leads often directly to perfection, and all the more to significant change, the longer the chain. It's clear that Spinoza made this obviously no wise either a priori nor a posteriori justified assertion only because he, like his predecessors, had to at whatever the cost throw from the path the magnum scientiae obstaculum, as he himself expresses it. Spinoza, like all philosophers, identified knowledge with una eademque ratio rerum qualiumcumque naturam intelligendi.[59] He was convinced that the very essence of knowledge is in explanation. One of the most remarkable traits of Spinoza's philosophy consists of the point that no one with such decisiveness and incisive definition followed the idea of the necessary connection of phenomena. As we know, in ethics he did not fear to extend his consistency to extreme limits.

> Quarto objici potest, si homo non operatur ex libertate voluntatis, quid ergo fiet, si in aequilibrio sit, ut Buridani asina? famene et siti peribit?[60]
>
> (Eth., Prop. 49, Scholium)

Again in Cogitata metaphysica he resolved the question of Burdian's ass another way:

> Si enim hominem loco asinae ponamus in tali aequilibrio positum, homo non pro re cogitante, sed pro turpissimo asini erit habendus, si fame et siti pereat.[61]
>
> (Cog. Met., II, 12, 10)

But in Ethics he already heads to the end:

> Dico, me omnino concedere, quod homo in tali aequilibrio positus (nempe qui nihil aliud percepit quam sitem et famem, talem cibum et talem potum, qui

<u>aeque ab eo disant) fame et siti perebit. Si me rogant, an talis homo non potius asinus quam homo sit aestimandus? Dico me nescire, ut etiam nescio, quanti aestimandus sit ille, qui se pensilem facit.</u>[62]

(Eth. II, Prop. 49, Scholium)

If you ask yourself, why Spinoza needed this harsh, stony consistency, you can give yourself only one answer: otherwise he would have had to reject the possibility of knowledge. And exactly that knowledge which alone Spinoza valued, scientific knowledge, constructed on principles, as mathematics is constructed.

All of reality ought to be inherent in nuce already in the first definitions, per Spinoza's ideal. Of course, Spinoza's ideal remained an ideal. He could not deduce reality from his definitions. The only thing that he could do was to utter sharp paradoxes, which by their sharpness underline his lack of desire to deal with this or that side of life. Put another way, Spinoza's consistency, so exalted by historians of philosophy, in no way deserves such astonishment. He went no further than the desire to be consistent and, perhaps, his glory for irrefutable logic is the best illustration of how weak and powerless men are in this regard. The condescension of historical evaluations, giving as many points for the unrealized intention as for the deed, is <u>testimonium pauperitatis</u> – testimony of the poverty of human reason. If Spinoza is the model of consistency – then, therefore consistency is – the fabled firebird, never yet having alit on earth. I cannot, of course, dwell in detail on the formal critique of the Spinozean system, nor is it necessary. For my goal the cited indices are sufficient. With just the allowance, <u>quod aliquid pluribus causus</u>,[63] etc., the Spinozean system is completely torn from its moorings. And what kind of affirmation is <u>Sentimur experimurque, nos eternos esse</u>?[64] On what basis does a doctrine, promising to attain all conclusions <u>more geometrico</u>, suddenly invoke the test of feeling? It's clear that the great significance of Spinoza, yielding him such passionate admirers as Schleiermacher and guaranteeing him such an outstanding role in history, is not rooted in his dialectical art. Logic played the same role for him, as the Church played for St Augustine. Under its cover and shade he could allow himself to believe and value that which was dear to him. He also sought authority – it also seemed to him that without eternal sanction, without approval, all the internal content of his life loses the very right to existence. One must force all to acknowledge his rightness. It is necessary that no one thinks otherwise than you think. And one must only allow oneself what you have the strength to demand from others. It stands to reason that the selected authority defines of itself both the character of possible claims and the opposite, of course.

Spinoza could suppress in himself everything <u>quo nos vituperabiles sumus</u> and let develop only that <u>quo nos laudabiles sumus</u>. Perhaps thanks to that, thanks to that strongly developed will, dealing with an uneasy temperament, one got the impression from Spinoza of the omnipotence of reason. This huge problem absorbed all his little strength. And just because he expended all his strength on it, he was accustomed to think that his task is the most important, the exhaustive task of life. So it is, I think, that Loofs vainly talks of Augustine's influence on Spinoza. It seems to me that Augustine's reasonings about virtue would rather have evoked Spinoza's dissatisfaction. For he taught that virtue demands no reward, that it is its own reward. Augustine could just not endure this idea. Self-righteous, autonomous virtue in his eyes was pride, superbia – the principle of any sin. He also attacked the Pelagians for this; all of Augustine's hope was that virtue could not and ought not to give satisfaction. And with malice he openly said to those who along with the Stoics affirmed the opposite – that they lie. Virtue – spiritual goods, accessible to men – is just as spectral and corruptible, as are material goods. If virtue can give so much, why do the Stoics flee from unsuccessful life? Why do they allow their own to commit suicide? The beginning of Augustine's faith is his conviction that people are incapable of doing good [творить добро] and create for themselves a worthwhile life.

And I suppose that if via Schleiermacher the modern Protestant theology has returned to Spinoza's idea of the self-righteousness of virtue, it only occurred after having submitted to the prestige of the modern scientific conquests and modern social organization. Protestant scholars lost the very capability of thinking of human existence as not secure.[65]

Schleiermacher still bowed before Spinoza – his heirs already preferred Kant, who, having preserved traditional Spinozean principles, completely cut them off from their natural roots. Spinoza was drowning, Spinoza felt himself hopelessly ill, dying – as it appeared from the above-adduced excerpts from his tract De Intellectus Emendatione.[66] And on this his philosophy grew. No matter how much he was fettered in his geometric truths, only a superficial glance could not see the suffering and penetrated soul under the steel armour.

Nothing so puts one off a correct understanding of Spinoza, as the striving to see in his ultimate conclusions a stable system of elevated noble truths. Although he himself did give sufficient basis to this understanding of his philosophy – albeit, so as not to search long – in such glorified words:

De affectuum natura et viribus, ac Mentis in eosdem potentia, eadem Methodo agam, qua in praecedentibus de Deo et Mente egi et humanas actiones atque appetitus considerabo perinde, ac si quaestio de lineis, planis, aut de corporibus esset.[67]

(Eth., III. introducto)

But hardly ought these and similar assurances to lead us into error. For the fundamental motif of his ethics is Cum Mens se ipsam, suamque agenti potentiam contemplatur, laetatur; et eo magis, quo se suamque agendi potentiam distinctius imaginatur[68] (Eth. III, 53). And its counterposition Cum Mens suam impotentiam imaginatur, eo ipso contristatur[69] (Eth. III, 55) – and, one might add, although Spinoza himself did not do this, eo magis quo suamque impotentiam distinctius imaginatur.[70] No matter how eloquently and sternly Spinoza demonstrated that he derived these positions with the same objectivity with which a geometer derives his theories on lines, planes and bodies, one can hardly not feel under them this extremely intense beating of life, which even the most believing pantheist will not seek out in geometric figures. The source of these adjustments has nothing in common with the sources from which the mathematician draws his knowledge. The ultimo ratio of Spinoza's philosophy emanates from the mysterious depth, inaccessible in words, of personal experiences – and thence emanates dispositions, not even cloaked in words, i.e., not deigning to condescend not at all to proof, but even to self-justification. These are not judgements, but exactly dispositions; these are not recherché truths; these are decrees, behests about truth. Whither did Spinoza assume this right, why does he speak as one having power? And isn't it clear that all his 'proofs', all attempts by more geometrico to compel his interlocutors to think like he thinks are only a conditional tribute to tradition and usage – rooted in the assurance that usage is and remains despot among men. For Spinoza himself this is obvious – (he no longer fears to draw from this source) he, approaching the source, in no way asks himself whether to consider its dew healing or destructive. He already internally disdains those people for whom such promises still exist. He has acquired a new assurance –the assurance of a man who is directed by a force which knows no mistakes. For him there can no longer be poisoned sources. Thus he dares affirm that rationes boni are alien to God. He says more: Si homines liberi nascerentur, nullum bona et mali formarent conceptum, quamdiu liberi essent[71] (Eth. IV, LXVIII): for freely born men the very opposition of good and evil disappears.

Saying all this, Spinoza supposes that he utters truths always equally obligatory for all men. He forgets that he didn't always think so, that at one time he could not think that way, and that, therefore, other people can now not think so, that for other people to say that the ratio boni is alien to God, or that a free man nullum bona et mali formarent is all the same as denying the existence of God. Along with Bl. Augustine and all the philosophers, Spinoza sets the ultimate goal of the philosopher as beatitudo, which he defines in the following manner: beatitudo nihil aliud est, quam ipsa animi acquiescientia, quia ex Dei intuitiva cognitione oritur[72] (Eth., IV, App. Chap IV). This, after all, is almost a paraphrase of the Augustinian tu fecisti nos ad te et inquietum est cor nostrum donec requiescat in te.[73] Repose of the soul is both a consequence and sign of knowledge of God. Cognition, put another way, accompanied by the condition of satisfaction and peace is the ultimate, final cognition. And all our activity ought to be directed to that goal. That's why Spinoza struggles with those affects which disturb spiritual peace. Spes et Metus affectus non possunt esse per se boni[74] (Eth. IV, Prop. 47). He explains why: quo magis ex ductu Rationis vivere conamur, eo magis spe minus pendere et Metu nosmet liberare et fortunae, quantum possumus, imperare conamur, nostrasque actiones certo Rationis consilio diregere[75] (d° Scholium). And again a few pages later he repeats anew: Qui Metu ducitur, et bonum, ut malum vitet, agit, is Ratione non ducitur[76] (Eth., IV, Prop. 63). We recall from the preceding how Spinoza in Tractatus de intellectus Emendatione tells the history of his spiritual struggle, i.e., the principle of his philosophy. For fear and hope were exactly those powerful movers which led his soul from the natural condition of equilibrium. If not for the constant alternation of despair and hope, Spinoza would have remained in that rut in which the accidental nature of birth and circumstance had put him in younger years.

There had to be an internal storm; there had to be a collision of opposite tendencies, so that the soul inclined to passive vegetation, firmly lowering its roots in the native land, getting in the ready rut, was expelled from the plane on which usual human existence was maintained. Coming to <u>aquiescentia</u> Spinoza forgot what had raised him above the level of the everyday. And forsooth, <u>aquiescentia</u> is in no way the exclusive prerogative of the philosophers.

Quite the converse, the condition of totally undisturbed tranquillity is observed in its pure form only in people who have never yet known doubt and struggle. The philosopher, who has set himself the goal of achieving tranquillity, dreams of <u>restitution in integrum,</u> of that condition, which is characteristic of and freely given to any, more or less limited and successful, i.e., bourgeois, existence. He who even once has soared on the wings of great despair and hope will not ever again return to stable tranquillity. Not in vain, even the Catholics pray: <u>credo, Domine, adjuva meam incredulitatem.</u>[77] And we encounter striking admissions in people of great religious experience, which cannot be ignored if you want to penetrate to the sources of philosophical creative work. Tertullian says: <u>timor fundamentum salutis est, praescriptio impedimentum salutis.</u>[78] Gregory the Great openly affirms: <u>Sancta ecclesia fidelibus suis spem miscet et metum.</u>[79]

And really, apparently, that spiritual seism, which is necessary for us to pull ourselves beyond the limits of the normal atmosphere allowed by reason and accessible to attainment, presupposes a special spiritual intensity, evoked in a man by irresistible fears – let them even be unfounded and unreasonable and great hopes, perhaps, just as spectral and just as little unfounded. And he who believes Spinoza's conclusions and accept his new-minted principles, while skipping the struggle, those depths of hope and despair, through which the philosopher had to pass before he learned his wisdom, will discover nothing from him. <u>Spei et metus affectus possunt esse per se boni</u> – more than that, they are necessary for any man; without these the ultimate attainments for man are absolutely impossible. Without them he doesn't even have the requirement to wrest out of the limits of the first, natural limitations of tranquillity – of that which Aristotle formulated in his philosophy of the mean, and which in modern theories of cognition continues to stubbornly justify the imaginary limits of ideal, perfect knowledge. In order to have the right to this or that philosophy, it's little to study it: one must <u>gustare et experiri</u>, that which is <u>extra verba et imagines percipitur</u>[80] (Tract. Theol. P., cap. IV, p 7).

VIII

I have so long dwelt on these questions in view of the point that the fate of philosophy hinges on them. Can a philosopher believe reason, on the proposition that in reason itself, as such, the source of cognition is inherent, or must he await <u>events</u>? It seems to me that if one so states the question, there can hardly be a possibility of giving two answers to it. It's clear that the readiness to seek the answer in reason, generally speaking, is the expression of the requirement to wall oneself off from all possible unexpected outcomes. One wishes to set a certain control apparatus over all life, defending the constructed existence from external storms.

A man knows what's good and what's possible – it seems to him that without this existence itself is unthinkable. To give oneself into the power of the unknown, who would undertake this? Bl. Augustine – true, under the shadow of the Catholic Church – resolved to set forth with a doctrine which seemed equally unacceptable for both Catholicism and Protestantism. With his rebuttals of the Pelagians he has as it were pulled the ground from under men's feet. We are all <u>massa perditionis, massa peccati</u> and, in essence, cannot <u>count on</u> anything; we are saved not by our efforts but by the grace of God. He first formulated grace as <u>gratia praeveniens</u>. God did not send man grace because man deserved it by his efforts, prayers or good deeds. Man cannot do it by effort, by prayer, not by doing good, unless God so wishes it.[81] That is, as opposed to Pelagius,[82] Bl. Augustine proposes, invoking the apostle Paul that the transgression of Adam led to all the human race being outside any kind of law.

> <u>Die Unruhe, der Hunger und Durst nach Gott, der Abscheu und Ekel vor den genossenen niederen Gütern ist nicht zu ersticken; denn die Seele, sofern sie ist, ist ja ex deo et ad deum. Aber nun fand er etwas Furchtbares: dass der Wille das factisch nicht will, was er will oder doch zu wollen scheint. Nein, es ist kein Schein es ist die fürchterlichste Paradoxie: wir wollen zu Gott und wir können nicht, das heisst, wir wollen nicht.</u>[83]
>
> (Harnack, III, 113)

And in fact, there is no exaggeration in these words. It's true, too, that Bl. Augustine experienced that terrible paradoxicality of man's position, who feels that all that the world gives cannot satisfy his unquenchable thirst for the eternal, and along with that is convinced, that it is not in his will to do even anything to in any way draw near to the source of eternal life which so attracts him. That which Augustine experienced by day, probably each man has to experience in dream. A terrible nightmare stifles you. You feel that this is a dream, that one can be rescued from the horror only by awakening. You make all possible effort to awaken, and you're convinced that all efforts are in vain, that your salvation is not in you but beyond you. Sometimes it happens that having made an effort at extreme intensity, you awaken asleep, arise from your bed, and it seems to you that all horrors have already passed, that you have returned to reality, that you are no longer in the power of an alien, cruel force. But a moment passes and you see that there was no awakening, that the awakening was imaginary, spectral. And again horrors, and again fear and consciousness of your helplessness, and along with that intensity of the whole impotent being. And only then, when on one hand you are convinced that with your own strength, no matter how you exert it, you will not be saved, and on the other hand when the torments and horrors of the dream attain the extreme degree of unendurability, real awakening occurs, the return to real life. It's not astounding that Augustine, having experienced the nightmare by day, a nightmare lasting years, then exclaims:

Unde hoc monstrum? et quare istuc? luceat misericordia tua, et interrogem, si forte mihi respondere possint latebrae poenarum hominum et tenebrosissimae contritiones filorum Adam. Unde hoc monstrum? et quare istuc?[84]

(Cond., VIII, 9)

Only he who has come at least somewhat close to the experiences of Bl. Augustine, only he who knows that such nightmares are possible by day, that it's not a myth, not an invention, not the thought experiment of a sly human spirit, would grasp the sense and meaning of the Augustinian conversion. And along with that, grasp what inspired him in his struggle with Pelagianism. True, in this struggle of St Augustine's the philosopher expressed himself, the true disciple of the Hellenes expressed himself. For Augustine's consciousness the question presented in the form in which Hellenic philosophy put it: on whose side is truth, on his side or Pelagius'? The right ought to be on his side or Pelagius' side.

The law of contradiction, the which Augustine did not doubt, did not lose its power and significance in this domain either. Thus he so passionately sought the condemnation of Pelagius and his confreres. It seemed to him that only after having driven his opponents off the road could he move unimpeded in the direction of the ultimate goal he'd set himself. We will limit ourselves here to this simple indication. The reader himself from this example will grasp in what manner people, by means of logical rework of their experiences, arrive at those judgements to which they consider they have the right to ascribe the predicate of general obligatoriness. It seemed to Augustine that if he succeeded in communing with higher consciousness then that means that by that alone he already knew all paths by which God draws men to him. He himself spoke so much on the inscrutable way to the Lord. It never entered his head that with such an allowance he limits the power of the Omnipotent, ascribing to Him only those possibilities which received preparatory sanction in the philosophical tracts of his Hellenic teachers. Pelagius established the general position that the sin of Adam <u>could not</u> harm any one of his descendants: that would be unjust. Augustine answered: the sin of Adam ruined all of humanity: if it ruined not everyone but only a part of humanity, that would be unjust. Both Bl. Augustine and Pelagius found in the Holy Writ sufficient texts in justification of their doctrines. But, Pelagius did not hear what Augustine was talking about – Augustine was deaf to the texts adduced by Pelagius. The human mind, even an outstanding mind, genius, cannot attain the multi-laterality which is characteristic of the Holy Writ. It seems to each man that from a point to a straight line one can erect only one perpendicular. And if factually it turns out, that one can erect not one, and not two, but a multitude of perpendiculars – this seems to people to be an obvious inconsistency. We all live in one defined plane and it is hardest of all to concede a multitude of planes and allow neighbours the freedom of movement in space. The further presentation will show, I hope, the false conclusion people are led to by this demand to limit everything, right to the power of God Himself. Meanwhile, we'll take up another side of Augustine's doctrine. We saw that he had to hack out of that plane in which his contemporaries lived. He was given to feel in his immediate experience the limitation of human strength. Living in this world, he was convinced, that he, per his most profound nature, belongs to another world to gustare et experiri, that which is extra verba et imagnes percipitur.⁸⁵ That only those who have hated it with all the strength of their soul can break out of everyday life.

> Fecerunt itaque civitates duas amores duo: terrenam scilicet amor sui usque ad contemptum Dei: caelestem vero amor Dei usque ad contemptum sui.⁸⁶
> (De civitate Dei, XIV, 28)

How to renounce self-love? How to make it so that love for God becomes the unique stimulus of all existence? Augustine in his experience was convinced that nothing can be attained by natural means, exercises of mind and will. The awakening, if it occurred, would be only seeming, only in dream. Then all would again go the old way: the power of sensuality cannot be overcome by usual internal struggle. Miracle, miracle alone can save man. And in the name of this miracle – Bl. Augustine renounces all conquests of the human mind – inasmuch, of course, as he had courage and self-renunciation. He wished to give his spirit into the hands of the Lord – and did give it – albeit, as I showed, with a certain looking back. Apparently, full trust in the Creator exceeds the strength of even such people as Augustine. Perhaps, that's why faith arrives only after such heavy experiences, which reduce the human soul to ashes. We won't even find words to tell the special condition, through which men must pass to liberate the emburdened soul from the ballast encumbering it to earth, purify it, and fly up to the heavens. We turn to the great psalmist. He, many millennia ago, first found actual words for the first aborning experiences. "I am poured out like water, and all my bones are out of joint: my heart is like wax; it is melted in the midst of my bowels" (Ps. 22, 14). And this is no metaphor, no conditional image. It must in fact be that the soul has poured out, that the bones are wracked, that the human heart has melted like wax among the internals.

Not in vain did Augustine so love the psalms – and not for nothing have the psalms remained ere now models of spiritual creative work unsurpassed by any man. And hardly can any man by his own strength rise to the height whither the calls of the great king beckon him. We can't even ascribe to the average man the most usual poetic talent, we are used to thinking that poetae nascuntur, and if this isn't accurate in essence, then it's accurate in the sense that no one knows what he must do to possess the mystery of inspiration. In what measure is the mystery of religious attainment more accessible to us – and have we the right there to count on existing validated planning methods for approaching the Divine? All observations on the life and internal experience of religious people show us that their 'methods' of seeking are the direct opposite to the very idea of planning. Internal dawnings come not when we await them, prepare for them: 'I am sought of *them that* asked not *for me*; I am found of *them that* sought me not' (Isa. 65, 1). All forms of exercitia spiritualia are more or less unsuccessful attempts at logical rework of those experiences, which in their very essence are at odds with any logic.

And here Augustine speaks directly of gratia praeveniens. Only the grace of God can tear the sullen and bound human soul out of the profound and tormenting unwakeable sleep. Faith is not the readiness to acknowledge these or those positions as true. No matter how many of this or that judgement you acknowledge true, you'll not get a step closer to God out of it. Faith is the transition to new life.

At one time God created the world, from dust, from nothing, He created man. Exactly so He creates, transforming the unbelieving sinner into a believer. And in such marvellous transformations, of course, human strength can have no significance, just as it had no significance when by the unlimited power of the Almighty their souls were brought forth from unbeing. Here's the essence of that experience which defined the conversion of Augustine. Here's why in his time Tertullian so boldly affirmed fiunt, non nascuntur christiani.[87] And this explains the readiness of Augustine to break with Pelagius, representing pagan wisdom. For Augustine, in actual fact, virtutes gentium splendida vitia erant.[88] All the moral force of Socrates, unusual from the point of view of mortal man, seemed as nothing to St Augustine. No matter what its dimensions, it does not raise men above earth, just as even the regal eagle, soaring above the clouds, on his own, so powerful wings, cannot fly past the limits of earth's atmosphere.

Of course, inasmuch as Bl. Augustine could and did express this his experience, he had to enter into the most implacable struggle with his confused opponents. They wished to attain the righteousness and justice of God – Bl. Augustine, following the Psalmists, prophet and great apostle – sought only to glorify it. And here, per the strange, paradoxical play of new creative work, Augustine with impassion insulting for his opponents falls to those utterances of Holy Writ, which most of all contradict the traditional concepts of the good and the rational. Man is saved by faith alone; faith is given not to him who sought it, not to him who worked at it, but to he whom God elected, prior to him in any way manifesting himself.

Electi sunt ante mundi constitutionem ea praedestinatione, in qua Deus sua future facta praescivit; electi sunt autem de mundo ea vocatione, qua Deus id, quod praedestinavit, implevit. Quos enim praedestinavit, ipsos et vocavit, illa scilicet vocatione secundum propositum, non ergo alios, sed quos praedestinavit ipsos et vocavit, nec alios, sed quos praedestinavit, vocavit, justificavit, ipsos et glorificavit, illo utique fine, qui non habet finem.[89]

(St Augustin, De praedestinatione sanctorum, 34. Harnack, III, 205)

This doctrine of predestination, which later attained with Luther and especially with Calvin an even sterner and sharper expression, strictly unendurable for healthy moral consciousness, was not invented by Augustine himself. It was taken by him whole from the Holy Writ.

These same prophets and apostles, unenlightened by Hellenic wisdom, taught Augustine to trust those his experiences which, per the previous criterion of truth, ought to be rejected as not consistent with either the nature of reason or the order of things. 'Verily thou *art* a God that hidest thyself, O God of Israel, the Saviour' (Isa. 45, 15). 'Woe to him, who spars with his Creator, crock of earthly crocks. Surely your turning of things upside down shall be esteemed as the potter's clay: for shall the work say of him that made it, He made me not? Or shall the thing framed say of him that framed it, He had no understanding?' (Isa. 29, 16). Or 'Who has searched the spirit of the Lord and who has given Him advice?'[90] and again: 'For who hath stood in the counsel of the LORD, and hath perceived and heard his word? Who hath marked his word, and heard *it*?' (Jer. 23, 18).

We recall again à propos of these words, installed by Socrates at the basis of Greek philosophy and coming down to us as principles in an unchanged form. Socrates disdained poets because although they knew the truth, they could not understand it. For Socrates – and after him for all philosophy – an incomprehensible truth is an unacceptable truth, a lie. We don't want to trust anything; we want to be convinced of everything. We count only on our own strength; we respect only our rectitude, rely only on our reason. Socrates doubtless would have relegated the prophets to the poets, and Plato would have resettled them out of his state. And actually Plato's sentence had been put into implementation by history. Prophets enjoy no right of citizenship in modern civilized states. They are only tolerated, as one tolerates the insane and possessed. Catholicism, as Dostoevsky correctly indicated, knew how to escort them to the county line of its doctrine. But Bl. Augustine, as we know, was simultaneously both Catholic and believer. Prophets inspired him with their nowise justified inspiration:

O profundas divitias tum sapientiae, tum cognitionis Dei! Quam imperscrutabilia sunt ejus judicia, et ejus viae impervestigabilia. Quis enim cognovit mentem Domini? Aut quis ei fuit a consilio.[91]
(Rom., XI, 33–4)

These words of the great apostle, inspired, along with the prophets extolling the unattainable wisdom of the Creator, and spoke more to Augustine's heart than all the philosophical systems of antiquity.

God elects whom He wished, no matter how much our reason is disturbed by the apparent injustice of just such a decision – Bl. Augustine is no longer disturbed by this. God is not under the jurisdiction of our reason and our justice.

Numerus ille justorum, qui secundum propositum vocati sunt ipse est (ecclesia). ... Sunt etiam quidam ex eo, numero qui adhuc nequiter vivant aut etiam in haeresibus vel in gentium superstitionibus jaceant, et tamen etiam illic novit dominus qui sunt ejus. Namque in illa ineffabili praescientia dei multi qui foris videntur, intus sunt, et multi, qui intus videntur, foris sunt.[92]
(St Augustin, De baptismo, V, 38. Harnack, III, 164)

So speaks Augustine that same Augustine, who as we recall, is completely legitimately considered the pillar and support of Catholicism. But yet in these words is the death of Catholicism! For they deprive the heir of Peter of that <u>potestas clavium</u>, without which all his power and all force are transformed into nothing!

For Augustine preaches the invisible church – i.e., rebels against the fundamental dogma of Catholicism, proclaiming the Church visible and the heir visible of God on earth, clothed in all fullness of power. All this is so, of course. But yet the doctrine of Augustine of <u>gratia praeveniens</u> and of salvation by faith alone so little comports with the theory and practice of Catholicism. Catholicism, no matter how much it expatiates on grace, in the final account puts the salvation of man dependent on his <u>merita</u> – merit.

And, if it renounced this, it couldn't hold off its multimillion herd for even a year. It's known, how they attempted to interpret Augustine's doctrine of grace:

> <u>quos Deus semel praedestinavit ad vitam, etiamsi negligant, etiamsi peccent, etiamsi nolint, ad vitam perducentur inviti, quos autem praedestinavit ad mortem, etiamsi currant, etiamsi festinent, sine causa laborant.</u>
>
> (Harnack, III, 248)

That is, those predestined by the decision of God to life, whether they will try or not, whether they sin or live righteously, they will be saved all the same. And, conversely, those whom God has predestined to death will perish all the same, no matter what efforts they make to please God and deserve his mercy. Logically this is a correct inference from Augustine's doctrine. It's clear, but it's no less clear what a threat such a doctrine presents for the whole extant construct and first of all for Catholicism itself. It's understandable that neither the Catholic nor the later Protestant church could ever relate serenely to such a sort of fearless consistency. And each time, when it had to make a choice between pure doctrine and retaining for itself the power to direct the souls of the pastorate, Catholicism did not hesitate. It was ready to entrust doctrine to God, but it always preferred to preserve its earthly power and its earthly goals by its own means.

But for us it is important to distinguish Catholicism from Bl. Augustine. I don't think that we can do as the Protestants do, reproach Bl. Augustine that he considered it necessary to support that vulgar Catholicism with which Luther had later to struggle. The further presentation will show that Luther had to do the same thing that Augustine did, that even liberal theology, having renounced vulgar Catholicism, had to rely on vulgar philosophy, the philosophy of common sense. More than that, we have already partially seen, and the further presentation will show it even more clearly that 'vulgar Catholicism' is not nearly as easy to shake off as it seems to Protestant theologians. They themselves, for all their freethinking, are far from free of those bonds for which they reproach Bl. Augustine. And this is no accident.

Before God a man, perhaps, would resolve in rare minutes of prayerful inspiration to be righteous and free, when He is attained <u>extra verba et imagines</u>. Nothing is fearsome before God. It's not even fearsome to acknowledge with Augustine that the very highest moral life does not yield internal satisfaction; it's not fearsome to discover that <u>rationes boni</u> are not characteristic of God; it's not even fearsome to utter the formula which so frightens everyone off – 'beyond good and evil'. Before the face of God, consciousness of one's helplessness and powerlessness might bring joy, even inspire.

Perhaps the source of the greatest pathos is to renounce for God all those 'natural' rights given by reason and morality. <u>Mihi adherere Deo bonum est</u>. To be in communion with the highest being signifies a readiness to renounce all that one had once wanted, and to want everything, that one had once feared. But it only takes averting one's eyes from the sky and looking at the earth, and everything changes. Faith seems madness and as a matter of fact becomes madness. You hear the murmur of the crowd <u>etiamsi negligent, etiamsi peccent.</u> And you feel that impassable abyss is dug between heaven and earth.

One has to deal with the crowd. Power is necessary over it, it needs acknowledged, proven, sanctioned truth. Only before such truth will it bow its obstinate head. Not in vain did Plato say that the crowd is an unbeliever, and Spinoza affirmed <u>terret vulgus nisi pascat,</u> and Dostoevsky, accusing and justifying his Grand Inquisitor, called people rebels. Here on earth what's necessary is powerful, dictatorial truth, brooking no objections.

On earth truth is necessary, on earth assurance is necessary, on earth the mean proclaimed by Aristotle ruled and always will rule.

Nor Augustine, nor Spinoza, nor all the greatest philosophical and religious geniuses ever were able to find a truth, equally necessary on heaven and earth. We now abandon Augustine and project the presentation forward a thousand years. We turn to one of his most remarkable disciples – to Luther, and we'll see, how he perceived that opposition between truth and faith, which was revealed to his teacher in the epistles of the Apostle Paul and in his own internal experience.

IX

I already indicated in one of the preceding chapters that the collision of Luther and Tetzel à propos indulgences could not be considered the real reason of the beginning of the Reformation. No matter how disturbing were the devices in and of themselves which Tetzel used, no matter how disturbing were they who sent him to turn around the people, it's quite possible that in other circumstances, Luther would have passed by them in complete equanimity. And it's also probable that those spirits which tore Luther from Rome could have made him a true son of the Catholic Church. The famous German historian Ranke finds that Luther's experiences extremely closely recall the experiences of Ignatius Loyola, founder of the Jesuit order. Both the one and the other strove to find, as religion demanded, reconciliation of the soul in God, and the usual paths indicated by the Church led neither the one nor the other to the desired goal.

<u>Auf sehr verschiedene Weise gingen sie aber aus diesem Labyrinth hervor. Luther gelangte zu der Lehre von der Versöhnung durch Christum ohne alle Werke: von diesem Punkte aus verstand er erst die Schrift, auf die er sich</u>

gewaltig stütze. Von Loyola finden wir nicht, dass er in der Schrift geforscht, dass das Dogma auf ihn Eindruck gemacht habe. Da er nur in inneren Regungen lebte, in Gedanken, die in ihm selbst entsprangen, so glaubte er, die Eingebung bald des guten, bald des bösen Geistes zu erfahren. Endlich ward er sich ihres Unterschiedes bewusst. Er fand denselben darin, das sich die Seele von jenen erfreut und getröstet, von diesen ermüdet und geängstigt fühle. Eines Tages war es ihm, als erwache er aus dem Traume. Er glaubte mit Händen zu greifen, das alle seine Peinen Anfechtungen des Satans seien. Er entschloss sich von Stund an, über sein ganzes vergangenes Leben abzuschliessen, diese Wunden nicht weiter aufzureissen, sie niemals wieder zu berühren. Es ist dies nich sowohl eine Beruhigung als ein Entschluss, mehr eine Annahme, die man ergreit, weil man will, al seine Ueberzeugung, der man sich unterwerfen muss.[93]

(Ranke, Die Römischen Päpste. I, 121)

Such an admission from an excellent Protestant historian deserves all attention paid it. One and the same internal experiences made Luther the enemy, Loyola the best support of the Catholic Church. The Reformation and the establishment of the Jesuit order, which set as its chief, if not sole goal, the struggle with the Reformation, are engendered by one and the same spirit of doubt, struggle and unrestrained seeking of ultimate truth.

Luther, like Loyola, felt himself in the power of the evil spirit and exerted all his strength to free himself from the terrible enemy. And it came to this – that the enemy is the Pope, the Catholic Church with its false doctrine. Truth can only be found in the Holy Scripture. Everything that contradicts the Holy Scripture is a lie and invented by the enemies of God. In this manner, Luther proclaimed what his heirs called the formal principle of Protestantism – i.e., the external criterion, which yields the possibility of distinguishing truth from falsehood in religious questions. Loyola too created his 'criterion'. In his Exercitia spiritualia there is a chapter, titled Ad motus animae quos diversi excitant spiritus discernendos, ut boni solum admittantur et pellantur mali – how to distinguish the different spirits influencing a man in order to accept only the good and reject the bad (Ranke, Ib, 121).

Luther – later we will speak of this in more detail – affirmed that the Gospel, i.e., his understanding of the Gospel, was given him by God himself. Loyola also attained his truth and the mystery of faith in supernatural vision (Ranke, Ib, 122). And it was so convincing for him that he no longer required any further confirmations – even the Holy Scripture:

his visis haud mediocriter tum confirmatus est[94] ut saepe etiam id cogitarit, quod etsi nulla scriptura mysteria illa fidei doceret, tamen ipse ob ea ipsa, quae viderat, statueret sibi pro his esse moriendum.[95]

(Loyola, Ranke I, 122)

Ranke makes a distinction between Loyola and Luther. Loyola only made a decision; Luther had created a 'conviction'. The Protestant historian supposes that by such a distinction he justifies Luther before the court of reason and hands Loyola his head. I think that the matter here is not that simple.

If we're already talking about court and those on trial, then at this point the historian in Ranke himself is threatened with the danger of falling from the judge's banc to the accused's bench. By what right does he impose his sentences? And in such a tone brooking no objection! As we know, not very long ago a whole series of well-known Germans scholars – historians and philosophers – raised a very noisy dispute on the methods of historical investigation proposed by Ranke.

One short phrase of Ranke's served as theme of the dispute – <u>bloss sagen will wie es eigentlich gewesen</u> – the historian ought to describe what was. The question arises – how to fulfil this commandment and what it actually demands from the historian. Ranke himself, speaking of how Loyola only made a decision, while Luther had created a conviction – does he describe what was, as he was supposed to in fulfilment of his self – proclaimed fundamental principle of historical investigation, or does he exceed the bounds of his rights, arbitrarily widening his competence? And how to verify, where the legitimate usufruct of his rights ends and usurpation begins? I remind you that Luther, whom Ranke depicts in the adduced excerpt as a man striving only to humbly obey the law, allowed himself to not accept the Epistle of the Apostle James as canonical and that he instead of any justification did not hold off, as motive of this decision, to quote the words of Horace – <u>sic volo, sic jubeo – sit pro ratione voluntas</u>. Doubtless, this was all known to Ranke the historian; why did the historical objectivity he elevated into law lose its power over him?

It's clear that this law, too, to which Ranke willingly and conscientiously subordinates himself in his historical storytelling has a limited sphere of application. Ranke doesn't try to say that the Peasant Wars took place in the seventeenth century, and the Thirty Years War in the sixteenth; he doesn't try to conceal the base origins of Luther, albeit, perhaps, it would be in his spirit to see a magisterial prince or count at the head of the Reformation movement. Within these limits the laws of objectivity still completely dominates him. But beyond a known marker the charm of the still recently untouchable truth disappears at once.

Neither objectivity nor law is any longer necessary for him. Expressing his judgements on Luther and Loyola, Ranke doesn't consider it necessary to even recall his own personal method of logical construction. Loyola, who per his own admission came wholly out of the same doubts and torments which drove Luther too off the high road of history well trodden through the ages, had no convictions, although he was prepared, as was Luther, to lay down his life for his task. It's clear that Ranke expresses himself so categorically and assuredly just because he feels that nothing any longer binds him here, that the moment of free decision has commenced: one can now no longer deal with any laws, for no matter how many new documents you discover in the archives, not one of them can dispute or affirm the judgements he expressed.

If you even succeeded in resurrecting Loyola and Luther, the matter would not be righted in any way, for no perspectival inquests would gather the material necessary for validation of Ranke's judgements. For him, Luther was and remains the representative of reason, Loyola the representative of passion. And Ranke values the right of such an arbitrary resolution so highly that he doesn't at all set himself the question that how did it occur that people so close in their experiences acted in the historical arena as implacable enemies? Why did the Jesuits and their order consider all means licit for struggle with the Reformation when Luther and Loyola proceeded from the same point and sought one and the same thing? Or do we have another gap in consistency? Here too identical principles yield different, directly opposite results. For the historian, who as a matter of fact would wish only to describe what was, such a conclusion ought to be more valuable than anything else in the world. For, if it's true, if the sphere of application of consistency of phenomena is limited, then as a matter of fact dreams of historic laws are a heavy interference for the historian in his investigations. That is, not in investigations, one must say, but in the attainment of the set goal – here's that magnum obstaculum scientiae of which Spinoza spoke.

Here we are presented a chance to be visibly convinced that the goals of knowledge and science might be directly opposed. For science everything that interferes with the coordination of events per a definite principle is an obstacle to be eliminated, a true stumbling stone. And an historian who wishes that his work be scientific cannot but exert all efforts to clear his path of these stones. If Loyola and Luther proceeded from the same place and strove for the same thing, it cannot be that the works of their life were so different. Therefore, one must at whatever cost introduce a new factor which explains what occurred.

Ranke does so. This means that even before he entered on formulation of his principle of historical method, before he said that the historian must describe what was, he already knew from somewhere that no matter what happened in the past, the general principle of appearance of consistency was not violated. Yes, as a matter of fact, let the historian try to renounce this principle – he couldn't write two words. How did one know whether the donatio Constantini (donation of Constantine) was false or not? For we verify this historical document and reject it only because we acknowledge the known unshakable criterion of truth, based on the proposition that a thousand years ago, just like now, there exists a definite unchangeable order of things. In Constantine's epoch they wrote like this, didn't know that, etc. If this were not acknowledged, then any kind of invention has the same rights, as the most accurate historical description. The tale of the witches on Bald Mountain, of the conquest of Zeus, of Mohammed's wonders, the tales of Swedenborg, etc., ought to be accepted by us with the same trust as the descriptions come down to us of Caesar's death or the campaigns of Alexander the Great. The criterion is the gate which bars the door of the temple of science against whole hordes of absurd and wild lies bursting in. Knock it down and all the barons with all their fantasies will seize the field of human truth. These considerations are as elementary as they are correct. And all the same, if the proposition turns out correct that the sphere of action of laws known to us, or even, that generally the sphere of consistency is limited, then science, with all its habits of credibility, falls into a tragic position: in order not to allow mistakes, it has to renounce knowledge, i.e., its main goal; everything, that turns out not susceptible to control, will be rejected by it. More than that, everything that is not susceptible to control and validation, by force of the acquired habit to seek out only the indubitable, turns out beyond the limits of not only human attainments but human searches. Instead of what is, we will see only that which, in our opinion, ought to be; i.e., in other words, science, which sought and seeks cognition of reality, will live in the fantastic domain of spectres and affirm the non-existent as that which exists. That it's just like that in actual fact – for me, that's almost indubitable. And in the given case, Ranke, that Ranke, who as a matter of fact wished to describe only that which is, fell into the deadfall set for us by all the extant theories of cognition. He still had the perceptivity and independence of judgement to see the kinship of the spiritual experiences of Loyola and Luther. But here the theory of cognition asserted its rights and Ranke begins to speak of the indubitable spectres in a tone such as though no one had the right for a minute to doubt their reality, just exactly as though they existed in actual fact.

Luther had a conviction, which he followed! Otherwise one couldn't write history. Otherwise how could such a great work as the Reformation be explained. For it's not the Jesuit order – which ought to receive no explanation, in punishment for its maleficent historical significance! To allow that the arbitrary and random were the beginning of the great historical event – thus to apply his principle of 'describe what was' – the genius German historian, for all the boldness and independence of his thought, didn't and couldn't go there.

It goes without saying that Catholic historians and theologians judge Luther completely differently than does Ranke. They consider Luther the student and follower of Occam. We already recall from the previous chapters that the fundamental trait of Occam's doctrine, so distinguishing him from Scholastics preceding him, was a principled unbelief in the rights of human reason. We can know, Occam taught, only that which is given us in the revelation of the Holy Scripture and personal experience. Human reason has a limited mission – only to attain and perceive what is given it. By force of its limitation, reason is not allowed to critique, or validate revealed truth, but only to subordinate itself to it, as indubitable, albeit it seems to it absurd and unnatural. The absurdity and unnaturalness of something is not an objection to it. Occam writes:

Non potest (libertas voluntatis) per aliquam rationem demonstrative probari, quia omnis ratio hoc probans accipiet aeque ignotum cum conclusione vel ignotius. Potest tamen evidenter cognosci per experientiam.[96]
(Occam, Quodlibet I, q. 16. Denifle, II. 336)

Occam's means of reasoning here corresponded like nothing else to the demand ripening in Luther for internal liberation. For him ratio was not a salvific mentor, but rather an evil despot, whose yoke must be thrown off whatever the cost. Luther felt that it was impossible to remain longer in the power of old presuppositions, which under the name rationes enchained all his being. And when Occam revealed to him that ratio accipiet acque ignotum vel ignotius cum conclusione – and all Occam's reasonings bore such a character – Luther heard good news in these words. Reason – with all its proofs – is a pretender (cf. Ritschl I, 98, 99 – on Luther's irrationalism). Reason does not know, it does not possess the truth, it posits positions as its suppositions that are just as little and even less founded than that conclusion to which it wishes by such means to compel us – on what basis to trust its decrees? For modern philosophers, ex officio studying the theory of cognition, just as for the majority of readers, it perhaps will not be completely clear why Luther connected so much with this or that resolution of the question of the prerogatives of rational thinking. It seems to everyone that this is a specialized, abstract problem, not, of course, bereft of theoretical interest, but practically completely indifferent. No one even suspects that great responsibility which Luther took on his soul when he affiliated with Occam's school. And I don't know whether there is a possibility of convincing the modern reader, or philosopher, that the fate of man, or even all of humanity, is connected with the doubts and hopes aborning in Luther's soul.

Where to go? Whom to follow? Whom to heed? If one accepts the philosophy of Aristotle embodied in Thomas Aquinas, one must submit in everything to the authority of the Catholic Church. Luther, of course, could not tell and circumstantially explain the historical connection between Aristotle and the Roman church – he was neither an historian nor a philosopher in the usual meaning of these words. But he felt with all the strength of his soul that it was not in vain that the Pope drew so near to the pagan teacher. Reason, elevated to the throne, laid limits to the searches and hopes of the human soul. Expressing it in Dostoevsky's words, Catholicism refused God the right of adding or taking away even anything from what they, Catholicism, once proclaimed as the ultimate truth. They, who within the limits delimned by the medieval church, found ample space for their experiences, blessed reason and its sanctions allowing for tranquillity. For under normal circumstances, nothing brings such joy and so eases the human soul – even the great ones – like limitation of possibilities.

We all know that the heavenly vault overturned over us is a fiction and a spectre, but nonetheless it soothes our view and we bless it, and we would not endure it if it suddenly disintegrated and our eye had to gaze on infinity. Thus the Hellenic spirit of Thomas Aquinas created the Summa, that magnificent and colossal Gothic cathedral of theological creative work. But, in Thomas' cathedral Luther could not pray. He stifled; he gasped under the imperial vaults. And he, albeit with a trembling horror, greeted the destructive work of Scholastic decadence. Ranke is not correct in supposing that Luther had a conviction created, that he knew to what the battle begun would lead. Luther, having begun his struggle, least of all supposed that he would have to undermine the very foundation of medieval Catholicism.

Now, looking back at the distant past, it would seem to the historian that he clearly sees the connection between the separate events of which the world phenomenon of Reformation was composed. But it was completely not visible to Luther what he had been fated to create – a new church or the Jesuit order. Luther rebelled against the Pope; Loyola applied all his great force at the foot of the Papal throne. The historian, who following Spinoza ought to think that res nullo alio modo, neque alio ordine a Deo produci potuerunt, quam productae sunt, exerts all his strength in order to see necessity defining the events of the past. Without this history, I repeat, there cannot be science. But what if this necessity is fiction? What then does history give us?

X

One must, obviously, free oneself from the Spinozean presupposition. Put another way, history in actual fact ought to be a depiction of what was. Where one can espy a connection of events – let's try to find it. But we also ought to be prepared to see an absence of connection, a break in the chain. I know that this is difficult; I know this is entailed with great, with the greatest risk. And I fully understand historians, who before they set to their work, consciously or unconsciously, take from their hands or other hands a series of ready presuppositions, which they no longer submit to any further validation. Without a compass, without a map, without a firm guide one cannot set out on the distant path. But in such a case one must beforehand tell oneself that huge domains of human existence and creative work must be forever closed.

If you value too much what you've already acquired, you will never discover anything new. In the case we're working, Luther, when he had to, staked everything he had, and if you wish to follow after him, you must be prepared for everything; you must not be afraid to jettison treasures into the sea in order to lighten and save the sinking boat. Doubtless, the Catholic theologians are correct when they affirm that Luther's struggle was a struggle against the church. It was not difficult for Dostoevsky, standing outside Catholicism and living in the nineteenth century to say that Catholicism committed the most terrible of crimes – put the Pope in the place of Christ, put itself in the place of God. Dostoevsky from the sidelines judged of others' sins and crimes. Luther himself was a believing Catholic and, before judging the Church to which he belonged, ought to have judged himself. For he was together with them, for he also taught for many years what they taught. The Catholic Church was the singular, ultimate haven for a soul; what must have been his horror, when he felt for the first time that he cowered in the shade of the Antichrist and that eternal perdition threatened his soul. True, already before Luther there were different people into whose soul such difficult suspicions had crept. In England Wycliffe, in Bohemia Hus had in much anticipated Luther. But no one of them found in themselves sufficient force to see and set the question in all its immensity. Protests were directed against individual malfeasances and injustices. But no one, apparently, could resolve to cast down the challenge against the Church itself – against the idea of the One, Holy, Infallible Church.

> True, Occam to a significant degree theoretically prepared the ground for Luther. He rebelled against the unlimited power of the church: Si Papa haberet talem plenitudenem potestatis a Christo, et evangelica lege, lex Evangelii esset intolerablis servitutis et multo majoris quam lex Mosaica, omnes enim essent per ipsam servi Papae[97]
> (Quaest. super potest. Papae. I,c.b; Goldast II,320. Denifle II, 376, 377)

And not only relative to the Pope, he affirmed almost the same thing also relative to the whole clergy: Totus Clerus non est illa Ecclesia, quae contra fidem errare non potest. And again: Omnes Episcopi possunt contra fidem errare cum omnibus clericis suis[98] (Dial., I, 1.5, pp 28–31; Goldast II, 497. Denifle II, 379).

In such cases the power of judgement devolves to secular persons.

Si omnes Praelati et Clerici mundi pravitate inficerentur haeretica, potestas judicandi omnes devolveretur ad catholicos laicos et fideles.[99] (Occam, Dialogues, I. I.5, p. 28; Goldast, II, 498, 18. Denifle, II, 375). Illae solae veritates sunt catholicae reputandae et de necessitate salutis credendae, quae in canone Bibliae explicite vel implicite asseruntur. And further: Omnes autem aliae veritates, quae nec in Biblia sunt insertae, nec ex contentis in ea consequentia formali et necessaria possunt inferri, licet in scripturis Sanctorum et definitionibus S. Pontificum assertantur, et etiam ab omnibus fidelibus teneantur, non sunt catholicae reputandae, nec est necessarium ad salutem eis per fidem firmiter adhaerere vel propter eas rationem vel intellectum humanum captivare.
(Dialogues, I, 1. 2, p. 1; Gold. II, 410. Denifle, II, 382)[100]

All this indicates that Occam's unconditional trust in the infallibility of the Catholic Church was already shaken. The authority of the Holy Scripture stood over him, as it later did Luther. It's most probable that the Catholics are right, that such affirmations of Occam strongly helped Luther in his boldness. Occam showed by his allowance that 'the Pope and all the clergy might fall away from the truth', that there can't even be talk about the ecclesiastical power and authority in the actual sense of the word. Apparently, Weiss is also right in his second affirmation: 'if one does not acknowledge the authority, neither for tradition nor for ecclesiastical decisions, nor for the faith of all, then the only support for the individual person is the Holy Scripture'.[101] In this Occam also converges with his great opponent Wycliffe and with all heretics, beginning with the time of Tertullian.

All the same, the difference between Occam and Luther is huge. Occam only pointed to the possibility that all Catholicism was in error. And in the case of such possibility they recommended to the believers the unique unshakable authority of the Holy Scripture. That which was possible for Occam became reality for Luther. Luther was convinced that the Church, that Church in which he sought salvation, was in the hands of the Antichrist.

I don't know whether many of our contemporaries are capable of understanding what this experience meant for the medieval monk. I do not wish to say by this that our contemporaries did not know profound experiences that move the soul. But it seems to me that they can hardly imagine that profound internal seism of this sort connected with thoughts of the role and significance of the Church. It would be a lot more comprehensible to us if we discovered that the revolution in Luther's consciousness was a consequence of a crime he committed. Like, let's say, that which Tolstoy described in Kreutzer Sonata, or in Power of Darkness, or Dostoevsky in Crime and Punishment, or Shakespeare in Hamlet.

For few of us are capable of conceding that to lose faith in the Church means to lose the ground under one's feet – nowadays thousands, even millions of people live excellently, not dwelling on the Church at all. They have other havens, to all appearances rather firm and reliable. But yet Luther entered the monastery because he found no other means to defend his weak and solitary soul from the dread danger advancing out of somewhere (he himself did not yet know whither). He broke with the whole world – the Church was all by which he lived, and on which he relied. And suddenly the suspicion, gradually transitioning to an unshakable conviction, that where he dreamt to find the Kingdom of God, there was the kingdom of Satan. Thence the beginning of Luther's apostasy. And, perhaps, in history we do not know of another case, when the meaning and significance of apostasy would have received a clearer and more omnilateral illumination.

That's why it's so mistaken to judge of Luther by Lutheranism. Lutheranism is already well organized; Lutheranism already has its past, its traditions, its foundations.

The essence and content of Luther's break consist in exactly the point, that it is bereft of the support of tradition, that those foundations which were created by thousand-year historical development were breaking up underneath him. Thus it is possible to not only agree with the Catholics, who affirm that Lutheranism renounced Luther and in its very essence turned to Catholicism; one can go further, one can say, that just as soon as Luther had to formalize his experiences and transform them into doctrine, he by that fact was compelled to renounce himself. In this apparently paradoxical transformation lay concealed the most profound mystery of religious experiences and religious creative work. Perhaps, one can also find in this an explanation of those eternal and irreconcilable contradictions, over which even until the present the theoreticians of not only Protestantism but of any religion have to occupy their heads. Here's why, if you wish to discover the history of the actual Luther, read, besides his own works, investigations on him, done not by his friends and followers, Protestants, but by his irreconcilable enemies – the Catholics. Although one cannot state the converse, in Protestants you will not find what is necessary to evaluate and understand Catholicism. Denifle's book, which I have already mentioned, as well as the huge investigation of Grisar, and the less significant, although very interesting works of French Catholics, in spite of all their enmity to Luther or, more exactly, thanks to this enmity, display the most grudge-filled, but alongside that the most significant inquests of the believing soul, solitary, left by himself.

That Luther was a believer, of that there can be no doubt, as there can be no doubt that he was an apostate. For Catholicism, faith and the Catholic Church have always been identified with one another even to the present day. Extra ecclesiam nemo salvatur (no salvation outside the Church).

The well-known Catholic theologian Albert Maria Weiss says directly: 'The present followers of Luther are divided from the Catholic not by a more or less significant difference of opinion in separate dogmatic questions, but by a complete and principled non-recognition of ecclesiastical authority.' And again:

An ein äusserliches, d.h. an ein von dem freien Willen der Gläubigen unabhängiges, an ein nicht durch sie übertragenes und nicht von ihrer Zustimmung bedingtes Recht, und demzufolge an eine Pflicht der Unterwerfung unter eine überlegene Macht kann hier nicht gedacht werden. Und das gilt dann nicht mehr bloss in foro externo, in rein rechtlichen Dingen, sondern auch in foro interno, soweit es sich um sittliche und religiöse Vorgänge im Gewissen handelt. Der Sazerdotalismus, wie sich in neuester Zeit George Tyrell ausdrückt, d.h. jene Grundlehre der katholischen Kirche, dass die Gewalt über die Seelen durch Gott selbst unmittelbar von oben gegeben wird, fällt dann gleichfalls als unmöglich hinweg.[102]

(Denifle und Weis, II, 411, 413)

You see that the modern Catholic almost literally reproduces the words of the Grand Inquisitor from Brothers Karamazov.

The most terrible crime of Luther consists in the fact that he could not acknowledge for the Catholic Church that fullness of power, that authority of infallibility – not only in material questions but also in spiritual questions, which it assumed for itself. The Catholic Church considers that it – and only it – receives that power unmediated from God. To it and it only is given the right to bind and loose – potestas clavium. And what it looses on earth, that will be loosed in heaven, and what it binds on earth, that will be bound in heaven. God delegated his power to the successor of the Apostle Peter and now He Himself cannot add or subtract anything from that which was once proclaimed. Here's how the well-known dogmatic Pohle formulates this potestas clavium of the Catholic Church:

Wenn Christus also dem Petrus 'die Schlüssel des Himmelreiches' übergibt so überträgt er ihm damit die Vollgewalt, in der Kirche Christi zu schalten und zu walten, in die Kirche einzulassen und Davon auszuschliessen, alle Personen zu regieren und alle Sachen zu verwalten. Gesetze zu erlassen und aufzuheben, Strafen zu verhängen und zu erlassen, kurz, die ganze Fülle königlichrichterlicher Gewalt über die ganze Kirche, d.i. über seine Mitapostel und die Gläubigen … Was immer aber Petrus in seiner Eigenschaft als oberster 'Schlüsselträger' (claviger) tut, *das heist Gott im Himmel gut.*

(Pohle, III, 420–1)

Weil diese wichtige Gewalt jedoch kein persönliches Privileg sein sollte, das mit dem Tode der Apostel erlosch, so folgt, dass es eine fortdauernde Macht der Sündenvergebung in der Kirche geben muss, und zwar einer wirklichen und wahren Vergebung, da die Lospechungen auf Erden auch im Himmel, d.i vor Gott (in foro divino) Gültigkeit besitzen sollen … Würde Gott wirklich eine (Tod) Sünde im Himmel binden, d.i.nicht verzeihen, welche die Kirche auf Erden rechtmässig gelöst, d.i. nachgelassen hat, so trügen die Verheissungsworte Christi den Stempel der Unwahrheit an sich.[103]

(Pohle, III, 422)

I think that now after the adduced examples from Weiss' and Pohle's works, it will be clear to anyone that the Grand Inquisitor of Dostoevsky accurately recounted the fundamental doctrine of Catholicism. The only difference is that Dostoevsky's Inquisitor speaks in the raised voice of a man who understands the whole burden – incommensurate with mortal strength – of the burden of responsibility taken on himself. Pohle and Weiss, obviously, don't suspect this. They are convinced that this power and these 'rights', as any sort of right and power, are well within range not only of those whom they consider infallible, in the capacity of the successor of the Apostle Peter, but even of themselves. If they were assigned to 'bind and loose', they would have serenely taken this obligation on themselves, as they would have taken on themselves the obligation of world judge, or boss of the earth – in full assurance that it is no more difficult than other human obligations – that they would have handled it no worse than the next guy. And their manner of speaking recalls the business-like tone of usual, everyday judgements on usual everyday themes. They have a precisely formulated definite doctrine – how hard can it be to apply general principles to specific situations?

The theologian, the doctor, the administrator, the world judge, they all have the same problems of subsuming the individual phenomenon under the rule. And the task of the Catholic theologian, it may be, is the simplest and clearest. Once the potestas clavium is in the hands of the infallible Pope, that means the theologian, unlike the doctor or engineer, cannot be mistaken. Everything that he does on earth will, as Pohle expresses it, be acknowledged by God in the heavens.

I remind the reader again that the idea of potestas clavium is taken by Catholicism; lock, stock and barrel from Hellenism. We know the reasoning of Socrates, Plato and Aristotle on eternal principles. Socrates built all of his philosophy on the position that men could know all things, that there exists an organic connection between this side and the other side and that, thus, man in his earthly life knows, what he ought to do, so as to secure his bliss in the life beyond the grave. For it's the same thing that Catholicism, too, affirms: only in place of the infallible Catholic Church Socrates has put reason, never mistaken and assuredly heading to its goal or, expressed more exactly, more precisely in chronological order – in place of the self-assured reason Catholicism has put the One, Infallible Church.

We recall that Plato said that there is no greater misfortune for a man than to become a hater of reason. The Catholic says there's no greater misfortune than to renounce the Catholic Church. Weiss exclaims with horror à propos the Reformation movement beginning, in his opinion, with Occam, Wycliffe and Hus and concluding with Luther: 'The fearsome disintegration of Christianity. We can destroy our neighbor, or lead him to danger and perdition. But, if the talk concerns the salvation of our neighbor, then they say: save yourselves, no one can help you, you must take care of yourselves.' It seems to the Catholic that if a man will not help a man, then he can depend on no one and nothing. This is strange, almost improbable, but it's so. Thence the dispute of Catholicism and Luther on the church visible. A Catholic cannot reconcile himself to the idea that Christ left men and did not leave in His place His deputy bedecked in fullness of power.

The dogma of the infallibility of the Pope, although promulgated only about fifty years ago, is only the final expression of that fundamental idea of Catholicism, taken by it whole from Hellenic philosophy.

The visible Church is embodied in the Pope and the thousand-year human anxiety for a finite goal, brooking no objections and putting an end to palpitations, achieves its resolution. Msgr. Bougaud, presenting the essence of the dogma of Papal infallibility, exclaims:

> Voilà, dans sa simplicité, dans sa netteté, dans sa grandeur, dans sa force, cette définition de l'infallibilité, attendue si impatiemment par les uns, et que les autres déclaraient impossible. Mais l'Eglise, qui sait ce qu'elle est, ce qu'elle possède, a le don de le dire. Ni emphase, ni exagèration, ni faiblesse. Une simplicité parfait, sous laquelle on sent une force surnaturelle. Et en même temps le voilà, ce grand privilège de l'infallibilité doctrinale, *sans laquel une religion ne se conçoit pas*, qu'aucune religion cependant n'a revendiqué; dont aucune secte n'a osé conserver le nom; que l'Eglise catholique seule réclame et exerce depuis dix-huit siècles et dont elle vient de déterminer avec une hardiesse superbe le siège et l'organe: hardiesse qui n'est pas d'une être humain et qui suffrait á elle seule à prouve sa divinité.[104]
>
> (Le christianisme et les temps présents, IV, 122)

I won't try to dispute the historical accuracy of the respectable prelate's point that not a single church besides the Catholic Church has ever laid claim to infallibility. For us it is much more important to establish that that same Socrates, whose philosophy is considered the official philosophy of Catholicism, claimed infallibility with no less boldness than the Pope in 1871. Huh, that serves as proof of the divinity of human reason? For Catholicism with the same assurance with which it affirms the great and marvellous prerogatives of the Pope contests the claims of all other people to infallibility? And here in this stubborn striving of Catholicism to find at whatever the cost and as fast as possible here on earth a visible, tangible, all-accessible authority, isn't what's displayed the whole depth of unbelief characteristic of the whole majority of people? How can one entrust one's fate to someone whom no one has seen or touched? Weiss goes into horror at the thought that man cannot help man; Bougaud triumphs at the thought that finally the man's been found, who can answer all questions. As the Hellenes in antiquity, in the epoch of paganism, so now people, having for almost two thousand years absorbed the books of the Holy Scripture, have not resolved to seek beyond the limits of the accessible and comprehensible. They invoke the name of God but live and wish to live only by their own mind. There've been bad, corrupt, talentless, avaricious Popes, and of course, there'll be more of these anon: better to trust such a Pope than that God, of whom it says in the Holy Scripture that one cannot look upon Him, that one who has looked upon Him can no longer live.

Catholicism did not renounce the Holy Scripture, but it knew how 'to interpret it', i.e., level it to the quotidian demands of man.

<u>A côté de chaque dogme terrible, Mgr Bougaud, il y a dans le catholicisme un second dogme qui l'adoucit, qui en rend la pointe moins pénétrante et moins dure. Et c'est par là que l'Eglise catholique ravit les âmes et les contient, les domine en les enchantant.</u>[105]

(Bougaud, IV, p. 298)

What can I say, it's a good device and yields brilliant results in practice. Catholicism could always enchant human souls and direct them to the desired side, adding to each terrible dogma another one that mollifies it. But this device has not always turned out to be the thing. There have been cases, when this 'mollification' of Catholicism turned out more unendurable than the most tormenting and merciless cruelty. Doesn't mollification and condescension indicate an exaggerated trust in the human and a fear to stand face to face with the Omnipotent Creator? Not only Catholicism knows this mollification; it has been communicated to Protestantism as well. Even the freethinking historian Harnack, we recall, allows faith to be supported on external authority. It would be too cruel to demand from weak, solitary man that he renounce all support, all ground. And Harnack also mollifies the 'terrible' truth and allows even Luther to seek his ultimate truth not in heaven but on earth.

XI

But life does not know the sentimentality and condescension characteristic of Catholic theologians. Life led Luther from completely the other end to those terrible dogmas, which Monsignor Bougaud covers up with a practised hand. The root question for each Christian was and is the question of salvation of the soul. Catholicism, considering that the <u>potestas clavium</u>, limited by nothing, belongs to it on earth, was convinced, of course, as well, that both its right and its obligation consist in utilizing the power belong to it in all its fullness. It opens the doors of the heavenly kingdom to the worthy and closes them to the unworthy. And it exactly, definitely knows who is worthy and who is unworthy. That's not all; it has worked out a clear and distinct scale, by which it directs, separating its children. In order to be saved, one must fulfil a series of conditions and requirements. True, Catholicism accepted wholly the interpretations proposed by Bl. Augustine of the epistles of Apostle Paul and his doctrine of <u>gratia praeveniens</u>. Both in the Middle Ages, as well as at the present time, Pelagianism and even semi-Pelagianism were condemned as harmful heresies. The favourite theme of Catholic theologians was reasonings about grace. But these reasonings only conceded what was and has even now remained the nerve of all Catholicism, and which found completely adequate expression in the formula <u>facienti quod in se est Deus infallibiliter dat gratiam</u>.[106] It stands to reason that this was indeed the complementary 'doctrine' of which Monsignor Bougaud spoke and which was intended to mollify the 'terrible doctrine' of <u>gratia praeveniens</u> (prevenient [antecedent] grace). If you ever take it in the mollified form, as Denifle demands, if you say <u>non denegat gratiam</u> (will not refuse grace), instead of <u>infallibiter dat</u> (surely give), the essence of the matter changes not a bit from this. All the same, to him who fulfils everything, which fulfilment is in his power, God will not refuse His grace. It's clear that the Pope, too, for all his infallibility, cannot get by without this 'mollification'; it's also clear that Catholics, too, can breathe easier when it's announced to them that, in the final account, salvation all the same is in their hands. The Pope had the entire fullness of <u>potestas clavium</u>, but this power with its fullness is transformed to an empty sound, once salvation of the soul completely depends on <u>gratia praeveniens</u>.

The Pope wished to make use of his power so as, threatening punishment to some and promising reward to others, to direct his flock on those paths which he considered the singularly true.

The flock, who in this respect differed in no way from its pastor, also demanded that there be issued <u>suum cuique</u> (to each his due), so that the workers were rewarded, those who refuse to work would receive their fitting retribution. The concept of the just reward, so intertwined with the ideas of earthly justice, naturally translated from the earthly life to the life beyond the grave. No one wished and no one could allow that the laws of justice and truth had limited significance, and beyond well-known temporal and spatial limits lost their power. If Thomas Aquinas said '<u>in operibus Dei non est aliquid frustra, sicut nec in operibus naturae</u>'[107] (C.G. 3, 156. Denifle, II, 314) – as we know, the favourite, and so characteristic analogy for Thomas – then with still more right one may say that the idea of justice, which is already on earth, and manifests itself in the actions and judgements of man, is all the more essential in the judgements of God. Only under such presupposition was the existence of Catholicism possible as well. Theoretically, the doctrine on <u>merita</u> seems like the pea hidden under eighty pillows, but factually <u>merita</u> and <u>satisfaction</u> dominated Catholic doctrine. As with Socrates, as in the Middle Ages, despite the epistle of the Apostle Paul and the works of Bl. Augustine and all those who followed him, people absolutely did not endure the idea that the resolution of the question as important for them as the question of the salvation of the soul did not lie in their hands.[108] They praised Bl. Augustine, but they believed Pelagius, reverently honoured the Apostle Paul, but followed Socrates.

Young Luther, in this respect, was no wise different than his (or our) contemporaneous Catholics. Although we cannot say with exactitude which circumstances exactly roused him completely unexpected for everyone, against the will of his father, to go while still completely a youth into the monastery, obviously, he resolved on this fateful step – no matter what the Protestants say – for he considered that only the monastic life is the perfect life, that only the monastery guarantees man perfect life, and that by this more perfect life he will be able to please God and earn forgiveness and eternal life. Consequently he himself affirmed that God sent him into the camp of the Antichrists just exactly so he could see with his own eyes the abomination of desolation in the place where the altar of the Lord ought to be located, and he proclaimed what he saw to the world. But, of course, he was a thousand versts from such suspicions when he stepped over the threshold of his new refuge. He was convinced that he was heading to the Holy place – to accomplish a great God-pleasing heroic exploit of self-renunciation, and by that remit from his soul some heavy, unendurable sin – his own or another's, we never have discovered. He was led to the monastery by the great thirst for heroic exploit, and the conviction that only by heroic acts could one be purified of sin. Apparently, such an urge to dedicate one's whole life to one's God deserves the highest praise. Apparently, the monastery was the most very suitable place for realization of such a laudable intention. But something truly improbable occurred with Luther. After ten or eleven years of monastic life, he began to feel that he served not God, but the devil, that what he did was not heroic exploit, but crime. Not that he was an insufficiently zealous monk. Even Catholics and such fierce slanderers of Luther as the recently deceased Dominican monk Denifle cannot impeach Luther on any serious accusations. With all the conscientiousness of which only a man with great will, and with sincerity unique of its kind is capable, he fulfilled the vows he had made at his tonsure. In the Catholic literature Luther is accused not because he evaded the stern prescriptions of the statutes of his order – on the contrary, he is reproached with the absence of the virtue of moderation. This same Dominican monk Denifle, sallying forth against Luther with such passion, exactly as though he were not a dead man, passing from the world several hundred years ago, but rather a live enemy, from whom one can expect every minute new and terrible onslaughts, this same Denifle, I say, dedicated dozens of pages of his book, in many respects really remarkable, to prove that Luther, allowing excess into the stern regime of his life, acted against the fundamental principles of monasticism. Denifle is a very learned man and an excellent connoisseur of the medieval. And he in point of fact has managed to collect a rather significant number of quotations supporting the correctness of his position. But, all the same, one cannot agree with them, as one cannot agree with his other affirmation that Catholic monks saw in their monasticism only the possibility of easier attainment of perfection – and not the beginning of perfection itself. The very tone of Denifle's book demonstrates the opposite. More than that, Denifle's very book and all his unrestrained hatred, hatred to the point of impropriety, of Luther is only explained by the fact that Luther resolves to acknowledge the uselessness of monastic labours. The monk Denifle, enduring to the end his temptations, cannot forgive the apostate Luther this, who arbitrarily released himself from imposed vows. If Luther is right, if the heroic exploit of monastic renunciation does not bring man nearer to God, if those who fulfil the difficult vows are just as little perfect, as those who are broken down under their weight, then what is all Denifle's life work worth? Luther dared write about the most perfect monk of the Middle Ages, about St Bernard of Clairvaux, who when he was near death, could say nothing other than that he had wasted all his years in vain, for he had lived badly – <u>nihil aliud sonuit quam confessionem hujusmodi: tempus meum perditi, quia perdite vixi</u>[109] (Denifle, I, 41). Denifle, disgracing the Protestant scholars, who accepted Luther's reference without verification, demonstrates that St Bernard pronounced these words not on his death bed but in a sermon on the theme of the Song of Songs, and that in the context they do not support the interpretation which Luther wishes to give them. And Denifle, of course, is right. Luther had no basis to interpret these words as he interpreted them, asserting that Bernard put his faith only on Christ, and not on this own works; he was praised not for vows of poverty, moderation, obedience to be ends, he called life in vows a bad life, <u>perdita vita</u>, and in this faith he preserved himself and saved himself along with other saints. Think you, that he lied, or told it in jest, that he destroyed his life? ... If you hear from the lips of the just man, that the vows and monastic life are rejected, that they have no significance for righteousness and salvation, then who will come to give vows and fulfill those given?

When Denifle hears such a thing, he loses all his self-control. For if Bernard of Clairvaux, to whom Luther too relates with reverent respect, was obliged to acknowledge, that <u>tempus meum perditi, quia perdite vixi</u>, then what is he, Denifle, to say? All of his difficult, tormenting life of the conscientious monk was for nothing. In the final moment he must acknowledge that at the Last Judgement he will have no advantage over those people who feckless, among light pleasures and amusements strolled their life paths. But Luther was not satisfied with such assertions. He saw terrible blasphemy in monastic vows. The monk giving his vows, in Luther's words, says: <u>Ecce, Deus, ego tibi voveo impietatem et idolatriam tota vita</u>.

Luther speaks without end on this theme. And Denifle himself collected a whole series of notations from Luther's works – probably so as to justify both his rage and his sentence on his opponent. For us what Luther said of monks presents special interest because what Luther said in his attacks does not proceed from the same considerations by which monasticism is usually used to subsist. Luther says little of the dissipation or corruption regnant behind the monastery walls. Those monks, who entered into the monastery for worldly goals, are not a worthy target for Luther's thunders, and if Luther recalls them, it's only in passing. Anyone can deal with them – Luther has another more difficult and more serious task.

He considers that actual, honourable monks, those before whom all bow, even atheists – that exactly these, offering their vows, enter into Satan's service. Not just anybody, I repeat, but Bernard of Clairvaux himself, whose personality impressed even Luther – he represents no exception. He too dedicated his whole life to the praise of dishonour and idolatry and only in the final minute repented and acknowledged that <u>perdidi annos meos, quia perdite vixi</u>, and thus saved his soul. And for this they bore terrible punishment while still alive. Many years after his first forays, Luther describes the life of the monks in such expressions:

<u>genus hominum perditissimum libidinibus, scortationibus et adulteriis, qui dies notesque tantum ludos suos venereos somniant ac imaginantur, quid ipsi facturi essent, si talis licentia (ut patriarchis) concederetur, ut singulis noctibus conjuges permutare possent, et cum eis ludere secundum flammas et ardorem carnis, sciut cum scortis duis ludunt.</u>[110]

(Opp. Exeg. Lat. VII, 277, Denifle, I, 313)

Citing this passage, Denifle spitefully asks, how the reformer knows what the innumerable monks, having given the vow of celibacy, dream of at night and what they see in their dreams. The question is doubtless legitimate and – let it not be said to insult Protestant theologians – the answer which Denifle gives must be accepted without any looking back or limitation. Yes, Luther learned everything of monks that he later told in his innumerable works exactly from his personal horrible experiences. Harnack says that to write his book, Denifle had to make Luther a monster. Denifle did not have to do that – Luther himself had to experience the horrible consciousness that he was the last of men, worse than the very last. No one else, he himself pronounced the terrible vow: <u>ecce, Deus, tibi voveo</u>, etc. This and only this that Luther not metaphorically, not only figuratively, but fully really fell into the power of Satan and was clearly conscious of this – explains that unusual spiritual uplift, which gave him the possibility to tear himself away from the ground on which he had grown up, which he had been used to consider native – and drew millions of men after him. If Harnack were right, if Luther sought authority for his faith, how could he rebel against his own birth mother? And yet the Catholic Church was mother to him – he ran first to her for defence when the strange visions visited him first in early youth, which were never later to quit him all his life. And it was not others but himself he condemned when he predestined monks to eternal perdition. This was not felt either by the Protestants, who wish to see models of all earthly virtues in their teacher, or by Denifle, who did not spare the black paints to depict Luther as the most repulsive possible. The Protestants justify, Denifle condemns Luther – just as though in actual fact the whole <u>potestas clavium</u> is in their hands, and that which Harnack or Denifle says attains in heaven the same indisputable recognition, which it claims on earth: depict him white – the gates of the heavenly kingdom are open to him; depict him black – he falls to hell. The sufferings and dissatisfaction of Denifle are comprehensible and psychologically explicable.

Denifle was already an old man when he wrote his book on Luther, how must it have been for him to hear such a terrible sentence over all his life, already finishing, into the past. Imagine that after the court had already pronounced their final sentence over him, they had demanded from Socrates an admission, that the sentence was not an act of violence of a crude and unenlightened crowd but rather the just punishment for all that 'good' which Socrates had done in the course of this whole life. That not only force but truth is not on his side but on the side of the disdained and unworthy Anitus and Melitus. For Socrates also thought that he had dedicated his whole life to good. And suddenly they would announce to him that he served evil, that he gave a vow to serve evil: <u>Ecce, Deus, voveo tibi voveo impietatem et idolatriam tota vita</u>. Even the very possibility of such a transformation is improbable. Denifle cannot, of course, remain in debt to Luther. Drawing himself up to his full height, not so small either, in a loud voice he pronounces his anathema on Luther. He, following Reigger, calls him <u>omnium bipedum nequissimus</u>[111] (Denifle, I, 319) and announces there is no place in heaven for Luther and for the monks relapsed after him, if they do not in their final hours renounce their blasphemous doctrine and life. So people thunder against one another (Catholic and Protestant) and each thunders in full conviction of his correctness. Both Luther and Denifle hurl their lightning in the name of the One, Omnipotent, Never-mistaken God. Where is truth, on whose side? And can it be these terrible anathemas are absolutely impotent, and heaven just as disinterestedly regards the thunders of monks arguing, as it regards the other sounds coming from earth?

I've purposely recalled Socrates and his opponents, for I know that the modern reader with a light soul sacrifices Luther to Denifle or the opposite and stands up for Socrates and his truth when Anitus and Melitus dare trespass on it. But it is a great mistake, explicable only by the inability to understand the past, to think that the argument of Denifle and Luther has become anachronistic and unnecessary for us. Only the words which they utter are archaic and anachronistic. The essence of the matter for which they struggle is no less near to us, even nearer, than that matter for which Socrates paid with his life. And just because Luther, and not Anitus and Melitus, rebelled against Socrates personified in Denifle, the argument acquires special significance and interest. For Denifle is not some superficial journeyman; it was not for transitory gain that he took on himself the defence of Catholicism against the long dead, yet still living enemy. He devoted his whole life to high service and before death came to the terrible, the ultimate battle with the spectre, poisoning the tranquillity of his elder years.

XII

Of what does the terrible crime of the monastics consist, which led Luther to the conviction, that the Pope and all of Catholicism had gone over to the Antichrist and leads humanity to eternal perdition? I repeat insistently that, if Luther had to indict the numerous malfeasances, which were as a matter of fact a usual phenomenon in the life of that clergy of his epoch – that would not have repelled him from the Catholic Church. One can struggle with malfeasances, with bad habits, and with bad people, without resorting to such heroic means as schism.

Where there's people, there's always filth, a lot of it. Luther, soon after his overt foray against the Pope, had to be convinced that his personal supporters were far from distinguished by only virtues alone. And there is no doubt that among the numerous nuns and monks, who had responded to Luther's call, there were very few who understood what Luther sought. The new word of freedom was interpreted by the crowd in the crudest sense, and Catholics, not diverging from historical truth, drew the most repulsive pictures of the dissipated life of Luther's first followers.

But Luther himself, although such sort of adherents were repulsive to him with his whole soul, was little disturbed by them. He headed to his goal, not looking back and not considering ahead the practical results to which his new doctrine ought to lead. No other way: Lot's wife, leaving Sodom, looked back and turned to a pillar of salt. If Luther had looked back, the same lot would have awaited him. And, to the extent he looked back, and, in the final end, when history entrusted him with the governance of the fate of nations, he would have to converse not only with God but with man as well. He himself would have been continuously horrified at his own visions. Denifle, and, yes, all Catholics, completely correctly assert that Luther's doctrine of salvation, which is the <u>articulus stantis et cadentis ecclesiae</u>[112] (Loofs, 741), was never accepted by a single Protestant in the form in which Luther presented it. One can say even more, one can say along with Denifle: <u>Luther hat der Kirche eine von ihm verzehrte Lehre untergeschoben, um fur sich die echt katholische in Pacht zu nehmen</u>[113] (Denifle, I, 220). And as a matter of fact, as we'll see now, not only the Lutherans but Luther himself did not know what to do in practical life with his doctrine of <u>sola fide</u>. When he was left alone with himself, when he looked forward into infinity, he felt that there faith is everything, that it and it alone gives both strength and hope, and even comfort. Just as soon as he turned back to men, he saw that the Catholics were right. Faith is terrible for men [Людям вера страшна] – men need authority, firm, unlimited, merciless, even unchanging power. And Luther began to converse in just such a language, just as though he had indeed never drawn near to Sinai and not heard the new words revealed to him in the storm and fury. He himself, like Lot's wife, turned into a pillar of salt. History never dealt with Luther the prophet. Prophets aren't necessary for it. It has always stoned them and always will. History needs reformers and people who want to and can look back, who possess the knack which gives them the possibility of previewing beforehand all the practical consequences of their doctrines and enterprises. History valued this side of Luther and for this the name of Luther is inscribed by the Germans in letters of gold along with the other brilliant names who facilitated the rebirth of the German nationhood. All the rest that Luther thought, felt and saw has been shaken down and measured by Protestantism, who relates to the actual Luther with no less enmity and hatred than does Catholicism. Of course, the good Luther stands way higher than Luther and his 'doctrine' and way nearer to that Catholicism, to whose defence Denifle rose.

Luther taught <u>hominem sola fide justificari</u>. That one little word <u>sola</u> had indeed dug an abyss between Catholicism and Luther – it then disappeared completely in Protestantism, as we'll see later. Even at the very beginning of his commentary on <u>Ad Romanos</u>, published even before Luther's break with Catholicism, you read the following lines:

<u>Inveniuntur sane multi, qui sinistraria bona i.e., termporalia propter Deum nihil reputent et bene perdant ut judei et heretici. Sed qui dextraria i.e., bona spiritualia et opera justa velint nihil reputare propter Christi justitiam acquirendam pauci sunt. Hoc einem judei et heretici non possunt. Et tamen nisi fiat, nemo salvabitur. Semper enim volunt et sperant ipsa coram Deo reputari et premiari. Sed stat fixa sententil: 'Non est volentis neque currentis, sed miserentis Dei'.</u>[114]
(Luther, <u>Ad Romanos,</u> I, 1; W 56, 159; Ficker, 3)

Pagans too are capable of renouncing usual earthly goods for the sake of the Lord, but you won't find many who are ready for the sake of Christ's truth to renounce spiritual goods and righteous deeds. Included in this affirmation already <u>in nuce</u> is not only all his commentary but everything that Luther came at any time at all to say about faith. Just so, the paradoxical, unacceptable for usual common sense becomes the most attractive for Luther. With the avidity of a man starving in the desert, he attacks the most mysterious places of the epistles of the Apostle Paul and not only does not try to accommodate them to the conditions of human understanding, as Catholicism did, but with all the strength of his colossal writer's talent he strove to display the complete impossibility of reconciling reason with faith. From all his most inspired writings there wafts the terrible incarnations of the prophet Isaiah and the Apostle Paul – I will destroy the wisdom of the wise and the reasons of the reasoners I will overturn (Isa. 29,14; I Cor. 1, 19).

He who counts on his wisdom, on his righteousness, on his strength, will never be saved. From this conviction came Luther's revulsion for Catholicism in general and for monasticism in particular. He, who counts on his merits, on his works, by that point displays his unbelief. Augustine said: <u>Initium omnis peccati superbia. Initium superbiae hominis apostatare a deo</u>[115] (De nat. et grat. 29, 33; Loofs, 382). Pride, i.e., assurance in oneself, that you know where to go and how to go, that you count on your reason and your skill to wrest out of those tight limits, in which mortal human beings are enclosed, is the beginning of the most terrible sin, threatening eternal perdition – the sin of apostasy from God. He who depends on himself has renounced God. For there can be nothing common between how man saves himself from his woes and how God saves man. The more a man makes an effort, the more intensely he applies himself to distinguish himself above and beyond others by his works, his heroic exploits, and to lay himself down a path to the heavenly kingdom, the more he moves away from God. <u>Opertet ergo hominem de suis operibus diffidere et *velut parlyticum* remissis manibus et pedibus gratiam operum artificem implorare</u> (Luther, Weimar, II, 420; Denifle, I, 581). Man ought not to trust his own works; just like a paralytic, without use of legs and arms, he ought to call to grace, the only one doing the works. Of course, this motif was not alien to Catholicism. Thomas à Kempis wrote: <u>Non superbiam de operibus tuis, quia aliter sunt judicia Dei, quam hominum, qui saepe displicet, quod hominibus placet.</u>[116] But the resemblance here is more external. Thomas à Kempis only wished to say by this that man is inclined to overvalue his works and still see merits where they no longer are, in other words, that the judgement of God is sterner and less hypocritical than human judgement. Luther though directly says that the judgement of God and human judgement have nothing in common. Here's what Spinoza expressed, as we recall, in his formula of the reason and will of God. God does not recompense – as earthly judges do – and does not punish. God creates, and the essence of grace consists in that, overshadowing the dead man, it gives him life. In the same commentary to the epistle to the Romans he writes:

> <u>Quid superbit homo de meritis suis et operibus, quae nullo modo placent, quia sunt bona vel merita, sed quia sunt a Deo electa ab aeterno ei placitura? Non ergo nisi gratias agendo bene operamur. Quia opera nos non faciunt bonos, sed bonitas nostra, immo bonitas Dei facit nos bonos et opera nostra bona. Quia non essent in se bona, nisi quia Deus reputat ea bona, et tantum sunt vel non sunt, quantum ille reputat vel non reputat.</u>[117]
>
> (Luther, Comm. ep. ad. Rom.; Denifle, I, 596; Ficker, 221; W 56, 394)

You see that in his doctrine of grace Luther has simply been transported out of the plane on which the eventual thought of the Catholic theologian operates. One can no longer bring Luther into agreement with Denifle. Denifle, like any other Catholic, is profoundly convinced, as Albert Weiss expresses it, of the organic connection between the natural and the supernatural. No matter how he bows before the greatness of the Creator, no matter how much he affirms the unsearchability of the paths of God, he always holds in his reserve the right to demand a just judge for himself, i.e., that judge, who maintains principles, which he (Denifle) honours as just. That is, using Socrates' expression, God loves the good because it is good, not that the good is good because God loved it. To Socrates and to the Catholics the opposite affirmation seems madness. In Luther it evokes a true access of rapture. The hairs stand on Denifle's head when he reads the feverish, really delirious speech of Luther. Quis enim eum potest amare, qui secundum justitiam cum peccatoribus vult agere? Haec exposito periculossissima est, praeterquam quod vana est; concidat enim occultum odium contra Deum et ejus justitiam[118] (Enarr. in Ps. 51; Denifle, I, 396). Luther tries even to 'provide a foundation', prove his correctness: si placet tibi deus indignos coronans, non debet etiam displicere immeritos damnans; si illic justus est, cur non justus erit.[119] I don't think that such 'proof' would seem convincing to anyone. But Luther's force and significance are not in the convincingness of his dialectic. If he, by force of habit, and so as not to give way to his opponents, then expounds an argument – then for the most part it's just as successful, as in the case cited. But perhaps his logical and dialectical helplessness the more attracts us to him. It does not have its source in an incapacity for consistent thought. It is a consequence of disdain for rational conclusions. Luther felt that his reason can give him just as little as his good works. Therein, too, the learned monastery of Aristotle, with its stern code of thought, not allowing scientifically unproven and unprovable truths behind the stone wall, evokes the same horror in his soul as did the Catholic monasteries. As long as you live by good works and logical (also good) reasoning, everything that is necessary to a man remains beyond the limits of attainability. Luther strives to burst out of the atmosphere in which men live. How to overcome the laws of gravity – when the very idea of overcoming the law is non sens and striving – insane. In his De servo arbitrio, one of his most remarkable books, answers to the deviationist Erasmus of Rotterdam, who resolved, finally, after long vacillations, per the insistence of highly placed contemporaries, to come up for overturning Luther's doctrine – Luther goes to the extreme limits of paradoxical affirmations. Even Protestants, and such as Otto Ritschl, would with pleasure give it to the property of Catholicism, but Luther speaks of it differently: nullum agnosco meum justum librum, nisi forte de servo arbitrio et catechismum[120] (Loofs, 761). And, really, these two of his books are the most remarkable – for Luther the religious thinker and Luther the reformer. We'll talk of catechistics further along. Now I'll adduce his following words from De servo arbitrio as explanation of what was said earlier about justitia Dei and faith: Hic est fidei summus gradus credere illum esse clementum, qui tam paucos salvat – justum, qui sua voluntate nos damnabiles facit[121] (Luther, De Serv. Arb. 124; W 18, 633). Who gave Luther the right to speak so? When they retorted to Luther, that he had no right to interject the word sola into the translation of Apostle Paul, we recall that he answered sit pro ratione voluntas.¹²²

In 1535 he wrote à propos his doctrine of sola fide: sum enim certus et persuasus per spiritum Christi meam doctrinam de Christiana justitia veram et certam esse.¹²³ This is his ultima ratio. He has no proofs and cannot – for he regards natural reason, the source of all truths, with unheard-of disdain. Frau Hulde, die naturliche Vernunft, diese Hure des Teufels und Erzfeindin des Glaubens¹²⁴ (Loofs, 7470). Luther toppled ratio from the throne. And to the vacant throne some other ruler ascended, in any case per his profile most of all similar to the capricious, changeable voluntas, than to the stultified and forever immovable control apparatus. It is the highest degree of faith – to acknowledge as beneficent Him who saves so few, to see justice in Him, Who created us sinners. You can retort to Luther that such an affirmation contains an odium occultum contra Deum et ejus justitiam (secret hatred of God and His justice). And your retort will be correct, but it won't stop Luther. Luther is not afraid of the arbitrariness of God – Luther fears human arbitrariness. And perhaps, one must experience for oneself, as Luther experienced, all the heavy and unendurable burden of human despotism and limitation, embodied in Catholicism and secular wisdom in order to feel readiness to devote one's whole soul to the unknown, and with faith that seems madness to men, to extinguish all the lights which illuminate the habitual life path, and head-down rush to the eternal darkness. He even says so directly in his Commentary to the Epistle to the Romans:

> ad primam gratiam sicut et ad gloriam semper nos habemus passive sicut mulier ad conceptum … Ideo licet ante gratiam nos oremus et petamus, tamen quando gratia venit et anima impregnanda est spiritu, oportet, quod neque oret, neque operetur, sed solum patiatur. Quod certe durum est fieri et vehementer affligit, quia animam sine actu intelligendi et volendi esse est eam in tenebras ac velut in perditionem et annihilationem ire.¹²⁵
>
> (Ad Romanos, 8, 26; Grisard, I, I, 201; W 56, 379; Ficker, 206)

Listen carefully to these words – they have special significance for us. To accept eternal darkness, perdition, annihilation – to go where, per human understanding there is not, nor can be salvation. The young Luther already felt this – he was thirty-three years old when he wrote his commentary from which the adduced excerpt is taken. Afterwards, when the movement of Schwarmgeisters began, under the influence of Luther's preaching, he wrote to Melanchthon: 'You want to know, when and how we gained God's revelation. When that occurred, of which it is said: like a lion, he crushed my bones' (Isa. 38, 13). The greatness of God cannot favourably speak with the old man, without having proactively crushed him (An Melanchthon; Grisar, I, 422). Ad primam gratiam … semper nos habemus passive, sicut mulier ad conceptum (Ad Romanos, W 56, 379). One ought to say that all the medieval mystics, in that number Tauler and the unknown author of Theologia Deutsch, who influenced Luther, i.e., all those people who claimed that they had to sense unmediated the Spirit of the Lord repeat the same thing that

Luther said and share the moment of passivity and reception of grace, as those supporting the words of the Apostle Paul, which Luther so often recollected in old age: 'No longer do I live, but Christ lives in me.'

In the modern, even Catholic tracts, a specific sign of mystical or supernatural conditions is the complete impossibility to evoke them by personal human efforts, even for a minute and even in a weakened form.[126] In order that the above-cited speeches of Luther become more comprehensible or, more accurately, more accessible – even Luther himself did not succeed in truly understanding them –we recall what Tolstoy said of his experiences in those works, which relate to the series Notes of a Madman.[127] Tolstoy speaks of this in Death of Ivan Il'ich. He doesn't do anything; it's done to him. All the horror of his position consists in that 'it (death – Trans) is here – and nothing can be done'. Any matters, any possibility of some kind of matters are over; this is as indubitable as anything might generally be indubitable for man. All of life one can improvise, search, find, defence, or complete matters – only to take matters in hand. Now, when days are numbered, one must get used to a new position – insane in its no-exit quality – to look in the face of horror, and do nothing, only wait. Any attempt to do something – not only does not ameliorate it, but if one here can allow comparative degree – still more worsens the position. Both Ivan Il'ich and Brekhunov are left with only one thing: to renounce, renounce and renounce these various devices of self-construction to which their long life has inured them. Father Sergei, who has accumulated in long years of monasticism so much spiritual treasure, has it no better than the predatory Vasily Andreevich Brekhunov or the well-intentioned Ivan Il'ich. All that was necessary and important there in church here has no significance. Completely, as Luther says nihil reputari: propter Christum bona spiritualia et opera justa. Sicut paralyticus manibus et pedibus omissis.[128] For the sake of what? He whom God has 'visited' has deigned His grace and cannot answer this question. Later, perhaps, he will repeat, following Bl. Augustine his gnarus and his ignarus – of that we'll speak further along. And it's doubtless difficult and a torment to renounce reason and head into darkness, just as to destruction and annihilation. But for Luther, as for Tolstoy, this is the necessary condition of faith; this is faith itself. That juxtaposition, which we have already encountered in Augustine: amor Dei usque ad contemptum sui et amor sui ad contemptum Dei (De civitate Dei, XIV, 28). One must go in love for God to self-forgetting – otherwise you will belong to the earth. While you listen to Luther – a scientifically educated man – your suspicion of the 'method' of the medieval monk might interfere with your hearing what is necessary. You would relate with the same unbelief, of course, if I began to tell you of the 'experiences' of Tauler, Meister Eckhart, St Theresa, and St John of the Cross. All probabilities are towards, that you are ready to apply your 'criterion of truth' to both the Apostle Paul and to the Biblical prophets, who told so much of the wisdom of man, whom the Lord had afflicted with madness.

But Tolstoy lived before your eyes. And he just as much trusted his reason, as you do, if not more. For him, Socrates was the ideal of the sage, and that doctrine of sola fide, which all the Lutheran sermons serve to illustrate, evoked the liveliest dissatisfaction in him. And nonetheless he affirmed all that Luther tells, everything that the apostles and prophets taught. The light flickers out before the human eyes wide open in horror, and this great darkness, so dread, so unendurable, absorbing all things equally, both the good, yeah the good, <u>summum bonum</u>, the works of Father Sergei, of Tolstoy himself – cutting off, as with a knife, from all that's past, comprehensible, explicable, human, it ought to be considered not the end, but the beginning? Ought to be considered – are these words acceptable? Don't they fall away of themselves, as soon as man has to step across the fatal line?

XIII

To the horror and dissatisfaction of the Protestants, Denifle cast Luther a terrible reproach: his doctrine of <u>sola fide</u> has its source not in strength but weakness. He could not fulfil his duty, he could not manage the vows he had voluntarily imposed on himself – he could not even force himself to fulfilment of the usual commandments and thus, to justify himself, created a doctrine founded on a false interpretation of the Holy Scripture, that man is not saved by works but by faith. A terrible accusation – but for him who is familiar with Luther's work, which are half a presentation of one uninterrupted and righteous confession, there can be no doubt that Denifle was right. Luther couldn't fulfil not only the so-called Gospel <u>consilia</u>, which are the source of monastic vows, but he felt, and admitted this, that at every step he violated commandments obligatory for every Christian. Just his commentary to Romans serves as sufficient proof of this.

If Denifle were not so blinded by his fantastic hatred of the irreconcilable enemy of Catholicism, the commentary to Romans would have evoked in him at least a feeling of sympathy for the unfortunate, albeit perhaps also mistaken brother.

Luther himself proceeded from the conviction that <u>facienti quod in se est Deus infallibiliter dat gratiam.</u>[129] But personal experience led him to a terrible consciousness – he had not the strength to do what, per the generally accepted opinion, which he shared, he had the strength to do. Denifle with the triumph of the savage steps on the chest of the fallen opponent seizes him by the throat. <u>Gott wollte das Seinige tun, aber Luther hat nicht das Seinige getan</u>[130] (Denifle, I, 453). Perhaps nowhere else in all Denifle's infinite reasoning has the spirit of Catholicism spoken out with such force as in these words. And yet it is the best way of overturning all those objections which Denifle presents against Luther's doctrine. Therefore, in the final account, the salvation of man is all the same in his hands. God wishes to do His part, but Luther <u>didn't do his</u>, and it didn't come out as God wanted. And what Denifle affirms, so must every Catholic. For if the <u>potestas clavium</u> is given to Catholicism, if the Pope is the successor of St Peter, then God's will cannot be hidden from a Catholic. For whom he condemns here on earth, God also condemns in heaven. And also – the main thing – that which Denifle says of Luther now, 400 years later, that Luther thought of himself. He literally thus represented his position to himself: God did His part; I didn't do mine; therefore, there is no salvation for me! The entire interest of Denifle's book consists in it producing anew over Luther that judgement, which Luther himself in his time produced on himself. The only difference is that Denifle judges another, Luther – himself.

This circumstance might have been fatal for Denifle's book, if this latter, as I already indicated, did not feel that his personal salvation depends on the outcome of his argument with Luther. It is necessary for Denifle, like Socrates, to be convinced that he fecit quod in se est. Otherwise he, yeah, ought to have to say of himself the same that he said of Luther – i.e., acknowledge himself condemned to eternal perdition. Or conversely, man, supposing that he has the strength to manage the problems imposed on him, creates a doctrine such that God will not refuse him His grace, he who too clearly feels his helplessness, and learns the unattainable and mysterious art of loving the Secret God [любить Бога Сокровенного] who tells not His will to humanity. Recall Pelagius and Augustine. Pelagius also did not reject grace – he only wished to see the incarnation of justice in God. For to condemn a man, who did all he could, doesn't this mean to commit the greatest act of injustice? But Luther could not count on Divine justice – for if God were just, there'd be no salvation for Luther, per his personal admission. Why did he so tormentingly feel his sinfulness? That he was a great sinner, there can be no doubt –below I cite a series of his most horrible admissions, which will convince any man, that Luther's sins were not conventional pastoral or professional ones. But here's the question, where exactly can Denifle, having accused Luther, on turning to God, say, putting his hand over his heart, I thank you, Lord, that I am not the same, as that Luther? I think that Denifle would not have the boldness to so define his relation to Luther. The sin of Adam, of which the Bible tells, lay with all its weight equally on Denifle, as on Luther as well. And this original sin, which becomes no easier, in that all men must bear it on themselves, was the source of Luther's torments and doubts. He was convinced by his personal experience, that what was told in the Bible was no myth and no invention. That we all have sinned and continue to sin together with Adam, and that each of us begins and continues the deed of our forefather. And that the greatest and most terrible sin is to think that by any possible means we can take off ourselves the burden of sins.

In other words, the greatest seduction is 'pride', superbia – and this pride, as Luther understood, consists in linking the grace of God with facere quod in se est:

> Ego stultus non potui intelligere, quomodo me peccatorum similem caeteris deberem reputare et ita nemini me praeferre, cum essem contritus et confessus; tunc enim omnia ablata putabam et evacuata, etiam intrinsece.[131]
> (Ad Romanos, 4; Denifle, I, 455)

So, too, thought Luther, so ought Denifle to think too, and each Catholic who professes the formula facere quod in se est and not allowing a gap between our 'works' and the grace of God. No matter how many excerpts Denifle adduces from the best Scholastics, the fact remains that people go into the monastery just so as to there acquire new and more significant powers with which to gain the grace of God. The monastic life seemed to them more perfect and thus revealing the path to the heavenly kingdom.

I could contrast to Denifle's quotations in their turn a whole series of excerpts from the works of Alphonse Liguori – the last Catholic doctor ecclesiae. His work La vera sposa de Gesu Christo is a guida spirituale for nuns. It explains to them what monasticism is and how one ought to live in a convent. And as opposed to what Denifle wishes to demonstrate in affirming that, in essence, there's no difference between the monk and the usual Christian, for one and the other strive for the same goal – only one has taken the easier, longer way, the other the more difficult, albeit shorter way – Liguori directly affirms that the whole meaning of monasticism is in this very difficulty:

> Egli è un gran pregio il martirio per la fede; ma lo stato religioso par che abbia qualche cosa piú eccelente del martirio. Il martire soffre i tormenti per non perder l'anima, ma la religiosa li soffre per rendersi più grata a Dio; ondè che se il martire è martire della fede, la religiosa è martire della perfezione. È vero che al presente lo stato religioso ha perduto molto del primiero splendore: tuttavia ben puo dirsi che anche al presente le anime più care a Dio che camminano con maggior perfezione e che più edificano col loro buon odore le chiesa, communemente parlando, non si trovano che nelle case religiose. Ed in fatti dove sono e quanto sono quelle persone anche spirituali nel mondo che levansi di 'notte a fare orazione ed a cantar le divine lodi? che impiegano cinque o sei ore del giorno in questi e simili sancta esercizi? che fanno tanti digiuni, astinenze e mortificazioni? And further: lo tengo per certo che la maggior parte delle sedie de serafini, lasciate vuote dagl'infelici compagni di Lucifero, non sarà occupata che dalle persone religiose. Nel secolo passato di sessanta persone poste dalla Chiesa nel catalogo de' santi o de' beati non più che cinque o sei non sono state religiose. Guai al mondo (disse un giorno Gesù a s. Teresa) se non vi fossero i religiosi![132]

(Liguori, I, 44–5)

I think that Liguori speaks of monasticism much better and more correctly and chiefly, openly, than does Denifle. This, of course, is explicable, as Liguori is preaching to the choir. He does not fear the inquisitive, incredulous gazes of the inimically inclined crowd of Protestant theologians before whom Denifle had to justify and defend Catholicism. He was convinced that those to whom he turned would understand and value him, for they trod the same path and know such things, which non-participating persons do not suspect. Of course, a monk is a voluntary martyr and, therefore, he cannot but value his work higher than anything else in the world. For to suffer for the faith, to accept torments and tortures on oneself, in order not to commit apostasy, although it is difficult, infinitely difficult, but all the same it's easier than to bear insuperably difficult labours and trials constantly, for years, decades without any external compulsion, from just the desire to please the Lord. And it's demanded from those who accept such labour on themselves that they consider themselves equal to all others and not marked out by God's index finger! Denifle affirms that they looked at it thus, but I say with conviction that it's not that he's mistaken – he intentionally conceals the truth.

I do not wish to accuse him. And one cannot accuse him. Such truth is revealed only to the initiate – before the person of Harnack, Loofs, Troeltsch, and the whole glorious herd of modern Protestant theologians one must be silent on it, one must deny it with all one's strength.

Here's what Liguori says to his nuns:

> Siccome gli ebrei erano nell'antica legge il popolo diletto di Dio a differenza degli egiziani, cosi lo sono nella nuova i religiosi a rispetto dei secolari.[133]
>
> (Liguori, I, 26)

Could it be Denifle didn't know <u>La vera sposa de Gesu Christo</u>? He did, knew it full well, but it was necessary for him that Harnack and his comrades didn't know this. To Harnack he only tells stories of <u>humilitas</u>, but to his spiritual daughters he says something else:

> E ciò appunto è quel che dice la monaca, allorchè riceve il velo dal prelate nella sua professione; Il mio sposo mi ha coperto il volto con questo velo, acciocchè io, non vedendo e non essendo veduta, non ammetta altro amante che solo esso Gesù mio sposo. Questa è la santa superbia, dice s. Girolamo, che dee sempre nudrire una sposa di Gesù Cristo nel suo cuore; Dei sponsa proferas, cosi egli parla, disce superbiam sanctam. Scito, te illis esse meliorem.[134]
>
> (Liguori, I, 23)

And Thomas Aquinas, too, of course, not in such expressions, but in his transparent, crisp language affirms the same:

> Ad quartum dicendum quod, sicut Philosophus dicit in IV Ethic. (cap. 3, circa med.) *honor proprie et secundum veritatem non debetur nisi virtuti.* Sed quia exteriora bona instrumentaliter deserviunt ad quosdam actus virtutum, ex consequenti etiam eorum excellentiae honor aliquis exhibetur; et praecipue a vulgo quod solam excellentiam exteriorem recognoscit. *Honori igitus qui a Deo et sanctis omnibus* exhibetur propter virtutem, prout dicitur in Ps. 138, 17: 'Mihi autem nimis honorati sunt amici tui, Deus', non competit religiosis abrenuntiare, qui ad perfectionem virtutis intendunt; honori autem qui exhibetur exteriori excelletiae, abrenuntiant ex hoc ipso, quod saecularem vitam derelinquunt; unde ad hoc non requiritur speciale votum.[135]
>
> (Sum. Theol. IIa, IIae, qu. 186, art. 7)

Here's what's concealed in the depth of the soul of the humble monk. 'Learn holy pride' and know that you are better. Monks, too, actual monks, those, yes, of whom Liguori tells, that they rise at night, in order to pray and sing praises to the lord, dedicate five to six hours a day to spiritual exercises, fast, torment themselves, these monks cannot not believe, that their labours are in vain and indifferent to God, that other people living in the world are just as good, as the heroic religious behind the stone wall. They have renounced material goods, but spiritual goods and rights to superiority – <u>ille esse meliores</u>, right to <u>sancta superbia</u>, this they will give up to no one. And Denifle will not give this up. His whole argument with Luther is an argument over the right to <u>sancta superbia</u>. But let's listen again to Liguori:

> <u>Ma quel che più rilieva è che non vi è lode bastante a spiegare il pregio della verginità: Non est digna ponderatio continentis animae. E perciò dice Ugon cardinale che negli altri voti si concede la dispensa, ma non già nel voto della verginità, perchè il pregio della verginità non v'è prezzo che possa adequarilo. Ciò ben lo diede ad intendere Maria santissima con quelle parole con cui ripose all' arcangelo: Quomodo fiet istud, quoniam virum non cognosco? Dimostrando esser ella pronta a rinunziare più presto la dignità di madre di Dio, che il pregio di sua verginità.</u>[136]
>
> (Liguori, I, 14)

Liguori tells us much that is highly instructive and significant on monastic life – the kind of thing that Denifle naturally considers necessary to protect from peripheral, idly curious people, especially from his hated liberal Protestant theologians.

We recall that Denifle rose up high against Luther's stories of those self-inflicted trials to which the future reformer submitted himself in the monastery. If, he says, what Luther says is true, then he has himself to blame for his woes. Catholicism has never allowed excess in self-inflicted trials and cannot take responsibility itself for the fact that Luther knew no feeling of measure and obeyed his own voice, and not the voices of the teachers of the church. Bernard of Clairvaux said:

> <u>discretio, quae mater virtutum est et consummatio perfectionis,</u> that <u>discretio omnivirtuti ordinem point.</u> ... Est ergo discretio non tam virus quam quaedam moderatrix et auriga virtutum, ordinatrixque affectuum et morum doctrix. Tolle hanc, et virtus vitium est.[137]

He adduces corresponding statements from Thomas à Kempis, Thomas Aquinas and the most ancient teachers of the Church – all in the same genre – variations on Aristotle's reasonings on φρόνσις (Eth. ad Nicom., V, 13).

> x. 8) <u>Unmöglich</u>, exclaims Denifle, <u>dass dieser gefeierte Mann sich hätte sollen durch den Heiden Aristoteles beschämen lassen, der doch wusste, dass das Gute und überhaupt die Tugend nicht möglich ist ohne die Klugheit</u> φρόνσις.[138]
>
> (Denifle, I, 383)

That Aristotle was the bard of common sense, no one, of course would take up disputing that, just as anyone ought to admit, that Catholicism in general sought and found an egress from its difficult position by means of the famous pagan philosopher. But the contradiction and irreconcilability of the official doctrine, rising not at Aristotle even, but at Socrates, with the spirit of the medieval, is just as obvious. In monasteries there lived the same insane Socrates, of whom we spoke at the beginning of the present book. That insane Socrates, reborn in Antisthenes, Diogenes and in their successors, who said, that he preferred to go out of his mind rather than experience pleasure. Read the biographies of St Anthony by Athanasius the Great, and you'll be convinced, how the model story of the ideal of the monk so little conformed to the presentation of Aristotle on φρόνσις [Trans – φρόνσις] or with the doctrine of St Bernard of Clairvaux that discretio mater omnium virtutum. On the contrary, measure is the enemy of all monastic virtues. Even Thomas Aquinas, to whom Denifle so willingly refers and who, as a matter of fact, as it were more than anyone justifies the theory of moderation – not in vain was he raised on Aristotle – but even he too saw in monasticism exactly the unusual, dissimilar to that which all Christians do.

Measure is for those who live in the world. They can calculate, foresee – which they do. The pathos of the monk is in the immeasurable, where the very idea of calculation and foresight loses any meaning. Not for nothing is St Theresa depicted with the inscription pati, domine, aut mori. Holy pride, sancta superbia of the monks had its source exactly in the consciousness that their virtues can have nothing in common with the virtues of secular folk.

> Religionis status, quatenus est quoddam holocaustum quo quis se totum Deo offert et quasi immolate, ex tribus votis, obedientiae videlicet, contientiae et paupertatis, in isque votis religionis perfectio consist.[139]
> (Sum. Theol., IIa IIae, qu. 186, art. 7, concl.)

This conclusion was well known to Denifle. He quotes neighbouring passages from the same questio 186. He knew that per Thomas' doctrine, the monk brings his whole self to God.

quasi immolat art, I (cf. the same quaestio – religio, quum sit status in quo homo se totum et sua omnia ad divinum cultum consecrat et quasi immolat ...).[140]

There, in the world – measure is necessary, limitations are necessary, because there physical force is necessary, health is necessary, there even material means are necessary. The monk has no necessity of anything, and in this is the consciousness of his superiority over others – illis meliores esse. Liguori edifies his flock:

> Dice s. Bernardo: 'Magis nocet domesticus hostis'. Una piazza assediata non ha peggiori nemici di coloro che tiene di dentro, poichè da essi è più difficile di guardarsi che dagli altri che stanno di fuori. Dicea pertano il b. Guiseppe Calasanzio; 'Non bisogna far più conto del corpo che d'uno straccio di cucina'. Ed in fatti cosi han praticato i santi con se stessi. Siccome gli uomini del mondo non istudiano altro che di soddisfare i loro corpi co'piaceri sensuali, cosi all'incontro le anime amanti di Dio non istudiano altro che di mortificare, sempre che possono, la loro carne. S. Pietro d'Alcantara diceva al corpo suo; 'Corpo mio, quietati, io in questa vita non voglio darti alcun riposo, altro da me non avrai che tormenti ...' Leggiamo pure le vite de' santi, e vediamo ivi le penitenze ch'essi han fatte, e vergogniamoci poi d'esser noi cosi delicati e

> riserbati nell'affliggere la nostra carne. Leggesi nelle vite de' padre antichi che vi era un monastero numeroso di monache le quali non gustavano nè frutti nè vino: alcune non prendeano cibo che da una serra all'altra, e non si cibavano se non dopo due o tre giorni di rigorosa astinenza: tutte poi vestivano di cilizio, e sopra il cilizio dormivano.[141]

(Liguori, I, 195–6)

Alphonse Liguori recommends such models of the holy life to his listeners. Denifle affirms and 'proves' that only irrational youth, giving it up to self-inflicted torments, exceeded the bounds of moderation and ruined their health. Liguori teaches otherwise:

> Santa Teresa ... cosi avvertiva le sue figlie; 'Siete venute non ad accarezzarvi ma a morire per Gesù Cristo. Se non ci risolviamo d'inghiottire il mancamento di sanità, non faremo mai niente. Che importa che muoiamo? Quante volte ci ha burlato questo corpo! e noi non ci burleremo alcuna volta di lui?' Dicea ancora il b. Giuseppe Calasanzio; Guai a quel religioso che ama più la santità che la santità! S. Bernardo stimava esser cosa indecente a' religiosi infermi il prender medicine di valore; dicea bastare ad essi i decotti dell'erbe ... Dice Salviano: 'Homines Christo dediti infirmi sunt et volunt esse; si fortes fuerint, sancti esse vix possunt'.[142]

(Liguori, I, 198)

But enough excerpts. It's clear, it seems, even for those who were never interested in the life of monks that exactly φρόνσις (Eth. ad Nicom. V, 13) and discretio least of all inspired these mysterious people. The most remarkable representatives of monasticism exerted all their strength exactly to burst out of those frames, in which reason and experience accessible to reason forcefully enclose human strivings. Neither sufferings, nor humiliations, nor sickness, nor even death was taken into account by those who set as their unique and ultimate goal the possession of the beloved spouse. Osculum suavissimum et secretissimum[143] – for this kiss Bernard of Clairvaux was willing to give up everything you please. He dedicated a whole series of his sermons to exegesis of the Song of Songs and even so did not get to the end of his works. And was it necessary for him to finish? When all his life was one eternal, incomprehensible love, alien to the great majority of men, love for the Invisible and Eternally Enigmatic? But, the world did not wish to leave Bernard of Clairvaux, as well as all his predecessors and successors, who were in communion with the great mystery contained in the Holy Scripture, in peace, alone with their unusual experiences. People around them powerfully demanded their participation in their own personal lives. Reveal us your secret; commune with us of your great joys. People do not allow the thought that possessors cannot share their pleasures with their neighbours. And yes, Bernard of Clairvaux and other saints are only men, i.e., political beings. And the conviction lived in them that what they had is the Truth and therefore might be embodied in word and transmitted to those who wished to listen and receive. Prophets, apostles, saints, desert hermits – all spoke and all listened to them. And the more they spoke, the more they demanded that the revealed be turned into truth, i.e., into what <u>semper, ubique, et ad omnibus creditum et credendum est</u>,¹⁴⁴ all the more did primordial revelation becomes similar to what was already known earlier, and all the less like unto itself.

XIV

Thus Liguori writes of monasticism – so Luther too imagined monasticism when he went away to the monastery.

<u>Nonne haec est religio sancta, in qua homo vivit purius, cadit rarius, surgit velocius, incedit cautius, irroratur frequentius, quiescit securius, moritur confidentius, purgatur citius, remuneratur copiosius.</u>¹⁴⁵

Even Bernard of Clairvaux (the words quoted belong to him), that ideal of the medieval monk, whom Luther dared not mock even at the time when in his frenzied outbursts against monasticism he exceeded all bounds of what's allowed, could not forget the generous reward – <u>remuneratur copiosius</u>. Luther had the right to expect rewards for himself for the vows he imposed on himself. He had the right to hope that having entered the monastery, he would live purer, fall more rarely, rise easier, act as convinced that the dew of celestial grace would more often water his parched soul, and that while still alive he would find that spiritual serenity, which would give him strength to await death with assurance. Denifle, in order to void Luther's stories of his monastic life, juxtaposes his early and later admissions on monastic life: they are mutually exclusive. Of course, they're exclusive. Luther could resolve to tell the truth of his monastic years only <u>after</u> he renounced monasticism. While he was a monk he tried with all his strength to assure himself and others that monasticism gave and could give what people expected of it, and of which before him Bernard of Clairvaux and Thomas Aquinas so eloquently told, with reference to the Aristotelian <u>honor proprie et secundum veritatem non debetur nisi virtuti</u>, and of which after them, the <u>doctor Ecclesiae</u> Alphonse Liguori related, extolling <u>sancta superbia</u>. In his early works, even as early as his <u>Vorlesung uber den Römerbrief</u>, Luther repeats everything that is usually said of monasticism, and with all the more conviction and passion, the less his words conformed to his internal condition.

<u>An ergo bonum nunc religiosum fieri? Respondeo: Si aliter salutem te habere non putas, nisi religiosis fias, ne ingrediaris. Sic enim verum est proverbium: Desperatio facit monachum, immo non monachum, sed diabolum. Nec enim unquam bonus monachus erit, qui ex desperatione ejusmodi monachus est, sed, qui ex charitate, scilicet, qui gravia sua peccata videns, et Deo suo rursum aliquid magnum ex amore facere volens, voluntarie resignat libertatem suam, et induit habitum istum stultum, et abjectis sese subjicit officiis.</u>¹⁴⁶

(<u>Ad Romanos</u>, 14, 1; Denifle, I, 35; W 56, 497; Ficker, 318)

Catholics and Denifle willingly quote the passage as proof that Luther, while he was a monk and had not broken with the Church, looked at monasticism completely differently than when he broke out against Rome. But listen carefully to these words: you will be convinced that here only the tone is different – the content is the same. It was just the same with Nietzsche when he wrote his magnificent articles on Wagner: only the consciousness that he had nowhere to go away from Wagner connected him to Wagner. And not a consciousness, but rather something unconscious, some kind of instinct. Just as Tolstoy too finished writing the lukewarm Anna Karenina and praised the life of the gentry – also only because it was not new, and he held on to the annealed old days – for a man needs to have something to hold onto. But if Luther is correct that desperatio facit diabolum, then we must acknowledge that just this happened to him. He only went into the monastery because he despaired of otherwise finding himself salvation. Tormented by his sins, he put on the stultum habitum in order that Deo suo aliquid magnum facere: he says this himself and Denifle quotes these words of his, completely forgetting that the whole horror of Luther's ensuing life had as source the conviction that he ought to and could do something good out of love for God – and the conviction, that a man has not the strength to do not just something great, but generally even anything for God. At the beginning, of course, Luther did not generalize and considered that not any man, but he (Luther) had not the strength to accomplish the exploit which might redeem his sins. Despair was the beginning of his monastic service; despair was his almost normal condition over the course of the fifteen years of his monastic life. It's audible, even in those of his works which were written dozens of years after his renunciation of monasticism.

Here are figures of his speeches as early as 1531:

Und mir ward auch also Gluck gewuntscht, da ich die Profession gethan hatte, vom Prior, Convent und Beichtvater, dass ich nu ware als ein unshüldig Kind, das itzt rein aus der Taufe käme. Und fürwahr, ich hätte mich gern gefreuet der herrlichen That, dass ich ein solcher trefflicher Mehsch wäre, der sich selb durch sein eigen Werk, ohn Christus Blut, so schon und helig gemacht hätte, so leichtlich und so balde. Aber, wiewohl ich solches süsses Lob und prachige Wort von meinem eigen Werk gern höretc, und liess mich also für einen Wunderthäter halten, der sich selbst so liederlicher Weise künnt helig machen, und den Tod fressen sampt dem Teufel u.s.w., so wollt es doch den Stich nicht halten. Denn wo nur ein klein Anfechtung kam vom Tod oder Sunde, so fiel ich dahin, und fand weder Taufe noch Müncherei, die mir helfen möcht; so hatte ich nu Christum und seine Taufe längest auch verloren. Da war ich der elendeste Mensch auf Erden. Tag und Nacht war eitel Heulen und Verzweifeln, dass mir niemand steuren kunnte[147]

(Luther, Kleine Antwort auf Herzog Georg's nähestes Buch
(Harnack, III, 821)

In the same work he says:

Ist je ein Münch gen Himmel kommen durch Müncherei, so wollt ich auch hinein kommen sein; das warden mir zeugen all meine Klostergesellen.¹⁴⁸
(Harnack, III, 821)

If you now compare the corresponding places from his Römerbrief you'll be convinced that as early as 1515, Luther was exactly in the position of which Ranke spoke: either he had to leave Catholicism – and leave, as he did leave, i.e., disgrace his previous holy of holies, or found something in the nature of the Jesuit order. For Luther there was no other way out, as with Loyola. One or the other – either in actual fact, having forgotten all measure, to slowly incinerate himself at the stake (holocaustum) and enjoying his torments, considering, as the Stoics considered, and after them, Thomas Aquinas and Liguori, that honor or sancta superbia non debetur nisi virtuti, and that the essence of human religious life in God is in this holy pride, in this internal consciousness of one's rightness, of one's moral superiority ille esse meliorem; or, if this is impossible, or, what's even worse, if this is not the essence of life in God, then it remains to trample one's false faith in the mud. For a cast-down idol is not God; a cast-down idol is the devil. All the great events in the human soul are accompanied by heartache [надрыв].

Deus enim nos non per domesticam, sed per extraneam justitiam et sapientiam vult salvare, non que veniat et nascatur ex nobis, sed que aliunde veniat in nos, non que in terra nostra oritur, sed que de coelo venit.¹⁴⁹
(Com. ep Ad Romanos., 1,1; Luthers Werks, W 56, 158; Ficker, 2)

As early as 1515 such ideas ruled Luther. Obviously, any sort of reminders of discretio and φρόνσις (Eth. ad Nicom., V, 13) could no longer hold back the flow and pressure of the new, internal stream. These firm dams, not made by hand, which seemed eternal and incorruptible in serene periods, during the big storm in a moment tore apart and burst into pieces. Luther himself treasured them and directed all his skill to buttress them. Thus he so rapturously extols the monastic life and himself invents and repeats others', good words of heroic religious exploits.

Quamobrem credo nunc melius esse religiosum fieri, quam in ducentis annis fuit; ratione tali videlicet, quod hucusque monachi recesserunt a cruce et fuit gloriosum esse religiosum. Nunc rursus incipiunt displicere hominibus, etiam qui boni sunt, propter habitum stultum. Hoc enim est religiosum esse, mundo odiosum esse ac stultum. Et qui huic sese ex charitate submittit, optime facit. Ego enim non terreor, quod episcopi persequuntur et sacredotes nos. Quia sic debet fieri. Tantum hoc mihi displicet, quod occasionem malam huic damus displicentie. Ceterum quibus non est data occasio et fastidiunt monachos, nescientes quare, optimi sunt fautores, quos in toto mundo habent religosi. Debernet enim gaudere religiosi tamquam voti sui compotes, si in suo isto voto pro Deo assumpto despicerentur confunderenturque, quia ad hoc habent habitum stultum, ut omnes alliciant ad sui contemptum. Sed nunc aliter agunt multo, habentes speciem solam religiosorum. Sed ego scio felicissimos eos, si charitatem haberent, et beatiores, quam qui in heremo fuerunt, quia sunt cruci et ignominie quotidiane expositi.[150]

(Com. ep. Ad Romanos, XIV, 1; Luthers Werke, W 56, 497; Ficker, 318)

You see Luther cares little for the usual difficulties which are loaded on the shoulders of monks. He adds new ones. No longer just secular folk, but also spiritual persons, bishops and priests, disdain monks, but it's all good. So it ought to be. That's why it's so useful now to enter the order, not like it was two hundred years ago, when monks were in general honour. The more humiliations, the better. Those who humiliate monks – without knowing it themselves – are the monks' best benefactors. And only those who just for appearance put on the cassock are oppressed by common disdain. Those who have actual love are the happiest and most blessed people, happier than even desert dwellers, for they submit themselves to everyday humiliation and disgrace. The whole work is full of this sort of intense and passionate hymn to monasticism.

Luther strained the strings of his soul to the ultimate degree – and you await in fear, to what it will lead – whether the strings will break, or will you hear a new accord, never heretofore heard in such beauty and power. He destroys and burns everything that he has, and still it seems that this is yet little, that something of his he neglected and thus ruined his work.

Non potest fieri, ut plenus justitia sua repleatur justitia Dei, qui non implet nisi esurientes et sitentes. Ideo satur veritate et sapientia sua non est capax veritatis et sapientiae Dei, que non nisi in vacuum et inane recipe potest. Ergo dicamus Deo: 'O quam libenter sumus vacui, ut tu plenus sis in nobis! Libenter infirmus, ut tua virtus in me habitet; libenter peccator, ut tu justificeris in me; libenter insipiens, ut tu mea sapientia sis; libenter injustus, ut tu sis justitia mea!'[151]

(Com. ep. Ad Romanos, III, 7: Luthers Werke, Weimar, 56, 219; Ficker, 59)

This is no longer the virtue of humility that speaks in Luther. Or, if you wish to preserve the word humility unchanged – if you please, it'll be even better. But here humility ceases to be a virtue, i.e., a laudable spiritual quality (Laudabitur). For how can one praise a man for his qualities – when he strives exclusively to void his soul? He wishes to be weak, sinful, unjust, ignorant, stupid – he wishes to eliminate all qualities, all virtues. Can one really praise him for this? And can anyone call such humility virtue? All the more so since everything for which he strove had already been realized. He, as a matter of fact, is infirmus, peccator, injustus, insipiens. His humility is only that he openly acknowledged his desolated soul. But there is no merit in this admission. For it is only the howl of a tormented soul. He can no longer pretend to be just, righteous, and wise – when his personal sinfulness has so clearly bared itself before him. Like Tolstoy's Father Sergei, like Tolstoy himself, Luther runs without looking back from undeserved awards, for these honours burn him, by reminding him that they only cover his shame. Luther did not desolate his soul out of humility – humility came when he felt that his soul was incinerated.

I repeat and insist: Denifle and the Catholics correctly limn the internal condition of Luther's soul. He was a monster; he was a man who had lost the right to sancta superbia, to honour. And the most important thing – he knew this. Protestants cannot endure this idea, as Catholicism cannot endure the idea that, per Dostoevsky's expression, it put itself in God's place, as Denifle cannot endure Luther's reproaches: ecce voveo tibi, Deus, etc. But that doesn't change the matter. Luther is correct in his accusations of Catholicism; Denifle is correct in his accusations of Luther. Luther himself acknowledges:

> Wir meinten, wir wollen mit dem Abbrechen so viel verdienen, dass wir dem Blut Christi wollten geleichtun. So hab ich armer Narr gelaubt … Ich hätte mich erwürgt mit Fasten, Wachen und Frieren. Or: Warum habe ich im Kloster die großsten Strengheiten ausgehalten? Weshalb habe ich meinen Körper mit Fasten, Wachen und Kälte beschwert? Weil ich darnach trachtete gewiss zu sein, durch solche Werke Vergebung der Sünden zu Erlangen.[152]
>
> (Denifle, I, 352)

Of course, while Luther was a monk, he would not dare to say such horrible things to himself. To acknowledge that he wished to put his works in place of the Blood of Christ. Not even to say it – he didn't even dare think it, by himself, so that no one heard that he put his exploit in place of the work of Christ.

Only a mysterious, unconscious feeling, embryonic in the depth of his soul said to him that he was on a false path and directly – to the abyss. But he did not at once take account of the reasons for the dissatisfaction living in the depth of his soul. It seemed to him that he insufficiently fervently fulfilled the obligations he had taken on himself. He multiplied his vigilance by two, by ten, but the more he tried, the more strongly grew his unease. He saw that his efforts only more and more led him to the cup that will not pass [в неприходимую чащу]. He sighed, cried, confessed – tormented his spiritual advisor with ceaseless complaints on his unfitness. Staupitz[153] did not understand where such unease in a young man came from. He counselled him, directed him, tried as he could to calm him, but all the words of the good, old, and experienced Staupitz bounced off Luther, just as though they weren't meant for him. Neither his own works nor other counsels gave him anything. With horror Luther was more and more convinced that concupiscentia invincibilis est – although there is a direct commandment: ne concupisces. In other words, he wished to head to God, but an incomprehensible force possessed him and drew him from God to his own sinful lust. Denifle's right again: the consciousness that concupiscentia invincibilis est; i.e., the consciousness of the impossibility of fulfilment of not only the monastic vows he imposed on himself but usual commandments as well was the beginning of Luther's apostasy. A consciousness, of course, that's terrible: I am no better than other men; I, who gave my whole life to the service of God, am just the same poor and pitiful sinner as other men. No, I am worse – worse than all others in the world: others, at least, didn't impose vows on themselves. I imposed them and did not fulfil them; I am a liar, an oath-breaker – there is no man in the world, who would have fallen so low as I have. Here's where the monastery gave Luther, instead of the right to sancta superbia and great honor premium virtutis, qui bonis attribuitur. Denifle enters into a theoretical theological argument with Luther. He proves to him that it is no sin that concupiscentia remains. That the problem of man is not to excise concupiscentia from oneself, but rather, despite it, not to give into temptation, and do what the commandments and self-imposed vows demand. Do your part; pray to God for help – all the rest will be added unto you [Делать свое, молиться Богу о помощи – все остальное приложиться]. The consciousness will be superadded that you have seen the work you began through to the end – and that God has not turned his face from you. Perhaps, in this argument of Luther's with Catholicism one of the most profound mysteries of human experience lies concealed.

When we become acquainted with the life of those people, who – beginning with Socrates, Stoics and Cynics, up to and including the monks of the Middle Ages – cultivated sancta superbia and for rights to this holy pride did not hesitate at any, sometimes straightly insane sacrifices, we cannot but be amazed at their exploits. And then those words which Luther cast at them, ecce voveo, etc., seem blasphemous to us. Doubtless that whatever Denifle said, they too felt that concupiscentia invincibilis est, their personal testimonies attest to this.

And if Luther allowed in a factual mistake, ascribing to the dying Bernard of Clairvaux the words perdidi tempus meum, quia perdite vixi (Denifle I, 41), then psychologically he was all the same correct: Ber. Clairvaux himself could better than anyone else, in the face of impending death, so deeply feel the vanity of all his great exploits.

Even such unusual people as St Theresa have acknowledged more than once, that they felt themselves the last, worst among people. And thus they felt that as a matter of fact there was an extreme duality in their soul. On one hand, they were drawn by all intents to God; on the other hand, their powerless flesh crushed them with its great weight and did not allow them to rise from the earth. What to do? Where to see one's essence – in the readiness to rise to heaven, or in the impossibility of escaping the earth? An actual monk, like Socrates, like the Stoics, like the Cynics, directed all the strength of his soul, so as to ascribe especial value to their strivings – to rise upwards. Virtus laudata crescit – it seems to people that one must by any means encourage virtue, praise it, hymn it, in order to ascribe it as much strength as possible, so that it can do its difficult task as well as possible. For monks virtue is no longer satisfied with the usual praises, usual sanction – it wishes to be holy. It's necessary for it that God Himself gazed upon it, that it is guaranteed the same triumph in Heaven, that it would have wished on earth. They are agreed in deferring its victory – but its victory they demand, for it cannot be that that work, to which they have devoted their best strength, in which they so believed, which they withstood with such heavy and tormenting sacrifices – would turn out – it's terrible even to say the word – to be unnecessary, indifferent and exactly unnecessary not on earth, which they've renounced, but in Heaven, which was for them the unique object of their hopes and dreams.

Catholicism by any means shamed paganism and fenced itself off from it, but all the same meekly following Socrates acknowledged that God, like men, acknowledged the superiority of norms of reason and morality over Him. Therefore they both strove to emphasize and value as highly as possible the principle of the conscious striving to victory over concupiscentia in both life and man's internal struggle. Allow that lusts live in us, allow that we have not the strength to excise the hated fomes peccati from ourselves – that's nothing. The chief thing – that we do not give them power over our actions. To all their demands we answer a categorical 'no', and by that already fulfil the chief problem of life – and then we can already entrust our faith to God – for facienti quod in se est Deus infallibiter dat gratiam.[154] God will not refuse grace to one who has done his part. The connection between heaven and earth is preserved and preserved for ages and ages. Even all modern Catholic theologians insist on this connection.

Rationis usus fidem praecidit et ad eam hominem ope revelationis et gratiae conducit. Ratio cum certitudine authenticitatem revelationis Judaeis per Moysen et christianis per Jesum Christum factae, probare valet.[155]
(Denzinger, § 124, 5–6 (1492–3), p 442)

I don't think that anyone who set himself the task of attentively and sympathetically looking into the life of the monks would decide to reject their work. And, along with that, hardly anyone would want to reject their right to sancta superbia. He who can do what the monks do can feel in himself a feeling of sancta superbia at the concupiscentia living in soul or body, that means that God Himself ordered it so. For to be a monk and not know holy pride is obviously impossible. Man rises to this pride, as on wings, over the grey and murky, often repulsive and unendurable reality, to that domain of the fantastic, which was, is and will be the ultimate goal for many.

One ought only not to think that here is the limit of human attainments, that men are completely not allowed to be awakened from the nightmare of reality. Let's follow Luther and we'll see that something is possible that's completely unlike what monks did and how they lived.

XV

As opposed to Denifle and those monks whom Luther takes under his defence, Luther in his internal struggle felt not so much the pride of victory when he succeeded in self – possession with his concupiscentia, as much as shame and denigration at its very presence. I did not submit; I did not violate the law with my external action – but internally, invisible to others, but tormentingly for myself, I am completely in the power of bad passions. With his characteristic righteousness he tells of his horrible conditions, thus preparing material for his future accusers. From Wartburg, when he composed his booked De vitis monachorum he wrote to Melanchthon: 'Ego hic insensatus et induratus sedeo in otio, proh dolor, parum orans, nihil gemens pro ecclesia dei, quin carnis meae in domitae uror magnis ignibus. Summa: qui fervere spiritu debeo, ferveo carne, libidine, pigritia, otio, somnolentia'[156] ad Melanchthon, Denifle, I, 79). It's difficult, of course, for the modern Lutheran to read these lines, used as he is to see in the founder of his faith a prophet, pure beyond reproach, always directing his eyes up to the hills, as it might have been difficult for admirers of Dostoevsky to read the aforementioned[157] letter of Strakhov or for admirers of Tolstoy to recognize their great teacher in the hero of Notes of a Madman. But, like it or not, one sometimes has to in actual fact see 'what was' and not what ought to have been, if the world were organized as it's supposed to be by human understanding.

Luther ought to have burned in spirit, but rather the flesh possessed him with its lusts, laziness, idleness, otiosity, somnolence. This is a horrible condition for Luther – even if he had had the strength to fulfil in the strictest manner to the end of his life all the demands of the monastic code – that no longer gave him any hope of those honours, which attended virtues, at that sancta superbia, which yet on earth crowns the work of the religious heroes. Can he experience holy pride, he who is considered carne, libidine, pigritia, otio, somnolentia? He thus pronounced a death sentence on himself. For if one can save oneself only through virtue, then there was no salvation for Luther.[158] When for Luther, as for those mystics whom he had to read, as for those Tolstoyan heroes of whom we spoke in the first part of this book,[159] his great apostasy began; he was really like a paralytic deprived of use of arms and legs. Some kind of unknown force carried him into impenetrable darkness. All of this is not images, not metaphors. All of this is reality, that which was in actual fact; i.e., reality not reworked and not smoothed over by any kind of human a priori, neither logical, nor moral.

Completely as Tolstoy tells of Ivan Il'ich, 'it (death) is here, and nothing can be done'. One cannot allow oneself the slightest movement; one cannot twitch one member. One must freeze in senseless and stupid fear and only wait. What? Await the miracle. And for Luther the miracle occurred. He dared alone – to rebel against the whole Catholic Church, the greatest force which the world had ever created. Harnack says, there is no faith without external authority. On Luther's example it is most visible of all, that the meaning and essence of faith consist in the fact that it proceeds without any external support. I recall the words of Ignatius Loyola – if the Holy Scripture were against him, he would not fear to go where the unknown voice bade him. He himself affirms this. Luther invokes the epistle of Paul.[160] True. But Luther rejected the epistle of James as apocryphal. More than that, Luther allowed himself to read and interpret the Apostle Paul, and when he needed to, not stopping, as we recall, before the authentic interpretation. And yes, to allow himself to read the Holy Scripture his own way doesn't this mean to usurp for himself the highest power to which a man may vaunt. Protestants compare the 'experience' of Luther with the experience of the Apostle Paul, and the work of Luther with the work of the apostle. Like Saul, who never saw and never heard Jesus, who dared to break away from the authority of the Jewish tradition, and at his own risk went to preach to the nations the news of Christ, just so Luther, believing his internal feeling, they say, threw down the challenge to Catholicism and preached to the world the new truth of the true God.

But, yes, if this is at least approximately accurate, then can one after this still speak of the significance of authority for faith? Isn't it clear, on the contrary, that the whole meaning of faith, its very essence, consists in that it tears away, not from this or that defined authority but with the very idea of authority. And this transformation, so unexpected, so little entering into men's calculations and hopes, that occurs with him, not just in spite of, but directly against his will, is indeed the great miracle of faith, which presents as absolutely impossible for those who have not experienced it. Just some support, some authority, some kind of criterion – one cannot all at once, completely break with them, with what we've grown up with, and with which we've grown together spiritually. A man suddenly begins to feel that no support, no infrastructure is necessary. The insane fear, which seizes man at the first feeling that the ground has fallen away from his feet – that passes. The habit of support is, as it were, our second, not our second, but rather our first nature, with which we are so connected, exactly as though it conditioned the very possibility of our existence, but it's only habit.

In Russia the simple folk think that the earth stands on three whales. Some kind of savage peoples, I read somewhere, also share the conviction of the three whales, but extend its curiosity further and ask what the whale stands on. And they answer: on a snail. Such an answer seems satisfactory and arouses no further inquisitivity. Isn't that the authority of which Harnack speaks – the little snail, which he installed under the usual whales?

To allow the idea that heaviness and lightness are not characteristics of bodies seemed unnatural to Aristotle. It just so seems to our contemporaries, that moral weight and lightness are essential to man. And that there is some principle of spiritual weight, equally powerful and unchangeable in both the visible and in the invisible world. Kant postulated God on this foundation. And, although he was a Protestant, he expressed by this in the most definitive manner the spirit of Catholicism – always so afraid to devote oneself without looking back, without criteria, without conditions on the will of the Creator.

Luther then, as monk, but not as reformer, had to do exactly the opposite: renounce any authority. <u>Deus nos non per domesticam se per extraneam justitiam vult salvare.</u>[161] That is, the only thing in common between our justice and God's justice is the name. Now choose – do you wish to live by your justice, which promises you <u>honores</u> and <u>sancta superbia</u>, those great goods, by which even Socrates and the Stoics seduced their listeners, or you, having abandoned hopes on your own strength, your reason, your skill, charge off with eyes closed there, where per your <u>understanding</u> nothing can be, for there the whole order, the whole construct has nothing in common with those orders, which you are used to value in your life as the highest good. In the interpretation of the Epistle to the Romans this striving of Luther had still attained a comparatively meek expression. He remained a good Catholic, i.e., he thinks that the authority of the Pope still holds for them. He still thunders on heretics, and most of all because they do not wish to acknowledge the authority of the successor of St Peter. He doesn't even suspect that the dread temptation will await him himself in the yet near future and that he'll have to choose between the authority seen and the beckoning of the not seen. He doesn't even guess that such a dilemma is possible. It seemed to him, as it does to Harnack now, that authority is inextricably linked with faith. That is, that authority supports faith on itself, as the little snail holds the whales. And probably, if in 1515–16 someone would have said to Luther that the support of his faith would be chopped away, he would simply have not understood what he was being told, just as for Harnack now, for all his reverent relation to Luther, would not understand a faith, not defended and not supported.

Of course, Luther the reformer gave Harnack sufficient pretext to think so of himself. But we ought to here, as far as possible, also follow that Luther, who was ready to introduce a new religion in Germany and enter into desperate struggle with omnipotent Rome. We ought to select those moments of his life, as we have done up until now, when no one looks at Luther, when he is alone with himself, when he is not thinking of people, but of his personal, weak and helpless soul. In his works traces are clearly visible of all those special experiences. And, if I were asked, by which 'criterion' to distinguish those places in Luther's work in which the believer speaks, from those places in which the reformer speaks – and if I've resolved to do it one time – ein Mal ist kein Mal[162] – to head to meet the usual reader's demands and give such a criterion, I would say: this criterion is the paradoxicality of the judgements uttered. There, where Luther speaks like everyone else, one can serenely pass by. That Luther does not tell but convinces – beckons followers, the human herd to his side. He knows that the Τοῖς δὲ πολλοῖς ἀπιστίαν παρέχει,[163] the crowd accepts only 'proven truths'.

But just as soon as he begins to speak the truth of himself, his speech becomes just as unusual as it is unattainable. The most remarkable of his works in this respect are, besides the commentary to Paul's Epistle to the Romans, from which I have already introduced so many excerpts, his works De vitis monachorum, De servo arbitrio, the commentary to Paul's Epistle to the Galatians.

In these words the history of Luther's evolution is bared before us to the smallest details. 'Mann muss in Gottes Sachen nicht unserem Urteil folgen, und nicht zum Maßtab der Definition das machen, was unserem Verstande hart, weich, schwer, leicht, gut, böse, gerecht, ungerecht scheinet.' And further 'denn wieviel Gutes du auch tust, wenn du auch dein Blut vergiessest immer und andauernd zuckt doch unruhig dein Gewissen und sagt: Wer weiss, ob dies Gott gefällt'[164] (Über die Mönchsgelübde, pp 241 and 243). You see that Luther has thrown overboard the most valuable, the only existing compass which helps to direct people on their path. Where to move? Where to go – if doubts are the eternal lot of man? And exactly in the most difficult life positions we have no possibility of verifying ourselves. That which seems to us good, necessary, by which we have always tried to be directed in our actions – in no way has unconditional significance. We lay down our lives, we shed our blood for that which we consider the truth – and it turns out that in the judgement of God it's not truth at all, but lie, not good, but evil. Just like it was with the Catholic monks, they gave vows of chastity, poverty and restraint and were convinced that they did something pleasing to God, and God in their vows heard only blasphemy: ecce Deus, tibi voveo, etc. It is not allowed for us to penetrate into the mystery of the will of God:

> Er ist Gott für dessen Willen man keine Ursache und keinen Grund angeben kann, die ihm wie eine Regel und Mass vorgeschrieben warden könnten; denn nichts ist ihm gleich oder höher als er, sondern sein Wille ist eben die Regel für alles. Denn wenn sein Wille eine Regel oder einen Maßtab hätte, einen Grund oder eine Ursache, so könnte er nicht mehr Gottes Wille sein. Denn nicht deswegen weil er so wollen soll, oder sollte, ist richtig was er will, sondern im Gegenteil, weil er selbst so will, deswegen soll recht sein, was geschieht. Dem Willen des Geschöpfes wird Grund und Ursache vorgeschrieben, aber nicht dem Willen des Schöpfers, es sei dann, dass du ihm einen anderen Schopfer vorziehest. [165]
>
> (vom Verkn. Willen, 390)

So crudely Luther answers the delicate Renaissance philosopher Erasmus of Rotterdam. Erasmus in his Diatribe directed against Luther and picked the doctrine of freedom of the will as the basic theme of his rebuttals. It seemed to him that he was unassailable on this ground and that, conversely, the very weakest place in Luther's doctrine is his doctrine of freedom of the will, that on this question classical philosophy will uphold an easy victory over the ignorant and crude theologian. Luther denies freedom of the will – we are not allowed to save ourselves by our effort; God saves us and condemns us. One must remark, and this might be one of the most remarkable moments in Luther's doctrine of servo arbitrio, that Luther posed the very question of freedom of the will completely differently than in ancient and modern philosophy. We all, up to the present time, suppose that it must be stated in the most general form – either man is free always and everywhere, or all his actions, entering into an unbroken chain of other phenomena, are precisely defined by the totality of causes. Kant had another statement of the problem. Man, as phenomenon, is submitted to the general principle of causality; as thing in itself, as cognizable [умопостигаемое] being, he is nowise bound and freely defines his decisions. Luther, not adhering to any defined philosophical school, and thus not obliged to consider age-old traditions, posed the question otherwise. To him it seemed not at all necessary to acknowledge that man is either a free or unfree being. He easily allowed full freedom of the will – and exactly where Kant feared to let it: in the world of phenomena. Man is free in all the quotidian events of life – he freely marries, acquires property, argues, reconciles, gambles, etc. How to reconcile such freedom with the general consistency of phenomena? Luther didn't much worry about this: let consistency bicker as much as it wanted with freedom – Luther's not going to burst into tears on this one and won't make the slightest effort, in point of fact, or at least in his imagination to eliminate this type of disharmony. Man is free in this world bound by laws – here there is nothing either insulting or mysterious for him, who is not educated in mathematics and natural sciences, who doesn't know at all, for what end one has to at any cost to overcome multiformity of principle of this sort. If there is multiformity in reality, let it be. And further: from the fact that man is free in many respects, it in no way followed for Luther that man is an absolutely free being. Up to certain limits he is given freedom – beyond certain limits it terminates. This sort of break aroused no unease at all in Luther and seemed to him neither unnatural nor insulting. On the contrary, the doctrine of continuity seemed to him savage, improbable and blasphemous; the order observable on earth is in no wise order <u>an sich</u>. He distinguished <u>potentia ordinata</u> from <u>potentia absoluta</u>.

God by his decision established a certain construct on earth. But to extrapolate thence from the <u>potentia ordinata</u> established, to the very essence of <u>potentia absoluta</u>, as philosophy has tried to do from the time of Socrates, only those so act, whom their poor experience has inspired with trust in the limited, in the finite, always and everywhere steady state. Kant sent freedom off to the cognizable world and that only after he had fettered it in the same chains of immanent principle, i.e., firmly linking it proactively with the orders of our world of phenomena. Erasmus wished the same: <u>potestas clavium</u> could thus have been given by God to men because men are allowed to attain the ultimate meaning of the will of God. Men know what good is, and what evil is, and they are allowed by their own will to realize the good and avoid the bad. Otherwise it would turn out that God, who sent us off on the false path, would then punish us for heading down that path. And in point of fact, per Luther's doctrine, that's the way it is. Once people can do nothing for their own salvation, once even the very striving to be saved by one's own efforts contains an insult to the Divinity, how then to find justice in the rewards prepared for some people and the terrible punishments for some others. All the more, reasons Erasmus, that in Scripture it is said: God desires not the death of the sinner (Ezek. 33, 11). It seems to Erasmus that nothing can withstand these considerations: 'What', he asks Luther, 'God sorrows on the death of his people, having sent them this death Himself? If God did not desire death, then, therefore, one must impute our perdition to our will. But how can one impute something to someone who likewise cannot do good or evil?'

To Erasmus these reasonings seem the apex of human wisdom and profundity. And, as a matter of fact, they are unconditionally irrefutable as long as we maintain on the plane of ordinary human thinking – as irrefutable as the position that from a point to a straight line one can draw only one perpendicular, as long as we don't abandon the fundamental position of planeometry in two dimensions. But Luther had long already been raised above the plane of ordinary thinking. We already recall that he saw exactly in this the essence of Divinity, that it is the source of all laws, without being itself bound in any way. '<u>Deum necessitari non posse. In anderer Weise muss man über Gott oder den Willen Gottes disputierin, der uns gepredigt, offenbart, angeboten, und (öffentlich) verehrt ist, und anders über den Gott, der nicht gepredigt, nicht offenbart, nicht angeboten, nicht (öffentlich) verehrt ist</u>'[166] (Vom Verkn. Willen, 343). This juxtaposition of <u>Deus absconditus</u> – God hidden, to <u>Deo revelato</u> – God revealed, is the nerve of Luther's whole sermon.

He feels a great, hidden mystery, knows that it is unattainable, knows that it is in contradiction with all our hallowed wishes and hopes – and nonetheless with all our heart and all our soul we strive for it. Present Protestants cannot endure such an intensity of faith. We recall that Albrecht Ritschl renounced Luther's book <u>De servo arbitrio</u>. In the edition of Luther's work which I use, the well-known theologian Scheel,[167] referring again to the better-known theologian Kattenbusch, tries any old way to weaken the impression from Luther's speech. It seems to him improbable that 'God is free of any norms'. He denotes in Luther <u>eine Unterströmmung</u> (undercurrent), which preaches a God, definable by ethical rules and by exactly such rules, which we too with our limited comprehension are capable of attaining.

The fear and revulsion of German theologians before <u>Deus absconditus</u>, not bound by any norms known to us and even generally by any norms at all, are comprehensible and licit. We recall that even the Jesuit Grisar, who like all other Catholics, is ready to ascribe to Luther anything you like, did not resolve to indict him on such a charge, terrible from the usual point of view. I think that now, after the adduced quotations, no one would come to argue that Luther's doctrine can be reduced to Nietzsche's formula 'beyond good and evil'. Luther's faith, and perhaps, any actual, bold faith, begins only when man dares to step over the fatal line, drawn for us by reason and good. To renounce postulates – to demand nothing, to set no conditions – only to accept. Just exactly, as transitioning from non-being to life, we did not know where and why fate led us, just so, transitioning from rational conscious life to faith (cf. I Letter of Paul to the Cor. 2, 9); we begin all anew and utterly cannot know by what means we might best 'guarantee' ourselves new existence. The work of faith is not to correct the sinful and weak man. Our sins, our weaknesses are so infinitely great that by no efforts will you gain anything, just as it is not in your power to call non-being to life. Faith, by its essence, has nothing in common with either our knowledge or our moral feelings.

In order to gain faith, one must free oneself from both knowledge and moral ideals. Man is not allowed to do this.

This Luther discovered by his personal experience of monastic life; this he read in the Epistles of the Apostle Paul, and in the Gospels, the prophets – in a word, in the great and unfathomable books of the Holy Scripture.

XVI

We see from the preceding that Luther was led to those outer limits of human life, on which the brightest light of reason has not the power to show with any kind of definition the outline of the new reality. No choice there – one must either accept the darkness, as the natural condition of existence, or renounce life itself. This is not Luther's invention – Luther only tells what happened to him, as Tolstoy's Ivan Il'ich, Brekhunov, Father Sergei and his other later heroes tell what happened to him.

Thus Luther with such avidity threw himself at once on just those places in the doctrine of the apostle Paul, which the Catholic Church tried and tries in any old way to obviate or mitigate by artificial interpretations taken by them from Hellenic wisdom. They are incomprehensible to reason – they are a challenge to reason; how to accept them?

It's clear to reason that man may attain something only when with planning he consciously strives to a definite goal. Thus Catholicism in the Holy Scripture always saw 'doctrine', i.e., a series of instructions, how man must live and think, so as to merit the Kingdom of Heaven. Erasmus and other opponents of Luther willingly referred to the existence of the commandments, to the words of Christ to the youth: if you wish to be perfect, sell your property and give it all to the poor. And really, the Holy Scripture abounds with such places, which can be taken as an admonition to a righteous life or as the path to salvation. Erasmus as proof of his correctness quotes a whole bunch of such places, which attest that one can be saved by only one path: fulfilling the behests of the law. And thence draw an inference consistent with reason that, if the law exists, if it's said in the Scripture, that the laws ought to be fulfilled then, therefore, those to whom the edicts of the law are addressed have the possibility of fulfilling or not fulfilling them. For what could be more absurd from the point of view of usual comprehension, than to address a being with these edicts, who has not the power to fulfil these edicts and is threatened with eternal perdition for nonfulfillment of the edict. It seemed to Erasmus, as it seems now to all Catholics, that this objection is obvious to such a degree, that no one would dare refute it. Bl. Augustine also wrote: 'Non igitur Deus impossibilia jubet, sed jubendo admonet et facere quod possis, et petere quod non possis' (De nat. et gratia. Denifle I, 705). And more strongly: Firmissime creditur, Deum justum et bonum impossibilia non potuisse praecipere; hinc admonemur, et in facilibus quid agamus, et in difficilibus quid petamus[168] (De nat. et gratia. Denifle I).

And really – approach from any side you like – how to allow that a good and just God demanded the impossible from men?

For such an admission in actual fact is equivalent to a complete renunciation of reason. Is this acceptable for people? Obviously, generally speaking, it's absolutely unacceptable. But Luther had to accept it.

The usual mitigatory interpretations of the Catholics about merita de congruo and merita de condigno, by which men strove to throw across a pontoon bridge from human reason to the divine, were clear self-deceptions for Luther. Once we are not allowed to deserve salvation before God – due to the point that we will call our merits not de condigno but de congruo, i.e., acknowledge them as quasi merits, we cannot impute any significance to them. Our merits mean just about nothing in the economy of divine creative work – one must openly acknowledge this; reality tears such an acknowledgement out of people who have walked through Luther's experience. And once it's so, then the enigma remains an enigma and one must not eliminate it from the field of view but rather put it in the most visible place. There can't even be conversations here of compulsoriness [долженствование].

Here everything reduces not to what ought to be but rather to that which is. He who can hide himself from the great mystery by reasonings on merita de congruo and merita de condigno – he will not hurry to commune with it. But – when and under what conditions we cannot define – the moment occurs for a man; he can no longer not see. Imo nobis, Luther admits, qui primitias spiritus habemus, impossibile est, ista perfecte intelligere et credere, quia fortissime pugnant cum ratione humana[169] (ad Gal. II, 34. Denifle, I, 702). It's impossible to completely understand, it's impossible to believe and all the same one must accept. This improbable paradox, this mystery of communion with the absolute, I underline the word absolute, i.e., not to some irrational, of which Kant spoke, drawing his Ding an sich, in the sphere in which all the same the humanly comprehensible moral law reigns, but to such an unknown, where it is allowable that God might demand the impossible from men – i.e., where, it means, there is no place not only for moral laws but for any laws at all. That domain which Nietzsche revealed, apparently independently from Luther – the domain, located beyond good and evil and any kind of persistent ever steady-state truth. That domain, where Tolstoy lived with his heroes, and where Dostoevsky's underground gentlemen rules, where Shakespeare's time is out of joint.

Denn es bleibt ungereimt, nach dem Urteil der Vernunft, dass jener gerechte und gute Gott vom freien Willen Unmögliches fordert, und obwohl der freie Wille nicht das Gute wollen kann, und notwendig der Sünde dient, dennoch es ihm anrechnet ... Dies wird nach dem Urteil der Vernunft nicht von einem guten und gnädigen Gott zeugen ... Aber der Glaube und der Geist urteilen anders; sie glauben das Gott gut ist, auch wen er alle Menschen verdürbe.[170]
(Vom Verknecht, Willen, 382)

Hour after hour it becomes more and more difficult. It might seem to the uninitiated man that Luther intentionally down-selects affirmations which fortissime pugnant cum ratione humana cast a challenge to human understanding. How to allow that God demands the impossible from man? While man reasons, while he bases his reasonings on self-evident truths – without which equally neither scientific nor Catholic philosophy can get around – just so long he has not renounced the conviction, that Deus impossibilia non jubet. And authority in such cases does not have the strength to overcome the natural conviction of man, striving to see in Divine justice only the logically perfect development of the idea of human justice.

And when reality presented to Luther with all its ineluctable conviction, when he felt in his experience, that despite the commandment: non concupisces all the same concupiscentia turned out invincible, only then he saw that all the so-called self-evident truths exist only until such time, and for such people, until they collide with the reality that does not fit into them. God on the lips of the apostles dreadfully demands the fulfilment of his commandment; human nature, to which these demands are presented under the fear of the cruellest retribution, refuses to fulfil them – and not because it does not want to – it wants to – but it cannot. I said and repeat that not the Protestants but the Catholics truly limned the Lutheran experience.

He was in no way a pure righteous man; he was a great and terrible sinner. And, perhaps, his entrance into the monastery – which, he hoped, and all hoped who entered the monastery, that it would help him in the work of self-perfection – for even the Catholics, who deny, like Denifle, that in the acceptance of the monastic there is already intrinsic meritum, they allow that monasticism is status perfectionis and eases the path to perfection – thus, perhaps, for Luther the acceptance of monastic vows, imposing on man the obligation to fulfil, besides the usual demands of the commandments and consilia evangelica (i.e., the obligation of poverty, continence and obedience), with special clarity underlined the opposition between Divine behests and the helpless of man attempting to fulfil them.

The fulfilment of the consilia is just as obligatory for the monk as the fulfilment of the usual Ten Commandments is for other Christians. Therefore, it cannot be that they are beyond human strength. But, in fact, they exceeded Luther's strength. Luther could still externally fulfil his obligations, but his internal nature did not hear the Divine voice; worse than that it, obviously, mocked and even cursed the behests from above. Again in the commentary ad Romanos you encounter the following admissions:

> Non est Deus noster Deus impatiente et crudelitatis, etiam super impios. Quod dico pro consolatione eorum, qui vexantur jugiter cogitationibus blasphemiarum et trepidant nimium cum tales blasphemiae, quia sunt violenter a diabolo hominibus invitis extorte, aliquando gratiores sonent in aure Dei quam ipsum Alleluja vel quecunque laudis jubilation.[171]
>
> (Ad Romanos, 9, 19; W 56, 401; Ficker 227)

As early as 1515, i.e., several years before his collision with Rome, Luther knew of these terrible experiences, when a man, against his will, violates the greatest commandment and begins to blaspheme. And already then he dares affirm that such involuntary blasphemiae sonent in aurae Dei gratiores quam ipsum Alleluja. If you want to imagine clearly what these words mean, recall the passage in Dostoevsky's Notes from Underground, where the Underground Man with horror and some incomprehensible triumph as well – no matter how strange, extreme horror is always accompanied by at least nascent triumph – says: the world can fall apart, or I can get my tea. Let the world go, just so I've got my tea.

This, literally, is what Luther says, and adds on his own, that his blasphemy is more willingly accepted by God than an Alleluia would be. No matter how used we are to the paradoxicality of the people of the borderlands, to the fantasticality of their experiences, but, seems to us, there ought to be a limit to everything. Yes, seems so – in fact, no limit. The most improbable, fantastic transformations occur before our eyes – and each new step in the darkness promises all new unexpectedness, not submissive to any foresight and calculation. Catholic theology, with its attempts to seize and fixate the infinite world of experiences of souls discovering the mystery of faith, seems so impotent and infantile. It also wishes to possess the criterion of truth, wishes, like men of science as well, to distinguish error-free the shalt from the shalt not, the true from the false, in this eternal darkness. It takes with it as dependable guide the great Aristotle, true praecursor Christi in naturalibus, and in order not to get off the path, agrees to put him in charge of the supernaturalibus, too.

Each time that Luther has to tell of something unusual and unseen in this naturalium world, which the Philosophus so skilfully described, Catholics howl – this cannot be – this is false, this is disturbing. And exactly, the hair stands on end on the heads of Catholic dogmatics on reading Luther's works. Luther says directly – not one man can fulfil the law. And the law is not given at all to be fulfilled. What then is the law for? Quid igitur Lex? And Luther answers in the words of the apostle Paul. Lex propter transgressionem apposita est[172] – thus he translates τῶν παραβάσεων χάριν προσετέθην, not transgressionem gratia, not by reason of transgression was the law given, but just such that transgressions became possible. Again you say that such a statement is insane. No doubt – everything that's healthy in a man howls against such an affirmation. That almost stands to reason of itself. On the path which Luther entered, you'll meet nothing but monsters. All the meek, soft, easy, habitual, he's left behind. One must track him, straining all spiritual force, to preserve any possible serenity. If I here recall the howls emanating from the Catholic camp, it's only so as to emphasize the traits of Luther's life understanding, which so repulses the average man from him. Catholicism, in this case, took on itself the role – in common opinion, playing out of position – of defender of simple common sense against the attempts of a madman to possess the throne from which the truth is proclaimed.

Catholicism steps up here, no matter how strange at first glance, as ally of scientific philosophy. Catholicism demands a criterion of truth and does not allow the very concept of a truth, which does not have criterion and ultimate sanction. Science does the same. Its ultimate goal is to prove the possibility of objective verification of truth. Only those judgements can be called true which are defended by defined norms. The affirmation lex propter transgressionem apposita est cannot be considered a correct translation of Paul's statement in that alone, that it cannot be harmonized with our criteria of truth and justice. As we recall, the Pelagian Julian of Eclanum said this as well. But they did not wish to hear him in the fifth century. Bl. Augustine succeeded in this epoch in bringing the Catholic Church over to his side. And in the sixth century, we read the conciliar statement, affirmed by Pope Boniface II.

> Si quis per invocationem humanam gratiam Dei dicit posse conferri, non autem ipsam gratiam facere, ut invocetur a nobis, contradicit Isaiae prophetae, vel Apostolo idem dicenti: Inventus sum a non quarentibus me, palam apparui his, qui me non interrogabant.[173]
>
> (Denz. XXII, 3, 146 p. 52)

Catholics, of course, have not renounced this position. Even now they are ready to repeat, following the prophet Isaiah and the apostle Paul; I reveal myself to those who sought me not and was found by those who sought me not. In the treasure house of Catholicism, of course, there are many riches preserved from the Holy Scripture, but they all lie under a rock [под спудом – upon this rock [Peter-petrus-pierre-stone] I will build My Church – Trans]. They dare not show them to people. And people themselves have not resolved to turn over the rock. Each time the breath of God reaches man, he tries to close his eyes and put his hands over his ears – the scene of the Hebrews on Sinai repeats. In fear and trembling they demand that Moses himself conversed with God, and he retransmitted to them in their language what was to be revealed to them.

Now the Pope has taken Moses' spot in Catholicism, but he, as Dostoevsky truly said in Grand Inquisitor, has not dared to himself approach closer to God and exchanges the eternal truth for the false money of his inventions.

No matter how hard it was for Luther to admit, he all the same, despite Catholicism and its favorited teacher Augustine, was convinced that Deus impossibilia jubet, that God does only demand from man the impossible, and here's how Luther describes the mission and meaning of the law:

> Oportet enim mundum repleri horribilibus tenebris ac erroribus ante novissimum diem. Qui igitur potest capere, capiat, quod lex in christiana theologia et sua vera descriptione non justificet, sed omnino contrarium effectum habeat. Ostendit enim nos nobis, Deum iratum exhibet, iram aperit, perterrefacit nos et non solum revelat, sed etiam abundare facit peccatum, ut, ubi prius peccatum erat parvum, per legem illuminantem fiat magnum, ut homo incipiat odisse et fugere legem, et perfecto odio horrere Deum, legis conditorem. Hoc certe non est justum esse per legem, id quod ipsa ratio etiam fateri cogitur, sed dupliciter peccare in legem, primum, non solum aversam a lege habere voluntatem, ut non possis eam audire, sed contra eam facere, imo diende etiam sic oddise, ut cuperes eam abolitam una cum Deo, ejus auctore, qui est summe bonus.[174]

(Ad Gal. II, 88)

In all the philosophical and theological literature I know no more horrible and shattering admission. Even Dostoevsky's Notes from Underground, written on the same theme, pales before Luther's adduced words. Dostoevsky for that dared not speak directly in the first person. He, besides that, considered it necessary to conceal – like with a fig leaf – with his well-known commentary to Notes from Underground.

Maybe only in Tolstoy, in some of his stories, does the pathos of hatred for the law and God attained such intense development in its desperate sense of the dead end [безысходность]. If man has come to this – where else to go? Convene all the wise of the world, who would resolve to allow that any kind of way out is possible from such a position? Man is turned into nothing, into that dust of which he was created.

Yes, says Luther, but that's what was necessary. Nothing, exactly nothing ought to remain with man – and while he still has anything – access to God is closed to him.

> Nam Deus est Deus humilium, miserorum, afflictorum, oppressorum, desperatorum et eorum, qui prorsus in nihilum redacti sunt, ejusque natura est exaltare humiles, cibare esurientes, illuminare caecos, miseros et afflictos

consolari, peccatores justificare, mortuos vivificare, desperatos et damnatos salvare etc. Est enim creator omnipotens ex nihilo faciens omnia.[175]

(Ad Gal. II, 70)

Here's what was revealed to Luther in the times of his nocturnal vigils and tormenting struggle with the unclean force. Not when he broke with monasticism, turning to those who had not followed him, did he exclaim ecce, Deus tibi voveo impietatem. He turned with these words to himself, when he was himself still a monk and considered the condition of his salvation to be the exact fulfilment of all the vows imposed on him. When first this horrible consciousness dawned its black light upon his tormented soul, he along with all Catholics saw in God a Being subordinate to general human norms. He saw in Him a stern but comprehensibly just being, for whom, as for man as well, norms existed that defined His actions. He could not demand the impossible; He would not refuses His grace to him, who did all that depended on him – like an earthly wise king, too, in his court. And thus, he ought to feel a special disposition to the monk, who voluntarily gives up his whole life to holy service. And the monk legitimately hopes, counts on special Divine good will, feels sancta superbia in himself, of which we spoke above. All people vituperabiles aut laudabiles sunt depending on their conduct. So thought Luther, so thought all, or almost all in the monastic order. And, for sure, all so formulated the motivation which guided them on entrance into monasticism.

Of course, it's not accidental that The Song of Songs so attracted the attention of the strongest representation of monasticism in Europe. Not accidentally, of course, the psalms furnished so much joy to the recluses, tormented by self-imposed vows, and by the struggle with their own powerlessness. And all the same this, per Luther's experience, is still not faith. Not in vain did he ascribe to Bernard of Clairvaux himself the words – perdidi tempus meum, quia perdite vixi. The summation of any heroic exploit – so Luther teaches – is the consciousness that all done by man is done in vain. Once again, one must remark the striking similarity with the admissions made by Tolstoy in Father Sergei. Looking back of the past, Father Sergei must admit in horror that his works were good things in men's valuation, but before God they were not only not of value, but yet included in themselves a barrier for attainment of some higher, unattainable goal. And Father Sergei every time in horror discovers in himself that sancta superbia, which in ordinary times is the source of human energy and vitality and so distinguishes its bearers from those run-of-the-mill exemplars of our genus, but at the last trial, and that Last Judgement, the very existence of which seems not even deserving of the attention of modern positive philosophy – then presents not as holy but is diabolical. Why? Est einem (Deus) creator omnipotens ex nihilo faciens omnia (Ad Gal. II, 70). That's Luther's answer. God is the great Creator, creating all from nothing. And further:

Ad hoc autem suum natural et proprium opus non sinit eum pervenire nocentissima pestis illa, opinion justitiae.

That is, that same sancta superbia, of which Liguori spoke, and which in modern times served in the form of ultimate sanction as the foundation of the Kantian doctrine of good and truth.

> quae non vult esse peccatrix, immunda, misera et damnata, sed justa, sancta etc. Ideo oportet Deum adhibere malleum istum, legem scilicet, quae frangat, contundat, conterat et prorsus ad nihilum redigat hanc belluam (monster!) cum sua vana fiducia, sapientia, justitia, potentia, etc.; ut tandem suo malo discat se perditam et damnatam.[176]
>
> (Ad Gal. II, 70)

The whole commentary to Galatians is permeated with this idea. God created from nothing and man only apperceives God when, prepared in a tormenting and terrible process of internal renunciation, he loses any hope in his personal creative work. And the law, demanding the impossible from man, leads us to God. The law is the hammer with which God smashes human pride to pieces. Self-assurance is flushed out of our consciousness by the law, assurance in all, created by us. The law turns even the great heroic exploit to sin. The law led the pious monk Luther to the consciousness that in imposing the most difficult vows on himself, he in fact renounced service to God: ecce, Deus, tibi voveo, etc. Luther cuts all the threads, which before him connected the religious life with the usual life, albeit it was also high in the moral respect. If, besides the aforementioned examples from modern experiences, others are necessary, I can point to Chekhov and Ibsen. When I in my time had to speak on Chekhov, I had to speak of 'creation from the void'.[177] And indubitably, if Chekhov were not a physician, used to formulating his thoughts in the learned language of the nineteen century, if he lived, like Luther, in the sixteenth century, and was raised on the philosophical and theological ideas of that time, he would speak of himself and his ideas in the language of Luther. He would admit that God does not touch the soul of man where man has hope of managing his life by his own efforts [Бог до тех пор не касается души человека, пока у человека есть надежда своими силами устроить свою жизнь]. 'If you hate not father, mother, etc.' Ibsen would have said the same, for whom in the last years of his life the unattainable became the only goal of the strivings. I could also point to Shakespeare. In his tragedies Julius Caesar and Hamlet, more fully than anywhere else stands reflected that process of transition from human creative work out of prepared material to creation out of nothing, which Luther tirelessly affirmed. Brutus still hopes to realize the ideal of the good and to find in the good the ultimate human ideal. Shakespeare pronounces solemn words over his grave, which ought to justify the high mission of man on earth. Hamlet already knows that there is no salvation for him, that the hammer of fate has shattered him and his dreams to pieces. He cannot look on the earth – and no longer looks upon it. All his gifts – which so advantageously distinguished him from other men, not in the eyes of his kin, whom he had so burdened with both his deeds and his existence – for himself have become an object of horror and revulsion. I do not justify him: he's not working for your justifications – he fears them more than anything else in the world. He needs to be guilty; he needs to renounce his talents and virtues. He acts without taking account of his own actions, for who in Hamlet's position could do that? – strives, as Luther says, to the abyss, to annihilation. Not to rectify, begin a better life, and meticulously fulfil the laws, by new good works rectify old misses, missteps, and transgressions. And man is inclined to such an understanding.

> Ego, inquit, si diutius vixero, emendabo vitam meam, hoc et hoc faciam. Item, ingrediar monasterium, parcissime vivam, contentus pane et aqua, nudis pedibus incendam, etc. Hic nisi omnino contrarium feceris, hoc est, nisi ablegaveris Mosen cum lege sua ad securos et induratos, et apprehenderis in istis pavoribus et horroribus Christum passum, crucifixum, mortuum pro peccatis tuis, plane *actum est de salute tua*.[178]
>
> (Ad Gal. II, 71)

XVII

You see how far Luther was carried off course of the usual representation of the problems and goals of the human soul. The normal theologian, following the testament of the normal philosopher, writes:

> Utitur tamen sacra doctrina etiam ratione humana, non quidem ad probandum fidem (quia per hoc tolleretur meritum fidei) sed ad manifestandum aliqua quae traduntur in hac doctrina. Cum enim gratia non tollat naturam, sed perficiat, oportet quod naturalis ratio serviat fidei; sicut et naturalis inclinatio vouluntatis subsequitur charitati.[179]
>
> (S. Thomae Aquinatis, Sum. Theol. Ia, Qu. I, art. VIII)

It goes without saying, how seductive Thomas Aquinas' reasonings are for man. The grace of God is not in contradiction with human nature and does not nullify it; it only develops and perfects it. Thence it follows that reason not only does not struggle with faith but serves and helps it. True it is, and Thomas so concedes, that the truth of revelation can be neither gained nor proven by reason – otherwise there would be no merit in faith. This consideration is very important for us and we will again return to it and we'll see in the final account Luther too could not get by without it. But right now let's turn our attention only to that opposition in the train of thought of Luther and Thomas Aquinas which is clearly seen in the aforementioned quotation. For Luther Deus est creator ex nihilo – God always created and continues to create from nothing, for Thomas Aquinas and for Catholicism, God only helps men to be perfected and attain the highest rung of spiritual development. In this approach the eternal and implacable enmity of two currents of the human spirit is most clearly expressed. We already saw at the beginning of the present book that these two currents don't even presuppose that they be represented by discrete representatives. The same Plato who so sharply rejected the Cynic Diogenes, who'd gone insane, by calling him an insane Socrates, bore in his own soul the rudiments of the most extreme and stormy cynicism. He taught, as we recall, that philosophy is nothing else than preparation for death and dying. It's comprehensible that those dying and those preparing to die serenely and even happily accept that which arouses tormenting anguish and panic fear in those living and those preparing to live a long time yet.

Plato, as we recall, also added on his own accord that the problem of philosophy was and always remains a great mystery for man. No matter how strange, a mystery as a matter of fact remained a mystery even after it was discovered. One must think that it will remain just as much a mystery until the end of the world, even if people agree to write it in letters 10-feet high on all visible spaces or shout it out from all the rooftops.

Lutheranism serves as the best proof of this. The most conscientious and sincere followers and students of Luther up to the present time react no less hostilely to Luther's doctrine than do the defenders of Catholicism. Gratia non tollit naturam – they, of course, do not repeat these words, but all their adherence to Luther begins from the moment when Luther, having abandoned his isolation, began to speak with the people in a commonly accepted and generally understood language.

Luther knew for himself that man's nature does not perfect itself that the grace of God does not consist in liberating man from sinfulness. Man until his death remains the same sinner he was born. Justificatio consists only in God not holding man guilty of his sins. That's why it was necessary for God to send His Son to earth. Christ took on Himself all human sins – and by His torments redeemed the guilt of Adam and his descendants. But man became no better for this: they're the same sinners they were. All their hope is, despite their personal voice of conscience, imputing them the very sternest sentence, in God, Who per His eternal mercy, by His strength and His wise decision, which no man can attain, deigned to save those whom he marked in his elect. It goes without saying that such doctrine casts both Luther's enemies and friends into horror. People can absolutely not be reconciled with the idea that before the highest judgement all – both sinners and righteous – are equal. That all must renounce their works and their merits, and await only, that Deus est creator ex nihilo of the human soul, would anew, as once, create something.

> Hoc fecit, writes Luther, Bernhardus, vir adeo pius, sanctus et castus, ut eum merito putem praeferendum omnibus monachis. Is cum semel graviter decumberet, ac de vita sua jam desperasset, non collocabat fiduciam in coelibatum, quem castissime servaverat, non in benefacta et officia pietatis, quae plurima fecerat, sed illis procul remotis ex oculis beneficium Christi fide arripiens dixit: Ego perdite vixi, sed tu Domine Jesu Christe duplici jure tenes regnum coelorum, primum quia filius Dei es, deinde, quia illud tua passione et morte acquisivisti ... Is non opposuit irae et judicio Dei monachatum et angelicam vitam suam, sed apprehendit illud unum, quod necessarium est, atque ita salvatus est.[180]
>
> (Ad Gal. II, 284)

One so irreproachable in human judgement, as Bernard of Clairvaux in the final moment did not counterpose his monasticism, his exploits, his angelic life, to the Divine ire and judgement. All that was just as useless for Bernard of Clairvaux as for any man of the most vulgar and repulsive life.

Not only the virtues of the pagans but the virtues of the Christians as well are only brilliant vices and at the Last Judgement give man no advantages and no hopes. To unite with God <u>unum necessarium est</u>, one thing is needed: faith, i.e., the readiness to burst out of the circle of all those ideas in which men ordinarily live. Or, expressing it more accurately, faith and salvation are synonyms. He who has come to believe is saved. He who is saved came to believe, i.e., felt that all the limiting laws, all the foundations, all the supports to which man holds, are broken, shattered, annihilated, that all the light bulbs are out, all the signs have disappeared – so it is written: the Lord said that it pleased Him to dwell in darkness (3rd Kings 8, 12).[181] That is, the Lord said that His native element is that darkness, which man fears more than anything on earth. Does He demand of us that we voluntarily go into this terrible darkness? Not either. God demands nothing from us. 'I am sought of *them that* asked not *for me*; I am found of *them that* sought me not', says the prophet (Isa. 65, 1).

Men demand. God only leads – leads by those paths incomprehensible, unattainable, terrible for the weak mortal, of which His elect have told us so much – Luther, Plato, Augustine, Tolstoy, Dostoevsky, Nietzsche, Chekhov and many others, whose names I've not mentioned here only because one cannot tell about all who have emulated [сподобился] the great mystery. My problem reduces only to showing by a series of examples, how real life does not fit in the frames of those <u>a priori</u> frames which are created by the human mind for trapping the ultimate mysteries of being.

Outside our general principles, past our cognizing reason, flow the most remarkable and significant events of our existence. One can say more strongly – at any attempt of our reason to verify by <u>its</u> criteria the reality of such experiences of ours – the very experiences in the moment turn into nothing, literally as if they never were. Here one cannot verify, cannot fixate. Here sanction is also unnecessary; here there can be no authority. Here there's no true and false, no struggle between good and evil, no mistakes, no errors, no triumph of truth, or defeat of untruth. Here there is only real life, new, unlike the previous, unlike to a greater degree than is the life of a baby at the breast to the life of a grown man. Here there is no law, no retribution for those rejecting it or reward for those fulfilling it.

<u>Thomas et alii scholastici</u>, writes Luther, <u>de abrogatione legis loquentes dicunt judicialia et ceremonalia post Chritsum mortifera, ideoque jam abrogata esse, non item moralia. Hi ignorant, quid loquantur. Tu vero cum voles de abrogatione legis loqui, disputa praecipue de lege proprie dicta ac spirituali, et complectere simul totam legem, nihil distinguens inter judicialem, ceremonialem et moralem. Nam cum Paulus ait nos per Christum a maledicto legis liberatos esse, certe de tota lege loquitur, ac praecipue de morali, quae vel sola accusat, maledicit et condemnat conscientias, non item reliquae duae species.</u>[182]

(Ad. Gal. II, 265)

And again:

> Non tantum caermonialia sunt lex non bona et praecepta in quibus non vivitur, sed et ipse decalogus et quicquid doceri dictarique intus et foris potest.[183]
>
> (Denifle, I, 569)

I know how tormentingly difficult it is for a man to acknowledge, following Luther and the Apostle Paul, that the law is adeemed that the difference between laudabiles et vituperabiles, between first and last, is wiped away. In my time I had to note à propos Nietzsche's experience, by which path man comes to the sort of internal admissions, or more accurately, by which path fate leads him to this ultimate degree of self-renunciation. Here the terrible hammer of God is necessary, of which Luther spoke so much, and of which Nietzsche too spoke in almost Luther's expressions. We have too much grown up with earthly ideas and thoughts of the true and just and no one, not even the strongest man, has sufficient strength to with his own hands cause himself that ultimate, unendurable pain, which accompanies the attempt to cut the live wires which connect us to habitual being. We ourselves do not do this, cannot do it. The most extreme asceticism, the most desperate self-mortification, halts at this limit. Just as we cannot by our own will step across the line separating unbeing from being, so we are not allowed to transgress by our own strength beyond the limits of 'good and evil'. Reason not only cannot by its own power direct man in this enigmatic and mysterious domain – on the contrary, it directs all its admonitory capabilities, all its 'proofs', to restrain men from the fatal step. In the eyes of reason, at its court and under its valuation, to fly across the border of good and evil means to cease to exist. Heaven reacts with disinterest to our own falls and crimes, as well as our religious exploits.

Even young Luther felt:

> Homo, quando facit, quod in se est, peccat, cum nec velle aut cogitare ex se ipso possit;[184]

In the commentary to the Epistle to the Romans, in expressions, bordering on insane despair, he writes:

> Idcirco illi periculosissime de bono disputant ex philosophia deducto, cum Deus illud *verterit* (God himself turned into!) in malum. Quia, etsi cuncta valde bona sint, tamen nobis nulla bona sunt; et si nulla ullo modo mala sint, tamen nobis omnia mala sunt. Et hoc totum, quia peccatum habemus; ideo oportet fugere bona et assumere mala, et hoc ipsum *non voce tantum et ficto corde*, sed pleno affectu confiteri et optare, nos perdi et damnari. Quia sicut agit, qui alium odit, ita et nos in nos agere oportet. Quia odit enim, non ficte sed serio cupit perdere et occidere et damnare eum quem odit. Si ergo et nos ipsos sic vero corde perdemus et persequemur, in infernum offeremus, propter Deum et justitiam ejus, jam vere satis fecimus justitiae ejus, et miserebitur atque liberabit nos.[185]
>
> (Ad Romanos, 9, 3; Denifle, I, 505; W 56, 393; Ficker, 220)

I understand full well that in these words of Luther, as well as in many words adduced earlier, there is no possibility of trapping some sort of general idea, or principle, which ought to direct man in his conduct. But this does not deprive Luther's admissions of their significance. He for all that tells what happened to him – and whether we want to or not – we ought to accept them, despite the fact, as is even visible from the adduced excerpt, Luther himself falls under the burden of his unusual experiences. One must avoid good and seek evil; one must wish condemnation and eternal perdition on oneself, and not in words only but in deed. One must act with oneself, as you act with your hated enemy – do all to destroy him, says he. And here he adds that only then does God have pity on you and save you. That means we know how to be saved? That means a ray of light has broken through the outer darkness? Luther has been seduced by Hellenic wisdom as he attains the goal?

Luther especially willingly recalls the imperfection of the saints:

Imo quandoque etiam accidit, ut sancti labantur et desideria ipsius carnis perficiant. Sicut David grandi et horribili lapsu cecidit in adulterium, item auctor fuit caedis multorum ... Lapsus est horribiliter et Petrus, cum negaret Christum etc.[186]

(Ad Gal. III, 31)

And all the saints, says Luther, were sinless only in man's imagination.

Itaque sophistarum (i.e., Catholics) sancti similes sunt sapientibus stoicorum, qui tales finxerunt sapientes, quales nulli unquam fuerunt in rerum natura, et hac stulta et impia persuasione, quae nata est ex enscitia hujus Paulinae doctrinae, adegerunt sophistae se ipsos et alios infinitos ad desperationem.[187]

(Gal., III, 33)

I myself, Luther tells further on, when I was a monk, dreamed of hearing and seeing such a saint.

Interim tamen somniabam talem sanctum, qui in eremo agens abstineret a cibo et potu et victitaret tantum radiculis herbarum et aqua frigida, et illam opinionem de monstrosis illis sanctis non solum hauseram ex libris sophistarum, set etiam partum. Nam alicubi s. Hieronimus sic scribit: de cibis vero et potu taceo, cum luxuria sit etiam languentes aqua frigida uti et coctum aliquid accepisse.[188]

(Gal., III, 34)

Such saints, who hope by stern restraint ('denial'), self-flagellation and other heroic exploits to merit salvation, seem monstrous to Luther. They themselves indeed ought ineluctably to head to despair and lead others to despair. They have no faith in God; they, like the Stoics, have faith in their strength – and this faith sooner or later will be crushed against the factual impossibility of doing anything. In summa, sancti sunt sanctitate passiva non activa. That is, in other words, God will only extend help to man, when man has finally despaired of himself, when he has dropped his hands, when he sees nothing before him, besides darkness and horror. Such was Luther's <u>experience</u>. While he struggled and strove by fulfilment of the law to gain sanctity, he fell deeper and deeper. And only when he felt that he had lost his last hope, when he was convinced that he was not the best, but the worst, not the strongest, but the weakest – completely powerless man, only then was he convinced that God alone could give him that which he had so vainly laboured on in the long years of his reclusion. Previously he dreamed to have at least one glance at a holy man – and saw only weak and unworthy people. Now, he tells:

> <u>laetus gratias ago Deo, quod supra modum abunde mihi donaverit, quod olim petit non ut viderem unum sanctum, sed multos, imo infinitus vere sanctos, … quorum et ego, gratia Dei, unus sum.</u>[189]

One must dwell attentively on these words, for hence Luther's doctrine of salvation <u>sola fide</u> takes its principle. Heretofore, I have culled from Luther's disparate works exclusively those places, in which he described the history of his conversion or, if you will, his apostasy. Now Luther approaches a new problem. He wishes to transform his experience into doctrine. That is, he wishes in his one man's experience to find such elements as making him generally interesting and significant. Luther repeats more than once that God leads men by unfathomable paths. And the path by which he was himself miraculously transformed from the last sinner into a righteous man was also unusual and miraculous, completely unattainable for human reason. It would seem Luther could be satisfied with a simple description of the history of his conversion. Perhaps, he could indeed have limited himself to this if he were fated to remain a simple monk. But fate decided otherwise. Fate entrusted him to lead man and create history; Luther had to enter into unequal struggle with omnipotent Rome. The infallible Pope and the whole Catholic Church cast at him the terrible accusation of heresy. He was informed that if he did not renounce his errors, he would be expelled from the Church and subject to anathema. And Luther picked up the gauntlet thrown his way, not suspecting even for a single minute that, if all that he was told was true of his visions and revelations, then his first and greatest problem ought to have been the readiness to decline the argument begun by Rome. Rome, remaining true to itself, was within its right to call Luther to court, for Rome, legitimately or illegitimately, claimed the full scope of <u>potestas clavium</u>. Rome considered that it alone was bequeathed the power of the keys, that it was right to bind and decide – could Luther lay claim to such a right?

We already recall that the very idea of <u>potestas clavium</u> first arose with Socrates and from him, through the Stoics, from whom Luther emancipated himself with such labour and then transitioned to Catholicism. For the power of the keys presupposes the continuity and hereditary connection between the human and divine – just exactly that, against which Luther rebelled with such magnificent inspiration and passion. Catholics could seek arguments in Hellenic philosophy, for Catholics reason was the ultimate instance. They knew only <u>Deus revelatus</u> – Luther felt on himself the power of <u>Deus absconditus</u>. Can one submit the will and foreshadowings of the mysterious God inhabiting the darkness to such logical rework as Catholicism worked out over the will of its revelatory God?

But here yet another question arises. Could Luther begin his struggle with Catholicism in the name of those mysterious revelations, untransmittable in words, of which he told so much in his best works? In order to overcome Catholicism, he ought to have contrasted a new doctrine to the old one. He proposed – Lutheranism has preserved this in principle even now – to consider the Holy Scripture the sole source of religious cognition. But, as is clear to anyone who is even a little acquainted with the Holy Scripture, Luther could not stop at this. The Holy Scripture evokes the most varied representations from different people. While Catholicism, assuming to itself the power of singular interpretation of Scripture, taught humanity truth, there could still be discussion of unity.

But, after Luther repelled against this prerogative of Rome, there were no longer any means to unify people in one truth. Luther had to choose one or the other – either renounce his claims or admit together with Catholicism that the right of teaching was really delegated by God not to all but only to the elect. Only on this condition was argument possible, was struggle possible with its, of course, accidents of success and failure. And Luther, I say, decided to accept the challenge – come what may.

The triumph of truth, as always happens, was dependent on the talents, energy and stubbornness of the disputing sides. And this just as little astonished Luther as it did the Catholics. We know the outcome of the struggle: neither one of the warring sides succeeded in gaining full victory. Luther and Lutheranism split off many hundred thousands of souls from Catholicism. But Catholicism preserved for itself a still large number of faithful sons. The struggle did not lead to full triumph 'of the truth' or even to its clarification. Opponents even now stand one against the other, armed from head to foot. And both are profoundly convinced that they once and for all have discovered eternal truth and given it adequate expression in words. Melanchthon, in one of his letters, thus formulates Luther's 'doctrine'.

<u>Quando Deus justificare vult hominem, terret ejus conscientiam per legem et facit, ut agnoscat peccata; hinc ille ad desperationem impellitur, nec est pax ulla conscientiae, nisi dominus dederit ei remissionem peccatorum per absolutionem, que est Evangelium.</u>[190]

(Denifle, I, 730)

You already note in these words, which at first glance so closely recall what we earlier heard from Luther, the presence of a new element, by which Melanchthon, unnoticed for himself, and, perhaps, for Luther himself, tries to connect and define the scattered statements of his teacher. Melanchthon already in exact and definite expressions defines the mechanism of the process of human salvation.

In order to save man, God ought to first shake his soul and crush it. God can save a man otherwise? Melanchthon knows this how? Melanchthon knows even more, i.e., he even more boldly begins to demarcate the limits of Divine omnipotence. In loci communes, which already makes the first attempt to substitute itself for the Roman catechism, he writes:

> Assensus seu fiducia in promissionem divinam, quod Christus pro me datus sit, quod Christus mea deleat peccata, quod Christus vivificat me, haec fides es illa Evangelii, quae sola justificat i.e., sola reputatur nobis a Deo pro justitia; opera quantumenis videantur bona pro justitia non reputantur.[191]

Here, too, as in the earlier adduced excerpt, all is so similar to what Luther said, that you'll not be astonished at all, that Luther considered Melanchthon his alter ego, and even affirmed that Melanchthon expressed his thoughts better than he himself did. And as a matter of fact, Melanchthon possessed one great advantage over Luther – Luther gained his material out of the depths of his own experience – crude, unpolished material, such as it was created in the depths of his own soul. He himself saw and heard what he said.

The material came to Melanchthon, albeit poor, but all the same reworked. No matter how sincere and truthful he was, all beginners, all activists, compelled to act on their own initiative, are especially truthful – but all the same he too could not say of himself only how it was and what happened. For, if he had set himself such a goal, no one would have listened to him. And Luther buffed and shined his experiences. Melanchthon understood his life work as namely to liberate Luther's beginning from all accreted escapes which insult human consciousness. And, before all, from such undefinition and arbitrariness, which really scares people.

One had to contrast a no less strong and exact doctrine to the stern and exact doctrine of Rome. Luther, too, as I indicated, well understood this. But Luther in the depth of his soul knew something else, too, for he experienced internal events which least of all harmonized with the representations of the existence of a definite mechanism in the universe. Luther could write:

> Justificatur quidem homo fide coram Deo etiamsi apud homines et in se ipso ignominiam tantum inveniat. Hoc est mysterium Dei sanctos suos mirificantis, quod non solum est impiis impossibile intellectu, sed etiam piis mirabile et difficile creditu.[192]

(Ritschl, I, 99)

Luther knew this full well – God saves a man, who in both his own eyes and the opinion of his neighbours has no hope of salvation. And the Divine mysteries are equally miraculous and unattainable not only for the impious but for the righteous. If that's so, then, obviously, Luther could juxtapose nothing to the Roman catechism, which was created by men who put their own understanding in place of Divine wisdom. Luther wasn't even afraid to say of Christ:

<u>Realiter et vere se in aeternam damnationem obtulit Deo patri pro nobis, et humana natura non aliter se habuit, quam homo aeternaliter damnandus ad infernum.</u>[193]

(<u>Ad Romanos</u>, 9, 3; Denifle, I, 506; W 56, 392; Ficker, 218)

You understand what a seism the man who dared to write down such lines must experience. And you now, perhaps, grasp that Melanchton's attempt to logically rework what Luther said, by means of generally accepted presuppositions, must unavoidably lead to substitution of living, eternal, and marvellous mystery by dead and mortifying words of lightly changed Catholic tradition.

Melanchthon, like all ensuing Protestantism as well, avidly searched in Luther's words for definition and clarity, in other words, for a new law. They did not wish to go where Luther had been, or they did not wish, as happened to Luther, to hear the voice of God in the storm, under the rolling thunder and in the blinding light of the lightning – that they feared more than anything else in the world. They needed someone to tell them 'in his own words' what Luther heard and saw.

'What is a man to do to be saved?' they asked him. You rejected the Catholic law – give us a new one. And when Luther said:

<u>Necesse st certa fide credere sese justificari et nullo modo dubitare, quod gratiam consequatur; si enim dubitat et incertus est, jam non justificatur, sed evomit gratiam.</u>[194]

(Loofs, 722)

And when Luther began to prescribe, the flock began to 'understand' him. When the '<u>assensus</u>' was demanded from them, they willingly agreed to give their acknowledgement, and their true spokesman, like that same Melanchthon, sought the most comprehensible and generally accessible formulae for Lutheran prescriptions.

Melanchthon wrote:

<u>Manifesta et horribilis impietas est dicere, omnibus hominibus etiam non credentibus remissa esse peccata.</u>[195]

(P.R.E., XVI, 507)

Melanchthon already knows not only who is saved and who is condemned to eternal perdition. Without any hesitation, when he needs to repel the attack of Catholicism, Melanchthon takes up rework of Luther's experience. 'Experience' in and of itself has no interest and no significance for people. Some experiences today, other ones tomorrow. To rest at '<u>mysterium Dei sanctos suos mirificantis</u>' means to rest at not a thing in man's general opinion. One must find an exact and defined order, forever indubitable and obligatory for all. In other words, one must turn life into 'truth' or find such elements in life which would serve as guarantee for tomorrow. Not in vain did Luther from the first days of their acquaintance feel what Melanchthon could give him, and tried with all its strength to bind the promising youngster to him. Melanchthon, as we know, was no theologian and connected his name with Luther's work accidentally. Melanchthon was an educated humanist, raised on Hellenic literature and philosophy. And thanks to him, Aristotle, thrown out the door by Luther, came in the window and submitted the activist of the great Reformation to his influence. Without Melanchthon, or, more accurately, without the Melanchtonian spirit, the Reformation would have been absolutely impossible. Men could not and cannot live without authority – and one had to install some other ruler on the throne of the deposed Pope. Luther felt this even before his collision with the <u>Schwarmgeisters</u>. As soon as he spoke in the new way, all at once streamed to him with the authoritarian demand to present his new element as truth, single and brooking no contradictions.

Luther said: <u>Sola fide justificari hominem</u>, i.e., men ought to devote himself to God and place all his hopes on the Almighty. But it's so high to God – God is infinitely remote from man: who can take such words of Luther as instruction? For, it's the opposite: in them inheres the refusal of any instruction.

Man is saved by faith; this means, don't seek signs of the path anywhere, for you'll all the same find nothing. In the Holy Scripture you encounter the law, but the law does not direct you but rather diminishes you. The more you listen closely to the law and apply it, the more you'll be convinced that it can give you nothing. You, like the paralytic, are deprived of both arms and legs. Around you the terrible impenetrable night thickens and you have to live in the gloom for years, as Luther himself did. And seek despair, destruction. For Christ too <u>humana natura non aliter habuit quam homo aeternaliter damnatus in infernum</u>. Such was Luther's experience, by such a path Luther came to his <u>sola fide</u> – one asks, can faith be <u>assensus in promissionem divinam</u>, as Melanchthon later taught, humouring Catholicism and Thomas Aquinas? Was Luther right to affirm that the conclusive <u>assensus in promissionem divinam</u>, torn away from all its preceding experiences, can have any kind of significance? And all the more the significance of the one eternal truth. Melanchthon, educated on Hellenic philosophers, could, of course, think no differently. For him <u>sola fide</u> is either truth or lie. That is, if Luther is correct, then all people who give their <u>assensus in promissionem divinam</u> are saved; those who refuse this <u>assensus</u> perish. Faith for Melanchthon, as for Thomas, is an <u>actus intellectus</u>. And he, following Thomas, can ask <u>utrum fides meritoria est</u> and, of course, answer the question in the affirmative.

And in this is inherent the transformation of faith into doctrine – that which happened to Luther, having undergone specific rework by means of accepted common presuppositions, was turned into truth, universal and obligatory: he who believes is saved; he who does not, is not. And the readiness to believe or not believe, obviously, is entirely dependent on the will of man. There doesn't remain a trace of <u>servo arbitrio</u> – man already freely gives his <u>assensus</u>. And when he gives his assent, he has done all that depends on him: <u>facienti quod in se est Deus infalliberer dat gratiam</u>. What was said earlier is also forgotten, that God from the beginning of the world in His wise, unfathomable decision predetermined which people are intended to be saved, which to perish. Melanchthon, like the Catholics, does not agree to entrust his fate to God. They want to know what awaits them – otherwise they cannot believe. They wish to know that faith yields salvation, and thus with joy and triumph accept Melanchton's affirmation that <u>horribilis impietas est dicere, hominibus etiam non credentibus remissa esse peccata.</u>[196] You see what happens with faith when they wish to turn it into 'truth'.

At any attempt to touch the callipers of reason to faith, faith perishes. It can live only in an atmosphere of madness. It shares its power with no one. And the question is posed exactly thus – either reason or faith.

Melanchthon affirms that it is the greatest impiety to think that the unbelievers will be absolved of their sins. And the prophet, by whose lips God speaks: I revealed myself to him who sought Me not. Don't the criteria of truth taken by Melanchthon from Hellenic philosophers allow the words of Isaiah through their wall? Of course not. And while these criteria exist, the word of God will not reach the human soul.

XVIII

We already see now how malevolently he snuck into Luther's experiences, that old serpent, who never did die, who even in Paradise seduced our forefather with the promise of knowledge. He bypassed Luther – and kept his promise. Luther himself will be as God, if not for himself – then for his followers. He got his and tore his <u>potestas clavium</u> from the hands of the Pope – the right to bind and resolve, <u>potestas legandi et solvendi</u>. Luther now is no longer an apostate, heading in horror to meet eternal perdition; Luther himself is indeed a saint and possesses the power to make other men saints. The victorious, acknowledged apostate becomes forever a prophet.

They chopped off Thomas Munzer's head; Karlstadt died in poverty and oblivion – a grateful posterity, though, erected an eternal, imperishable monument to Luther. And, understandably, not because he penetrated, communed with the eternal mystery. All that he himself lived by was rejected by history. Put another way, from the moment that life drew Luther from the isolation of his monastery cell and required him to common service, he had to, willingly or unwillingly, fixate his revelations into definite and clear expressions and turn them into universal and obligatory truth. We recall how Luther oft said that his visions were given him by God. It goes without saying, no one's in a position to rebut Luther on this affirmation of his.

More so, anyone who reads his works could not but get the impression that Luther touched the sources of living water, invisible for the great majority of people. But this seemed little to Luther. Having believed Aristotle, that knowledge is knowledge of the general, and having believed people around him, that faith ought to be knowledge of the transliminal, he considered it possible to use his experience the same way, as all men use usual empirical evidence. By the relics of one excavation, the geologist judges of the fauna of the prehistoric period. Such random finds are valuable exactly because they give us basis for generalizing conclusions. No matter how Luther warred with Aristotle and that old whore reason, he could not renounce that sovereign right of generalization. Yes, I add, people would not have allowed him that. They gave him the power to direct historical events only because they saw in him not as an individual case of the dawning of Divine Grace – and only because, by a train of thought characteristic of people, they saw a manifestation of the general in the individual. If Luther by this and that path came to the source then, therefore, any man, following Luther, could get there on the same path.

So people thought, so Luther himself came to think a little bit. It goes without saying that for anyone who attentively followed at least the excerpts I adduced of Luther's admissions, it ought to be completely clear that this conclusion is completely false.

Just the contrary, the experience of Luther attests exactly, most of all, that there is a whole domain of human experience, absolutely inaccessible to that logical rework which is so successfully applied by us to quotidian empirical experience. Here we are concerned with, expressing it in the language of the Scholastics, not with potentia ordinata but with potentia absoluta (limited power, absolute power).

And just hear one must recall Occam's principle: Deum necessitari non posse. God is not compelled – and from the moment, when man encounters the breath of God, the end of all common rules begins. If you wish ineluctably to speak of rules, then one has to establish that possibilities that are nowise limited begin. And how much Luther himself told us exactly of those unlimited possibilities, excluding any kind of human foresight at all! For that's why he spoke of sola fide, that fides, as opposed to ratio, completely precludes foresight. How warmly Luther rebelled against the catholic fides formata caritate[197] – i.e., against the doctrine that faith alone is not enough, that it's necessary that faith be accompanied by love. And yet he didn't protest against fides formata and defend fides informis because the first commandment was alien or hateful to him. He was just convinced that men could rise to God only on the wings of faith, i.e., not when man himself decided to head to God does he go, but when God calls him to Himself. I repeat once more that Luther's experience showed him that the manifestation of faith in his soul was just as unexpected for him, as his own birth is for man born on earth. Perhaps, man transitions just as painfully from unbeing to being, as from knowledge to faith. We recall that to head to faith, per Luther, meant in tenebras ac annihilationem ire[198] – head to darkness and annihilation, that man is turned into nothing and, sicut paralyticus manibus et pedibus omissis[199] submits to the Divine will. That one has to renounce both morality and knowledge, yielding foresight – to go blind, go deaf, etc. Even the Law revealed on Sinai is not intended to guide man in the task of his salvation. The law, we recall, is given for increase of sin.

In a word, all that Luther told us of himself reduced to not how we saved himself but only to how God saved him. Every time that Luther himself wished to save himself, he sunk ever deeper into the abyss of sin.

The mystery of his salvation was and remained a mystery, known only to God. The only 'conclusion' which Luther might draw from his experiences ought to be reduced to the affirmation that Deus est creator omnipotens ex nihilo creans.[200]

Any attempt by man to guess the path which would quicker lead him to God is only self-deception, is a denial of faith, falling away from God. Self-deception is, perhaps, negatively useful, in that it leads man to new sin and brings him near to ultimate despair, but it has no positive significance.

Here's what, actually speaking, Luther could have and ought to have said, if he resolved to limit itself to only such affirmations as his experiences gave him rights to. He wasn't even within his rights to launch on Catholicism, either. For it doesn't at all follow from the fact that he, Luther, did not succeed in saving himself by his own efforts that no one is allowed to save themselves by their own efforts.

If we can in no way constrain God, if, as Luther himself taught, our merits are valued in the eyes of God as He wishes, then who dares to indicate to God that He can never condescend to the efforts of man and accept them as merit, and not only de congruo but de condigno as well. Luther, when he was a simple monk, had not yet allowed himself pretensions to the right of interpretation of the Lord's will. He did then feel that he made contact with other worlds and knew something that many people don't even suspect. And it didn't enter his head to consider his knowledge exhaustive and final. That which God revealed to him was only personal, individual revelations and Luther could then be grateful to God for such kindness. But that which could satisfy the monk was already insufficient for the reformer. Melanchthon and the whole growing audience of Luther did not understand limited truth. They demanded full, exhaustive, powerful, autocratic truth – they wished, I repeat, that he who taught them was himself all-knowing, like God.

And they got what they wanted. Luther as early as 1535 writes: Ego omnino nihil audio contrarium meae doctrinae; sum enim certus et persuasus per spiritum Christi meam doctrinam de christiana justita veram et certam esse[201] (Ad Gal. I, 288; Loofs, 744). Here's when Luther spoke up in that language which through the ages people considered the sole diction worthy of ultimate truth. It's no longer simply that the grace of the Spirit dawned on him – no, he received immediately from God a doctrine, doctrina – just as if God were a professor of philosophy, teaching assiduous students. But, as a matter of fact, nothing like that happened. What happened was, God reduced Luther to despair, shattered him with His hammer. What happened was, Luther descended to blasphemy, to self-hatred, etc. The doctrine doctrinam was created by Luther himself, created by those rules which were worked out by his eternal enemy Aristotle. And here occurred the earthly triumph of the weak monk – having united with Aristotle, he gained that force which gave him the possibility to struggle with Catholicism. An authority was created, on which men might rely, an incline up which all his disciples and followers could hurriedly scramble – right up to modern liberal theologians, who proclaim from the lips of Adolf Harnack that there is no faith without authority. Of all that Luther told, people absorbed only the conviction that the old authority of Catholicism ought to be overturned and Le roi est mort, vive le roi – a new authority ought to be established at his vacated space. Luther himself, at the news of Zwingli's death, with whom he had not converged on several questions of dogmatics (on the question of transubstantiation), did not fear to announce that

Zwingli's salvation, if he were saved, had to be extra regulam. This means that the paths of God became just as clear and definite for Luther, as if he, instead of the Pope, had received the inheritance of St Peter.

We observe here one of the most remarkable cases of the transformation of human visions and revelations into doctrine, into 'truth'. And, along with that, on Luther's example we can be convinced with especial self-evidence how little men value the attainment of eternal truth. Men do not need eternity and the unlimited – men seek limitation. The process of rework of experience into science, of which Kant speaks so much in his critique of pure reason, and which reduces to the insertion of all the complexity and all the multiformity of real life into a schema of principles to which no exceptions are granted, also presented in Luther. And Luther valued only those judgements which excluded any possibility of contradiction: ego omnino nihil audio contrarium meae doctrinae. As it seemed to Socrates and Plato, it also seemed to the reformer Luther that all that originates from God ought to bear the character of 'truth' in the human sense, i.e., of universal and obligatory judgement. And, conversely, he was sure that the absence of signs of universality and the obligatory discredit any affirmation. All the upheavals, all the usual experiences which fell to Luther's lot, could not, as we see, wipe out those paths which people from Socrates to modern times had laid for themselves, so as at least in their imagination to represent real life in agreement with bourgeois ideals of serenity and unchangeability. Plato hymned Eros – the most capricious and inconsistent divinity, and all the same concluded with 'ideas' – you won't squeeze any generally obligatory and universal principles out of Eros. Au contraire, the characteristic of Eros consists in the point that its affirmations have no need at all of general acknowledgement. He who has loved knows that love cannot find support from without – and along with that, not only has no need of such support but even avoids it. The affirmations and judgements of one in love are not all like the affirmations and judgements of sober and everyday people – but the condemnation of the whole world holds no terror for them. Socrates, and after Socrates, Kant and almost all of philosophy, in attempting to synthesize, i.e., converge to a single principle, hallowed by reason, all the luxurious and multifarious multiformity of the world, usually tries to crowd out of his field of view the rebellious little divinity – and with even greater sternness they persecute pure faith as well. Philosophy asks cui est credendum; they wish to subordinate man to their control even in these rare, higher minutes of spiritual uplift, when he, having forgotten all the threats and dangers of our miserable existence, recklessly charges to the eternally mysterious and unknown. It fears to let men even for a minute into that infinite world of possibilities, literally sure, that without its protection man couldn't exist even a moment. Look into the relations of the Catholic Church, to which all so willingly ascribe an attraction to the miraculous, to those of her children, who are fated to really touch the extraordinary and miraculous. We are used to Catholicism encouraging such experiences with joy. But this is a mistake. Catholicism, just like secular philosophy, is armed with a complete and very complex system of criteria, which give it the possibility of distinguishing beyond a doubt the true and the false in man's experience. And these criteria differ not a whit in their logical construction from their secular brethren. And here in the first place is the principle of universality and general obligatoriness. If someone has to experience something not corresponding to the principles established by Catholicism, then no matter how unusual his experience, Catholicism rejects it.

So that the similarity between spiritual and secular criteria is clearer, I will cite examples. That scholar, without vacillation, will reject any communiqué on a phenomenon, which presupposed a violation of continuity of the causal chain. With the same assurance the Catholic knows that if in a vision of God the Catholic doctrine of the Holy Trinity were not observed, i.e., if there were no <u>Spiritus sanctus procedeus ex parte filioque</u>,[202] then there's no need to further heed the narrator; he's either inventing it or is conscientiously self-deceived. The Catholic investigator of mysticism, Professor Zahn, says directly (p. 69) that not one heresy stands in sharper opposition to the Catholic Church and Christianity than mysticism, which has renounced its historical objective basis, i.e., the dogmata of Catholicism.

Just as the scholars affirm that all human experience ought to be subsumed in those judgements which are collected by Kant into the special category of synthetic judgements <u>a priori</u>, just so the Catholic scholar applies exact and definite criteria to the events of man's eternal life, by means of which he distinguished with high assurance the true from the false. Those who wish may be convinced of this, by getting acquainted with either the work of Zahn cited above, or the tract of the Jesuit Pulan, or at least with the little booklet of the recently deceased Cardinal Penari: <u>De falso misticismo</u>. The cited works, and many others, strive not so much to describe the experiences of the mystics as to verify them. Professor Zahn especially prides himself and underscores the methodological carefulness of Catholic investigators about unusual phenomena. He affirms that Catholicism no less sternly and demandingly than the most pedantic scholar approaches phenomena it studies. And he, by his own lights, of course, is correct. Catholicism, sharp-eyed and unsleeping, guards the walls of its doctrine, and Dostoevsky hardly exaggerated that it would refuse Christ himself the right to enter that domain, where the infallible <u>pontifex maximus</u> rules. And this is just as necessary for it, this is the <u>conditio sine qua non</u> for it, as its presuppositions, its doctrine of synthetic judgements <u>a priori</u> are for science. Logically the representation of Catholicism and the representations of men of science of the character and fundamental signs of truth do not differ from one another. Truth gives the right to affirm <u>ego omnio nihil audio contrarium doctrinae meae</u>. That is, a man decides to only utter his judgement when he is convinced that he has the right to no longer consider anything that does not agree with his utterance. One can say it even more strongly – and this more accurately expresses the nature of the human condition of 'truth' – he who utters any kind of judgement, as truth, supposes that by this utterance he deprives all people, all rational beings of the right to utter otherwise. If we affirm that rays of light move in straight lines, then anyone who affirms they move in crooked lines is no longer in truth but in lie.

This means that he who possesses the truth is conscious that his judgement is hallowed with some higher power so powerful that nothing in the world can oppose it. This gives him the right to that sancta superbia, of which the last doctor ecclesiae Liguori, spoke so much, and which, as we saw earlier, embryonic in Socrates, flowered so luxuriantly in the doctrine of the Stoics. Bl. Augustine and Luther himself hated Stoics. But they could not renounce the ultimate sanction or even share the right to the sanction with other people.

In order to become a teacher of humanity for the ages, one must convince all that you possess exclusive rights. When Luther said certus et persuasus sum per spiritum Christi meam doctrinam veram esse, he like all other teachers as well, no longer just retransmitted what was revealed to him in vatic and exclusive experiences – he interpreted the events of his internal life. And he interpreted with the help of presuppositions wholly received from the traditions of Hellenic philosophy. He, who had fought so much with reason, proceeded from the proposition that God, like men as well, is obliged to be subordinate to general norms and that, consequently, all that men hears from God ipso facto, by its very origin, can be easily transformed into a general affirmation, equally obligatory for all. That is, he, whom the word of God reaches, hears not only what is said to him but also something supplemental, and exactly, that the revelation is not revealed to him as such but as truth. Example: Luther heard that his monastic service was rejected by heaven. He was allowed to grasp that pronouncing his vows, he said ecce Deus tibi voveo, etc. Luther was not satisfied to see in this voice from above a forewarning for him. He 'concluded' thence that all monks give a vow of impiety. Thus concluding, he, without suspecting it himself, gave himself up to the power of the hated Aristotle. He no longer valued the revelation itself in the revelation – but rather the law, rule, general judgement, norm, i.e., just exactly against which he always so passionately and unrestrainedly protested. He, like modern gnoseologues as well, considered that the light of reason is not allowed to deal with the multiformity of reality otherwise than with the help of universal and obligatory judgements – and, outdoing the gnoseologues, extrapolated this proposition from men to Creator. Not only man – God himself is lost in the multiformity of the existent and can orient himself in it only with the help of general judgements. Luther transformed his revelations into truths and, bit by bit, insofar as he more and more had to step up to the role of leader of men, got used to think that all which he received from above was already received by him as truth. That is, each revelation was not a revelation for him but a general rule for all men. The same process we observed in Plato. Eros thus also was turned into truth and engendered a whole complex of immobile and eternal ideas.

The Lutheran faith underwent the same kind of metamorphosis and was changed into a doctrine, definite and exact, supported on sancta superbia as its ultimate foundation. Thence the Lutheran catechisms, of which he, and even more his followers, clear up to Adolf Harnack, are so proud. And exactly these catechisms are models of their type, and there is nothing astonishing that Protestants educated in these catechisms over the course of 400 years have so advantageously shared their moral qualities among the European nations. But, in order to write these catechisms, Luther had to renounce all his exceptional experiences. Here Luther speaks, as though he never ever suspected what he said in De votis monachorum, and De servo arbitrio, and his commentaries and other works. The decalogue established by Moses is the foundation of the catechism: Luther point for point repeats: thou shall not, thou shall not – completely forgetting those frenzied fits of rage which possessed him in other moments just at the recollection of Moses and his commandments.

Here's how he teaches them to understand the commandments in the shorter catechism: 'God threatens to punish those who transgressed these commandments, therefore we ought to tremble before His rage and not regress from the commandments. God promises kindness and all goods to those who fulfill these commandments, thus we ought to love Him, trust Him, and willingly live by His commandments.' You recall, with what pathos Luther related that man is not destined to fulfil the commandments, that no one is saved by the law. There is no talk of this in the Catechisms. There even directly, just like in Thomas Aquinas, faith is counted as merit – before God faith makes men holy, as conscientious fulfilment of the commandments is counted as merit: 'Know, that the Lord speaks to you, Luther exclaims, – and demands obedience to Himself; obey Him, and you will be His beloved son; disdain Him – and your lot will be disgrace, sorrow and torments.' This is the fundamental tone of the catechism. 'I, the Lord, your God, am a jealous God, for the sins of the fathers punishing the children to the third and fourth generation of those that hate Me, and working kindness to the thousandth generation of those that love Me and observe my commandments' (Exod. 20; 5 and 6).

He clarifies that these dread words relate not only to the first but to all commandments. In these words, he says, there is united

> enraged threat and friendly promise, in order to forewarn and scare, but at the same time attract ... His word we ought to accept in all His majesty and divine sternness, for He Himself speaks what meaning he attributed to the commandments, and as unfailingly as He will demand their fulfillment, so terribly and mercilessly will He punish those who transgress or disdain them, and how generously He rewards and how he will share all goods with those who fulfill his commandments and will live by them.

Luther, once he became a reformer, was compelled to minimize all that he attained in the minutes of his highest dawnings and uplifts. Jacob Boehme said that he himself didn't understand his words when God took his right hand away from his desk. And Luther ought to have said the same. But Boehme was only a believer; Luther was a reformer. A believer is allowed to give himself up to God's will. The historical activist considers himself responsible both for his words and for his works. Luther had to guard his doctrine with all his strength – how could he make admissions like those we hear from Boehme's lips.

The believer strives to efface the borders of the visible and invisible worlds. In his cell Luther blessed his weakness and the infinite might of the Creator. Before men he himself indeed had to step up in the omnipotence of the perfect gift of knowledge. Previously he did not fear a rift between the visible present and the mysterious future – on the contrary, in the mysteriousness of the future he saw the promise of something better. Now mysteries scare him; he avoids rifts; he strives as the Catholics do too to see one organic whole in universal life, so as to conclude with assurance from that known to him to the unknown. He wishes here on earth to hear the word of his justification and here on earth to have the power to lead his neighbours to salvation.

Of course, you won't get there sola fide. Faith gives neither serenity, nor assurance, nor stability. Faith does not base itself on consensus omnium,[203] faith knows no end or limits. As opposed to knowledge, it is never allowed the triumph of self-satisfaction. It is trembling, expectation, anxiety, strength, hope, constant presentiment of great unexpectedness, anxiety and dissatisfaction with the present and impossibility of penetrating into the future. Luther accepted such faith for himself, but for men it turned out unacceptable. People demand ultimate resolutions in their life. Could Luther say to them that there are no ultimate resolutions in life. That is, he did say that, but in the system of his doctrine, in loci communes, so masterfully composed to his astonishment by Melanchthon, all this wasn't a fit. The same thing happened to Luther that happened to Plato. It forever remained and, apparently, remains a mystery that faith, like philosophy for Plato, is only preparation for death and dying. Like Socrates and Plato, having attained this truth, the 'ultimate' for man, could not share it with men. So, likewise Luther left his sola fide for himself. He spoke of it, a lot, passionately, and strongly – more than Plato on his 'mystery'. But truth, even uttered, does not cease to be mystery. Philosophers in the Platonic definition did not discover truth – neither did Protestants discover truth in Luther's sola fide. They returned to the foundations of Catholicism – to its authority and criteria. And now Protestantism is only simplified Catholicism, as all Catholic theologians completely correctly affirm. The victor here too, as always in history, was not the insane but the common-sense Socrates, and the ultimate mystery left the unbelieving crowd for its eternal isolation – Τοῖς δὲ πολλιος ἀπιοστίαν παρέχει- (unbelieving crowd – Phaedo 69e).

XIX

It seems to me that the material collected in the preceding pages sufficiently clarified how unendurably difficult, one might say, straight impossible it is for man to transition from the usual condition of trust in his reason and his strength to faith in the omnipotence of God. Both our conscience and reason are so constructed that the necessity to give oneself over to the unknown seems to us the most horrible, most improbable misfortune. The unknown is a synonym of perdition [гибель] for us. We wish to support ourselves on what we have already seen and experienced, we even demand a guarantee from the heavens, and all the yet unseen and not experienced repulsed us with much greater force than even that which is known to be difficult. Only in rare minutes of exceptional spiritual uplift and seism does there awake in man a hazy and unclear consciousness that stability and organization which he has succeeded in gaining by his own strength are only a gift of our limitation [ограниченности – Trans.] and weakness. The Gothic cathedral and Summa Theologiae of Thomas Aquinas can just as little resist the destructive influence of time and eternity, as can the pitiful hovels of aboriginal people, as the lairs of the beasts, and the nests of the birds. Only the uncreated, only that is not made by hand, may oppose all trials and temptations to which the descendants of Adam are submitted on earth.

The most profound and the most mysterious story of the Bible, of the world created from nothing, and of original sin – so little comprehensible for a mind educated on modern apodictic truths – begins then to instil more trust than the 'proven' system of scientific philosophy. Man, shocked out of the habitual rut, begins to see and feel things which even the day before seemed to him fantastic and incompatible with the fundamental ideas of the very essence of truth. The experience and inferences of an entire, sometimes long life, even the whole millennial history of humanity are flensed, sometimes in a moment, as false and unnecessary. All that bore the honourable name of 'authorities', all criteria which guaranteed man the utilization of truth, lose meaning and significance. Truth in order to be truth has no need at all of general acknowledgment, and still less of any kind of validation. Jacob Boehme, in one of those moments of enlightenment, did not fear to say that man can say nothing to man of the divine. That is, that the Divine, per its essence, is such that it cannot find expression in idea, in principle, in affirmation, i.e., in not one of the forms in which man ought to bedeck his experiences so as to share them as truths with neighbours.

God is Creator – and all emanating from God is created anew. The creative work of the Almighty, as opposed to the creative work of mortals, is distinguished in that it is not subject to norms and limitations. Between earth and heaven is a profound abyss, break – and thus there can't even be talk here of gradual ascent. Here only raptum is possible – rapture, sudden and inexplicable transition from one condition to another. And thus, any attempt to prepare oneself or others for faith is fruitless.

Not in vain did Tertullian say: fiunt, non nascuntur Christiani.[204] Those means, by which the Creator prepares man for a new life, seem horrible and improbable from our human point of view. The divine hammer of which Luther tells, the madness of abandonment and solitude, which Tolstoy depicted in his stories, the experiences of the Cynics, of Bl. Augustine, the 'beyond good and evil' of Nietzsche, and others contain per our human scale so much cruelty, unreason, crudeness, that if we were allowed to judge, we would without vacillation condemn Him, who brought such torment into our life. Therefore, both Catholicism and Protestantism, equally interested in justifying their doctrines before men, write up 'mitigating dogmata', of which we spoke above. And first of all they insist on the possibility of finding a path to truth. But neither the exercita spiritualia of Loyola, in their straight-line sternness imitating the cruelty and implacability of nature, nor the sermons of Adolf Harnack, hoping by the path of humanist and rational convictions to lead man to what he considers the 'true faith', can move the inert soul of man off the spot. The mystery of faith remains a mystery for the ages, and all attempts of reason to find means of conversion of men lead to nil, and can lead only to nil, for, one must think, the very essence of rational devices, the very desire to find a true path to the problematic and unknown, excludes the possibility and implementability of the stated problem.

All the preceding presentation ought to illustrate the position stated here. Only, by the way, illustrate. There can be no proofs here. For the very domain of eternal darkness, in which we had to and have to grope along, to move without any instructions, is the domain of darkness because one can distinguish nothing there. There is nothing constant in it, nothing defined, nothing amenable to precalculation. There all is unexpected, fantastically random, in essence inexplicable. Perhaps, this is the root of the reason for eternal arguments on ultimate truth, that men, in place of the ultimate mystery, not amenable to definition and limitation, like all the living, demand precisely fixed judgements. Thus, one must think, the majority of believers have to be apostates and outcasts. The Catholic Church condemned Luther to anathema. The victorious Luther in his turn demanded unconditional subordination to himself and did not halt at persecutions. Calvin, having fortunately avoided the Catholic court, burned Michael Servet. True disciples of Aristotle, they were all convinced that truth needs human defence. If they did not support it with their weak arms, it will perish! And they, of course, were correct: the truth which they proclaimed and defended would doubtless have perished if it had not been protected by means of compulsion. The Catholic Inquisition was necessary to Catholicism in the same measure as Aristotle needed his conclusions and proofs in defence of the philosophical scheme he established. But that which people defended with these proofs of reason and sword was in no way what they lived by. That's why I the whole time over the course of this book tried to separate the internal lives of men from the truths they proclaimed. Internally they all were alien to any norms, general positions – when stepping out before men, they arrayed themselves in prepared schemes of generally obligatory positions. Here's why solitude, deeper than any on earth or at the bottom of the sea, is the principle and condition of drawing near the ultimate mystery.

No one will support you, all will rise up against you, all will condemn you – i.e., you will be left outside the protection of all laws, you will embody lawlessness in yourself – as Tolstoy, Luther, Nietzsche and others told, and only then will you understand what the psalmist said: if God is with me, I need no one. It's not even necessary that men acknowledge that God is with me. It's not necessary that God armed up on those who are against me. It's not necessary that everyone's like me, that I have means to lead men after me. A man can lead and unite men for a human task. But man comes to God only when God calls him, when God leads him to Himself. The ultimate truth is born in most profound mystery and solitude. It not only does not demand, it does not allow the presence of bystanders. Thus it does not endure proofs and most of all fears what usual empirical truths, admissions of human and final sanction live by.

I well understand that in taking away from truth its fundamental prerogatives, heretofore considered inseparable, its right to high sanction, to universal acknowledgement – I discredit it in men's eyes. And I am almost convinced that for the huge majority of people, truth, which has lost its right to general acknowledgement, seems a king without a crown, salt which has lost its savour. And all the same I can think and say no other [Ich kann nicht anders]. And I add that all those people of whom we spoke above felt, in the moment of contact with truth, as opposed to the consolidated opinion, that its meaning and significance were not at all in that it wished to be one and the same for all. As it's indifferent for a man in love, whether all men see the best woman in his beloved, just so for him that seeks the truth, general acknowledgement loses any significance. Let them turn away from him, let them unload jeers and threats on him – what's all this to him, if God is with him. He does not seek support and knows that men have just as little need of his support in the ultimate terrible hours of transition from unbelief to faith, as he has no need of it himself either. I think that it would not be otiose, besides those people of whom I've already had to speak, to point too at the conclusion of the present work to the history of a now little-known but nonetheless remarkable man, Michael de Molines. His doctrine left no noticeable tracks in history and hardly could anyone could wish that it were accepted by humanity. It seems to me that he too well understood that that which he knew was no good for guidance of man. Although he did write his guida spirituale, che disinvolge l'anima e la conduce per l'interior camino all'acquisto della perfetta contemplazione, del ricco tesoro della pace interiore,[205] i.e., as though promises in the very title of the book to lead the human soul by an internal path to perfect contemplation and to the rich treasure of internal peace, but this promise, as anyone who becomes acquainted with the content of the book may easily convince himself, is only given because, per accepted usage, every guida spirituale ought to promise something. Molinos himself knew well that his guida spirituale could do nothing in this sense. A Dio solo tocca, non alla Guida Spirituale, il promover l'anima dalla meditazione alla contemplazione: perchè se il Signore non la chiama con sua special gratia a questo stato d'orazione non farà niente la Guida con tutti i suoi documenti, e col suo sapere[206] (Molinos Libros, I, cap. XVI, 119). God alone is allowed to lead man from reasoning to contemplation and, if the Lord does not call man, no guide with all its instructions and scholarship will help him.

You will ask, why then a guide, why write books? Indeed the very content of the book gives you an answer to your question. One doesn't write this sort of book to show a man how and where he ought to go, what to seek and what to work on – not even the very wisest can do this. The problem of a spiritual guide inheres only in helping one's neighbour free himself from the usual wisdom, which has become as it were second human nature. Here too man might be necessary and useful to man. He who discovered the vanity of human wisdom, the vanity of prepared paths in the desert, can in a difficult minute support and comfort the beginner. Molinos' whole book, like the best and most remarkable places as well from Luther's works, says that man must head forward, not fearing the storm, not hoping on the promises of wisdom.

Finalmente devi sapere, che la maggior tentazione è lo star sena tentazione; e perciò devi rallerati quando ti assalira.[207]

(Molinos Libros 1, cap. X, 630)

The greatest temptation, he says, is when there are no temptations, and thus one must rejoice at temptations. He calls man to the final solitude – there, whither, as we recall Tolstoy's heroes and Tolstoy himself went with such horror against their will – only there in that divine solitudine can man find what is necessary to him.

> O dilettevole solitudine e cifra di eterni beni! O specchio, in cui di continuo si mira l'eterno Padre! con ragione ti chiami solitudine, perchè stai tanto sola, che appena vi è un'anima, che ti cerchi et che ti ami et ti conosca.
> (Ib. Lib. III, cap. 12, 119)[208]

You at once, per the small adduced excerpts, see how Molinos distanced himself from the usual human ideals and reasonings on good. He glorifies that terrible solitude, where not one soul will follow after us, where no one loves us, nor knows us. That which is considered the most terrible and unendurable punishment he … … …

NOTES

Lev shestov, by faith alone (Sola Fide)
Translator's Introduction

1. Emperor of the Earth, Modes of Eccentric Vision, Shestov, or the Purity of Despair, pp. 99–119.
2. N. Baranova-Shestova, Zhizn' L'va Shestova, La Press Libre, Paris, Religio-Philosophical Series, 1983, (Life of Lev Shestov, translated 2017–2018).
3. A key phrase, originally from War and Peace, where Tolstoy presents Pierre Bezukhov's peregrinations. [странствование по душам].
4. Baranova, Ch VI, p. 13.
5. (Recontres avec Léon Chestov, p. 42).
6. Lev Shestov, in Job's Balances. On the Sources of the Eternal Truths, Athens, Ohio University Press, 1975, p. 57. Trans. Camilla Coventry.
7. Lev Shestov, Potestas Clavium, Chicago, Henry Regnery Company, 1970. pp. 47–56. Trans. Bernard Martin.
8. Lev Shestov, Athens and Jerusalem, Athens, Ohio University Press, 1966, Trans. Bernard Martin.
9. Fotiade, Ramona Conceptions of the Absurd. *From Surrealism to the Existential Thought of Chestov and Fondane*, Legenda, European Humanities Research Centre, University of Oxford, 2001.
10. Alexis Philonenko 'Chestov et la philosophie' in Ramona Fotiade (ed). The Tragic Discourse, Shestov and Fondane's Existential Thought.

    Pour comprendre Chestov et Luther, *une même disposition d'esprit est nécessaire*. C'est moins dans les *contenus* que dans la structure de l'intention formelle que se manifeste la coïncidence; le postulat commun est que l'attitude se profile dans l'aptitude et réciproquement. Ce qui compte n'est pas l'Être, mais la manière d'exister. Le lieu privilégié de Chestov sera celui des joies et des souffrances des philosophes: leur histoire et parfois même leurs histoires entrecroisées.

    (p. 31)
11. Finkenthal, Michael, Lev Shestov. Existential Philosopher and Religious Thinker, New York, Peter Lang Publishing, 2010.

YMCA editor's introduction

1. This preface accompanied the Russian YMCA Press (1966) edition of Sola Fide.

Part I

1 Μανια – inspiration. Zeller (II-1, 511) in the second commentary says: "generally, religious inspiration, or in art, was named madness by the Greeks."
2 'Allein Niemand verachtet ungestraft Vernuft und Wissenschaft' (Harnack, Dogmengeschichte; III, 869) no one unpunished disdains reason and science.
3 Alles religiöse – nicht nur die Religionen – ist, gemessen an der sinnlichen Ehrfahrung und dem exacten Wissen, Paradox (Harnack, W.d.Chr. 44). (All that is religious, not just religions, as evaluated by sensual experience and exact knowledge, is Paradox.)
4 "Ich kann die katolischen Kritiker sehr wohl begreifen, wenn sie in jenen Briefen einen „wahrsinnigen Hochmuth" bemerken. Es bleibt in dur That nur die Wahl, diesen Luther so zu beurtheilen oder anzuerkennen, dass es mit ihm eine besondere Bewandtniss in der Geschichte der christichen Religion hat (Harnack, D.G. III, 813). (I can fully understand Catholic critics when they see an 'insane mania for greatness' in these letters. Really, one choice remains: so judge Luther, or acknowledge that he represents a special phenomenon in the history of Christian religion.)
5 Never yet in the world has there been a strong religious faith, which in the fundamental, decisive moment would not invoke external authority. Only in the pale reasonings of religious philosophers, or in the polemical conclusions of Protestant theologians, are religions constructed which would draw their stability exclusively from personal internal experiences … Jesus Christ invoked the authority of the Old Testament, the first Christians – invoked the foretellings, Augustine – invoked the Church, even Luther invoked the written word of God.
6 Cf. Harnack III, 507.
7 The crowd destroys all unless held in fear.
8 Eutiphrones para 10.
9 Tixeront, II.
10 Ibid.
11 Forerunner of Christ, not only in the natural, but in the supernatural.
12 Ordained power.
13 Absolute power.
14 First live and then philosophize.
15 First live and then philosophize.
16 Triumph of the cross.
17 Is the exercise of free will necessary for justification of the sinner? Here's his answer: God Himself justifies the sinner as said in the Epistle to the Romans 4, 5. God moves everything, considering the specifics of its nature, as we see this in the natural order of things, where He differently moves heavy and light bodies because their nature is not the same. Similar to this, He directs people to righteousness, considering the characteristics of human nature, but man is gifted from nature with free will; therefore when the matter concerns man, possessing free will, God leads him to righteousness through the cooperation of free will.
18 Note in margin: 'Quod veritati fidei christianae non contrariatur veritas rationis. Quamvis praedicta veritas fidei christianae humanae rationis capacitatem excedat, haec tamen quae ratio naturaliter indita habet, huic veritati contraria esse non possunt' (The truths of the Christian faith do not contradict the truths gained by reason. Although the aforementioned truths of the Christian faith exceed the possibility of understanding for human reason, it is impossible that the natural characteristics of reason contradict Christian truths.)

19 We conclude that man is justified without acts of the law.
20 Man is justified by faith alone.
21 Prince of scholastics.
22 As we see in the natural.
23 In the natural.
24 Precursor of Christ in the natural.
25 Precursor of Christ in the supernatural.
26 In the natural.
27 Natural.
28 As he sees in the natural.
29 ἆρα τὸ ὅσιον ὅτι ὅσιον ἐστιν φιλεῖται ὑπὸ τῶν θεῶν ἢ ὅτι φιλεῖται ὅσιόν ἐστιν.
30 Not thanks to knowledge ... but per divine inspiration (Ion.534 b; Zeller II-1, 498).
31 Δοκεῖ δὲ τοῖς πολλοῖς περὶ ἐπιστήμης τοιοῦτόν τι, οὐκ ἰσχυρὸν οὐδ᾽ ἡγεμονικὸν οὐδ᾽ ἀρχικὸν εἶναι (Protagoras 352 b). The opinion of the crowd on knowledge that it has no force, no power, and no authority.
32 Gorgias, 471 a.
33 To the philosopher, who worked his own task, specific to him.
34 God will unquestionably give grace to him who does what he can.
35 'And the goals which the crowd follow, not only do not give means for preservation of our essence, but rather interfere, being often the cause of destruction of those who are under their power.'
36 'The love of an eternal and infinite thing feeds the soul with only joy, it is free from any sorrow, it's what one must strongly wish and seek with all one's strength.'
37 For the philosopher, who worked his own personal task.
38 Trubetskoi, Prince Evgeni, author of 'Meaning of Love' – Trans.
39 Unbelieving crowd (Phaedo 69 e).
40 Before one's eyes.
41 So I wish, so I order, that will has primacy over reason.
42 πάντων γὰρ λόγον ἀξιοῦσιν οὗτοι εἶναι.. ..... λόγον γὰρ ζητοῦσιν ὧν οὐκ ἔστι λόγος ἀποδείξεως γὰρ ἀρχὴ οὐκ ἀπόδειξίς ἐστιν.
43 περὶ πάντον γὰρ ἀδύνατον ἀπόδειξιν εἶναι.
44 ἔστι γὰρ ἀπαιδευσία τὸ μὴ γιγνώσκειν, τίνων δεῖ ζητεῖν ἀπόδειξιν καὶ τίνων οὐ δεῖ.
45 Metaphysics IV, 3.1005b, 25.
46 One can say directly: philosophy begins where man ceases conversation not only with others but also with himself (cf. Sophists).
47 It is characteristic of matter to be passive and be moved. To act and to move belongs to another force.
48 Moderate in the extreme.
49 Over the entrance to Plato's academy was the inscription: 'Entry forbidden to those not knowing geometry' (μηδεὶς ἀγεωμέτρητος εἰσήτω).
50 Transition from one kind to another.
51 Introduction.
52 War of all against all.
53 Consensus of the wise.
54 Implicitly or explicitly.
55 Οὐδεμία γὰρ ἐνέπγια τέλειος ἐμποδιζομέη, ἡ δ᾽ εὐδαιμονία τῶν τελείων. διὸ προσδεῖται ὁ εὐδαίμων τῶν ἐν σώματι ἀγαυθῶν καὶ τῶν ἐκτὸς καὶ τῆς τύχης, ὅπως μὴ ἐμποδίζηται ταῦτα. 3 Οἱ δὲ τὸν τροχιζόμενον καὶ τὸν δυστυχίαις μεγάλαις

περιπίπτοντα εὐδαίμονα φάσκοντες εἶναι, ἐὰν ἢ ἀγαθός ἢ ἑκόντες ἢ ἄκοντες οὐδὲν λέγουσιν (Eth. Nic. VII, 13.2 – Zeller II-2, 620–1).

56 The mean is that which good sense ordains.
57 Voluntarily or involuntarily spoke rubbish.
58 As opposed to Antisthenes' μανείν μᾶλλον ἢ ἡσθείην (Zeller II–1, 260 – better to lose my mind than experience pleasure).
59 Philosophia Aristotelis seu doctrina magis debet dici opinio quam scientia. (Aristotle's philosophy or his doctrine ought to be called an opinion, rather than science.)
60 Eutiphrones 10a.
61 The truths of Christian faith do not contradict the truths of reason.
62 The son of God was crucified: it is not shameful because it is shameful; the son of God died: it is more probable because it is absurd; He arose from the grave: credible because it is impossible (Tertullian. De Carne Christi, V).
63 All else that is of God is good because it is pleasing to God and not the converse; for God all is good insofar as it corresponds to His will and not the converse. Therefore also Christ's sacrifice was good insofar as it was accepted by God and insofar merited, inasmuch as it was acknowledged by God; acknowledgement by God is the most powerful reason and the basis of any good.
64 Acknowledgement by God is the most powerful reason and the basis of any good.
65 There is no basis for why His will wished this, for just His will is His will.
66 Thus He (God) could act otherwise; He could proclaim another law just, inasmuch as established by God, in that no law can be just if it derives not from the Divine will.
67 Kattenbusch (Romische Kirche, PRE v XVII, p. 107) even tries to tie to Catholics the idea of God as the incarnation of arbitrariness in order to have the right to say of Catholicism (Durche solche Vorstellung wird die Gottesidee … dessittlichen Nervs beraubt. Such an idea of God as presented is bereft … of its moral nerve).

Catholics not without reason are disturbed by the article of Kattenbusch. The whole characterization of the Catholic representation of God he's done is completely incorrect. And, chiefly, ideas are ascribed to Catholicism which Luther preached with special pathos and which are not repulsive to the whole treasure of doctrine of the Catholic Church. Why did Kattenbusch need this?

68 Es ist ein echt scotistischer Gedanke, dass der absolute göttliche Wille nicht unter das Mass unserer ethischen Denkgewohnheiten (!) gestellt werden könne. (It's a completely Scotian idea that the absolute Divine will is not subsumed under the measure of our ethical capability of thinking.) After the word Denkgewohnheiten Harnack throws in an exclamation point on his own.
69 The Catholic Church considers as truth "quod semper, quod ubique, quod ab omnibus creditum est" (In which always, everywhere, everyone believed). KATTENBUSCH, Die Romische Kirche, PRE XVII, 104.
70 As visible in the natural.
71 To him who does what is within his power, God will certainly grant grace.
72 From nature no one can be worthy of eternal life even in possession of whatever gifts received from God. He only deserves eternal life in the case, per such gifts, if God freely and mercifully ordered this; nothing can compel God to give anyone eternal life.
73 One cannot prove by evidence that a singular God exists.
74 One cannot prove in the natural manner that desire cannot be fulfilled and stilled by anyone except God.
75 One cannot prove satisfactorily that God is the ultimate cause.

76 He allows and does not find it unseemly that the creature will might hate God, without falling in sin, because God could prescribe this.
77 God can prescribe that a rational being hate God and this obedience will be greater service than love for God because this being will obey with greater effort, for he acts against his inclinations.
78 It is an article of faith that God took human nature, and there would be no contradiction if God took the nature of an ass or the nature of rock or tree.
79 Characterization of Occam: Werner, Thomas Aquinas III, p. 120.
80 No natural thinking can demonstrate the existence of several persons in the Godhead [Божество]; therefore that there are several persons, of which one is the Father and the other Son, and that the Son is truly begotten from the Father is an affirmation of faith alone.
81 οὐδέ ἄλλο τι τῶν ὄντων ... ἐξάγει τήν ὑπέρ πάντα καί λόγος καί νοῦν κρυφιότητα τῆς ὑπέρ πάντα ὑπερουσίως ὑπερούσης ὑπερθεότητος (De Divinis Nominibus, XXX, 3).
82 Unattainable light, which not one man has seen or can see.
83 One can attain super-rational knowledge through unknowing (De Mystica Theologia I, 3).
84 In divine things, to know is to know that we do not know.
85 Trans – Prof. **Emil Heinrich du Bois-Reymond** FRSF or HFRSE (7 November 1818–26 December 1896) was a German physician and physiologist, the co-discoverer of nerve action potential, and the developer of experimental electrophysiology.
86 Why Werner allows this exception is completely unclear to me. We recall that Occam allowed that if God would command to hate Him, then he who obeyed this commandment would be more right than he who despite it would continue to love God more than anything.
87 Trans – **Socinianism** is a system of Christian doctrine named for Italians Lelio Sozzini (Latin: Laelius Socinus) and Fausto Sozzini (Latin: Faustus Socinus), uncle and nephew, respectively, which was developed among the Polish Brethren in the Minor Reformed Church of Poland during the sixteenth and seventeenth centuries and embraced by the Unitarian Church of Transylvania during the same period. It is most famous for its nontrinitarian Christology but contains a number of other unorthodox beliefs as well.
88 God cannot be compelled.

Part II

1 Grisard, III, 438–9. So I wish, so I order – to privilege will over reason.
2 Reuter (38ᵉ Augustine Studien) says of Pelagius and Celsetius:
Der gewohnheitsmässige Gehorsam gegen die Autoritat der Kirche was auch der ihrige. Beide Männer verfolgten als gute K a t h o l I k e n augenscheinlich eine kirchliche k o n s e r v a t I v e Tendenz; von irgendwelchen schismatischen Neigungen finden wir bei denselben kiene Spur.
(They too had the habitual obedience to the authority of the Church. Both followed, apparently, as good Catholics, the Church conservative tendency; we don't find even a trace in them of any kind of heretical tendency.)
3 Augustine, who attained virtue, passing through vice, and who emerged from his error only thanks to the feeling that the hand of God guided him with great power, was obliged to his personal experience for the profound feeling of human helplessness [немощ] and divine help [помощ].

4 By means of His doctrine and His revelation, God now opens for us the eyes of our heart, now shows the future, in order that we not be busied with the task of the present, now reveals the intrigues of the devil, now illumines by the multiform and ineffable [Trans – неослабным – неославным] gift of heavenly grace ... Does it seem to you that he who affirms this rejects grace?

5 Nihil potest per Sanctas Scripturas probare, quod justitia non potest tueri. (Julian, Op. imperf. II. 17, cited by Harnack III, 197). (Nothing can be proven by Holy Writ that cannot be justified by justice.)

6 In truth, those will be rewarded, who, using well freedom of the will, deserve the grace of God and keep his commandments.

7 Thus, God beforehand knew who would eventuate in the future holy and without sin through the service of his free will and thus elected those before the creation of the world in his own great knowledge, which knew beforehand that they would become thus. Consequently, He selected them before they became such, foreordaining for sonhood those he beforehand knew as future saints and sinners. In any case, He did not commit this but foresaw what they would become, but He did not create them thus.

8 Pagan virtues are splendid vices.

9 Adam, being created mortal, had to die, whether he sinned or not.
Because the sin of Adam doomed him, and not the human race.
Because thus the law may lead to the kingdom as well as does the Gospel.
Because before the coming of Christ there were men without sin.
Because children are born in the same condition Adam was before his disobedience.
Because it is not due to the death and disobedience of Adam that the whole human race dies, as it does not arise from the resurrection of Christ.
Man, if he wishes, can be without sin.
Children, although not baptized, have eternal life.
If the baptized rich men do not renounce all their goods, even though it seemed that they do something good, it will not be credited to them, and they cannot receive the Kingdom of God.

10 Man can be without sin and easily follow the commandments of God, if he wishes.

11 Augustine said of him: 'Pelagii nomen cum magna ejus laude cognovi' (Harnack, III, 172). I heard the name of Pelagius with great praise of him.
Harnack says:
Der Ernst und die 'Heligkeit' das Pelagius sind vielfach bezeugt, vor Allen von Augustin selbst und Paulin von Nola (Harnack III, 169). (The seriousness and holiness of Pelagius was multiply attested, first of all by Augustine himself and Paulin von Nola.)

12 Any good or evil, for which we might be praised or condemned, does not arise with us but is performed by us. We are receptive to one and the other, but it is not inborn in us.

13 When I speak of morality and of the principles of holy life, I first of all foreground the capacities embedded in human nature and show what man can do, such that the striving of his soul to virtue does not weaken, due to the soul considering itself less capable, and such that it does not consider the possibility embedded in it to be non-existent.

14 Freedom of the will, through which God gave man independence, consists in the point that man may accept sin or refrain from it.

15 Only he is worthy to extend his hands to God and in good conscience pour forth prayer, who can say: Thou knowest, Lord, how holy, innocent, and pure from all impurity, injustice, and predation are the hands, which I extend to Thee, and how righteous and free from all untruth are the lips, by which I offer Thee prayers, so Thou hast mercy on me.

16 Why did Harnack not undergo these great experiences, which would have opened his eyes to all objective 'miracles'? Perhaps, he never was seriously 'sick'. Perhaps, 'he never stood on the edge of the infernal abyss'; perhaps he was never completely 'nothing'. Only they can attain the mystery of Divine Redemption inaccessible to Harnack, who have not only the sins of Harnack (moral stains of 'unconsciousness and hurriedness'), but also 'bloody' red sins, vices, horrors, before which the educated and respected teacher (i.e., Harnack) is in horror.

17 One in being.

18 ὁμοούσιος.

19 Cf. 'The works and life of our holy father Athanasius the Great' v.III, p. 257 (pub. Moscow Spiritual Academy): 'And the Son of God so as to become the son of man, that the sons of man, i.e., the sons of Adam became [сделались] [or co-created [соделались] – Trans] sons of God. For the word unsayable, inexplicable, unattainable, eternally born from above of the Father, born below in time from the Virgin Mary, Mother of God, so that those born firstly below are born again [вторично] from above, that is, of God.'

20 Contrary to reason (Ger).

21 He says: <u>Ego vero Evangelio non crederem, nisi me catholicae (ecclesiae) commoveret auctoritas</u> (Harnack III, 79). (Of course, I would not have believed in the Gospel, if the authority of the Catholic Church had not impelled me to it.)

22 'My ears were already overfull of such matters.'

23 I had distanced myself in the garden in my spiritual tumult, in such a place where no one could disturb me until my struggle had passed, the upshot of which, of course, was visible to You, <u>my God</u>, but I saw it not. My <u>frenzy was salvific</u> for me, and the lethal anxiety acted on me in a life-saving way. *I was conscious of my unhappy position but did not see that is served me as transition to the better* (Bl. Augustine, <u>Confessions</u>, p. 203).

24 You yourself rouse him, so as to find joy in Your glorification, for You created us for Yourself and our heart is restless until it finds rest in Thee.

25 Peace of rest, Peace of Sabbath, peace without evening.

26 The seventh day has no evening; it is endless. You illuminated it and blessed it for eternal Sabbath (Gen. 2,3; EVR 4,1–10). And Your word elevates us, so as You rested on the seventh day from all Your works, so beautifully and so marvellously created by You, although You created it without any violation of Your rest; so as we, per completion of our works, which are good among us, in that they are the gift of Your grace, abide in Your rest and remain at peace in Your sabbathitude of eternal life (The Confessions of the Blessed Augustine, Translation Edition of the Journal 'Church' Moscow, 1914).

27 Φήσας πειρᾶσθαι το ἐν ἡμῖν θεῖον ἀνάγειν πρὸς τὸ ἐν τῷ παντὶ θεῖον (Porphyre, Vie de Plotin, p. 2).

28 This is in contradiction with all the direction of classical thought and is the decisive convergence to the Eastern mode [образ] of thought, when Plotinus, following Philo, finds the ultimate goal of philosophy only in such a gaze [воззрение] on the divine,

per which any definition of thought and any clarity of consciousness of self disappears in mystical ecstasy.
29 Ὅσω δ ἂν εἰς ἀνείδεον ἡ ψυχή ἴῃ, ἐξαδυνατούσα περιλαβεῖν τῷ μν ὁρίζεσθαι καὶ οἷσον τυποῦσθαι ὑπὸ ποικίλον τοῦ τυποῦνυος ἐξολισθάνει καὶ φοβεῖται, μὴ οὐδὲν ἔχῃ.
30 That time had passed for Augustine when he said to himself: <u>Mihi persuasi dicentibus potius quam jubentibus esse credentum</u> (PRE II, 262). (I was convinced that one must believe the teacher, and not the orderer.)
31 The ignorant arise and ravish the sky. And you and I with all our old knowledge wallow along in flesh and blood! Isn't it shameful for us to follow their example only because they righted themselves before us? But isn't it more shameful for us to not follow at all in their traces? I said to him a few more similar words – don't even remember what myself. Disturbed by the struggle of thought and feeling, I left him. Struck with astonishment, he only looked at me and fell silent. And really, I was then in unusual disturbance, and my speech was not as usual. The disturbance of my soul was more expressed by forehead, cheeks, eyes, as well as the colour of my face, change of voice, than by the words which I then spoke.
32 You then, Lord, are good and merciful. You saw the whole depth of my fall and with Your mighty right hand you led me from the abyss, into which I was hurled down as in the grave. I did not want what You wanted, and wanted what You did not. Now I have ceased to want what I previously wanted and have come to wish that pleasing to you.
33 Union of opposites.
34 Preserve the sole hope of the whole world. That which you annihilate is dishonour necessary for faith. What is unworthy of God is useful to me. <u>And more</u>, I am saved if I am not ashamed of my God.
35 In the Russian edition, the 28th verse of the 73rd Psalm.
36 It is possible for man to be without sin and keep God's commandments.
37 O, how accursed I was as a youth, most accursed of all mortals. Even in early youth I asked you to give me chastity and called to You: 'Give me chastity and virtue, but not *just* yet [sed noli *modo*]'. I feared lest You attended to my request at once and healed me to quickly from the sickness of lust, which I would rather sate than extinguish.
38 Nothing can be proven by the Holy Writ that cannot be justified by justice.
39 Justice, whose duty consists in awarding each his own.
40 Really, man has no other motive for philosophizing besides the attainment of bliss. That which makes him blissful, is of itself the attainment of the good. Thus, there is no other reason to philosophize than the attainment of the highest degree of good. Consequently, a sect which does not strive for the attainment of good, can in no way be called philosophy.
41 As concerns those who consider that good and evil are attained in the present life, be that in body or spirit, or who presuppose them in one or the other, that is, to express oneself more clearly, in lust or in virtue, or all together in one or the other, or even in tranquillity or virtue, if not in the two all together, even further in the natural principles or virtues, or in the two together, then they wish to be happy here, and per striking vanity from their side, become blessed by their own strength.
42 So, for such time as this we have intrinsic this weakness, this impotence, this enervation, how can we consider we are already saved? If such salvation still does not exist, how can we call ourselves blessed in this final bliss? For that virtue too, whose name is force of soul (in the manifestation of any wisdom) is the most obvious witness of human misfortunes, which they are compelled to bear with patience.

43 And they are not ashamed to call such a life blessed, consisting of such calamities! Oh, how blessed is a life which requires the help of death to finish it! If it is blessed, let us remain in it, if due to calamities they flee from it, how can it be called blessed? How not to call evil that which conquers the force of the soul and arouses this force not only to destroy oneself, but to go insane to such a degree, that the one and the same life is considered blessed and at the same time convince a man to flee from it. Who is blind enough not to notice that if it is blessed, there's no need to run from it. However, if per reason of the weight of the infirmity crushing this life, they are conscious that one ought to run from life, then why, having thrown off all pride, do they not acknowledge that such a life is misfortune? Tell me, Cato killed himself from endurance or from lack of endurance? He would not have committed it, if he could have reconciled himself with Caesar's victory. Where is his force now? It retreated, humbled itself, was conquered such that it abandoned its fortunate life in the world, dropped it and fled from it. And, perhaps, it was not fortunate? In that case, it was misfortune. Wasn't misfortune the reason one had to flee this unfortunate life?
44 Lev Shestov, 'Tolstoy and Nietzsche,' p. 209.
45 I acknowledge that the opinion which subordinates all to the indifferent divine will, and allows that all depends on this arbitrariness, is less far from the truth than the other opinion, which affirms that God acts in everything in agreement with the good.
46 Neither reason nor will were extended over God's divine nature.
47 For will and reason compelling God, are as far from our reason and will as from the sky, and in nothing except name can be likened; nor more than the Dog star is like the barking dog.
48 Nothing can be proven by Holy Writ, which cannot be justified by justice.
49 The movements of youth are innocent, but their spiritual characteristics are not.
50 Trans – In Christian theology, traducianism is a doctrine about the origin of the soul (or synonymously, 'spirit'), holding that this immaterial aspect is transmitted through natural generation along with the body, the material aspect of human beings.
51 Who affirmed quod ratio arguit, non potest auctoritas vindicari (Loofs, 431). What reason affirms – cannot be destroyed by authority.
52 O, Lord God of ours, under the cover of Thy wings we hope, defend us and carry us. You will carry us from childhood to old age, as our strength is only in You, without You it is only weakness.
53 Things could not be created by God other, nor in another order, than in the order that they were created.
54 Laws and rules of nature are everywhere and always the same; therefore there ought to be one unique means of understanding the essence of things, whatsoever they are.
55 Sub specie aeternitatis seu necessitatis (Ethics IV, 62). (From the point of view of eternity or necessity.)
56 The order and consistency of ideas, the same as the order and consistency of things.
57 Thought is an attribute of God; put another way, God is a thinking being. Extension is an attribute of God; put another way, God is an extensive thing.
58 As established in propositionibus 21, 22, 23 that action is most perfect which is produced by God unmediated, and the more intermediate links are required between God and the thing created by Him, the more imperfect will the thing be.
59 One unique means to understand things, whatever they are.
60 Fourth, one can rejoin that if a man does not act by free will, then what happens in the case if he is in such a position [equilibrium] as Burdian's ass? Will he perish from hunger and thirst?

61 If we put a man instead of an ass in such a position, he cannot be considered a thinking thing but rather a disdained ass, if he perishes from hunger and thirst.
62 I fully agree that a man, put in such a position of equilibrium (that is feeling nothing but hunger and thirst, when food and drink are located equidistant from him), will perish from hunger and thirst. If they ask, wouldn't such a man be considered more an ass than a man? I would say, I don't know, as I know not how one must evaluate a man who hangs himself.
63 That there are multiple causes [Trans].
64 We feel and reveal that we are eternal.
65 <u>Deutlich ist, dass die Erbsünde der Grund alles Sündigens ist, und dass es sich mit ihr ganz anders verhält, als mit den actuellen Sünden, weil hier die schlecht gewordene Natur das ganze Wesen inficirt. Dass das aber eine unerhörte Neuerung in der Kirche ist, ist unverkennbar (Harncak, III, 211).</u>

It's clear that original sin is the basis of all sinfulness and the case is different with it than with the presently existing sins because here corrupted nature infects the entire being. But it's indubitable that this is an unheard-of innovation in the Church.
66 The talk is <u>inter alia</u> of the following excerpt (cf. p 36):

<u>Videbam enim me in summo versari periculo, et me cogi, remedium, quamvis incertum, summis viribus quaerere; voluti aeger lethali morbo laborans, qui ubi mortem certam praevidet ni adhibeatur remedium, illud ipsum, quamvis incertum, summis viribus cogitur quaerere, nempe in eo tota ejus spes est sita; illa autem omnia, quae vulgus sequitur, non tantum nullum conferunt remedium ad nostrum esse conservandum, sed etiam id impediunt et frequenter sunt interitus eorum, qui ea possident, et semper causa ineritus corum, qui ab iis possidentur</u> (Spinoza, De Intellectus Emendatione, introductio 7, 9).

(I really saw myself submitted to the greatest danger and compelled to seek help with all my strength, albeit not reliable help; thus, like a sick man, infected by a lethal disease, foreseeing sure death, if he resorts not to the help of medicine, is compelled to seek this medicine with all his strength, albeit this help were dubious; because all his hope is upon it. And the goals, which the crowd follows, not only do not give means for preservation of our essence but rather interfere with it, being often the cause of destruction of those who rule them, and are always the cause of destruction of those who are under their power.)
67 I will reason of the nature of attachments and of their force, of the power of the soul over them per the same method by which in the preceding chapters I reasoned of God and of the Soul and will survey human actions and impulses, as though the question concerned lines, planes or bodies.
68 When the soul cognizes itself and cognizes its power of action, it rejoices, and all the more, the clearer it recognizes itself and its power of action.
69 When the soul cognizes its powerlessness it is saddened.
70 All the more that it no longer clearly represents its powerlessness to itself.
71 If men were born free, they could not create any concept of good and evil, while they would remain free.
72 The bliss of man is nothing other than internal satisfaction, which is engendered of an intuitive cognition of God.
73 You created us for Yourself, and our souls are restless until it finds rest in You.
74 *Affects of hope and fear cannot be good in and of themselves.*
75 The more we try to live directed by reason, the more we can apply efforts to be less dependent on hope, free from fear, and as much as possible, guide fate and direct our actions in agreement with the true advice of reason.

76 He who, directed by fear, acts in agreement with God, in order to avoid evil, is not guided by reason.
77 Lord, I believe, help my unbelief.
78 Fear is the basis of salvation, its absence a barrier to salvation.
79 The Holy Church gives its adherents an admixture of hope and fear.
80 To taste and experience that which is perceived beyond words and images.
81 Sunt omnes homines una quaedam massa peccati, supplicium debens divinae summaeque justitiae, quod sive exigatur sive donetur, nulla est inquitas (St Augustine, De Diversis Quaestionibus.; Loofs, 380).
82 Si Adae peccatum etiam non peccantibus nocuit, ergo et Christi justitia etiam not credentibus prodest; nulla ratione conceditur, ut Deus, qui propria peccata remittit, imputet aliena (Loofs, 422).

Non solum magna sed etiam minima bona esse non possunt nisi ab illo, a quo sunt omnia bona, hoc est deo (Loofs, 378).
83 Restlessness, hunger and thirst for God, revulsion at experienced, lowly goods cannot be stifled because the soul while it exists originates from God and heads to God. But now it reveals something horrible. The will, which factually does not wish what it wishes, or seems that it wishes. No, this is not appearance; it's the most horrible paradox: we strive to head to God and we cannot; this means that we do not wish to.
84 And what kind of unusual phenomenon is this? Whither is it, why, what reason for it? Yes, illumine me your mercy. Perhaps I will find answers to these questions in the sacred mystery of human ills, as the most sorrowful punishments of the sons of Adam. Whither this phenomenon, what for?
85 To taste and experience that which is perceived beyond words and images.
86 Consequently two loves erected two cities. The city, named earthly, created love for self, reaching to disdain for God, and the City of God created love for Him reaching to disdain for self.
87 Men are not born but become Christians.
88 Pagan virtues were splendid vices.
89 They were elected before the creation of the world, in the force of predestination, by which God had established beforehand His future deeds. They were elected and separated from the remaining world, in agreement with that vocation, with which God filled those whom he predestined. Really, those whom He predestined, He drew them to this vocation in agreement with His forward plan. Consequently not others, but those whom He predestined and called, justified and glorified, in agreement with that forward plan, which has no other goal than Him alone.
90 Кто исследовал дух Господень и кто преподал Ему совет is a Google singleton to this book (2018) – Trans.
91 O depth of wealth and wisdom and guidance of God! How unattainable is His justice and inscrutable are his paths! For who has known the mind of the Lord? Or was his counselor?
92 For per the ineffable providence of God, many of those who are apparently outside the Church are in it, and those apparently inside, who are outside it.
93 They exited from the labyrinth by completely different paths. Luther adjoined to the doctrine of remission of sins by faith in Christ and not by good works. He understood the Holy Writ thus, on which he firmly relied. Of Loyola one cannot say that he investigated the Scripture, that dogmata influenced him, as he lived only by internal motivations and ratiocinations occurring inside himself; he considered that he was inspired now by a good, now by an evil spirit; finally he learned their distinction. He found it, in that one brings joy and comforts the soul, and the other exhausts and tires

it. Once it seemed to him that he was awakened from sleep. He thought to grasp that all his sorrows are temptations of Satan. He decided from that hour to quit with all his past life, to not debride the wounds further, to never more touch them. This was not so much pacification, but rather a decision, more than that, a decision which was taken as conviction, to which one must be subordinated.

94 In the original stronger still: y le dieron tanta confirmacione siempre de la fe.
95 After what he had seen he was completely convinced of the idea which often occurred to him; although no place in the Holy Scripture taught these mysteries of faith, all the same, as he had seen it, he decided, he ought to die for it.
96 It (freedom of the will) cannot be proven by rational thinking, for any proof should have to accept that which is not clear, and what's more by unclear means. But it can be known by help of experience.
97 If the Pope received from Christ and from the Gospel law such a fullness of power, then the Gospel law would be unendurable slavery, even more than the Mosaic law because thanks to it everyone would be slaves of the Pope.
98 All the clergy does not comprise that church, which cannot be in error in questions of faith. And again: all the bishops can be in error on questions of faith, just as priests can.
99 All the bishops can be in error on questions of faith, just as priests can. If all the prelates and all the clergy were infected with the heretical corruption of the world, then the power to judge ought to have by right to devolve to all Catholics, both lay and clergy.
100 Only those truths ought to be considered Catholic and necessary for salvation which are clearly expressed or implied on the foundation of the Bible. And again: But all other truths, which are not founded on the Bible, and which cannot be derived from its content, as an exact and necessary conclusion, even if it is affirmed in the Holy Scripture, and in the definitions of the Pope, and even if everyone belonging to the Church believes in it – even in that case they ought not to be considered Catholic and it is not necessary for salvation of the soul to unite behind them, firmly believing in them and because of them holding reason in captivity.
101 De sola Sacra Scriptura Novi et Veteris Testamenti est illicitum dubitare, utrum sit verum vel rectum, quicquid in ea scriptum esse constiterit. Ergo de omnibus scripturis Conciliorum Generalium et similium, et quorumcumque aliorum expositorum Scriptorae divinae ac etiam Romanorum Pontificum et quorumlibet historiographorum, post canonem confirmatum editis, non est illicitum dubitare et discrepare, an a veritate exorbitent antequam Scripturae Novi et Veteris Testamenti consona demonstretur (Denifle II, 382–3). Only in the Holy Scripture (the Old and New Testament) is it not allowed to doubt and reason as true or false, what is contained in its writings. Thus, it is licit to doubt in all the writings of the ecumenical councils or other interpreters and even in the writings of the original Roman saints and their historians. All these writings were introduced after the foundation of the Bible. If their correspondence with the Holy Scripture were not proactively proven, then it is completely licit to doubt them and necessarily survey whether they diverge from the truth.
102 One cannot even think of subordination to an external law; that is a law not promulgated by them and not attested with their agreement, and as a consequence of that agreed to the obligation of subordination to a higher power. And this has force not only in the material respect (in foro extero), in simple legal questions, but also in spiritual questions (in foro interno), concerning the moral and religious experiences

of the conscience. Sazer dotalismus (power of the clergy), as expressed in modern times by Georges Tyrrell, is that fundamental doctrine of the Catholic Church, per which power over souls in given unmediated by God Himself from above. This also falls away as an impossibility.
103 When Christ transferred to Peter these keys of the heavenly kingdom, then He by that transferred to him the executive power in the Church of Christ: to admit to the Church and exclude from it, to order all people and direct all things, to issue laws and abolish them, to impose punishments and forgive, in a few words, transferred the whole fullness of regal and judicial power over the whole Church, that is, over his co-apostles and believers. What Peter does as superior bearer of the keys that God approves in the heavens ... As this full power ought not to have been a personal privilege, which would cease with the death of the apostle, then the constant power to forgive sins ought to have remained in the Church, that forgiveness, actual forgiveness, so that remission of sins on earth ought to be equivalent in heaven (in foro divino) ... If God really did not forgive in Heaven a mortal sin which the Church justly remitted on earth, then the words of the promise of Christ would bear on themselves the imprint of untruth.
104 Here in its simplicity, in its clarity, in its greatness, in its force – the definition of infallibility, which was so impatiently awaited by some and which others claimed impossible. But the Church, knowing what it is and what it possesses, has the gift to express this; there is neither decoration, nor exaggeration, nor weakness – full simplicity, beneath which one feels superhuman force. Here it is, this great privilege of dogmatic infallibility, without which one cannot attain religion, and which not one religion has accepted, and whose name not one sect has resolved to preserve; which only the Catholic Church proclaims and which it has pursued for eighteen centuries, and for which it has now defined space and voice with magnificent boldness, not proceeding from man; this boldness alone would be sufficient to demonstrate its divinity.
105 Along with each terrible dogma in Catholicism, there is another dogma which mollifies it, which makes its point less penetrating and less stern. And just by this does the Catholic Church seize souls, holds them back, and has power over them, enchanting them.
106 To he who does what is within his power, God will certainly grant grace.
107 In God's creation there is nothing in vain, as in the creatures of nature.
108 Ivan Il'ich in Tolstoy – it [death] is here – and nothing can be done.
109 He made no other admission than the following: I wasted time because I had lived badly (De votis monasticis indicium).
110 This is a genus of lost men, thanks to fleshly lusts, voluptuousness and adultery. People who spend days and nights in dreams of love impulses, and imagine what they would do themselves, if they were presented the same freedom as the patriarchs: the possibility of swapping a spouse every night and cavorting with them in the whole flame and ardour of the flesh, like they enjoyed themselves with whores.
111 Most evil of all two-legged animals.
112 Article of faith, on which depends the life and death of the Church.
113 Luther passed counterfeit on the Church with his perverted doctrine in order to take the actual catholic for himself.
114 Of course, there are many people who consider the 'left' goods (i.e., temporal goods) as nothing and willingly sacrifice them for closeness to God; so do the Jews and heretics, but few people there are who consider 'right goods' (i.e., spiritual goods)

as nothing for attainment of the righteousness of Christ. The Jews and the heretics cannot do this. And all the same without this no one can be saved. They always wish that God honoured and rewarded them for their acts and depend on this. But the word is unshakably firm: 'Mercy depends not on wishing it, and not on heroic exploit, but on God merciful' (Epistle to the Romans, IX,16).
115 The beginning of all sin is pride. The beginning of man's pride is denial of God.
116 Do not take pride in your works, for the justice of God is other than human justice, and often God is not pleased with what pleases man.
117 Why does man pride himself on his merits? For works please God not because they are good or salvific but because they are elected by God from eternity and pleasing to Him. And thus we only do good when we impute gratitude because works do not make us better, but rather our goodness and even more the goodness of God do; and this makes our works good because they are good not of themselves but because God considers them good. They are good or not good inasmuch as God approves or approves not.
118 Who can love him who wants to act with the sinner, as per justice? Such a relation is very dangerous and in vain to boot; it engenders secret hatred of God and His justice.
119 If you consider it just that God rewards the unworthy, then it ought to please you when He condemns those who do not deserve condemnation; if He is just in the first case, He is also just in the second case.
120 I do not call even one of my books good with the exception of 'De servo arbitrio' and 'Catechesis'.
121 The highest degree of faith is to believe that he is merciful, who so few save and so many condemn, that he is just, who per His decision created us sinners.
122 Let will be first over reason.
123 I am assured and convinced by the spirit of Christ that my doctrine of Christian justice is faithful and correct.
124 Mrs. Hulde, natural reason, that devils' whore and enemy of faith.
125 On reception of first grace as well as on reception of God's glory, we ought to be passive as a woman at conception … We can ask and plead for grace, but then grace comes and the soul is filled with the Holy Spirit, then ought it not to pray, or act, but simply be silent. This, of course, is hard to submit to and this brings great sorrow because if the soul renounces any knowledge and manifestation of spirit, then this means the following: it ought to be engulfed in darkness, perish and be annihilated.
126 <u>On appelle mystiques des actes ou états surnaturels que nos efforts, notre industrie ne peuvent pas réussir à produire, et cela même faiblement, même un instant</u> (Aug. Poulain, Des graces d'oraison). We call supernatural actions and conditions mystical, which are impossible to evoke neither by our efforts nor by art even in <u>a weakened form, and even for a minute</u>.
127 Cf. Lev Shestov, 'In Job's Balances', p. 94. Trans. – after SF.
128 To consider spiritual goods and just works as nothing for Christ's sake. Like a paralytic with useless arms and legs.
129 To him who does what is within his power, God will certainly grant grace.
130 God wished to do His part, but Luther did not do his.
131 I, stupido, cannot understand that I ought to consider myself a sinner like others and thus not exalt myself before anyone else, after I have repented and confessed – I did think that all is forgiven, internally as well.
132 I am convinced that the thrones of the Seraphim, abandoned by the unfortunate followers of Lucifer, will be occupied, in large part, by the souls of the nuns. In the

last century the Church inscribed sixty new names in the catalogue of the Holy or Blessed; of this number only five or six did not belong to monasticism. Christ said to St Theresa: 'It would be a misfortune for the world, were there no monks.'
133 According to the ancient law, the Hebrews were a people chosen by God, in contrast to the Egyptians. According to the new law, the chosen of God are the monks, as opposed to secular folk.
134 The nun says just this at her tonsure by the prelate: 'Jesus, my spouse, imprint Your sign on my face, covering it with this veil, so that, seeing Him and visible to Him alone, I agreed to be loved only by Him. O, holy pride, which as St Jerome says, the spouse of Christ ought to experience in her heart. "You are the spouse of God" says he to her, "learn holy pride. Secular women are praised for their marriage with noble and rich men. But, know, you are worth more than them".'
135 Fourthly, one must say that per Aristotle's doctrine (IV Eth. 3), speaking the truth, *only virtues deserve honours*. If external goods, especially significant ones, bring honours from the average people to those who possess the goods, these average people know no other excellence. This happens in the final account because it gives the possibility of accomplishing certain virtuous acts. Monks, who strive for perfection in virtue, ought not to renounce *honours which God and the saints present to virtues*, which is visible from the following words: 'I highly honour Your friends, My God' (Ps. 138, 17). As concerns honours, which surround external greatness, monks have renounced them, shedding secular life. Therefore they need not give a special vow.
136 The excellence of virginity is especially expressed in the statement of the Holy Spirit: 'no treasure is equal a chaste soul' and in consequence of this no praise corresponds to its dignity. That's why, says Cardinal Hugues, 'as distinct from other vows, there is no dispensation from the vow of complete chastity, because no one will ever find an equal substitute'. Mary in her answer to the angel Gabriel also reveals to us the incomparable value of virginity: 'How can this be, since I know not man.' Mary was prepared to sacrifice even the dignity of Mother of God to virginity.
137 Moderation – mother of virtue and incarnated perfection … moderation gives order to any virtue … moderation is not of itself a virtue but rather director of virtue; it introduces order in our feelings and gives rules for our mores. If you lose moderation, there will be no more virtue.
138 One cannot concede that this glorified man was disgraced by the pagan Aristotle: he knew that good and especially virtue are impossible without the participation of reason.
139 Monasticism is a certain form of offering by which man wholly gives himself to God and, so to say, brings himself as sacrifice, following three vows: obedience, chastity and poverty. In these vows the perfection of monasticism consists.
140 Man consists in man dedicating himself wholly, with all that belongs to him, to the service of God and, so to say, offers himself as sacrifice to God.
141 St Bernard says: 'An internal enemy causes more evil than an external one.' A besieged fortress is susceptible to the greatest danger from an internal enemy because it is harder for it to defend against it than against an external one. If this is so, then St Joseph of Calasanz was correct in saying: 'One need not take more account of our body than of a kitchen rag.' That's exactly how the saints took care of themselves. The chief worry of secular people is to afford their body sensual pleasure. On the contrary, the souls loving God take advantage of any occasion to mortify their flesh. St Peter of Alcantara said to his body: 'Don't worry, I'll give you no rest in this life; you'll get only

torments from me.' We will read the Lives of the Saints, we'll see what epithemia they imposed on themselves, and we'll blush at our tenderness and how we spare ourselves in mortification of the flesh. In the lives of the Desert Fathers it speaks of a great monastic commune, in which not one of the sisters used either fruits or wine; many ate only once in the evening or ate only every second or third day after the most stern restraint; all wore hair shirts and slept on hair bags.

142 St Theresa ... directs the attention of her nuns to the following: 'Tell yourselves decisively, my sisters, that you have come to die for Jesus Christ, and not for an easy life. If we do decide once for all to accept death and lose our health, we will never do anything. And what of it, if we die? How many times has our body failed on us, can't we laugh at it once? St Joseph of Calasanz for his part says: "That monk is unfortunate, who worries more about his health. How about sanctity". St Bernard considers that a sick monk should not take expensive medicines, but rather be satisfied with simple infusions ... People devoted to Jesus Christ, says Salvien – are sick and weak, and they wish to be so; in good health it's not easy to attain sanctity.'

143 Sweetest and most mysterious kiss.

144 What is believed always, everywhere, by all.

145 Is not that religion holy in which man lives purer, falls more rarely, rises easier, moves more carefully, is blessed more often, rests in greater security, dies with greater assurance, purified quicker and rewarded more generously?

146 Is it good at the present time to become a monk? I answer: if you think that you cannot be saved outside of monasticism, then do not go into the monastery because then will the adage be justified: 'Despair makes a man a monk.' Rather not a monk but a devil. He will never be a good monk, whom despair led to monasticism, only he will, who is directed by love, and seeing his heavy sins, comes to the joyful decision to bring God his great attestation of love, and by his will, renouncing freedom, will don this stupid outfit and impose the most menial duties on himself.

147 The abbot, monks and father wished me luck, when I accepted monasticism and said that I am now like an innocent child who has just been baptized. True, I would willingly have enjoyed such a magnificent affirmation that I am a wonderful man, who himself by his work, in place of the blood of Christ, became wonderful and holy, so easily and so quickly. And though I willingly listened to such magnificent words and sweet praise of my activity, and came to consider myself a miracle worker who myself could become holy and devour death along with the devil, etc., all this is not sustained by experience. For when there was just a small temptation from death and sin, I gave in to it and neither baptism nor monasticism helped me: I had already long ago lost Christ and his baptism. I was the most unfortunate man on earth, day and night I spent in vain sobbing and in despair; no one could help me.

148 If some time a monk through monasticism fell to the sky, then I ought to fall there; my monastic comrades can attest to this for me.

149 Thus God wishes to serve us not by our individual righteousness and wisdom but by justice, which proceeds not from us, and has its beginning not in us, but which comes to us from without; it rises not on our earth but comes from heaven.

150 Therefore I think that it is better to be a monk now than 200 years ago, and just because to the present day monks have walked away from the cross and were praised for being a monk. But now they again do not please people; even those who are really honourable because their outfit is considered the fool's and to be a monk means to be hated by secular folk and in their representation be a fool. He who submits himself to this out of love acts well. I, in any case, do not fear

the persecution of the bishops and clergy because so it ought to be. What doesn't please me is that we incur this persecution by such bad conduct. However, those too, whom are not given such pretext, hate monks all the same, not knowing why. They are the best helpers that monks have in the world; in truth, members of the order ought to rejoice; they only fulfil their vow, when from this vow, which they take on themselves per Divine behest, they are looked at with disdain and they are dishonoured. Just for this they do wear this fool's outfit, to attract the disdain of all upon them. Now they act completely differently; they wear only the appearance of the monastic life. But I know that they would be the happiest men, if they had love, and were happier than recluses in the desert because they bear the cross and are submitted to daily abuse.

151 It is impossible that Divine justice penetrate in him, who is full of his own justice. God sates only the hungry and thirsty. He who is sated with his own truth and wisdom will not attain Divine truth and wisdom. *Because they can only be received where there is an empty space for them [Trans]*. And so will we turn to God: 'O, how willingly we are empty, that you may fill us; I am willingly weak, that Your power may live in me; I am willingly stupid, that You be my wisdom; I am willingly unjust, that you may be my wisdom.'

152 'We thought that by deprivation, we deserve so much, that we can put our action in place of the Blood of Christ. So I thought, poor stupid me. I went overboard on fast, vigil, and cold.' Or, 'Why did I submit myself to the greatest severities in the monastery? Why did I oppress my body with fast, vigil, and cold? Because I was convinced by such works to merit forgiveness of sins.'

153 Johann von Staupitz, O.S.A. was a Catholic theologian, university preacher, and Vicar General of the Augustinian friars in Germany, who supervised Martin Luther during a critical period in his spiritual life – Trans.

154 To him who does what is within his power, God will certainly grant grace.

155 The use of reason precedes faith and leads man through it to revelation and grace. Reason with assurance proves the original nature of revelation, made to the Jews through Moses and to Christians through Jesus Christ.

156 As concerns me, I am here an unreasoning and hardened sinner, sunk in idleness, o woe! Praying little, not worrying on God's Church and burning with all the fires of my unrestrained flesh. Generally I, who ought to have been enflamed in spirit, am enflamed in flesh, lust, laziness, otiosity, somnolence.

157 Cf. 'In Job's Balances', p. 98.

158 <u>Ego monachus putabam statim actum, esse de salute mea</u> (ad Gal. III, 20 Denifle I, 437). (When I was still a monk, I often thought that I ought to perish.)

159 Cf. 'In Job's Balances', p. 94.

160 <u>Nec ego ausim ita legem appellare, sed putarem esse summam blasphemiam in Deum, nisi Paulus prius hoc fecisset</u> (Gal. II, 207) – I would not have so dared call the law; this would be the most terrible blasphemy if not the Apostle Paul had done it before me.

161 God wishes to save us not by our justice, but by justice which is external to us.

162 First one's free.

163 The unbelieving crowd (Phaedo 69e).

164 In Divine matters we ought not to follow our judgement and define, what per our reasoning is hard, soft, difficult, easy, good, evil, just, unjust … No matter how much good you did, even if you shed your blood, all your conscience uneasily wavers and says: 'Who knows whether this is pleasing to God.'

165 For the will of God there exist neither reasons nor foundations, which could be prescribed to him as rule and measure. Because nothing is equal to Him and nothing is higher than Him, but His will is law for everyone. Because if his will were subordinated to will and scale, it would have foundation and reason, then it would no longer be God's will. That which he wishes is not just because he ought to or ought not to so wish; but quite the converse, because He wishes it, then that which occurs ought to be just. The will of creation is prescribed foundation and reason, but not so the will of the Creator, as if you prefer another creator to him.

166 God cannot be subordinated to necessity. We otherwise ought to reason of a Divine will and of a God, which is proclaimed, presupposed and publicly honoured, and of a God, who is not proclaimed, not revealed, not presupposed, and not publicly honoured.

167 We're speaking of the commentary given by Scheel to p. 243 of the book 'Vom Verknechteten Willen'.

168 God does not demand the impossible, He bids you do what you can, and ask for what you cannot do … We clearly see that a good and just God could not prescribe the impossible; therefore he teaches us what we can do in the limits of the possible and how we ought to ask for the impossible.

169 To us who are dominated by the first presuppositions of reason, it is impossible to either understand or fully believe these things because they are in the strongest contradiction with human reason.

170 Because it is not in agreement with reason that a just and good God demand the impossible from free will; and although free will cannot wish good and per necessity serve evil, however it is blamed for this … All this, in agreement with reason, does not attest to good and merciful God … But faith and Spirit judge otherwise. They believe that God is good, even if he destroyed all men [Он погубил всех людей].

171 Our God is not a God of impatience and cruelty, even relative to the atheists. This I say to comfort those who are constantly tormented with blasphemous thoughts and on top of that are too fearful; yet such blasphemy, which the devil fastens on people against their will, resounds ofttimes more pleasantly in God's hearing than even the Allilueias of other solemn doxology.

172 Letter to the Galatians, 3, 17.

173 If the grace of God could be conferred per human invocation, not done by grace in and of itself, but invoked by us, this would contradict the prophet Isaiah, as well as the apostle Paul, who said: I reveal myself to those who sought me not, was found by those, who sought me not – Trans.

174 Thus, the world ought to be filled with fearsome, horrible gloom and errors before the day of the Last Judgement. Therefore, he who can, let him understand that the law, in agreement with Christian theology, does not justify per justice but rather creates the opposite: and namely opens our eyes and shows who we are, frightens us and reveals to us not only sins and Divine wrath but makes sin greater and more powerful: sin which earlier was light and insignificant becomes large and heavy when the law illuminates it. Then man begins to hate the law and flee from it and hate God Himself, Who gave the law. This means to not become righteous before the law; reason itself must admit this, but twice sin before the law. First, that man feels revulsion at the law, acts against it, cannot accept it, and secondly, that he becomes the greatest enemy and hater of the law such that he wishes that neither the law nor God, Who gave the law, existed, albeit God is indeed the highest good.

175 Because God is the God of the downtrodden, unfortunate, oppressed, despairing. The essence of God is so as to elevate the downtrodden, feed the hungry, return sight to the blind, comfort the unfortunate and sorrowing, justify the sinners, resurrect the dead, save the accursed and hopeless. He is indeed the omnipotent Creator, creating all from nothing.
176 But the most maleficent monster does not allow [man] to this His substantial work – this monster, the self-opinion of righteousness, which does not wish to be sinful, unclean, pitiful, and condemned, but rather just and holy. Thus God must resort to that hammer, namely the law, which shatters, crushes and *turns to nothing that monster* with his self-assurance, wisdom, justice, and power, that it knows it is lost and accursed from the evil in it.
177 Lev Shestov, 'Beginnings and Endings'.
178 I wish, said he, if it were meet for God to give me time enough to rectify my life; I wish to do much: enter the monastery, be satisfied with the very least, feed on bread and water, go in a rough shirt, go barefoot, etc. If you do not begin to do the opposite, that is, if you do not remove Moses and his law from yourself, which was created for self-assured and firm people, and you do not in horror and fear recognize Christ suffering, crucified, dying for your sins, you never will be saved.
179 All of theology uses human reason. The Truths of Revelation, of course, cannot be demonstrated by reason (there would be no merit), but reason can illumine certain aspects of the dogmatic. As the grace of God is not in contradiction with human nature, but only develops it, so the duty of reason is to serve faith, as the natural inclination of the will accompanies love.
180 Here's how St Bernard acted, a man so honourable, holy and chaste that, I think, he could be justly preferred to all monks. When he was once very ill and despaired for his life, he did not trust his chastity, which he observed in the very strictest manner, nor his numerous good works, but eliminated all this and held only to faith in Christ. He said: 'I, a poor sinner, conducted my life badly, but You, Jesus Christ, have the Kingdom of Heaven. First, because You are the Son of God; second, You deserved it by Your sufferings and death.' ... He did not juxtapose his monastic and angelic life to Divine ire and justice; he understood that one thing only is needed and thus was he saved.
181 1 Kgs, 8,12: Then spake Solomon, The LORD said that he would dwell in the thick darkness. – Trans.
182 When Thomas along with other Scholastics says how the law ought to be abolished, and affirms that secular laws (judicialia) and laws on ceremonies (ceremonialia) ought to be eliminated and abolished after the coming of Christ and that the Ten Commandments (moralia) ought not to be nullified, they themselves do not understand what they say or what they propose. You then, when you wish to speak of the nullification of the law, seize all law without distinction between secular law, ceremonial and the Ten Commandments. Because when Paul said that we are rescued by Christ from the curse of the law, he spoke of the whole law and especially of the Ten Commandments (moralia), which alone terrify and accuse the conscience before God, unlike the other two.
183 Not only are the laws on ceremonies not good and contain principles destroying life, but the Decalogue, too, and all that might be externally or internally taught is not good.
184 Man, when he does what is within his power, sins, because he cannot independently either wish or think.

185 Therefore this is very dangerous boldness, when they argue on 'The Good,' derived from philosophy, such that God turned the good into evil. Even when all is very good, then for us all the same nothing is good, and even, if there were things, which from some point of view would not be bad, then all the same for us all is bad. And all of this because we are sinners. Therefore we must avoid good and accept evil. And this is not only in words and with a hypocritical heart, but with full internal devotion, to acknowledge and wish that we were irretrievably condemned and accursed. We ought to act in relation to ourselves, as one acts who hates another. He who hates, wishes not only for appearance, but to seriously destroy, kill and accurse him whom he hates. If we will destroy and persecute ourselves with all our heart, if we give ourselves up to hell for God and His justice, then we have truly given satisfaction to His righteous judgement and he will have pity and free us.

186 Yes, it may happen that the saints fall into sin and submit to carnal temptations. Like David, acting horribly became the disgrace of marriage, which brought upon him the killing of many ... Just so profoundly Peter fell, renouncing Christ.

187 Holy Sophists (LS – i.e., Catholics) are like the sage Stoics: the Stoics reasoned about the wisest man, whose like has never been on earth. By such stupid and dishonourable reasonings, engendered by not knowing Paul's doctrines, Sophists led both themselves and many others to despair.

188 I dreamed of such a saint, who lived in the desert, would feed on roots and drink cold water; this opinion of so monstrous saints I drew not from the Sophists' books but also from the books of the fathers. St Hieronymous writes in one place of the desert elders: 'I am silent on food and drink, for to drink water and eat cooked food, even when we are very weak, is sin.'

189 Happy, I thank God, that he gave me in abundance, what I had once asked him for: to see not one saint but a large group of people really and profoundly holy ... I'm in their number, thank God.

190 When God wishes to justify man, He scares his conscience with the law and leads him to admission of sins: after which man comes to despair and there is no more peace in his soul; unless God grant him forgiveness through justification (<u>absolutionem</u>) through the Gospel.

191 Acceptance or trust in the Divine promises that Christ came for me, Christ takes away my sins, Christ gives me life – this faith, the faith of the Gospel, which divine justification, i.e., it alone is accounted by God, as justification. Our works, no matter how good they seem, are of no account.

192 Man is justified by faith before God, even if he is dishonoured by men and dishonours himself. Such is the mystery of God, glorifying His saints – a mystery, which is not only impossible to attain for the impious but which for the pious as well is astonishing and difficult to accept.

193 Really and truly, he gave himself up to us to God the Father for eternal curse. His human nature was no different than of any man sentenced to hell eternally.

194 It is necessary to believe profoundly that you are justified and not doubt that grace will descend upon you; if there is doubt and distrust, you will not be justified and will reject grace.

195 It is clear and horrible impiety to say that sins are remitted of all men, even unbelievers.

196 It is the most horrible impiety to say that even the sins of unbelievers are remitted.

197 Faith accompanied by love.

198 To walk in darkness and annihilation.

199 Like a paralytic with useless arms and legs.
200 God in the omnipotent Creator, creating from nothing.
201 I hear nothing that is not in agreement with my doctrine. I am fully convinced by the spirit of Christ that my doctrine of Christ's justice is completely right and true.
202 Holy Spirit, proceeding from the Father and the Son.
203 Agreement of all.
204 Men are not born but become Christians.
205 A spiritual guide, which eases the soul hampered by mediocrity and leads it by an internal path to perfect contemplation of the rich treasure of internal peace.
206 Only God is allowed to lead man from reasoning to contemplation, and if God does not overshadow him with His grace in time of prayer, no guide with all its instruction and scholarship will help him.
207 In the final end the greatest temptation is the condition without temptation, and thus you must rejoice when there are temptations.
208 O beautous solitude – source of eternal goods! O mirror, in which the eternal Father is constantly reflected! You have been justly named solitude because you are so vacuous that it's difficult to find a soul which seeks you and loves you and knows you.

Bibliography

1   **Dr Martin Luthers Werke, Kritische Gesamtausgabe**, Hermann Böhlaus, Weimar. This edition was begun in 1883 and is not yet completely finished. It ought consist of eighty volumes. Luther's works are given in chronological order. There are also three addenda to this edition:

   1° **Die Deutsche Bibel**, v1, 1906 v. IX, 1937.

   2° **Tischreden**, Kroker,v.1, 1912; v. Vi with chapters, 1921.

   3° **Correspondence** (18 vols, 1884–1923).

BIBLIOGRAPHY OF CITED WORKS

a) Luther's works

1° *Commentarium in Epistolam S. Pauli ad Galatas.*

References are given to the following editions (three small volumes): ERLANGAE sumtibus Caroli Heyderi, 1843 ad 1844. Curavit Dr. J.C. IRMISCHER.

These books also enter into the Erlangen edition (this edition consists of thirty-five volumes in Latin and sixty-seven volumes in German). In the WEIMAR[1] edition, the Commentaries are found in volume 40 (part I and part II) under the title Grosser Galatenkommentaur. We have not given references to these last two editions.

This book also exists in German translation: Dr. Martin Luthers Ausführliche Erklärung dei Epistel an die Galater, Berlin, Verlag von Gustav Schlawitz, 1856.

2° *Epistola beati Pauli apostoli ad Romanos. (1515–1516)*

References are given to the second volume of the following edition, consisting of two volumes: Luthers Vorlesung über den Romerbrief. Ausgegeben von Ficker, (Dieterich Verlag, Leipzig, 1908) (Erster Teil: Die Glossen; Zweiter Teil: Die Scholien).

In the Weimar edition this work in included in the fifty-sixth volume, issued in 1938, under the title Der Brief an der Römer. We also give references to this edition.

This book also exists in German translation. It exists in:

Martin Luther, Ausgewählte Werke. Ausg. Borchard und Mertz. Kaiser Verlag, München – ('Müncher Lutherausgabe'). Die Ausgabe enthält 7 Hauptbände und 3 Ergänzungsbände. Der Ergänzungsband II enthält nur die Römerbriefvorlesung (2-e Auflage 1937). Dieser Band enthält nur die **Scholien**; er ist durch Ed. ELLWEIN übersätzt und erschien früher (1927) in dem selben Verlag. Eine neuere Münchnere Luterausgabe enthält 7 Bänder und 4 Ergänzungsbänder.

3° *De Servo Arbitrio. (1525)*

For Latin texts, references are given to the following books:

3-er Band von **Luthers Werke in Auwahl** – in 8 Bänden herausgegeben von Otto Clemen, Verlag Gruyter, Berlin (1930–1934), und 18-er Band de Weimarausgabe.

For German texts (translations from the Latin), references are given to:

Ergängzungsband 2 von Luthers Werke für das Christliche Haus (Vom Verknechteten Willen). Diese Ausgabe enthält 8 Bänder (Ausgabe Buchwald, Köstlin, Kawerau etc.).

und zwei Ergängzungsbänder (Ausgabe Otto Scheel, Verlag Heinsius, Leipzig, ohne Jahresangabe).

There also exists a translation into contemporary German, done in 1926. It is printed in Ergangzungsband I Münchener Lutherausgabe, mentioned earlier. We have not given references to it.

We also note that this book was translated into French.

(Le Serf Arbitre Editions **Je Sers**. Paris 1936. Traduction Denis de Rougemont).

4º De votis monasticis indicium. (1521)

The Latin text is in:

Band 2 (S 188-298) **Luthers Werke in Auswahl** – herausgegeben von Otto Clemen. Verl. W. de Gruyter, Berlin 1934, und Band 8 der Weimarausgabe (S 573-669).

For the German text (translation from Latin) we refer to:

Martin Luthers Urteil über die Mönchsgelübde. Ergängzungsband I von Luthers Werke für das Christliche Hause (S 209-376).

b) Works of other authors

ANSELME DE CANTERBURY. Proslogion. ARISTOTE. **Ethique de nicomaque**. Texte grec et traduction française. Ed. Garnier. Paris 1950.

AQUIN (saint Thomas d') **Somme Théologique**. Texte latin et traduction.

Traité de Dieu (1 a, q. 1-11) Desclée, Paris, 1947.

La Grace, 1a-2ae, q. 109-14) Desclée, Paris, 1948.

Traité de la Vie Humaine, (2a-2ae, q. 179-89) Desclée, Paris, 1926.

ATHANASE (saint) De incarnatione Dei Verbi et Contra Arianos, patrologie greque de, t. 26, colonne 996.

AUGUSTIN (saint). **La Cité de Dieu**. (3 vol.), traduit par L. MOREAU, 4* éd. Avec le texte latin, Paris, Garnier Frères, 1899.

AUGUSTIN (saint) **Confessions** (2 vol.) texte latin et traduction par P. de LABRIOLLE, ed. Les Belles Lettres, Paris, 1925 et 1926.

BOUGAUD (Mgr.). Le Christianisme et les temps présents, tome III,

Les dogmes du Credo, 1 vol., 290 pp. Poussielgue, 1907; t. IV.

L'Eglise, 1 vol., 612 pp. Poussielgue, 1907.

DENIFLE, **Luther und Lutherum**, 3 Bände von 400 seiten:

Erster band (I Abteilung), erster band (Schluss Abt.),

Zweiter band (**Denifle und Weiss**),

2* auflage, Frazk Kircheim, Mainz, 1904 und 1907.

L. DUCHESNE, **Histoire ancienne de l'eglise** (3 vol.), Paris, Fontemoine, vol. I, 1906; vol. II, 3-eme éd. 1908; vol. iii, 4-eme éd., 1911.

DENZINGER, **Enchiridion symbolorum et definitionem**, Wirceburgi, 1865.

GRISAR (Hartmann) **Luther**. Drei Bände von 600 seiten.

1 band: **Luthers Werden. Grundlegung der spaltung bis 1513**;

2 band: **Auf der Höhe des Lebens**;

3 band: **Am Ende der Bahn**. Freiburg in Breslau. Herdersche Verlagshandlung, 1911.
HARNACK (Adolf von) **Lehrbuch der Dogmengeschichte** (Samml. der theologischen Lehrbücher), 3 Bände:
1-er band, **Die Entstehung des kirklichen Dogmas**, 820 S.
2e band, **Die Entwicklung des kirklichen Dogmas**, I, 538 S.
3e band, **Die Entwicklung des kirklichen Dogmas**, II-III, 959 S.
Verlag J.C.B Mohr (P. Siebeck) Tubingen 1909-10.
HARNACK (Adolf) **Das Wesen des Christentums**, 1 band, 189 S.
Verl. J.C. Hinrichssche Buchhandl, 1906.
LIGUORI (St. Alphonse-Marie de) **La vera sposa di Gesu Cristo** (in Italian).
Two volumes, 350 and 400 pp. Marietti-Torino-Roma – 1904.
La vraie épouse de Jésus-Christ, traduit en francais par P.F. Delerue, 2 vol. in – 16* (Castermann, Paris, 1936).
LOOFS (Friedrich) **Leitfaden zum Studium der Dogmengeschicte**, 1 band, Niemeyer, Halle a/S, 1906.
LOYOLA (S. Ignatii de) **Exceritorium Spiritualium**, Edition princeps qualis in lucem prodit Romae 1548, 1 vol., Herder, 1910.
LOYOLA (St Ignace de) **Exercices spirituels**, traduits par le P. Jennesseaux, annotés par le P. Roothaan. 1 vol. de Gigord. Paris, 1913.
MOLINOS (Miguel de) **Guida Spirituale**.
NATORP (Paul) **Platos Ideenlehre** – Leipzig, 1903.
PLOTIN. **Ennéades,** Précédé de la vie de Plotin par Porphyre (p. 1 à 39 du vol. I) Textes greque et francais. Vol. I (1924): vol. VI (1938) Ed. Les Belles Lettres, Paris.
POHLE (Joseph) **Lehrbuch der Dogmatik in sieben Büchern**. 3 Bände: 590, 635, 824 Seiten. Verlag Ferdinand Schönigh. Paderborn 1911/1912
POULAIN (R.P. Aug.) **Des graces d'oraison** (Traité de théologie mystique). 2-e éd. Ed. Ed. Beauchesne. Paris, 1922.
PRE **Herzogs Realencyklopädie für Protestantische Theologie und Kirche**.
RANKE (Leopold von), **Die Römischen Päpaste in den letzen vier Jahrhunderten**. Three volumes of 336, 377, 538 pp. Verlag. Duncker and Humbolt, Leipzig, 1907.
REUTER (Herrmann) **Augustinische Studien**, 1 band, 516 S. Verl. Perthes, Gotha, 1887.
RITSCHL (Otto) **Dogmengeschichte des Protestantismus**, 4 Bände, Leipzig, 1908:
I. **Biblizismus und Traditionalizmus**, Leipzig, 1908;
II. **Die Theologie der Deutschen Reformation**, 1912;
III. **Die reformierte Theologie des 16 und 17 Jhrh**, 1926;
IV. **Das orthodoxe Lutherum**.
RUPPRECHT (ed.) **Das Christentum von Ad. Harnack**, 1 Band, 278 seiten. Verl. Carl Bertelsmann, Gütersloh, 1901.
SEEBERG (R) **Die Theologie die Johannes Duns Scotus**.
SEEBERG (r) **Dogmengeschichte**. 5 Bände, I, II, III, IV.
SPINOZA, **Ethique**, texte latin et traduction, 2 vol., ed. Garnier, Paris, 1953.
SPINOZA, **Traité de la Reforme de l'Entendement**, texte latin et traduction, ed. Vrin, Paris, 1951.
SPINOZA, **Cogitata Metaphysica** (Ben. de Spinoza opera, Band III). M. Nijhoff, Hague, 1895
SPINOZA. **Tract. Theol. Pol.** (Ben. de Spinoza opera, Band II). Verlag M. Nijhoff, Hague, 1895.
TERTULLIEN **De carne Christi**.
TIXERONT **Histoire des Dogmes**. 3 vol. Paris, Lecoffre, 1905 et 1909, et Gabalda, 1931.

WALTER (Dr. Wilh.) **Ad. Harnack's Wesen des Christentums.** 1 Band. 168 seiten. Verl. A. Deihart (Georg Böhme) Leipzig, 1901.

WERNER (Dr. Karl) **Die Scholastik des späteren Mittelalters**:

I. **Johannes Duns Scotus**, 1881, 571 seiten.

II. **Die Nachscotistiche Scholastik**, 1883, 575 S.

III. **Der Augustinismus in der Scholastik der späteren Mittelalters**, 1883, 309 S.

IV. (1 Abt.) **Der Endausgang der Mittelalt. Scholastik**. 1887. Verlag Wilhelm Braumüller. Wien.

ZAHN (J.) **Einführung in die Christliche Mystik**. Verlag Ferd. Schöningh., Paderborn, 1908.

ZELLER (Dr. Ed.) **Die Philosophie der Griechen**, 3-e Auflage, 3 Teile in 5 Bänden, Fuch's verlag, Leipzig:

I. **Allgemeine Einleitung. Vorsokratische Philosophie**. 1876 (4-e Auflage)

II(1). **Sokrates und die Sokratiker. Plato und die alte Akademie**,1876 (3-e Auflage)

II(2). **Aristoteles und die alten Peripatetiker**, 1879 (3-e Auflage)

III(1). **Die Nacharistotelische Philosophie**, 1-er Teil, 1880 (3-e Auflage)

III(2). **Die Nacharistotelische Philosophie**, 2-er Teil, 1881 (3-e Auflage).

Publisher's Commentary

- Quotations from other works given by Shestov are given per Shestov's manuscript. They were verified, when possible, against the books indicated in the bibliography. In this verification it turned out that several words of the Latin quotations were written differently in the manuscript and the source books. In the majority of cases, we used the orthography used in the books. In certain cases (e.g., in the adduced excerpts from Luther's Commentary to the Epistle of St. Paul to the Romans), we preserved Shestov's orthography.
- Translation of the quotations into Russian was done with minor exceptions, after Shestov's death, by ANNA ELEAZAROVNA SHESTOVA. Please notify the publisher of any inaccuracies noted.
- After Shestov's death, his library was donated to the Sorbonne. The majority of the books cited in the bibliography are in the library of the Sorbonne.

INDEX

Ambrose 19
Anaximander 16, 117
Anselm of Canterbury 25, 70, 71, 72, 76, 78, 99, 115, 117
Anthony, St. 108, 157
Antisthenes 13, 15, 16, 108, 157, 204
Aquinas, St. Thomas 2, 4, 14, 20, 22, 25, 26, 29, 30, 31, 32, 70, 72, 74, 75, 76, 78, 79, 80, 134, 142, 155, 156, 157, 159, 161, 179, 188, 195, 197, 205
Aristotle 4, 13, 14, 15, 16, 25, 31, 32, 33, 34, 35, 36, 37, 43, 48, 54, 56, 57, 58, 59, 60, 61, 62, 63, 64, 66, 67, 68, 69, 70, 71, 72, 73, 73, 75, 77, 78, 79, 80, 95, 98, 99, 100, 104, 105, 106, 107, 109, 115, 117, 122, 129, 134, 139, 149, 156, 157, 167, 174, 188, 189, 191, 194, 198, 215
Athanasius the Great, St. 19, 98, 99, 157, 207
Augustine, Bl. 3, 4, 5, 19, 22, 23, 24, 44, 71, 79, 87, 88, 90, 91, 92, 93, 96, 97, 100, 101, 102, 103, 104, 105, 106, 107, 108, 109, 100, 111, 112, 113, 114, 115, 116, 119, 120, 121, 123, 124, 125, 126, 127, 128, 129, 141, 142, 148, 151, 153, 172, 175, 176. 181, 194, 197, 202, 205, 206, 207, 208, 211

Berezovskaya, Anna Eleazarovna [Shestov] 2
Bernard of Clairvaux, St. 143, 148, 156, 157, 158, 159, 164, 177, 181, 201, 215, 216, 219
Bloechl, Jeffrey 8
Boehme, Jakob 55, 56, 195, 197
Bois-Reymond, Emil du 78, 205
Boniface II, Pope 175
Brandes, Georg 2
Buddha 21
Bulgakov, Sergei 7

Camus, Albert 6
Catholic Church 5, 15, 17, 23, 29, 30, 72, 84, 87, 88, 90, 91, 93, 99, 100, 109, 114, 115, 123, 129, 130, 134, 135, 136, 137, 138, 139, 140, 145, 146, 166, 171, 175, 184, 192, 193, 198, 204, 205, 207, 213
Celsetius 93
Chekhov, Anton Pavlovich 4, 8, 93, 178, 181
Cicero 101, 112
Cynics 13, 14, 15, 44, 54, 67, 69, 106, 164, 180, 197

David, King 20, 101, 106, 183, 220
Denifle, Heinrich Seuse 76, 79, 85, 86, 133, 135, 136, 138, 141, 142, 143, 144, 145, 146, 147, 148, 149, 152, 153, 154, 155, 156, 157, 158, 159, 160, 163, 164, 165, 166, 172, 173, 174, 182, 185, 193, 212, 217, 223
Diogenes 13, 15, 16, 29, 49, 50, 60, 157, 180
Dionysus the Areopagite 78, 104
Dostoevsky, Fedor Mikhailovich 1, 2, 4, 5, 7, 83, 84, 85, 88, 100, 101, 127, 129, 135, 139, 166, 176, 181
Duchesne, Louis Marie Oliver 90, 91, 92, 93, 94
Duns Scotus 22, 70, 71, 72, 73, 75, 77, 79, 224, 225

Einstein Albert 5
Epictetus 54
Erasmus of Rotterdam 79, 149, 169, 170, 172
Ezekiel 13, 14

Fedorov, Nikolai Fedorovich 7
Finkenthal, Michael 7, 201
Florentine Uniates 17
Fondane, Benjamin 5, 8, 201
Fotiade, Ramona 6, 8, 201

Index

Gregory the Great, St. 29, 76, 77, 115, 122
Grisar, Hartmann 90, 137, 150, 171, 205
Gurian, Sorana 7

Harnack, Adolf von 15, 16, 17, 18, 19, 20, 21, 22, 23, 24, 73, 74, 75, 77, 78, 79, 80, 90, 91, 92, 93, 94, 95, 96, 97, 98, 99, 100, 115, 123, 126, 127, 141, 145, 155, 160, 161, 166, 168, 202, 204, 206, 207, 224
Hart, Kevin 14
Hegel, Georg Wilhelm Friedrich 19, 20, 30
Heraclitus 41, 58, 59, 98, 117
Husserl, Edmund 14, 72

Iraneus 19
Isaiah 5, 18, 20, 21, 106, 148, 175, 189, 218

Jakim, Boris 8
Jeremiah 18, 21
Jesus 19, 22, 24, 74, 166, 202, 215, 216, 217, 219, 224
Job 1, 5, 9, 80, 201, 214, 217
John of the Cross, St. 32, 151
Julian of Eclanum 90, 95, 115, 151, 175, 206

Kant, Immanuel 5, 26, 28, 36, 59, 65, 66, 67, 113, 167, 169, 170, 193
Karlstadt, Andreas 24, 189
Kierkegaard, Soren 4, 5, 7
Koteliansky, S.S. 8

Lawrence, David Herbert 8
Liguori, St. Alphonse-Marie de 154, 155, 156, 157, 158, 159, 161, 178, 194, 224
Loofs, Fredrich 73, 94, 148, 149, 150, 155, 187, 191, 211, 224
Lowtzsky G.L. 2, 9
Luther, Martin, 1, 2, 3, 4, 5, 6, 7, 8, 9, 10, 17, 18, 19, 20, 21, 22, 23, 24, 32, 73, 74, 79, 81, 83, 84, 85, 86, 87, 88, 89, 90, 100, 126, 128, 129, 130, 131, 132, 133, 134, 135, 136, 137, 138, 139, 141, 143, 144, 145, 146, 147, 148, 149, 150, 151, 152, 153, 156, 159, 160, 161, 162, 163, 164, 165, 166, 167, 168, 169, 170, 171, 172, 173, 174, 175, 176, 177, 178, 179, 180, 181, 182, 183, 184, 185, 186, 187, 188, 189, 190, 191, 192, 194, 195, 196, 197, 198, 201, 202, 204, 211, 213, 214, 217, 222, 223
Lycurgis 57

Marcus Aurelius 55, 57, 113
Martin, Bernard 3, 8, 201
Melanchthon, Philip 150, 165, 166, 185, 186, 187, 188, 189, 191, 196
Miłosz, Czesław 1, 7
Mohammed 21, 132
Moses 32, 106, 176, 195, 217, 219
Munzer, Thomas 24, 189

Natorp, Paul 35, 36, 37, 47, 48, 52, 224
Nietzsche, Friedrich Wilhelm 2, 5, 74, 89, 90, 113, 160, 173, 181, 182, 197, 198

Occam, William of 22, 70, 73, 74, 75, 76, 77, 78, 79, 80, 87, 133, 135, 136, 139, 205
Origen of Alexandria 22

Pascal, Blaise 1, 5
Paul, Apostle 3, 5, 9, 18, 23, 30, 31, 79, 85, 87, 88, 89, 90, 123, 129, 141, 142, 148, 150, 151, 166, 171, 175, 182, 217, 218, 219, 225
Pelagius 44, 88, 90, 91, 92, 93, 94, 95, 96, 97, 100, 109, 110, 111, 123, 124, 142, 153, 205, 206
Philonenko, Alexis 6, 201
Plato 1, 4, 13, 14, 15, 16, 28, 32, 33, 34, 35, 36, 37, 38, 39, 40, 41, 43, 44, 46, 47, 58, 49, 52, 53, 54, 55, 56, 57, 58, 59, 60, 61, 62, 64, 66, 67, 70, 79, 94, 95, 96, 98, 99, 104, 105, 106, 111, 117, 127, 129, 139, 180, 181, 192, 194, 196, 225
Plotinus 1, 67, 104, 105, 106, 107, 108, 114, 117, 207
Pohle, Joseph 29, 138, 139, 224
Pushkin, Aleksandr Sergeevich 40, 56

Ranke, Leopold von 129, 130, 131, 132, 133, 134, 161, 224
Renan, Ernest 15, 16, 18, 19, 35, 95, 100
Richert, Hans 28

Ritschl, Albrecht 19, 79, 134, 149, 171, 186, 224

Savonarola, Girolamo 29
Schelling, Friedrich Wilhelm Joseph 5
Schleiermacher, Friedrich 19, 37, 114, 119, 120
Schopenhauer, Arthur 27, 28, 48, 49
Seeberg, Reinhold 72, 73, 76, 224
Seneca 101
Sève, Sophie 9
Shakespeare, William 2, 9, 136, 178
Socrates 13, 14, 15, 16, 21, 24, 28, 29, 30, 31, 34, 36, 38, 39, 40, 41, 42, 43, 44, 46, 47, 48, 49, 50, 51, 52, 53, 54, 55, 56, 58, 60, 61, 63, 65, 66, 67, 69, 70, 71, 72, 74, 75, 76, 79, 92, 93, 94, 95, 96, 97, 100, 110, 111, 112, 113, 126, 127, 139, 142, 145, 146, 149, 151, 153, 156, 164, 165, 167, 170, 180, 184, 192, 194, 196
Spencer, Herbert 18
Spinoza, Baruch 5, 37, 44, 45, 46, 65, 113, 114, 116, 117, 118, 119, 120, 121, 122, 129, 132, 134, 148, 224
Stoics 15, 44, 54, 55, 95, 106, 112, 120, 161, 164, 169, 183, 184

Tejerizo, Margaret 8
Tertullian 3, 32, 71, 77, 99, 101, 109, 122, 126, 136, 197, 204
Tetzel, Johann 85, 86, 129
Theresa, St. 13, 15, 16, 32, 151, 157, 164, 215, 216
Thomas a Kempis 148, 156
Tolstoy, Count Lev Nikolaevich 2, 4, 5, 8, 50, 80, 87, 88, 89, 90, 93, 113, 136, 151, 152, 160, 162, 166, 173, 176, 177, 181, 197, 198, 200, 201, 209, 213
Troeltsch Ernest Peter Wilhelm 155
Turgenev, Ivan Sergeevich 2

Voltaire [Francois-Marie Arouet] 30

Weiss, Albert Maria 79, 104, 136, 137, 139, 140, 149, 168, 223
Werner, Karl 73, 74, 76, 77, 78, 79, 80, 205, 225

Zahn Theodor 17, 18, 193, 225
Zeller Eduard 13, 16, 19, 20, 39, 57, 59, 62, 69, 104, 105, 201, 203, 204, 225

www.ingramcontent.com/pod-product-compliance
Lightning Source LLC
Chambersburg PA
CBHW071834300426
44116CB00009B/1536